Hands-On Unsupervised Learning with Python

Implement machine learning and deep learning models using Scikit-Learn, TensorFlow, and more

Giuseppe Bonaccorso

BIRMINGHAM - MUMBAI

Hands-On Unsupervised Learning with Python

Copyright © 2019 Packt Publishing

All rights reserved. No part of this book may be reproduced, stored in a retrieval system, or transmitted in any form or by any means, without the prior written permission of the publisher, except in the case of brief quotations embedded in critical articles or reviews.

Every effort has been made in the preparation of this book to ensure the accuracy of the information presented. However, the information contained in this book is sold without warranty, either express or implied. Neither the author, nor Packt Publishing or its dealers and distributors, will be held liable for any damages caused or alleged to have been caused directly or indirectly by this book.

Packt Publishing has endeavored to provide trademark information about all of the companies and products mentioned in this book by the appropriate use of capitals. However, Packt Publishing cannot guarantee the accuracy of this information.

Commissioning Editor: Sunith Shetty
Acquisition Editor: Porous Godhaa
Content Development Editors: Pratik Andrade, Pooja Parvatkar
Technical Editor: Snehal Dalmet
Copy Editor: Safis Editing
Project Coordinator: Namrata Swetta
Proofreader: Safis Editing
Indexer: Pratik Shirodkar
Graphics: Jisha Chirayil
Production Coordinator: Deepika Naik

First published: February 2019

Production reference: 1270219

Published by Packt Publishing Ltd.
Livery Place
35 Livery Street
Birmingham
B3 2PB, UK.

ISBN 978-1-78934-827-9

www.packtpub.com

mapt.io

Mapt is an online digital library that gives you full access to over 5,000 books and videos, as well as industry leading tools to help you plan your personal development and advance your career. For more information, please visit our website.

Why subscribe?

- Spend less time learning and more time coding with practical eBooks and Videos from over 4,000 industry professionals

- Improve your learning with Skill Plans built especially for you

- Get a free eBook or video every month

- Mapt is fully searchable

- Copy and paste, print, and bookmark content

Packt.com

Did you know that Packt offers eBook versions of every book published, with PDF and ePub files available? You can upgrade to the eBook version at www.packt.com and as a print book customer, you are entitled to a discount on the eBook copy. Get in touch with us at customercare@packtpub.com for more details.

At www.packt.com, you can also read a collection of free technical articles, sign up for a range of free newsletters, and receive exclusive discounts and offers on Packt books and eBooks.

Contributors

About the author

Giuseppe Bonaccorso is an experienced manager in the fields of AI, data science, and machine learning. He has been involved in solution design, management, and delivery in different business contexts. He got his M.Sc.Eng in electronics in 2005 from the University of Catania, Italy, and continued his studies at the University of Rome Tor Vergata, Italy, and the University of Essex, UK. His main interests include machine/deep learning, reinforcement learning, big data, bio-inspired adaptive systems, neuroscience, and natural language processing.

About the reviewer

Chiheb Chebbi is a Tunisian infosec enthusiast, author, and technical reviewer with experience in various aspects of information security, focusing on investigations into advanced cyber attacks and research into cyber espionage. His core interests lie in penetration testing, machine learning, and threat hunting. He has been included in many halls of fame. The proposals he has put forward with a view to giving presentations have been accepted by many world-class information security conferences.

Packt is searching for authors like you

If you're interested in becoming an author for Packt, please visit authors.packtpub.com and apply today. We have worked with thousands of developers and tech professionals, just like you, to help them share their insight with the global tech community. You can make a general application, apply for a specific hot topic that we are recruiting an author for, or submit your own idea.

Table of Contents

Preface — 1

Chapter 1: Getting Started with Unsupervised Learning — 7
- **Technical requirements** — 8
- **Why do we need machine learning?** — 8
  - Descriptive analysis — 10
  - Diagnostic analysis — 11
  - Predictive analysis — 12
  - Prescriptive analysis — 16
- **Types of machine learning algorithm** — 17
  - Supervised learning algorithms — 17
    - Supervised hello world! — 20
  - Unsupervised learning algorithms — 21
    - Cluster analysis — 22
    - Generative models — 23
    - Association rules — 24
    - Unsupervised hello world! — 24
  - Semi-supervised learning algorithms — 29
  - Reinforcement learning algorithms — 30
- **Why Python for data science and machine learning?** — 31
- **Summary** — 32
- **Questions** — 32
- **Further reading** — 33

Chapter 2: Clustering Fundamentals — 35
- **Technical requirements** — 35
- **Introduction to clustering** — 36
  - Distance functions — 39
- **K-means** — 42
  - K-means++ — 43
- **Analysis of the Breast Cancer Wisconsin dataset** — 45
- **Evaluation metrics** — 51
  - Minimizing the inertia — 51
  - Silhouette score — 58
  - Completeness score — 60
  - Homogeneity score — 62
    - A trade-off between homogeneity and completeness using the V-measure — 63
  - Adjusted Mutual Information (AMI) score — 64
  - Adjusted Rand score — 66
  - Contingency matrix — 67

Table of Contents

K-Nearest Neighbors	68
Vector Quantization	74
Summary	82
Questions	82
Further reading	83
Chapter 3: Advanced Clustering	**85**
Technical requirements	86
Spectral clustering	86
Mean shift	92
DBSCAN	97
Calinski-Harabasz score	100
Analysis of the Absenteeism at Work dataset using DBSCAN	101
Cluster instability as a performance metric	109
K-medoids	112
Online clustering	117
Mini-batch K-means	118
BIRCH	119
Comparison between mini-batch K-means and BIRCH	122
Summary	125
Questions	126
Further reading	127
Chapter 4: Hierarchical Clustering in Action	**129**
Technical requirements	130
Cluster hierarchies	130
Agglomerative clustering	131
Single and complete linkages	133
Average linkage	134
Ward's linkage	135
Analyzing a dendrogram	136
Cophenetic correlation as a performance metric	143
Agglomerative clustering on the Water Treatment Plant dataset	145
Connectivity constraints	154
Summary	160
Questions	161
Further reading	161
Chapter 5: Soft Clustering and Gaussian Mixture Models	**163**
Technical requirements	164
Soft clustering	164
Fuzzy c-means	166
Gaussian mixture	172
EM algorithm for Gaussian mixtures	174
Assessing the performance of a Gaussian mixture with AIC and BIC	181

[ii]

Component selection using Bayesian Gaussian mixture	184
Generative Gaussian mixture	190
Summary	195
Questions	196
Further reading	196

Chapter 6: Anomaly Detection — 197

Technical requirements	198
Probability density functions	198
Anomalies as outliers or novelties	200
Structure of the dataset	202
Histograms	203
Kernel density estimation (KDE)	206
Gaussian kernel	206
Epanechnikov kernel	208
Exponential kernel	209
Uniform (or Tophat) kernel	210
Estimating the density	210
Anomaly detection	217
Anomaly detection with the KDD Cup 99 dataset	219
One-class support vector machines	227
Anomaly detection with Isolation Forests	233
Summary	238
Questions	239
Further reading	240

Chapter 7: Dimensionality Reduction and Component Analysis — 241

Technical requirements	242
Principal Component Analysis (PCA)	242
PCA with Singular Value Decomposition	245
Whitening	246
PCA with the MNIST dataset	249
Kernel PCA	253
Adding more robustness to heteroscedastic noise with factor analysis	256
Sparse PCA and dictionary learning	259
Non-Negative Matrix Factorization	262
Independent Component Analysis	264
Topic modeling with Latent Dirichlet Allocation	270
Summary	276
Questions	277
Further reading	277

Chapter 8: Unsupervised Neural Network Models — 279

Technical requirements	280
Autoencoders	280

Example of a deep convolutional autoencoder	282
Denoising autoencoders	287
Adding noise to the deep convolutional autoencoder	288
Sparse autoencoders	290
Adding a sparseness constraint to the deep convolutional autoencoder	291
Variational autoencoders	292
Example of a deep convolutional variational autoencoder	294
Hebbian-based principal component analysis	**299**
Sanger's network	300
An example of Sanger's network	302
Rubner-Tavan's network	307
An example of a Rubner-Tavan's network	309
Unsupervised deep belief networks	**312**
Restricted Boltzmann Machines	312
Deep belief networks	314
Example of an unsupervised DBN	315
Summary	**318**
Questions	**319**
Further reading	**319**

Chapter 9: Generative Adversarial Networks and SOMs — 321

Technical requirements	**321**
Generative adversarial networks	**322**
Analyzing a GAN	324
Mode collapse	326
Example of a deep convolutional GAN	328
Wasserstein GANs	337
Transforming the DCGAN into a WGAN	339
Self-organizing maps	**347**
Example of a Kohonen map	350
Summary	**354**
Questions	**355**
Further reading	**355**

Appendix A: Assessments — 357

Chapter 1	357
Chapter 2	358
Chapter 3	359
Chapter 4	359
Chapter 5	360
Chapter 6	361
Chapter 7	361
Chapter 8	362
Chapter 9	363

Other Books You May Enjoy — 365

Index 369

Preface

Unsupervised learning is an increasingly important branch of data science, the goal of which is to train models that can learn the structure of a dataset and provide the user with helpful pieces of information about new samples. In many different business sectors (such as marketing, business intelligence, strategy, and so forth), unsupervised learning has always had a primary role in helping the manager to make the best decisions, based both on qualitative and, above all, quantitative approaches. In a world where data is becoming more and more pervasive and storage costs are dropping, the possibility of analyzing real, complex datasets is helping to transform old-fashioned business models into new, more accurate, more responsive, and more effective ones. That's why a data scientist might not have a clear idea about all the possibilities, focusing on the pros and cons of all methods and increasing their knowledge about the best potential strategies for every specific domain. This book is not intended to be an exhaustive resource (which is actually impossible to find), but more of a reference to set you off on your exploration of this world, providing you with different methods that can be immediately employed and evaluated. I hope that readers with different backgrounds will learn worthwhile things for improving their businesses, and that you'll seek more study of this fascinating topic!

Who this book is for

The intended audience of this book is data scientists (both aspiring and professional), machine learning practitioners, and developers who want to learn how to implement the most common unsupervised algorithms and tune up their parameters in order to provide valuable insights to different stakeholders from all business areas.

What this book covers

Chapter 1, *Getting Started with Unsupervised Learning*, offers an introduction to machine learning and data science from a very pragmatic perspective. The main concepts are discussed and a few simple examples are shown, focusing attention particularly on unsupervised problem structures.

Chapter 2, *Clustering Fundamentals*, begins our exploration of clustering algorithms. The most common methods and evaluation metrics are analyzed, together with concrete examples that show how to tune up the hyperparameters and assess performance from different viewpoints.

Chapter 3, *Advanced Clustering*, discusses some more complex algorithms. Many of the problems analyzed in Chapter 2, *Clustering Fundamentals*, are re-evaluated using more powerful and flexible methods that can be easily employed whenever the performances of basic algorithms don't meet requirements.

Chapter 4, *Hierarchical Clustering in Action*, is fully dedicated to a family of algorithms that can calculate a complete clustering hierarchy according to specific criteria. The most common strategies for this are analyzed, together with specific performance measures and algorithmic variants that can increase the effectiveness of the methods.

Chapter 5, *Soft Clustering and Gaussian Mixture Models*, is focused on a few famous soft-clustering algorithms, with a particular emphasis on Gaussian mixtures, which allow the defining of generative models under quite reasonable assumptions.

Chapter 6, *Anomaly Detection*, discusses a particular application of unsupervised learning: novelty and outlier detection. The goal is to analyze some common methods that can be effectively employed in order to understand whether a new sample can be considered as valid, or an anomalous one that requires particular attention.

Chapter 7, *Dimensionality Reduction and Component Analysis*, covers the most common and powerful methods for dimensionality reduction, component analysis, and dictionary learning. The examples show how it's possible to carry out such operations efficiently in different specific scenarios.

Chapter 8, *Unsupervised Neural Network Models*, discusses some very important unsupervised neural models. In particular, focus is directed both to networks that can learn the structure of a generic data generating process, and to performing dimensionality reduction.

Chapter 9, *Generative Adversarial Networks and SOMs*, continues the analysis of some deep neural networks that can learn the structure of data generating processes and output new samples drawn from these processes. Moreover, a special kind of network (SOM) is discussed and some practical examples are shown.

To get the most out of this book

This book requires a basic knowledge of machine learning and Python coding. Moreover, a university-level knowledge of probability theory, calculus, and linear algebra is needed in order to have a full understanding of all theoretical discussions. However, readers who are not familiar with such concepts can skip the mathematical discussions and focus only on the practical aspects. Whenever needed, reference to specific papers and books is provided so as to allow a deeper understanding of the most complex concepts.

Download the example code files

You can download the example code files for this book from your account at `www.packt.com`. If you purchased this book elsewhere, you can visit `www.packt.com/support` and register to have the files emailed directly to you.

You can download the code files by following these steps:

1. Log in or register at `www.packt.com`.
2. Select the **SUPPORT** tab.
3. Click on **Code Downloads & Errata**.
4. Enter the name of the book in the **Search** box and follow the onscreen instructions.

Once the file is downloaded, please make sure that you unzip or extract the folder using the latest version of:

- WinRAR/7-Zip for Windows
- Zipeg/iZip/UnRarX for Mac
- 7-Zip/PeaZip for Linux

The code bundle for the book is also hosted on GitHub at `https://github.com/PacktPublishing/HandsOn-Unsupervised-Learning-with-Python`. In case there's an update to the code, it will be updated on the existing GitHub repository.

We also have other code bundles from our rich catalog of books and videos available at `https://github.com/PacktPublishing/`. Check them out!

Download the color images

We also provide a PDF file that has color images of the screenshots/diagrams used in this book. You can download it here: `http://www.packtpub.com/sites/default/files/downloads/9781789348279_ColorImages.pdf`.

Conventions used

There are a number of text conventions used throughout this book.

`CodeInText`: Indicates code words in text, database table names, folder names, filenames, file extensions, pathnames, dummy URLs, user input, and Twitter handles. Here is an example: "Mount the downloaded `WebStorm-10*.dmg` disk image file as another disk in your system."

A block of code is set as follows:

```
X_train = faces['images']
X_train = (2.0 * X_train) - 1.0

width = X_train.shape[1]
height = X_train.shape[2]
```

When we wish to draw your attention to a particular part of a code block, the relevant lines or items are set in bold:

```
import tensorflow as tf

session = tf.InteractiveSession(graph=graph)
tf.global_variables_initializer().run()
```

Bold: Indicates a new term, an important word, or words that you see onscreen. For example, words in menus or dialog boxes appear in the text like this. Here is an example: "Select **System info** from the **Administration** panel."

Warnings or important notes appear like this.

Tips and tricks appear like this.

Get in touch

Feedback from our readers is always welcome.

General feedback: If you have questions about any aspect of this book, mention the book title in the subject of your message and email us at `customercare@packtpub.com`.

Errata: Although we have taken every care to ensure the accuracy of our content, mistakes do happen. If you have found a mistake in this book, we would be grateful if you would report this to us. Please visit `www.packt.com/submit-errata`, selecting your book, clicking on the Errata Submission Form link, and entering the details.

Piracy: If you come across any illegal copies of our works in any form on the Internet, we would be grateful if you would provide us with the location address or website name. Please contact us at `copyright@packt.com` with a link to the material.

If you are interested in becoming an author: If there is a topic that you have expertise in and you are interested in either writing or contributing to a book, please visit `authors.packtpub.com`.

Reviews

Please leave a review. Once you have read and used this book, why not leave a review on the site that you purchased it from? Potential readers can then see and use your unbiased opinion to make purchase decisions, we at Packt can understand what you think about our products, and our authors can see your feedback on their book. Thank you!

For more information about Packt, please visit `packt.com`.

Getting Started with Unsupervised Learning

In this chapter, we are going to introduce fundamental machine learning concepts, assuming that you have some basic knowledge of statistical learning and probability theory. You'll learn about the uses of machine learning techniques and the logical process that improves our knowledge about both nature and the properties of a dataset. The purpose of the entire process is to build descriptive and predictive models the can support business decisions.

Unsupervised learning aims to provide tools for data exploration, mining, and generation. In this book, you'll explore different scenarios with concrete examples and analyses, and you'll learn how to apply fundamental and more complex algorithms to solve specific problems.

In this introductory chapter, we are going to discuss:

- Why do we need machine learning?
- Descriptive, diagnostic, predictive, and prescriptive analyses
- Types of machine learning
- Why are we using Python?

Technical requirements

The code presented in this chapter requires:

- Python 3.5+ (Anaconda distribution: https://www.anaconda.com/distribution/ is highly recommended)
- Libraries:
    - SciPy 0.19+
    - NumPy 1.10+
    - scikit-learn 0.19+
    - pandas 0.22+
    - Matplotlib 2.0+
    - seaborn 0.9+

The examples are available in the GitHub repository: https://github.com/PacktPublishing/HandsOn-Unsupervised-Learning-with-Python/tree/master/Chapter01.

Why do we need machine learning?

Data is everywhere. At this very moment, thousands of systems are collecting records that make up the history of specific services, together with logs, user interactions, and many other context-dependent elements. Only a decade ago, most companies couldn't even manage 1% of their data efficiently. For this reason, databases were periodically pruned and only important data used to be retained in permanent storage servers.

Conversely, nowadays almost every company can exploit cloud infrastructures that scale in order to cope with the increasing volume of incoming data. Tools such as Apache Hadoop or Apache Spark allow both data scientists and engineers to implement complex pipelines involving extremely large volumes of data. At this point, all the barriers have been torn down and a democratized process is in place. However, what is the actual value of these large datasets? From a business viewpoint, the information is valuable only when it can help make the right decisions, reducing uncertainty and providing better contextual insight. This means that, without the right tools and knowledge, a bunch of data is only a cost to the company that needs to be limited to increase the margins.

Machine learning is a large branch of computer science (in particular, artificial intelligence), which aims to implement **descriptive** and **predictive** models of reality by exploiting existing datasets. As this book is dedicated to practical unsupervised solutions, we are going to focus only on algorithms that describe the context by looking for hidden causes and relationships. However, even if only from a theoretical viewpoint, it's helpful to show the main differences between machine learning problems. Only complete awareness (not limited to mere technical aspects) of the goals can lead to a rational answer to the initial question, Why do we need machine learning?

We can start by saying that human beings have extraordinary cognitive abilities, which have inspired many systems, but they lack analytical skills when the number of elements increases significantly. For example, if you're a teacher who is meeting his/her class for the first time, you'll be able to compute a rough estimate of the percentage of female students after taking a glance at the entire group. Usually, the estimate is likely to be accurate and close to the actual count, even if the estimation is made by two or more individuals. However, if we repeat the experiment with the entire population of a school gathered in a courtyard, the distinction of gender will not be evident. This is because all students are clearly visible in the class; however, telling the sexes apart in the courtyard is limited by certain factors (for example, taller people can hide shorter ones). Getting rid of the analogy, we can say that a large amount of data usually carries a lot of information. In order to extract and categorize the information, it's necessary to take an automated approach.

Before moving to the next section, let's discuss the concepts of descriptive, diagnostic, predictive, and prescriptive analyses, originally defined by Gartner. However, in this case, we want to focus on a system (for example, a generic context) that we are analyzing in order to gain more and more control over its behavior.

The complete process is represented in the following diagram:

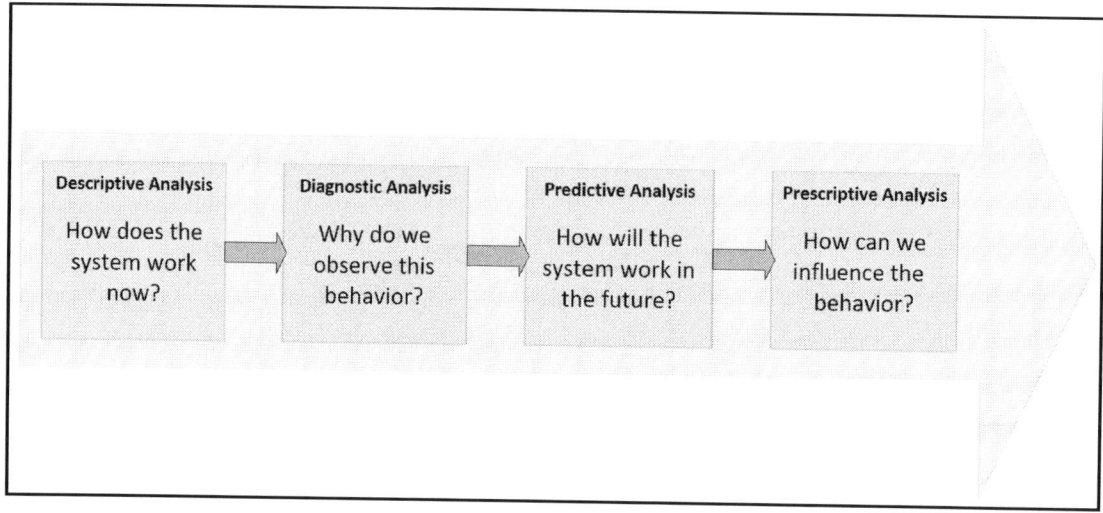

Descriptive, diagnostic, predictive, and prescriptive flow

Descriptive analysis

The first problem to solve in almost any data science scenario concerns understanding its nature. We need to know how the system works or what a dataset is describing. Without this analysis, our knowledge is too limited to make any assumption or hypothesis. For example, we can observe a chart of the average temperature in a city for several years. If we are unable to describe the time series discovering the correlation, seasonalities, and trends, any other question remains unsolved. In our specific context, if we don't discover the similarities between groups of objects, we cannot try to find out a way to summarize their common features. The data scientist has to employ specific tools for every particular problem, but, at the end of this stage, all possible (and helpful) questions must be answered.

Moreover, as this process must have clear business value, it's important to involve different stakeholders with the purpose of gathering their knowledge and converting it into a common language. For example, when working with healthcare data, a physician might talk about hereditary factors, but for our purpose, it's preferable to say that there's a correlation among some samples, so we're not fully authorized to treat them as statistically independent elements. In general, the outcome of descriptive analysis is a summary containing all metric evaluations and conclusions that are necessary to qualify the context, and reducing uncertainty. In the example of the temperature chart, the data scientist should be able to answer the auto-correlation, the periodicity of the peaks, the number of potential outliers, and the presence of trends.

Diagnostic analysis

Till now, we have worked with output data, which has been observed after a specific underlying process has generated it. The natural question after having described the system relates to the causes. Temperature depends on many meteorological and geographical factors, which can be either easily observable or completely hidden. Seasonality in the time series is clearly influenced by the period of the year, but what about the outliers?

For example, we have discovered a peak in a region identified as winter. How can we justify it? In a simplistic approach, this can be considered as a noisy outlier that can be filtered out. However, if it has been observed and there's a ground truth behind the measure (for example, all the parties agree that it's not an error), we should assume the presence of a **hidden** (or **latent**) cause.

It can be surprising, but the majority of more complex scenarios are characterized by a huge number of latent causes (sometimes called **factors**) that are too difficult to analyze. In general, this is not a bad condition but, as we're going to discuss, it's important to include them in the model to learn their influence through the dataset.

On the other hand, deciding to drop all unknown elements means reducing the predictive ability of the model with a proportional loss of accuracy. Therefore, the primary goal of diagnostic analysis is not necessarily to find out all the causes but to list the observable and measurable elements (known as **factors**), together with all the potential latent ones (which are generally summarized into a single global element).

To a certain extent, a diagnostic analysis is often similar to a reverse-engineering process, because we can easily monitor the effects, but it's more difficult to detect existing relationships between potential causes and observable effects. For this reason, such an analysis is often probabilistic and helps find the probability that a certain identified cause brings about a specific effect. In this way, it's also easier to exclude non-influencing elements and to determine relationships that were initially excluded. However, this process requires a deeper knowledge of statistical learning methods and it won't be discussed in this book, apart from a few examples, such as a Gaussian mixture.

Predictive analysis

Once the overall descriptive knowledge has been gathered and the awareness about the underlying causes is satisfactory, it's possible to create predictive models. The goal of these models is to infer future outcomes according to the history and the structure of the model itself. In many cases, this phase is analyzed together with the next one because we are seldom interested in a *free evolution* of the system (for example, how the temperature will change in the next month), but rather in the ways we can influence the output.

That said, let's focus only on the predictions, considering the most important elements that should be taken into account. The first consideration is about the nature of the processes. We don't need machine learning for deterministic processes unless their complexity is so high that we're forced to consider them as black boxes. The vast majority of examples we are going to discuss are about stochastic processes where the uncertainty cannot be removed. For example, we know that the temperature in a day can be modeled as a conditional probability (for example, a Gaussian) dependent on the previous observations. Therefore, a prediction sets out not to turn the system into a deterministic one, which is impossible, but to reduce the variance of the distribution, so that the probability is high only for a short range of temperatures. On the other hand, as we know that many latent factors work behind the scene, we can never accept a model based on spiky distributions (for example, on a single outcome with probability 1) because this choice would have a terribly negative impact on the final accuracy.

If our model is parameterized with variables subject to the learning process (for example, the means and covariance matrices of the Gaussians), our goal is to find out the optimal balance in the so-called **bias-variance trade-off**. As this chapter is an introductory one, we are not formalizing the concepts with mathematical formulas, but we need a practical definition (further details can be found in *Bonaccorso G., Mastering Machine Learning Algorithms, Packt, 2018*).

The common term to define a statistical predictive model is an **estimator**. Hence the **bias of an estimator** is the measurable effect of incorrect assumptions and learning procedures. In other words, if the mean of a process is 5.0 and our estimations have a mean of 3.0, we can say the model is biased. Considering the previous example, we are working with a biased estimator if the expected value of the error between the observed value and the prediction is not null. It's important to understand that we are not saying that every single estimation must have a null error, but while collecting enough samples and computing the mean, its value should be very close to zero (it can be zero only with infinite samples). Whenever it is rather larger than zero, it means that our model is not able to predict training values correctly. It's obvious that we are looking for **unbiased estimators** that, on average, yield accurate predictions.

On the other hand, the **variance of an estimator** is a measure of the robustness in the presence of samples not belonging to the training set. At the beginning of this section, we said that our processes are normally stochastic. This means that any dataset must be considered as drawn from a specific data-generating process p_{data}. If we have enough representative elements $x_i \in X$, we can suppose that training a classifier using the limited dataset X leads to a model that is able to classify all potential samples that can be drawn from p_{data}.

For example, if we need to model a face classifier whose context is limited to portraits (no further face poses are allowed), we can collect a number of portraits of different individuals. Our only concern is not to exclude categories that can be present in real life. Let's assume that we have 10,000 images of individuals of different ages and genders, but we don't have any portraits with a hat. When the system is in production, we receive a call from our customer saying that the system misclassifies many pictures. After analysis, we discover that they always represent people wearing hats. It's clear that our model is not responsible for the error because it has been trained with samples representing only a region of the data generating process. Therefore, in order to solve the problem, we collect other samples and we repeat the training process. However, now we decide to use a more complex model, expecting that it will work better. Unfortunately, we observe a worse validation accuracy (for example, the accuracy on a subset that is not used in the training phase), together with a higher training accuracy. What happened here?

When an estimator learns to classify the training set perfectly but its ability on never-seen samples is poor, we say that it is **overfitted** and its variance is too high for the specific task (conversely, an **underfitted** model has a large bias and all predictions are very inaccurate). Intuitively, the model has learned too much about the training data and it has lost the ability to generalize. To better understand this concept, let's look at a Gaussian data generating process, as shown in the following graph:

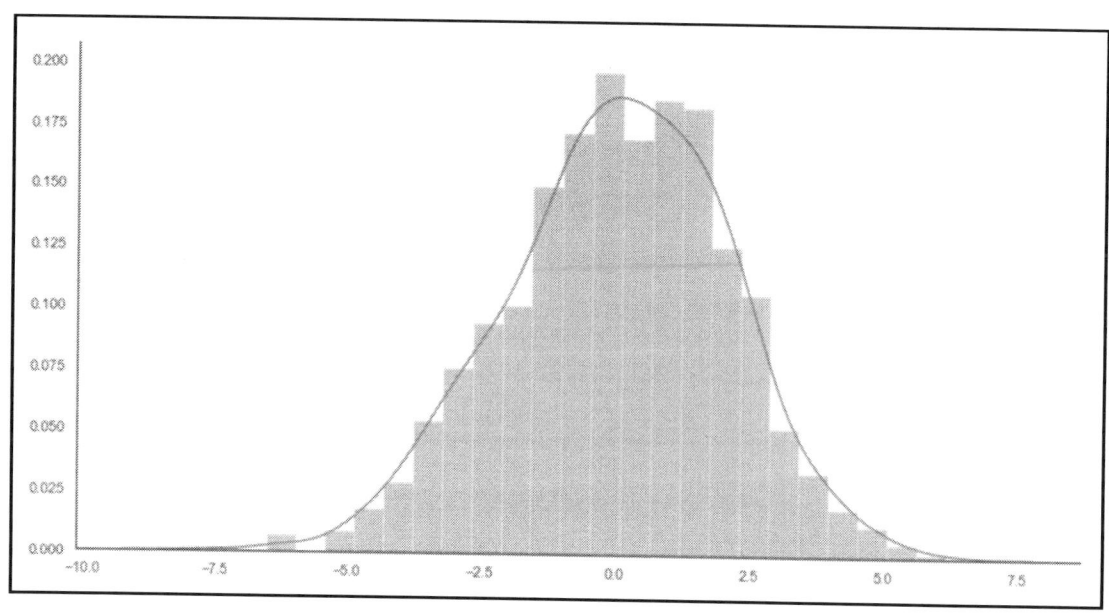

Original data generating process (solid line) and sampled data histogram

If the training set hasn't been sampled in a perfectly uniform way or it's partially unbalanced (some classes have fewer samples than the other ones), or if the model is prone to overfitting, the result can be represented by an inaccurate distribution, as follows:

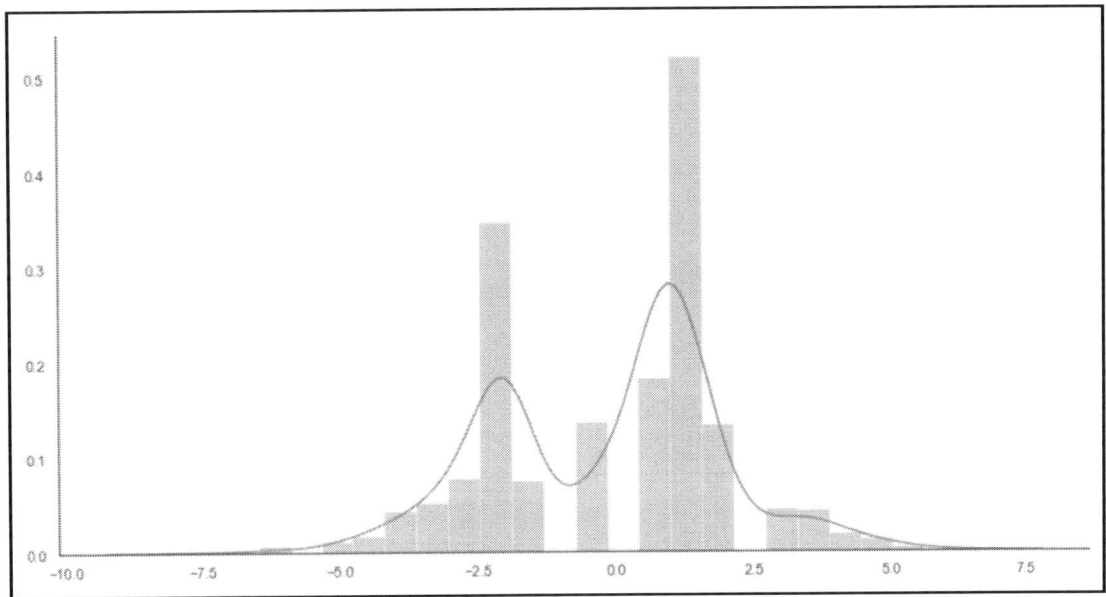

Learned distribution

In this case, the model has been forced to learn the details of the training set until it has excluded many potential samples from the distribution. The result is no more Gaussian, but a double-peaked distribution, where some probabilities are erroneously low. Of course, the test and validation sets are sampled from the small regions not covered by the training set (as there's no overlap between training data and validation data), therefore the model will fail in its task providing completely incorrect results.

In other words, we can say that the variance is too high because the model has learned to work with too many details, increasing the range of possibilities of different classifications over a reasonable threshold. For example, the portrait classifier could have learned that people with blue glasses are always male in the age range 30-40 (this is an unrealistic situation because the detail level is generally very low, however, it's helpful to understand the nature of the problem).

We can summarize by saying that a good predictive model must have very low bias and proportionally low variance. Unfortunately, it's generally impossible to minimize both measures effectively, so a trade-off must be accepted.

A system with a good generalization ability will be likely to have a higher bias because it is unable to capture all the details. Conversely, a high variance allows a very small bias, but the ability of the model is almost limited to the training set. In this book, we are not going to talk about classifiers, but you should perfectly understand these concepts in order to be always aware of the different behaviors that you can encounter while working on projects.

Prescriptive analysis

The primary goal of this is to answer the question How can I influence the output of the system? In order to avoid confusion, it's preferable to translate this concept into pure machine learning language, hence the question could be Which input values are necessary to obtain a specific output?

As discussed in the previous section, this phase is often merged together with predictive analysis because the models are generally employed for both tasks. However, there are specific situations where the prediction is limited to a *null-input* evolution (such as in the temperature example) and more complex models must be analyzed in the prescriptive stage. The main reason resides in the ability to control all the causes that are responsible for a specific output.

Sometimes, when not necessary, they are only superficially analyzed. It can happen either when the causes are not controllable (for example, meteorological events), or when it's simpler to include a global latent parameter set. The latter option is very common in machine learning and many algorithms have been developed to work efficiently with the presence of latent factors (for example, EM or SVD recommendation systems). For this reason, we are not focusing on this particular aspect, (which is extremely important in system theory) and, at the same time, we are implicitly assuming that our models provide the ability to investigate many possible outputs resulting from different inputs.

For example, in deep learning, it's possible to create inverse models that produce saliency maps of the input space, forcing a specific output class. Considering the example of the portrait classifier, we could be interested in discovering which visual elements influence the output of a class. Diagnostic analysis is generally ineffective because the causes are extremely complex and their level is too low (for example, the shape of a contour). Therefore, inverse models can help solve the prescriptive problem by showing the influence of different geometric regions. However, a complete prescriptive analysis is beyond the scope of this book and, in many cases, it's not necessary, hence we are not considering such a step in upcoming chapters. Let's now analyze the different types of machine learning algorithm.

Types of machine learning algorithm

At this point, we can briefly introduce the different types of machine learning, focusing on their main peculiarities and differences. In the following sections, we'll discuss informal definitions followed by more formal ones. If you are not familiar with the mathematical concepts involved in the discussion, you can skip the details. However, it's highly advisable to study all unknown theoretical elements, as they are fundamental to understanding the concepts analyzed in the next chapters.

Supervised learning algorithms

In a supervised scenario, the task of the model is to find the correct label of a sample, assuming that the presence of a training set is correctly labeled, along with the possibility of comparing the estimated value with the correct one. The term **supervised** is derived from the idea of an external *teaching agent* that provides precise and immediate feedback after each prediction. The model can use such feedback as a measure of the error and, consequently perform the corrections needed to reduce it.

More formally, if we assume a data generating process, $p_{data}(\bar{x}, y)$ the dataset is obtained as:

$$X = \{(\bar{x}_1, y_1), (\bar{x}_2, y_2), \ldots, (\bar{x}_N, y_N)\} \text{ where } (\bar{x}_i, y_i) \sim p_{data}(\bar{x}, y) \text{ and } \bar{x}_i \in \mathbb{R}^M, y_i \in (0, 1, \ldots, M) \text{ or } y_i \in \mathbb{R}$$

As discussed in the previous section, all samples must be **independent and identically distributed** (IID) values uniformly sampled from the data generating process. In particular, all classes must represent the actual distribution (for example, if p(y=0) = 0.4 and p(y=1) = 0.6, the proportion should 40% or 60%). However, in order to avoid biases, when the discrepancies between classes are not very large, a reasonable choice is a perfectly uniform sampling and has the same number of representatives for y=1, 2, ..., M.

A generic classifier $c(\bar{x}; \bar{\theta})$ can be modeled in two ways:

- A parametrized function that outputs the predicted class
- A parametrized probability distribution that outputs the class probability for every input sample

Getting Started with Unsupervised Learning

In the first case, we have:

$$\tilde{y} = c(\bar{x}; \bar{\theta}) = f(\bar{x}; \bar{\theta}) \text{ and } d_e(y, \tilde{y}) \text{ is an error measure (e.g. squared error)}$$

Considering the whole dataset X, it's possible to compute a global cost function L:

$$L = \frac{1}{N} \sum_{i=1}^{N} d_e(y_i, \tilde{y}_i) = \frac{1}{N} \sum_{i=1}^{N} d_e(y_i, f(\bar{x}_i; \bar{\theta}))$$

As L depends only on the parameter vector (x_i and y_i are constants), a generic algorithm must find the optimal parameter vector that minimizes the cost function. For example, in a **regression** problem (where the labels are continuous), the error measure can be the squared error between the actual value and prediction:

$$L = \frac{1}{N} \sum_{i=1}^{N} d_e(y_i, \tilde{y}_i) = \frac{1}{N} \sum_{i=1}^{N} (y_i - f(\bar{x}_i; \bar{\theta}))^2$$

Such a cost function can be optimized in different ways (peculiar to specific algorithms), but a very common strategy (above all in deep learning) is to employ the **Stochastic Gradient Descent (SGD)** algorithm. It consists of an iteration of the following two steps:

- Computing the gradient ∇L (with respect to the parameter vector) with a small batch of samples $x_i \in X$
- Updating the weights and moving the parameters in the opposite direction of the gradient $-\nabla L$ (remember that the gradient is always directed towards a maximum)

Instead, when the classifier is probabilistic, it should be represented as a parametrized conditional probability distribution:

$$c(\bar{x}; \bar{\theta}) = p(\tilde{y}|\bar{x}; \bar{\theta})$$

In other words, the classifier will now output the probability of a label y given an input vector. The goal is now to find the optimal parameter set, which will obtain:

$$p(\tilde{y}|\bar{x};\bar{\theta}) \twoheadrightarrow p_{data}(y|\bar{x})$$

In the preceding formula, we have expressed p_{data} as a conditional distribution. The optimization can be obtained using a probabilistic distance metric, such as the **Kullback-Leibler divergence** D_{KL} (which is always non-negative $D_{KL} \geq 0$ and $D_{KL} = 0$ only when the two distributions are identical):

$$L = D_{KL}(p_{data}||p) = \sum_{i=1}^{N} p_{data}(y_i|\bar{x}_i) \log \frac{p_{data}(y_i|\bar{x}_i)}{p(\tilde{y}_i|\bar{x}_i;\bar{\theta})}$$

With a few simple manipulations, we obtain:

$$L = \sum_{i=1}^{N} p_{data}(y_i|\bar{x}_i) \log p_{data}(y_i|\bar{x}_i) - \sum_{i=1}^{N} p_{data}(y_i|\bar{x}_i) \log p(\tilde{y}_i|\bar{x}_i;\bar{\theta}) = -H(p_{data}) + H(p, p_{data})$$

Therefore, the resulting cost function corresponds to the difference between the cross-entropy between p and p_{data} up to a constant value (the entropy of the data generating process). Therefore, the training strategy is now based on representing labels using one-hot encoding (for example, if there are two labels $0 \rightarrow (0, 1)$ and $1 \rightarrow (1, 0)$, so that the sum of all elements must be always equal to *1*) and using an intrinsic probabilistic output (such as in a logistic regression) or a softmax filter, which transforms M values into a probability distribution.

In both cases, it's clear the presence of a *hidden teacher* provides a consistent measure of the error, allowing the model to correct the parameters accordingly. In particular, the second approach is extremely helpful for our purposes, therefore I recommend studying it further if it's not known well (all the main definitions can also be found in *Bonaccorso G., Machine Learning Algorithms, Second Edition, Packt, 2018*).

We can now discuss a very basic example of supervised learning, a linear regression model that can be employed to predict the evolution of a simple time series.

Supervised hello world!

In this example, we want to show how to perform a simple linear regression with bidimensional data. In particular, let's assume that we have a custom dataset containing 100 samples, as follows:

```
import numpy as np
import pandas as pd

T = np.expand_dims(np.linspace(0.0, 10.0, num=100), axis=1)
X = (T * np.random.uniform(1.0, 1.5, size=(100, 1))) + 
    np.random.normal(0.0, 3.5, size=(100, 1))
df = pd.DataFrame(np.concatenate([T, X], axis=1), columns=['t', 'x'])
```

 We have also created a pandas DataFrame because it's easier to create plots using the seaborn library (https://seaborn.pydata.org). In the book, the code for the plots (using Matplotlib or seaborn) is normally omitted, but it's always present in the repository.

We want to express the dataset in a synthetic way, as follows:

$$x(t) = at + b$$

This task can be carried out using a linear regression algorithm, as follows:

```
from sklearn.linear_model import LinearRegression

lr = LinearRegression()
lr.fit(T, X)

print('x(t) = {0:.3f}t + {1:.3f}'.format(lr.coef_[0][0], lr.intercept_[0]))
```

The output of the last command is the following:

```
x(t) = 1.169t + 0.628
```

We can also get visual confirmation, drawing the dataset together with the regression line, as shown in the following graph:

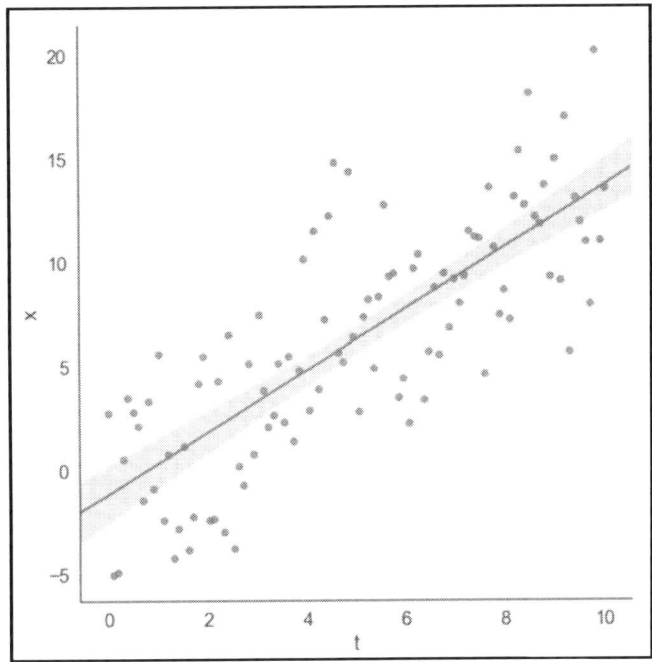

Dataset and regression line

In this example, the regression algorithm minimized a squared error cost function, trying to reduce the discrepancy between the predicted value and the actual one. The presence of Gaussian (with null mean) noise has a minimum impact on the slope, thanks to the symmetric distribution.

Unsupervised learning algorithms

In an unsupervised scenario, as it's easy to imagine, there is no hidden teacher, hence the main goals cannot be related to minimizing the prediction error with respect to the ground truth. Indeed, the same concept of ground truth has a slightly different meaning in this context. In fact, when working with classifiers, we want to have a null error for the training samples (meaning that other classes than the true ones are never accepted as correct).

Conversely, in an unsupervised problem, we want the model to learn some pieces of information without any formal indication. This condition implies that the only elements that can be learned are the ones contained in the samples themselves. Therefore, an unsupervised algorithm is usually aimed at discovering the similarities and patterns among samples or reproducing an input distribution given a set of vectors drawn from it. Let's now analyze some of the most common categories of unsupervised models.

Cluster analysis

Cluster analysis (normally called just **clustering**) is an example of a task where we want to find out common features among large sets of samples. In this case, we always suppose the existence of a data generating process $p_{data}(\bar{x})$ and we define the dataset X as:

$$X = \{\bar{x}_1, \bar{x}_2, \ldots, \bar{x}_N\} \text{ where } \bar{x}_i \sim p_{data}(\bar{x}) \text{ and } \bar{x}_i \in \mathbb{R}^M$$

A clustering algorithm is based on the implicit assumption that samples can be grouped according to their similarities. In particular, given two vectors, a similarity function is defined as the reciprocal or inverse of a metric function. For example, if we are working in a Euclidean space, we have:

$$d(\bar{x}_i, \bar{x}_j) = \sqrt{\sum_k \left(x_i^{(k)} - x_j^{(k)}\right)^2} \text{ and } s(\bar{x}_i, \bar{x}_j) = \frac{1}{d(\bar{x}_i, \bar{x}_j) + \epsilon}$$

In the previous formula, the constant ε has been introduced to avoid division by zero. It's obvious that $d(a, c) < d(a, b) \Rightarrow s(a, c) > s(a, b)$. Therefore, given a representative of each cluster $\bar{\mu}_i$, we can create the set of assigned vectors considering the rule:

$$C_i = \{\bar{x}_j : d(\bar{x}_j, \bar{\mu}_i) < d(\bar{x}_j, \bar{\mu}_k) \; \forall \, k \in (1, 2, \ldots, i-1, i+1, \ldots, N_c)\}$$

In other words, a cluster contains all those elements whose distance from the representative is minimum compared to all other representatives. This implies that a cluster contains samples whose similarity with the representative is maximal compared to all representatives. Moreover, after the assignment, a sample gains the *right* to share its feature with the other members of the same cluster.

In fact, one of the most important applications of cluster analysis is trying to increase the homogeneity of samples that are recognized as similar. For example, a recommendation engine could be based on the clustering of the user vectors (containing information about their interests and bought products). Once the groups have been defined, all the elements belonging to the same cluster are considered as similar, hence we are implicitly authorized to *share the differences*. If user A has bought the product P and rated it positively, we can suggest this item to user B who didn't buy it and the other way around. The process can appear arbitrary, but it turns out to be extremely effective when the number of elements is large and the feature vectors contain many discriminative elements (for example, ratings).

Generative models

Another unsupervised approach is based on **generative models**. The concept is not very different from what we have already discussed for supervised algorithms, but, in this case, the data generating process doesn't contain any label. Hence the goal is to model a parametrized distribution and optimize the parameters so that the distance between candidate distribution and the data generating process is minimized:

$$q(\bar{x}; \bar{\theta}) = p(\bar{x}; \bar{\theta})$$

The process is generally based on the Kullback-Leibler divergence or other similar measures:

$$L = D_{KL}(p_{data} || p) = \sum_{i=1}^{N} p_{data}(\bar{x}_i) \, log \frac{p_{data}(\bar{x}_i)}{p(\bar{x}_i; \bar{\theta})}$$

At the end of the training phase, we assume $L \to 0$, so $p \approx p_{data}$. In this way, we have not limited the analysis to a subset of possible samples, but rather to the entire distribution. Using a generative model allows you to draw new samples that can be very different from the ones selected for the training process, but they always belong to the same distribution. Therefore, they are (potentially) always acceptable.

For example, a **Generative Adversarial Network (GAN)** is a particular deep learning model that is able to learn the distribution of an image set, producing new samples that are almost indistinguishable (from a visual semantic point of view) from the training ones. As unsupervised learning is the main topic of this book, we won't dwell further on GAN in this introduction. All these concepts will be extensively discussed (with practical examples) in all the next chapters.

Association rules

The last unsupervised approach we're considering is based on the discovery of **association rules** and it's extremely important in the field of data mining. A common scenario is represented by a collection of commercial transactions made up of a subset of products. The goal is to find out the most important associations between products (for example, the probability of buying P_i and P_j is 70%). Specific algorithms can efficiently mine a whole database, highlighting all the relationships that can be taken into account for strategic and logistic purposes. For example, an online store can employ this method to promote all those items that are frequently bought together with other ones. Moreover, a predictive approach allows simplifying the provisioning processes by suggesting all those products that are very likely to be sold out, thanks to an increase in the sales of other items.

At this point, it's helpful to introduce the reader to a practical example of unsupervised learning. No particular prerequisites are needed, but it's preferable to have a basic knowledge of probability theory.

Unsupervised hello world!

As this book is completely dedicated to unsupervised algorithms, I've decided not to show a simple cluster analysis as a hello world! example, but rather a quite basic generative model. Let's assume that we are monitoring the number of trains that arrive at a subway station every hour because we need to ascertain the number of security agents required at the station. In particular, we're asked to have at least one agent per train and whenever there are fewer, we're going to pay a fine.

Moreover, it's easier to send a group at the beginning of every hour instead of controlling the agents one by one. As the problem is very simple, we also know that a good distribution is the Poisson one, parameterized with μ, which is also the mean. From the theory, we know that such a distribution can effectively model the random number of events happening in a fixed time frame, under the main assumption of independence. In general cases, a generative model is based on a parameterized distribution (for example, with a neural network) and no specific assumptions are made about its family. Only in some particular cases (for example, Gaussian mixture), is it reasonable to pick distributions with particular properties and, without loss of rigor, we can consider this example as one such scenario.

The probability mass function of a Poisson distribution is:

$$p(k; \mu) = \frac{\mu^k}{k!} e^{-\mu} \quad where \ k \in \mathbb{N}$$

This distribution describes the probability of observing k events in a predefined interval. In our case, the interval is always one hour and we're keen to estimate the probability of observing more than 10 trains. How can we obtain the correct figure for μ?

The most common strategy is called **Maximum Likelihood Estimation** (MLE). It collects a set of observations and finds the value of μ that maximizes the probability that all the points have been generated by our distribution.

Assuming we have collected N observations (each observation is the number of arrivals in one hour), the **likelihood** of μ with respect to all samples is the joint probability of all samples (for simplicity, assumed to be IID) under the probability distribution computed using μ:

$$L(\mu; k_1, k_2, \ldots, k_N) = p(k_1, k_2, \ldots, k_N; \mu) = \prod_{i=1}^{N} \frac{\mu_i^k}{k_i!} e^{-\mu}$$

As we are working with a product and exponential, it's a common rule to compute the **log-likelihood**:

$$\log L(\mu; k_1, k_2, \ldots, k_N) = \log \prod_{i=1}^{N} \frac{\mu_i^k}{k_i!} e^{-\mu} = \sum_{i=1}^{N} \log \frac{\mu_i^k}{k_i!} e^{-\mu}$$

Once the log-likelihood has been computed, it's possible to set the derivative with respect to μ equal to 0 in order to find the optimal value. In this case, we omit the proof (which is straightforward to obtain) and arrive directly at the MLE estimation of μ:

$$\mu_{opt} = \frac{1}{N} \sum_{i=1}^{N} k_i = Avg(k_i)$$

We are lucky! The MLE estimation is just the average of the arrival times. This means that, if we have observed N values with average μ, the Poisson distribution, which is the most likely to have generated them, has μ as the characteristic coefficient. Therefore, any other sample drawn from such a distribution will be *compatible* with the observed dataset.

Getting Started with Unsupervised Learning

We can now start with our first simulation. Let's assume we've collected 25 observations during the early afternoon of a business day, as follows:

```
import numpy as np

obs = np.array([7, 11, 9, 9, 8, 11, 9, 9, 8, 7, 11, 8, 9, 9, 11, 7, 10, 9,
10, 9, 7, 8, 9, 10, 13])
mu = np.mean(obs)

print('mu = {}'.format(mu))
```

The output of the last command is as follows:

```
mu = 9.12
```

Hence, we have an arrival average of about nine trains per hour. The histogram is shown in the following diagram:

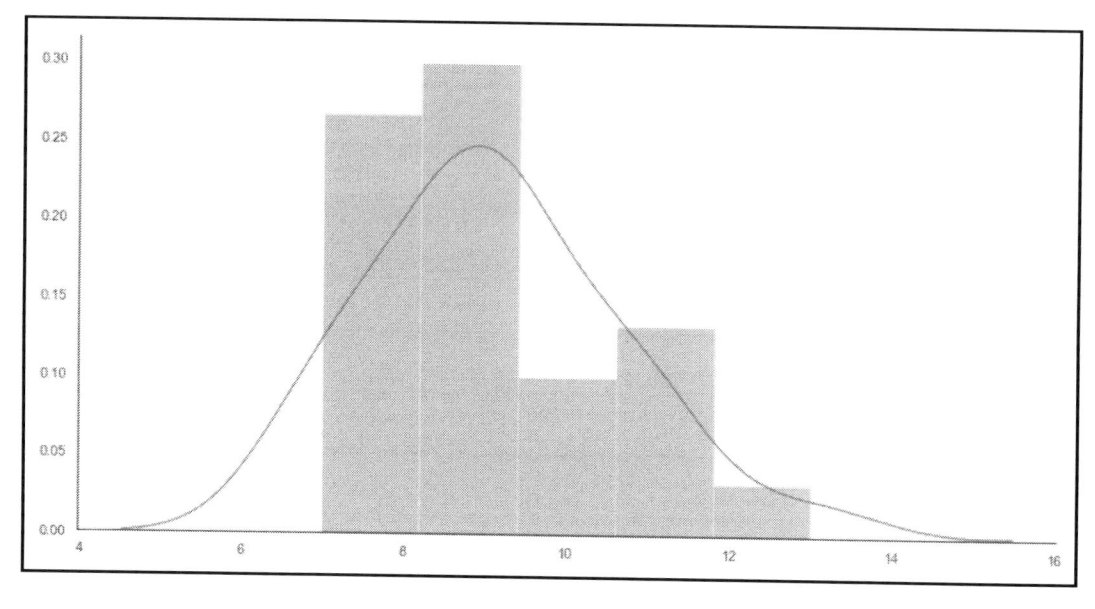

Histogram of the initial distribution

To compute the requested probabilities, we need to work with the **Cumulative Distribution Function** (**CDF**), which is implemented in SciPy (in the `scipy.stats` package). In particular, as we are interested in the probability of observing more trains than a fixed value, it's necessary to use the **Survival Function** (**SF**), which corresponds to *1-CDF*, as follows:

```
from scipy.stats import poisson

print('P(more than 8 trains) = {}'.format(poisson.sf(8, mu)))
print('P(more than 9 trains) = {}'.format(poisson.sf(9, mu)))
print('P(more than 10 trains) = {}'.format(poisson.sf(10, mu)))
print('P(more than 11 trains) = {}'.format(poisson.sf(11, mu)))
```

The output of the preceding snippet is as follows:

```
P(more than 8 trains) = 0.5600494497386543
P(more than 9 trains) = 0.42839824517059516
P(more than 10 trains) = 0.30833234660452563
P(more than 11 trains) = 0.20878680161156604
```

As expected, the probability of observing more than 10 trains is low (30%) and it doesn't seem reasonable to send 10 agents. However, as our model is adaptive, we can continue collecting observations (for example, during the early morning), as follows:

```
new_obs = np.array([13, 14, 11, 10, 11, 13, 13, 9, 11, 14, 12, 11, 12, 14,
8, 13, 10, 14, 12, 13, 10, 9, 14, 13, 11, 14, 13, 14])

obs = np.concatenate([obs, new_obs])
mu = np.mean(obs)

print('mu = {}'.format(mu))
```

The new value for μ is as follows:

```
mu = 10.641509433962264
```

Now the average is almost 11 trains per hour. Assuming that we have collected enough samples (considering all potential accidents), we can re-estimate the probabilities, as follows:

```
print('P(more than 8 trains) = {}'.format(poisson.sf(8, mu)))
print('P(more than 9 trains) = {}'.format(poisson.sf(9, mu)))
print('P(more than 10 trains) = {}'.format(poisson.sf(10, mu)))
print('P(more than 11 trains) = {}'.format(poisson.sf(11, mu)))
```

The output is as follows:

```
P(more than 8 trains)  = 0.7346243910180037
P(more than 9 trains)  = 0.6193541369812121
P(more than 10 trains) = 0.49668918740243756
P(more than 11 trains) = 0.3780218948425254
```

With the new dataset, the probability of observing more than nine trains is about 62%, (which confirms our initial choice), but the probability of observing more than 10 trains is now about 50%. As we don't want to risk paying the fine (which is higher than the cost of an agent), it's always better to send a group of 10 agents. In order to get further confirmation, we have decided to sample 2,000 values from the distribution, as follows:

```
syn = poisson.rvs(mu, size=2000)
```

The corresponding histogram is shown in the following diagram:

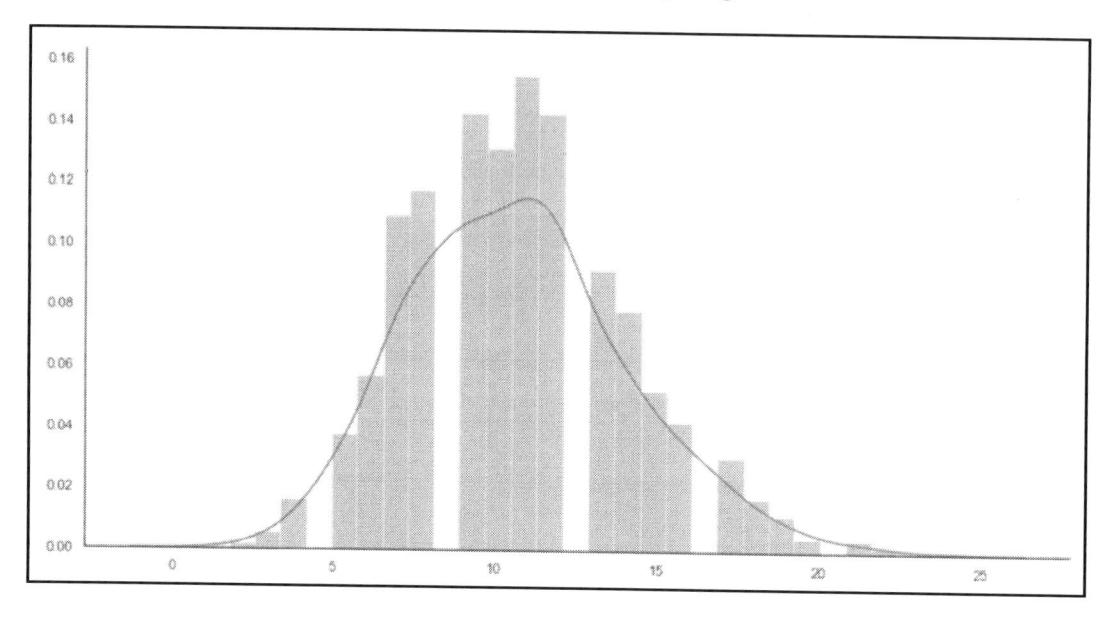

Histogram of 2000 points sampled from the final Poisson distribution

The diagram confirms a peak slightly after 10 (very close to 11) and a rapid decay starting from $k = 13$, which has already been discovered using a limited dataset (compare the shapes of the histograms for further confirmation). However, in this case, we are generating potential samples that couldn't be present in our observation set. The MLE guarantees that the probability distribution is consistent with the data and that the new samples are weighted accordingly. This example is clearly extremely simple and its goal was only to show the dynamics of a generative model.

We are going to discuss many other more complex models and examples in the next chapters of the book. One important technique, common to many algorithms lies in not picking a predefined distribution (which implies an apriori knowledge) but rather in using flexible parametric models (for example, neural networks) to find out the optimal distribution. The choice of a predefined prior (as in this case) is justified only when there's a high confidence degree about the underlying stochastic process. In all other situations, it's always preferable to avoid any assumption and rely only on the data in order to find the most appropriate approximation of the data generating process.

Semi-supervised learning algorithms

A semi-supervised scenario can be considered as a standard supervised one that exploits some features belonging to unsupervised learning techniques. A very common problem, in fact, arises when it's easy to obtain large unlabeled datasets but the cost of labeling is very high. Hence, it's reasonable to label only a fraction of the samples and to propagate the labels to all unlabeled ones whose distance from a labeled sample is below a predefined threshold. If the dataset has been drawn from a single data generating process and the labeled samples are uniformly distributed, a semi-supervised algorithm can achieve an accuracy comparable with a supervised one. In this book, we are not discussing these algorithms; however, it's helpful to briefly introduce two very important models:

- Label propagation
- Semi-supervised Support Vector Machines

The first one is called **label propagation** and its goal is to propagate the labels of a few samples to a larger population. This goal is achieved by considering a graph where each vertex represents a sample and every edge is weighted using a distance function. Through an iterative procedure, all labeled samples will send a fraction of their label values to all their neighbors and the process is repeated until the labels stop changing. This system has a stable point (that is, a configuration that cannot evolve anymore) and the algorithm can easily reach it with a limited number of iterations.

Label propagation is extremely helpful in all those contexts where some samples can be labeled according to a similarity measure. For example, an online store could have a large base of customers, but only 10% have disclosed their gender. If the feature vectors are rich enough to represent the common behavior of male and female users, it's possible to employ the label propagation algorithm to guess the gender of customers who haven't disclosed it. Of course, it's important to remember that all the assignments are based on the assumption that similar samples have the same label. This can be true in many situations, but it can also be misleading when the complexity of the feature vectors increases.

Another important family of semi-supervised algorithms is based on the extension of standard **SVM**, (short for **Support Vector Machine**) to datasets containing unlabeled samples. In this case, we don't want to propagate existing labels, but rather the classification criterion. In other words, we want to train the classifier using the labeled dataset and extend the discriminative rule to the unlabeled samples as well.

Contrary to the standard procedure that can only evaluate unlabeled samples, a semi-supervised SVM uses them to correct the separating hyperplane. The assumption is always based on the similarity: if A has label 1 and the unlabeled sample B has $d(A, B) < \varepsilon$ (where ε is a predefined threshold), it's reasonable to assume that the label of B is also 1. In this way, the classifier can achieve high accuracy on the whole dataset even if only a subset has been manually labeled. Similar to label propagation, these kinds of model are reliable only when the structure of the dataset is not extremely complex and, in particular, when the similarity assumption holds (unfortunately there are some cases where it's extremely difficult to find a suitable distance metric, hence many similar samples are indeed dissimilar and vice versa).

Reinforcement learning algorithms

A reinforcement learning scenario can be considered as a supervised one where the hidden teacher provides only approximate feedback after every decision of the model. More formally, reinforcement learning is characterized by continuous interaction between an agent and an environment. The former is responsible for making decisions (actions), finalized to increase its return, while the latter provides feedback to every action. Feedback is generally considered as a reward, whose value can be either positive (the action has been successful) or negative (the action shouldn't be repeated). As the agent analyzes different configurations of the environment (states), every reward must be considered as bound to the tuple (action, state). Hence, the final goal is to find a policy (a strategy that suggests the optimal action in every state) that maximizes the expected total reward.

A very classical example of reinforcement learning is an agent that learns how to play a game. During an episode, the agent tests the actions in all encountered states and collects the rewards. An algorithm corrects the policy to reduce the likelihood of non-positive actions (that is, those whose reward is positive) and increase the expected total rewards obtainable at the end of the episode.

Reinforcement learning has many interesting applications, which are not limited to games. For example, a recommendation system can correct suggestions according to binary feedback (for example, thumb up or down) provided by the user. The main difference between reinforcement and supervised learning is the information provided by the environment. In fact, in a supervised scenario, the correction is normally proportional to it, while in a reinforcement learning one it must be analyzed considering a sequence of actions and future rewards. Therefore, the corrections are normally based on the estimation of the expected reward and their effect is influenced by the value of the subsequent actions. For example, a supervised model has no memory, hence its corrections are immediate, while a reinforcement learning agent must consider the partial rollout of an episode in order to decide whether an action is actually negative or not.

Reinforcement learning is a fascinating branch of machine learning. Unfortunately, this topic is beyond the scope of this work, therefore we are not discussing it in detail (you can find further details in *Hands-On Reinforcement Learning with Python, Ravichandiran S., Packt Publishing,* 2018 and *Mastering Machine Learning Algorithms, Bonaccorso G., Packt Publishing,* 2018).

We can now briefly explain why Python has been chosen as the main language for this exploration of the world of unsupervised learning.

Why Python for data science and machine learning?

Before moving on with more technical discussions, I think it's helpful to explain the choice of Python as the programming language for this book. In the last decade, research in the field of data science and machine learning has seen exponential growth, with thousands of valuable papers and dozens of complete tools. In particular, thanks to its efficiency, elegance, and compactness, Python has been chosen by many researchers and programmers to create a complete scientific ecosystem that has been released for free.

Nowadays, packages such as scikit-learn, SciPy, NumPy, Matplotlib, pandas, and many others represent the backbone of hundreds of production-ready systems and their usage keeps growing. Moreover, complex deep learning applications such as Theano, TensorFlow, and PyTorch allow every Python user to create and train complex models without any speed limits. In fact, it's important to note that Python is not a scripting language anymore. It supports dozens of specific tasks (for example, web frameworks and graphics) and it can be interfaced with native code written in C or C++.

For such reasons, Python is an optimal choice in almost any data science project and due to its features all programmers with different backgrounds can easily learn to use it effectively in a short time. Other free solutions are also available (for example, R, Java, or Scala), however, in the case of R, there's complete coverage of statistical and mathematical functions but it lacks the support frameworks that are necessary to build complete applications. Conversely, Java and Scala have a complete ecosystem of production-ready libraries, but, in particular, Java is not as compact and easy to use as Python. Moreover, the support for native code is much more complex and the majority of libraries rely exclusively on the JVM (with a consequent performance loss).

Scala has gained an important position in the big data panorama, thanks to its functional properties and the existence of frameworks such as Apache Spark, (which can be employed to carry out machine learning tasks with big data). However, considering all the pros and cons, Python remains the optimal choice and that's why it has been chosen for this book.

Summary

In this chapter, we have discussed the main reasons that justify the employment of machine learning models and how a dataset can be analyzed in order to describe its features, enumerate the causes behind specific behaviors, predict future behavior, and influence it.

We also explored the differences between supervised, unsupervised, semi-supervised, and reinforcement learning, focusing on the first two models. We also used two simple examples to understand both supervised and unsupervised approaches.

In the next chapter, we'll introduce the fundamental concepts of cluster analysis, focusing the discussion on some very famous algorithms, such as k-means and **K-Nearest Neighbors (KNN)**, together with the most important evaluation metrics.

Questions

1. Unsupervised learning is the most common alternative when supervised learning is not applicable. Is it correct?
2. The CEO of your company asks you to find out the factors that determined a negative sales trend. What kind of analysis do you need to perform?

3. Given a dataset of independent samples and a candidate data generating process (for example, a Gaussian distribution), the likelihood is obtained by summing the probabilities of all samples. It is correct?
4. Under which hypothesis can the likelihood be computed as a product of single probabilities?
5. Suppose we have a dataset of students containing some unknown numerical features (for example, age, marks, and so on). You want to separate male and female students, so you decide to cluster the dataset into two groups. Unfortunately, both clusters have roughly 50% male and 50% female students. How can you explain this result?
6. Consider the previous example, but repeat the experiment and cluster into five groups. What do you expect to find in each of them? (List some reasonable possibilities.)
7. You've clustered the customers of an online store. Given a new sample, what kind of prediction can you make?

Further reading

- *Machine Learning Algorithms Second Edition, Bonaccorso G., Packt Publishing,* 2018
- *Hands-On Reinforcement Learning with Python, Ravichandiran S., Packt Publishing,* 2018
- *Hands-On Data Analysis with NumPy and pandas, Miller C., Packt Publishing,* 2018

Clustering Fundamentals

In this chapter, we are going to introduce the fundamental concept of cluster analysis, focusing the attention on our main principles that are shared by many algorithms and the most important techniques that can be employed to evaluate the performance of a method.

In particular, we are going to discuss:

- An introduction to clustering and distance functions
- K-means and K-means++
- Evaluation metrics
- **K-Nearest Neighbors (KNN)**
- **Vector Quantization (VQ)**

Technical requirements

The code presented in this chapter requires:

- Python 3.5+ (Anaconda distribution: `https://www.anaconda.com/distribution/` is highly recommended)
- Libraries:
    - SciPy 0.19+
    - NumPy 1.10+
    - scikit-learn 0.20+
    - pandas 0.22+
    - Matplotlib 2.0+
    - seaborn 0.9+

The dataset can be obtained through UCI. The CSV file can be downloaded from `https://archive.ics.uci.edu/ml/machine-learning-databases/breast-cancer-wisconsin/wdbc.data` and doesn't need any preprocessing except for the addition of the column names that will occur during the loading stage.

The examples are available on the GitHub repository:

`https://github.com/PacktPublishing/HandsOn-Unsupervised-Learning-with-Python/Chapter02`.

Introduction to clustering

As we explained in Chapter 1, *Getting Started with Unsupervised Learning*, the main goal of a cluster analysis is to group the elements of a dataset according to a similarity measure or a proximity criterion. In the first part of this chapter, we are going to focus on the former approach, while in the second part and in the next chapter, we will analyze more generic methods that exploit other geometric features of the dataset.

Let's take a data generating process $p_{data}(x)$ and draw N samples from it:

$$X = \{\bar{x}_1, \bar{x}_2, \ldots, \bar{x}_N\} \ \ where \ \ \bar{x}_i \sim p_{data}(\bar{x}) \ \ and \ \ \bar{x}_i \in \mathbb{R}^M$$

It's possible to assume that the probability space of $p_{data}(x)$ is partitionable into (potentially infinite) configurations containing K (for K=1,2, ...) regions so that $p_{data}(x; k)$ represents the probability of a sample belonging to a cluster k. In this way, we are stating that every possible clustering structure is already existing when $p_{data}(x)$ is determined. Further assumptions can be made on the clustering probability distribution that better approximate $p_{data}(x)$ (as we're going to see in Chapter 5, *Soft Clustering and Gaussian Mixture Models*). However, as we are trying to split the probability space (and the corresponding samples) into cohesive groups, we can assume two possible strategies:

- **Hard clustering**: In this case, each sample $x_p \in X$ is assigned to a cluster K_i and $K_i \cap K_j = \emptyset$ for $i \neq j$. The majority of algorithms we are going to discuss belong to this category. In this case, the problem can be expressed as a parameterized function that assigns a cluster to each input sample:

$$k = c(\bar{x}; \bar{\theta}) \ \ where \ \ k = 0, 1, 2, \ldots, K$$

- **Soft clustering**: It is often subdivided into **probabilistic** and **fuzzy** clustering and such an approach determines the probability $p(x)$ of every sample $x_p \in$ X belonging to predetermined clusters. Hence, if there are K clusters, we have a probability vector $p(x) = [p_1(x), p_2(x), ..., p_k(x)]$, where $p_i(x)$ represents the probability of being assigned to the cluster i. In this case, the clusters are not disjointed and, generally, a sample will belong to all clusters with a *membership degree* that is equivalent to a probability (this concept is peculiar to fuzzy clustering).

For our purposes, in this chapter we simply assume that the dataset X is drawn from a data generating process whose space, given a metric function, is splittable into compact regions separated from each other. In fact, our main objective is to find K clusters that satisfy the double property of **maximum cohesion** and **maximum separation**. This concept will be clearer when discussing the K-means algorithm. However, it's possible to imagine clusters as blobs whose density is much higher than the one observable in the space separating two or more of them, as shown in the following diagram:

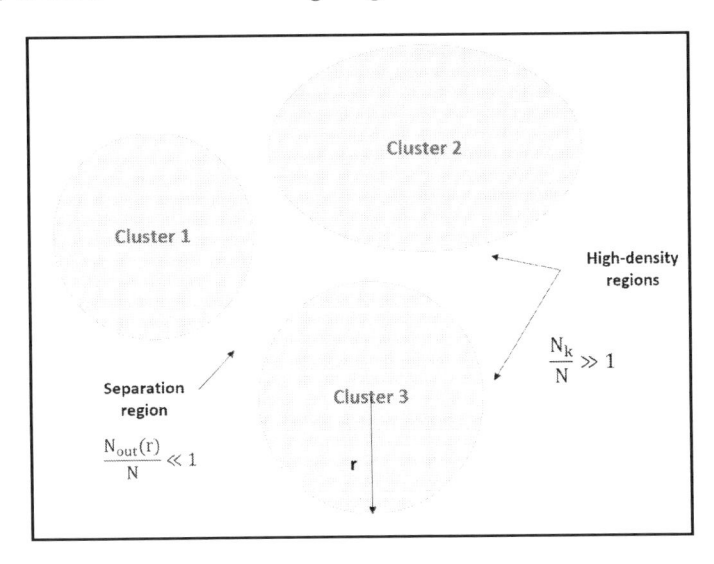

Bidimensional clustering structure obeying the rule of maximum cohesion and maximum separation. N_k represents the number of samples belonging to the cluster k while $N_{out}(r)$ is the number of samples that are outside the balls centered at each cluster center with a maximum radius r

In the preceding diagram, we are assuming that the majority of samples will be captured by one of the balls, considering the maximum distance of a sample from the center. However, as we don't want to impose any restriction on the growth of a ball (that is, it can contain any number of samples), it's preferable not to consider the radius and to evaluate the separating region by sampling small subregions (of the whole space) and collecting their densities.

In a perfect scenario, the clusters span some subregions whose density is D, while the separating region is characterized by a density $d \ll D$. The discussion about geometric properties can become extremely complex and, in many cases, it's extremely theoretical. Henceforth, we consider only the distance between the closest points belonging to different clusters. If this value is much smaller than the maximum distance between a sample and its cluster center for all clusters, we can be sure that the separation is effective and it's easy to distinguish between clusters and separating regions. Instead, when working with a distance metric (for example, in K-means), another important requirement we need to consider is the **convexity** of the clusters. A generic set C is convex if $\forall x_1, x_2 \in C$, and all the points belonging to the segment connecting x_1 and x_2 belong to C. In the following diagram there's a comparison between convex and non-convex (concave) clusters:

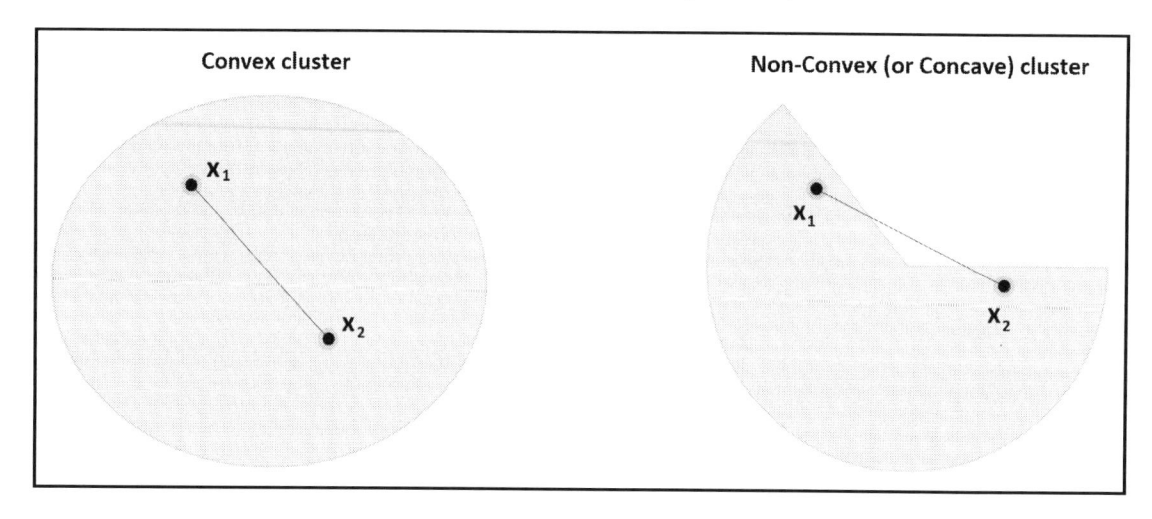

Example of a convex cluster (left) and a concave one (right)

Algorithms such as K-means are unfortunately unable to manage non-convex clusters because of the symmetry of the distance functions. In our exploration, we are going to show this limitation and how other methods overcome it.

Distance functions

Even if generic definitions of clustering are normally based on the concept of **similarity**, it's quite easy to employ its inverse, which is represented by **distance function** (dissimilarity measure). The most common choice is the **Euclidean distance**, but before choosing it, it's necessary to consider its properties and their behaviors in high-dimensional spaces. Let's start by introducing the **Minkowski distance** as a generalization of the Euclidean one. If the sample is $x_i \in \Re^N$, it is defined as:

$$d_p(\bar{x}_1, \bar{x}_2) = \left(\sum_{i=1}^{N} |\bar{x}_1^{(i)} - \bar{x}_2^{(i)}|^p \right)^{\frac{1}{p}}$$

For p=1, we obtain the **Manhattan** (or **city block**) distance, while p=2 corresponds to the standard Euclidean distance. We want to understand the behavior of d_p when $p \to \infty$. Let's suppose we're working in a bidimensional space and have a cluster whose center is x_c=(0, 0) and a sample point x=(5, 3), the distances $d_p(x_c, x)$ with respect to different values of p are:

$$\begin{cases} d_1(\bar{x}_c, \bar{x}) = 8 \\ d_2(\bar{x}_c, \bar{x}) \approx 5.83 \\ d_5(\bar{x}_c, \bar{x}) \approx 5.075 \\ d_{10}(\bar{x}_c, \bar{x}) \approx 5.003 \\ d_{100}(\bar{x}_c, \bar{x}) \approx 5.0 \end{cases}$$

It's clear (and very simple to prove) that if $|x_1^j - x_2^j|$ is the largest component absolute difference, $p \to \infty$, $d_p(x_c, x) \to |x_1^j - x_2^j|$. This means that, if we are considering the similarity (or dissimilarity) as the result of the differences due to all components, we need to pick a small value for p (for example, p=1 or 2). On the other hand, if two samples must be considered different only according to the largest absolute difference between components, higher values for p are suitable. In general, this choice is very context-dependent and cannot be easily generalized. For our purposes, we often take into account only the Euclidean distance, which is reasonable in the majority of cases. On the other hand, choosing larger values for p has important consequences when $N \to \infty$. Let's start with an example. We want to measure the distance between the 1N-vector (a vector belonging to $\Re^N$ with all components equal to 1) from the origin for different values of p and N (using a log-scale to compress the y axis), which can be done as follows:

```
import numpy as np

from scipy.spatial.distance import cdist
```

```
distances = np.zeros(shape=(8, 100))

for i in range(1, distances.shape[0] + 1):
    for j in range(1, distances.shape[1] + 1):
        distances[i - 1, j - 1] = np.log(cdist(np.zeros(shape=(1, j)),
np.ones(shape=(1, j)),
                                                 metric='minkowski',
p=i)[0][0])
```

The distances are shown in the following plot:

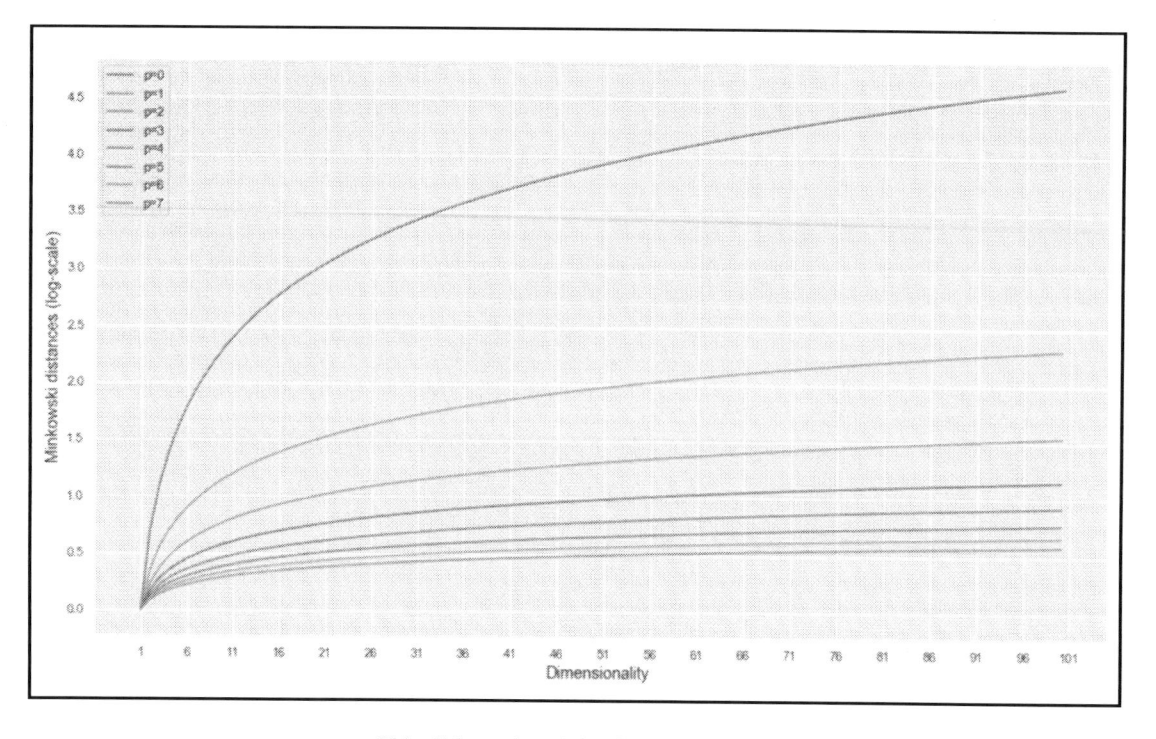

Minkowski distances (log-scale) for different values of p and N

The first result is that if we pick a value for N, the distances contract and saturate when $p \to \infty$. This is a normal consequence of the structure of the Minkowski distance, but there's another element that sharp-eyed readers could have noticed. Let's imagine setting one of the components of the *1N*-vector equal to *0.0*. This is equivalent to moving from a vertex of the N-dimensional hypercube to another one. What happens to the distance? Well, it's easy to prove with an example that, when $p \to \infty$, the two distances converge to the same value. In particular, Aggarwal, Hinneburg, and Keim (in *On the Surprising Behavior of Distance Metrics in High Dimensional Space, Aggarwal C. C., Hinneburg A., Keim D. A., ICDT* 2001) proved an important result.

Let's suppose we have a distribution $p(x)$ of M binary samples $x_i \in (0, 1)^d$. If we employ the Minkowski metric, we can compute the maximum (D_{max}^p) and minimum (D_{min}^p) distance between two points sampled from $p(x)$ and the origin (in general, this distance can be computed analytically, but it's also possible to use an iterative procedure that continues sampling until D_{max}^p and D_{min}^p stop changing). The authors proved that the following inequality holds:

$$C_p \leqslant \lim_{d \to \infty} E\left[\frac{D_{max}^p - D_{min}^p}{d^{\frac{1}{p} - \frac{1}{2}}}\right] \leqslant (M-1)C_p \text{ where } C_p \geqslant 0$$

In the previous formula, C_p is a constant dependent on p. When $p \to \infty$, the limit of the expected value $E[D_{max}^p - D_{min}^p]$ is captured between the boundaries $k_1 C_p d^{1/p - 1/2}$ and $(M-1)C_p d^{1/p - 1/2}$. As the term $d^{1/p - 1/2} \to 0$ when $p > 2$ and $d \to \infty$, the expected value of the difference between the maximum and minimum distances converges to 0. This means that, independently from the samples, when the dimensionality is high enough and $p > 2$, it's almost impossible to distinguish between two samples using the Minkowski distance. As we are finding the similarity on a distance function, this theorem warns us about the choice of large values for p when $d \gg 1$. The common choice of the Euclidean metric is quite reliable also when $d \gg 1$ (even if $p=1$ would be the optimal choice) because it has a minimum effect on the weight of the components (it's possible to assume that they have the same weight) and guarantees distinguishability in high-dimensional spaces. Conversely, $p \gg 2$ in a high-dimensional space yields indistinguishable distances for all samples where the maximum component is kept fixed and all the other ones are modified (for example, if $x=(5, 0) \to (5, a)$ where $|a| < 5$), as shown in the following example:

```
import numpy as np

from scipy.spatial.distance import cdist

distances = []

for i in range(1, 2500, 10):
    d = cdist(np.array([[0, 0]]), np.array([[5, float(i/500)]]),
metric='minkowski', p=15)[0][0]
    distances.append(d)

print('Avg(distances) = {}'.format(np.mean(distances)))
print('Std(distances) = {}'.format(np.std(distances)))
```

Clustering Fundamentals

The output is as follows:

```
Avg(distances) = 5.0168687736484765
Std(distances) = 0.042885311128215066
```

Hence, for p = 15, all samples *(5, x)* for *x ∈ [0.002, 5.0)* has distance from the origin whose mean is about 5.0 and the standard deviation is about 0.04. When p becomes larger, Avg(distances) = 5.0 and Std(distances) = 0.04.

At this point, we can start discussing one of the most common and widely adopted clustering algorithms: K-means.

K-means

K-means is the simplest implementation of the principle of maximum separation and maximum internal cohesion. Let's suppose we have a dataset $X \in \mathfrak{R}^{M \times N}$ (that is, *M* *N*-dimensional samples) that we want to split into *K* clusters and a set of *K* **centroids** corresponding to the means of the samples assigned to each cluster K_j:

$$M^{(0)} = \left\{ \bar{\mu}_0^{(0)}, \bar{\mu}_1^{(0)}, \ldots, \bar{\mu}_K^{(0)} \right\} \quad where \quad \bar{\mu}_i^{(t)} \in \mathbb{R}^N$$

The set *M* and the centroids have an additional index (as a superscript) indicating the iterative step. Starting from an initial guess $M^{(0)}$, K-means tries to minimize an objective function called **inertia** (that is, the total average intra-cluster distance between samples assigned to a cluster K_j and its centroid μ_j):

$$S(t) = \sum_{k=1}^{K} \sum_{\bar{x}_i \in K_j} \left\| \bar{x}_i - \bar{\mu}_k^{(t)} \right\|^2$$

It's easy to understand that S(t) cannot be considered as an absolute measure because its value is highly influenced by the variance of the samples. However, S(t+1) < S(t) implies that the centroids are moving closer to an optimal position where the points assigned to a cluster have the smallest possible distance to the corresponding centroid. Hence, the iterative procedure (also known as **Lloyd's algorithm**) starts by initializing $M^{(0)}$ with random values. The next step is the assignment of each sample $x_i \in X$ to the cluster whose centroid has the smallest distance from x_i:

$$c(\bar{x}_i; M^{(t)}) = argmin_j^{(t)}\ d\left(\bar{x}_i, \bar{\mu}_j^{(t)}\right)$$

Once all assignments have been completed, the new centroids are recomputed as arithmetic means:

$$\bar{\mu}_j^{(t)} = \frac{1}{N_{K_j}} \sum_{\bar{x}_i \in K_j} \bar{x}_j = \langle \bar{x}_j \rangle_{K_j}$$

The procedure is repeated until the centroids stop changing (this implies also a sequence $S(0) > S(1) > ... > S(t_{end})$). The reader should have immediately understood that the computational time is highly influenced by the initial guess. If $M^{(0)}$ is very close to $M^{(t_{end})}$, a few iterations can find the optimal configuration. Conversely, when $M^{(0)}$ is purely random, the probability of an inefficient initial choice is close to 1 (that is, every initial uniform random choice is almost equivalent in terms of computational complexity).

K-means++

Finding the optimal initial configuration is equivalent to minimizing the inertia; however, Arthur and Vassilvitskii (in *K-means++: The Advantages of Careful Seeding, Arthur D., Vassilvitskii S., Proceedings of the Eighteenth Annual ACM-SIAM Symposium on Discrete Algorithms*, 2007) have proposed an alternative initialization method (called **K-means++**), which can dramatically improve the convergence speed by choosing initial centroids with a higher probability of being close to the final ones. The complete proof is quite complex and can be found in the aforementioned paper. In this context, we are providing directly the final results and some important consequences.

Let's consider the function $D(\bullet)$ defined as:

$$D(\bar{x}, i) = min_i\ d(\bar{x}, \bar{\mu}_i)\ \forall\ i \in [1, p]\ where\ p \leqslant K$$

$D(\bullet)$ represents the shortest distance between a sample $x \in X$ and a centroid already selected. Once the function has been computed, it's possible to determine a probability distribution $G(x)$ as follows:

$$G(\bar{x}) = \frac{D(\bar{x}, i)^2}{\sum_{j=1}^{M} D(\bar{x}_j, i_j)^2}$$

The first centroid μ_1 is sampled from a uniform distribution. At this point, it's possible to compute $D(\bullet)$ for all samples $x \in X$ and, therefore, the distribution $G(x)$. It's straightforward that if we sample from $G(x)$, the probability of selecting a value in a dense region is much larger than the probability of uniform sampling or of picking a centroid in a separating region. Hence, we continue by sampling μ_2 from $G(x)$. The procedure is repeated until all K centroids have been determined. Of course, as this is a probabilistic approach, we have no guarantee that the final configuration is optimal. However, the employment of K-means++ is $O(log\ K)$-competitive. In fact, if S_{opt} is the theoretical optimal value for S, the authors proved that the following inequality holds:

$$E[S] \leqslant 8 S_{opt}(log\ K + 2)$$

As S is decreased by a better choice, the previous formula sets an upper bound for the expected value $E[S]$ roughly proportional to $log\ K$. For example, for $K=10$, $E[S] \leq 19.88 \cdot S_{opt}$ and $E[S] \leq 12.87 \cdot S_{opt}$ for $K=3$. This result reveals two important elements. The first one is that K-means++ performs better when K is not extremely large and the second, probably also the most important, is that a single K-means++ initialization cannot be enough to obtain the optimal configuration. For this reason, common implementations (for example, scikit-learn) performs a variable number of initializations and select the one whose initial inertia is the smallest.

Analysis of the Breast Cancer Wisconsin dataset

In this chapter, we are using the well-known **Breast Cancer Wisconsin dataset** to perform a cluster analysis. Originally, the dataset was proposed in order to train classifiers; however, it can be very helpful for a non-trivial cluster analysis. It contains 569 records made up of 32 attributes (including the diagnosis and an identification number). All the attributes are strictly related to biological and morphological properties of the tumors, but our goal is to validate generic hypotheses considering the ground truth (benign or malignant) and the statistical properties of the dataset. Before moving on, it's important to clarify some points. The dataset is high-dimensional and the clusters are non-convex (so we cannot expect a perfect segmentation). Moreover our goal is not using a clustering algorithm to obtain the results of a classifier; therefore, the ground truth must be taken into account only as a generic indication of a potential grouping. The goal of such an example is to show how to perform a brief preliminary analysis, select the optimal number of clusters, and validate the final results.

Once downloaded (as explained in the technical requirements section), the CSV file must be placed in a folder that we generically indicate as `<data_folder>`. The first step is loading the dataset and performing a global statistical analysis through the function `describe()` exposed by a pandas `DataFrame`, as follows:

```
import numpy as np
import pandas as pd

bc_dataset_path = '<data_path>\wdbc.data'

bc_dataset_columns = ['id','diagnosis', 'radius_mean', 'texture_mean',
'perimeter_mean',
 'area_mean', 'smoothness_mean', 'compactness_mean', 'concavity_mean',
 'concave points_mean', 'symmetry_mean', 'fractal_dimension_mean',
 'radius_se','texture_se', 'perimeter_se', 'area_se', 'smoothness_se',
 'compactness_se', 'concavity_se', 'concave points_se', 'symmetry_se',
 'fractal_dimension_se', 'radius_worst', 'texture_worst',
'perimeter_worst',
 'area_worst', 'smoothness_worst', 'compactness_worst', 'concavity_worst',
 'concave points_worst', 'symmetry_worst', 'fractal_dimension_worst']

df = pd.read_csv(bc_dataset_path, index_col=0,
names=bc_dataset_columns).fillna(0.0)
print(df.describe())
```

I strongly suggest using a Jupyter Notebook (in this case, the command must be only `df.describe()`), where all the commands yield inline outputs. For practical reasons, in the following screenshot, the first part of the tabular output (containing eight attributes) is shown:

	radius_mean	texture_mean	perimeter_mean	area_mean	smoothness_mean	compactness_mean	concavity_mean	concave points_mean
count	569.000000	569.000000	569.000000	569.000000	569.000000	569.000000	569.000000	569.000000
mean	14.127292	19.289649	91.969033	654.889104	0.096360	0.104341	0.088799	0.048919
std	3.524049	4.301036	24.298981	351.914129	0.014064	0.052813	0.079720	0.038803
min	6.981000	9.710000	43.790000	143.500000	0.052630	0.019380	0.000000	0.000000
25%	11.700000	16.170000	75.170000	420.300000	0.086370	0.064920	0.029560	0.020310
50%	13.370000	18.840000	86.240000	551.100000	0.095870	0.092630	0.061540	0.033500
75%	15.780000	21.800000	104.100000	782.700000	0.105300	0.130400	0.130700	0.074000
max	28.110000	39.280000	188.500000	2501.000000	0.163400	0.345400	0.426800	0.201200

Statistical report of the first eight attributes of the dataset

Of course, I invite the reader to check the values for all attributes, even if we are focusing our attention only on a subset. In particular, we need to observe the different scales existing among the first eight attributes. The standard deviations range from 0.01 to 350 and this means that many vectors could be extremely similar only because of one or two attributes. On the other side, normalizing the value with a variance scaling will give all the attributes the same responsibility (for example, `area_mean` is bounded between `143.5` and `2501`, while `smoothness_mean` is bounded between `0.05` and `0.16`. Forcing them to have the same variance can influence the biological impact of the factors and, as we don't have any specific indication, we are not *authorized* to make such a choice). Clearly, some attributes will have a higher weight in the clustering process and we accept their major influence as a context-related condition.

Let's start now a preliminary analysis considering the pair-plot of `perimeter_mean`, `area_mean`, `smoothness_mean`, `concavity_mean`, and `symmetry_mean`. The plot is shown in the following screenshot:

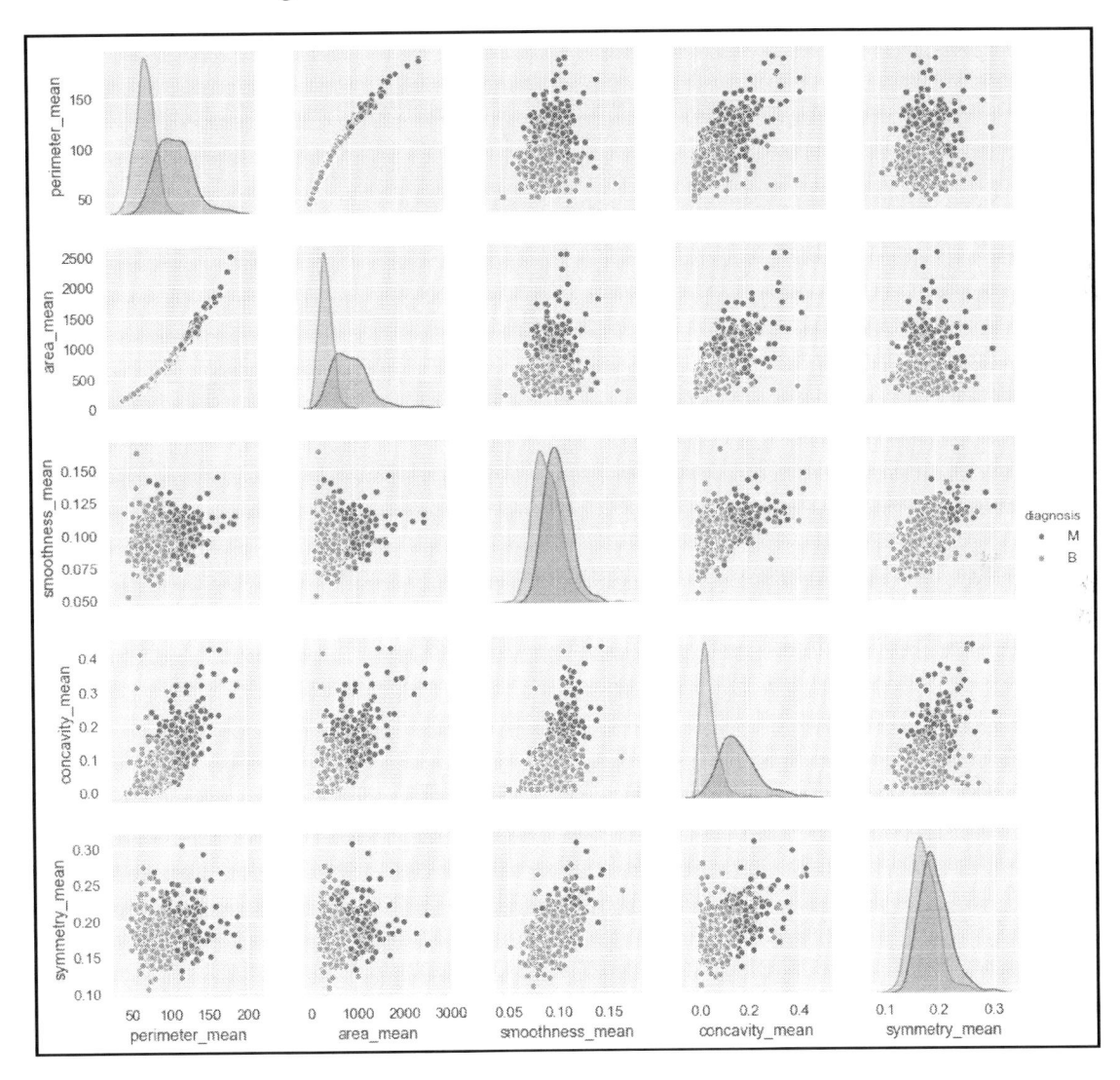

Pair-plot of perimeter mean, area mean, smoothness mean, concavity mean, and symmetry mean

The diagram plots each non-diagonal attribute as a function of all the other ones, while the diagonal plots represent the distributions of every attribute split into two components (in this case, this is the diagnosis). Hence, the second non-diagonal plot (top-left) is the diagram of `perimeter_mean` as a function of `area_mean`, and so on. A rapid analysis highlights some interesting elements:

- `area_mean` and `perimeter_mean` have a clear correlation and determine a sharp separation. When `area_mean` is greater than about 1,000, obviously also the perimeter increases and the diagnosis switches abruptly from benign to malignant. Hence these two attributes are determinant for the final result and one of them is likely to be redundant.
- Other plots (for example, `perimeter_mean`/`area_mean` versus `smoothness_mean`, `area_mean` versus `symmetry_mean`, `concavity_mean` versus `smoothness_mean`, and `concavity_mean` versus `symmetry_mean`) have a horizontal separation, (which becomes vertical inverting the axis). This means that, for almost all values assumed by the independent variable (x axis), there's a threshold that separates the values of the other variable in two sets (benign and malignant).
- Some plots (for example, `perimeter_mean`/`area_mean` versus `concavity_mean`/`concavity_mean` versus `symmetry_mean`) show a slightly negative sloped diagonal separation. This means that when the independent variable is small the diagnosis remains constant for almost all values of the dependent variable, while, on the other side, when the independent variable becomes larger and larger, the diagnosis switches proportionally to the opposite value. For example, for small `perimeter_mean` values, the `concavity_mean` can reach its maximum without affecting the diagnosis, (which is benign), while `perimeter_mean > 150` yields always a malignant diagnosis independently on the `concavity_mean`.

Of course, we cannot easily draw our conclusions from a split analysis (because we need to consider all the interactions), but this activity will be helpful in order to provide each cluster with a semantic label. At this point, it's helpful to visualize the dataset (without the non-structural attributes) on a bidimensional plane through a **t-Distributed Stochastic Neighbor Embedding (t-SNE)** transformation (for further details, please check *Visualizing Data using t-SNE, van der Maaten L., Hinton G., Journal of Machine Learning Research 9, 2008*). This can be done as follows:

```
import pandas as pd

from sklearn.manifold import TSNE

cdf = df.drop(['diagnosis'], axis=1)
```

```
tsne = TSNE(n_components=2, perplexity=10, random_state=1000)
data_tsne = tsne.fit_transform(cdf)

df_tsne = pd.DataFrame(data_tsne, columns=['x', 'y'], index=cdf.index)
dff = pd.concat([df, df_tsne], axis=1)
```

The resulting plot is shown in the following screenshot:

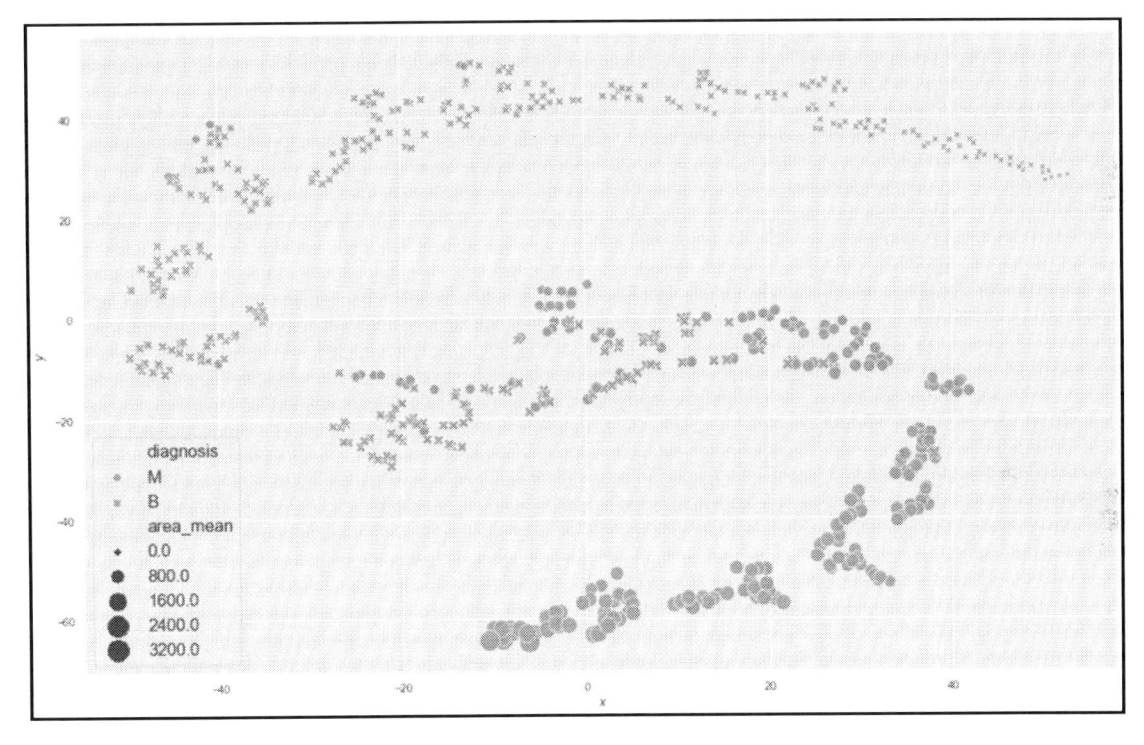

Bidimensional t-SNE plot of the Breast Cancer Wisconsin dataset

The diagram is highly non-linear (don't forget this a projection from $\Re^{30}$ to $\Re^{2}$), but the majority of malignant samples are in the half-plane $y < 0$. Unfortunately, also a moderate percentage of benign samples are in this region, hence we don't expect a perfect separation using $K=2$ (in this case, it's very difficult to understand the real geometry, but t-SNE guarantees that the bidimensional distribution has the smallest Kullback-Leibler divergence with the original high-dimensional one). Let's now perform an initial clustering with $K=2$. We are going to create an instance of the KMeans scikit-learn class with n_clusters=2 and max_iter=1000 (the random_state will be always set equal to 1000 whenever possible).

Clustering Fundamentals

The remaining parameters are the default ones (K-means++ initialization with 10 attempts), as follows:

```
import pandas as pd

from sklearn.cluster import KMeans

km = KMeans(n_clusters=2, max_iter=1000, random_state=1000)
Y_pred = km.fit_predict(cdf)

df_km = pd.DataFrame(Y_pred, columns=['prediction'], index=cdf.index)
kmdff = pd.concat([dff, df_km], axis=1)
```

The resulting plot is shown in the following screenshot:

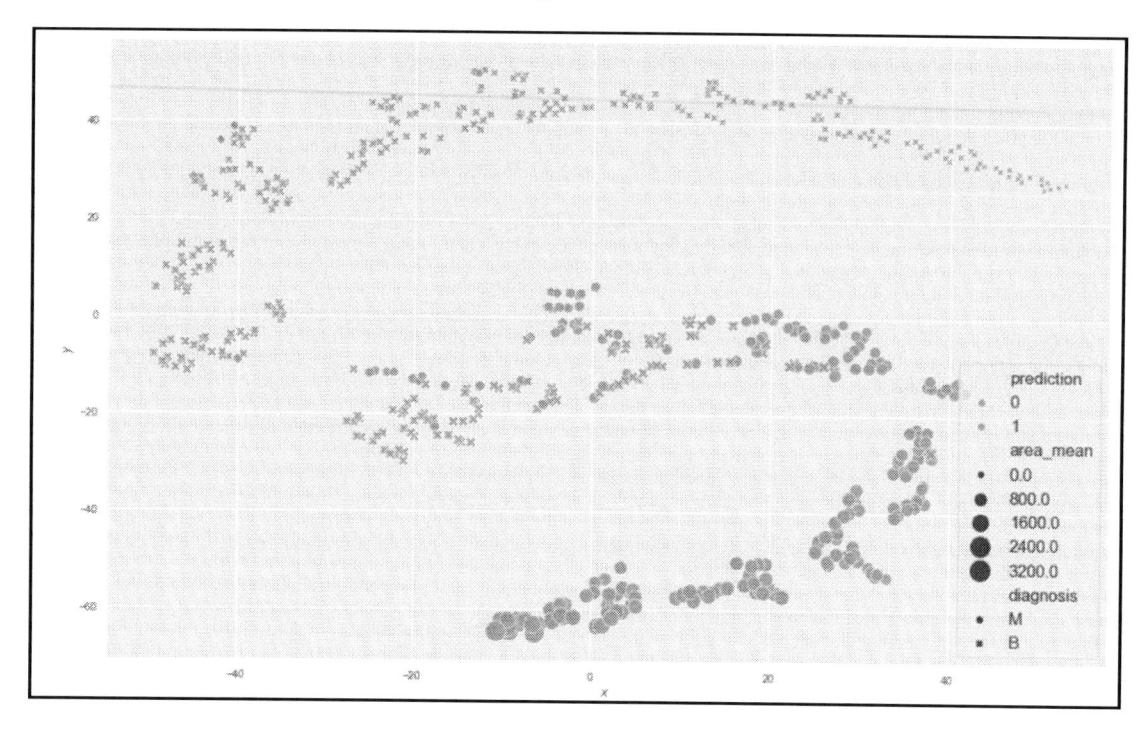

K-means clustering (with K=2) of the Breast Cancer Wisconsin dataset

Not surprisingly, the result is rather accurate for $y < -20$, but the algorithm is not able to also include the boundary points ($y \approx 0$) into the main malignant cluster. This is mainly due to the non-convexity of the original sets and it's very difficult to solve the problem using K-means. Moreover, in the projection, most of the malignant samples with $y \approx 0$ are mixed with benign ones, so the probability of error is high also with other methods based on the proximity. The only chance of correctly separating those samples is derived from the original distribution. In fact, if the points belonging to the same category could be captured by disjoint balls in $\Re^{30}$, K-means could also succeed. Unfortunately, in this case, the mixed set seems very cohesive, hence we cannot expect to improve the performance without a transformation. However, for our purposes, this result allows us to apply the main evaluation metrics and then, to move from $K=2$ to larger values. With $K>2$, we are going to analyze some of the clusters, comparing their structure with the pair-plot.

Evaluation metrics

In this section, we are going to analyze some common methods that can be employed to evaluate the performances of a clustering algorithm and also to help find the optimal number of clusters.

Minimizing the inertia

One of the biggest drawbacks of K-means and similar algorithms is the explicit request for the number of clusters. Sometimes this piece of information is imposed by external constraints (for example, in the example of breast cancer, there are only two possible diagnoses), but in many cases (when an exploratory analysis is needed), the data scientist has to check different configurations and evaluate them. The simplest way to evaluate K-means performance and choose an appropriate number of clusters is based on the comparison of different final inertias.

Let's start with the following simpler example based on 12 very compact Gaussian blobs generated with the scikit-learn function `make_blobs()`:

```
from sklearn.datasets import make_blobs

X, Y = make_blobs(n_samples=2000, n_features=2, centers=12,
                  cluster_std=0.05, center_box=[-5, 5], random_state=100)
```

Clustering Fundamentals

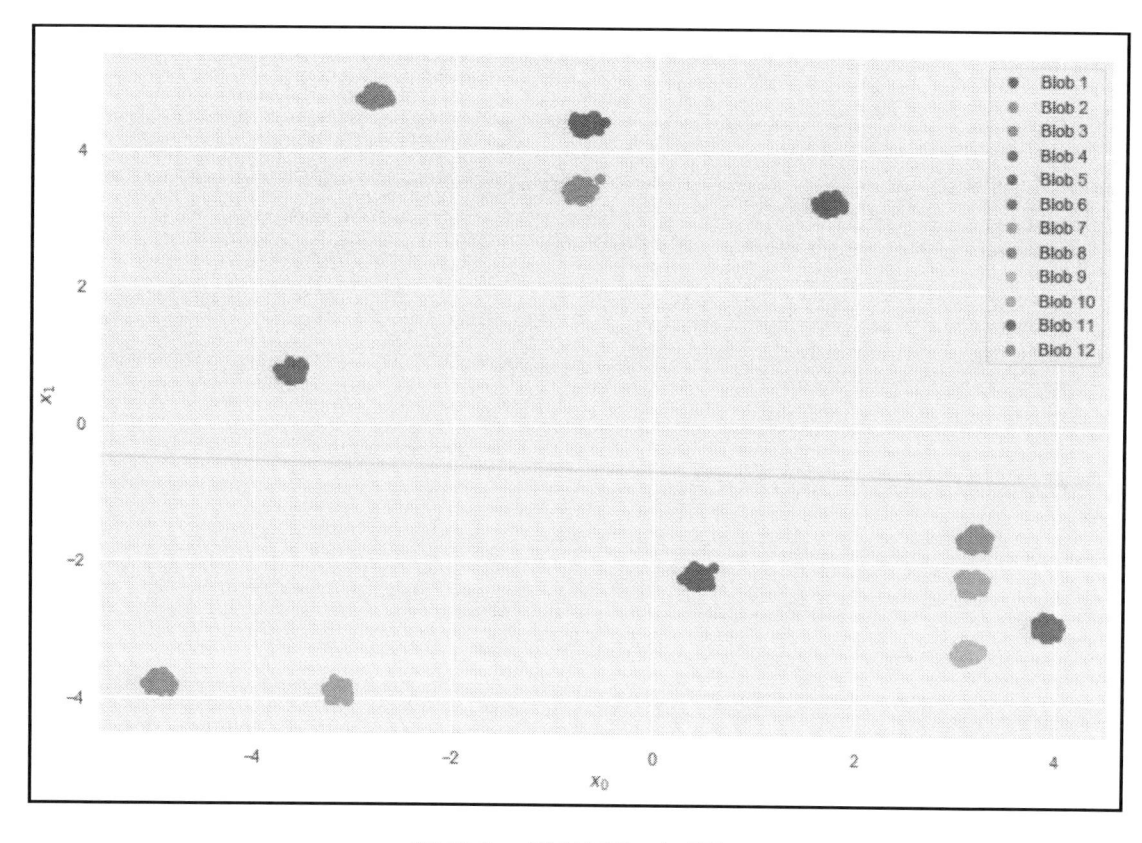

The blobs are represented in the following screenshot:

Dataset made up of 12 disjoint bidimensional blobs

Let's now compute the inertia (available as an instance variable `inertia_` in a trained `KMeans` model) for $K \in [2, 20]$, as follows:

```
from sklearn.cluster import KMeans

inertias = []

for i in range(2, 21):
    km = KMeans(n_clusters=i, max_iter=1000, random_state=1000)
    km.fit(X)
    inertias.append(km.inertia_)
```

The resulting plot is as follows:

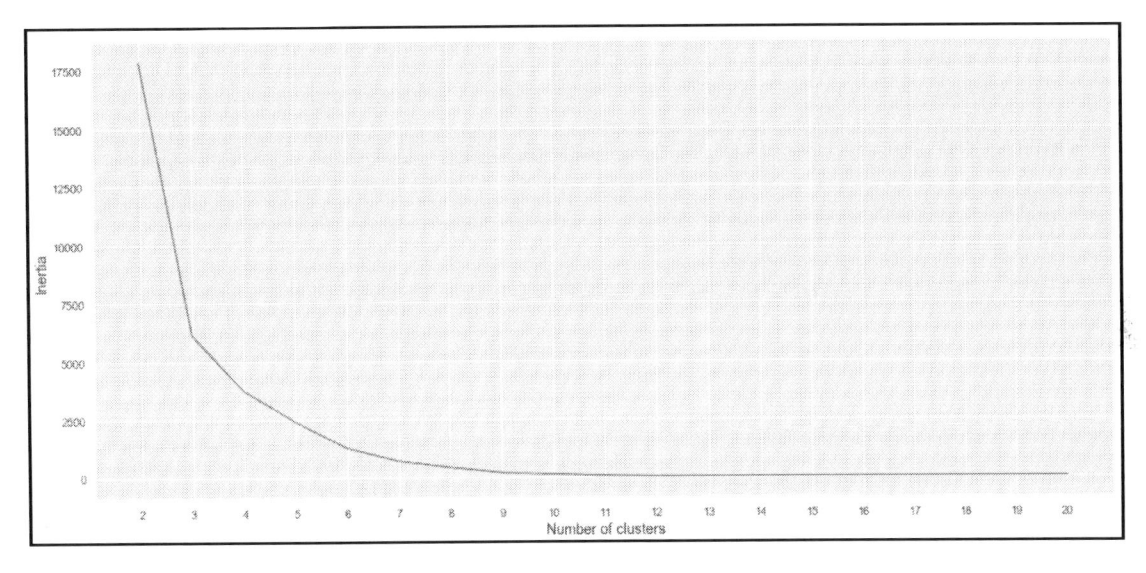

Inertia as a function of the number of clusters

The previous plot shows a common behavior. When the number of clusters is very small, the density is proportionally low, hence the cohesion is low and, as a result, the inertia is high. Increasing the number of clusters forces the model to create more cohesive groups and the inertia starts to decrease abruptly. If we continue this process and $M \gg K$, we will observe a very slow approach toward the value corresponding to a configuration where $K=M$ (each sample is a cluster). The generic heuristic rule (when there are no external constraints) is to pick the number of clusters corresponding to the point that separates the high-variation region from the almost flat one. In this way, we are sure that all clusters have reached their maximum cohesion without internal fragmentation. Of course, in this case, if we had selected $K=15$, nine blobs would have been assigned to different clusters, while, the other three would have split into two parts. Obviously, as we are splitting a high-density region, the inertia remains low, but the principle of maximum separation is not followed anymore.

Clustering Fundamentals

We can now repeat the experiment with the Breast Cancer Wisconsin dataset with $K \in [2, 50]$, as follows:

```
from sklearn.cluster import KMeans

inertias = []

for i in range(2, 51):
    km = KMeans(n_clusters=i, max_iter=1000, random_state=1000)
    km.fit(cdf)
    inertias.append(km.inertia_)
```

The resulting plot is shown in the following screenshot:

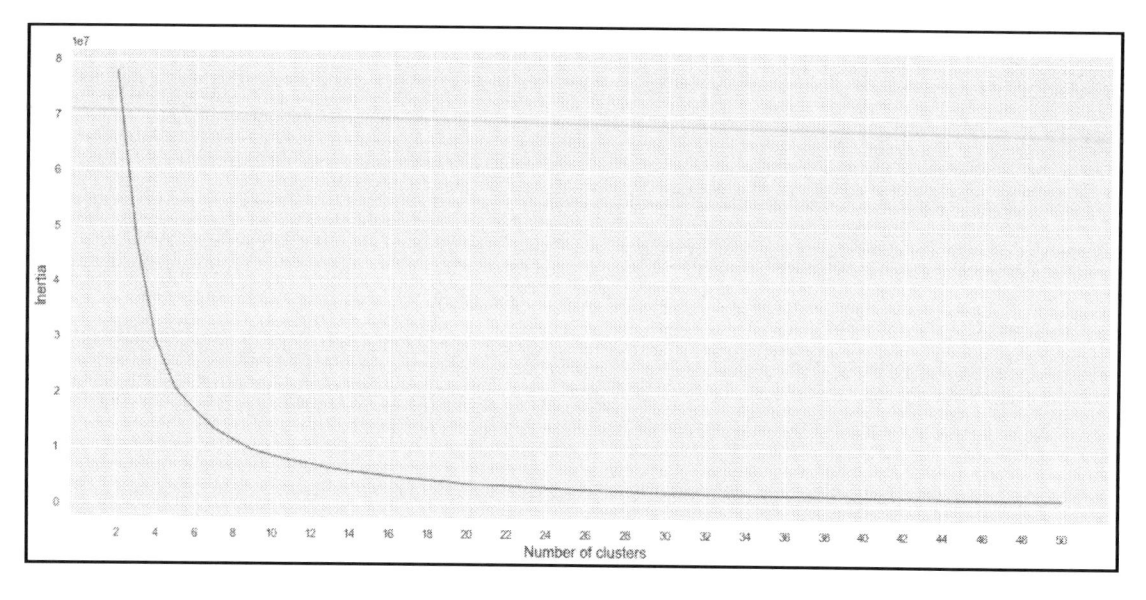

Inertia as a function of the number of clusters for the Breast Cancer Wisconsin dataset

In this case, the ground truth suggests that we should cluster into two groups corresponding to the diagnoses. However, the plot shows a drastic descent that ends at $K=8$ and continues with a lower slope until about $K=40$. During the preliminary analysis, we have seen that the bidimensional projection is made up of many isolated blobs that share the same diagnosis. Therefore, we could decide to employ, for example, $K=8$ and to analyze the features corresponding to each cluster. As this is not a classification task, the ground truth can be used as the main reference, but a correct exploratory analysis can try to understand the composition of the substructures in order to provide further details for the technicians (for example, physicians).

Chapter 2

Let's now perform a K-means clustering with eight clusters on the Breast Cancer Wisconsin dataset in order to describe the structure of two sample groups, as follows:

```
import pandas as pd

from sklearn.cluster import KMeans

km = KMeans(n_clusters=8, max_iter=1000, random_state=1000)
Y_pred = km.fit_predict(cdf)

df_km = pd.DataFrame(Y_pred, columns=['prediction'], index=cdf.index)
kmdff = pd.concat([dff, df_km], axis=1)
```

The resulting plot is shown in the following screenshot:

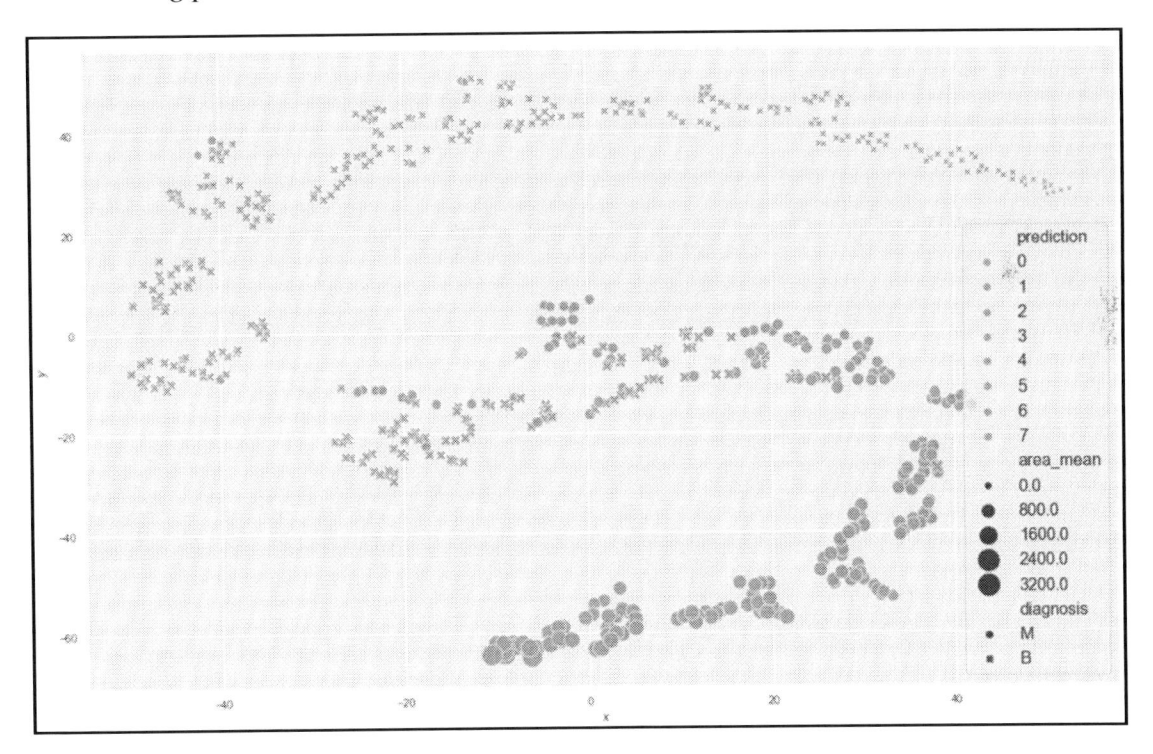

K-means clustering (with K=8) result for the Breast Cancer Wisconsin dataset

Clustering Fundamentals

Let's now consider the subcluster located in the bottom part of the plot (-25 < x < 30 and -60 < y < -40), as follows:

```
sdff = dff[(dff.x > -25.0) & (dff.x < 30.0) & (dff.y > -60.0) & (dff.y < -40.0)]
print(sdff[['perimeter_mean', 'area_mean', 'smoothness_mean',
            'concavity_mean', 'symmetry_mean']].describe())
```

A print-friendly version of the statistical table is shown in the following screenshot:

	perimeter_mean	area_mean	smoothness_mean	concavity_mean	symmetry_mean
count	58.000000	58.000000	58.000000	58.000000	58.000000
mean	129.822414	1199.527586	0.100231	0.176981	0.193281
std	6.503630	98.030806	0.010427	0.063437	0.027702
min	110.000000	904.600000	0.080200	0.086900	0.142800
25%	125.675000	1138.000000	0.091568	0.134600	0.176925
50%	130.000000	1210.500000	0.100200	0.161000	0.189750
75%	133.800000	1271.750000	0.107600	0.212650	0.209100
max	143.700000	1386.000000	0.128600	0.375400	0.290600

Statistical description of a malignant cluster

From the ground truth, we know that all these samples are malignant, but we can try to determine a rule. The ratio `area_mean/perimeter_mean` is about `9.23` and the relative standard deviations are very small compared to the means. This means that these samples represent extended tumors in a very narrow range. Moreover, both `concavity_mean` and `symmetry_mean` are larger than the overall values. Hence (without the presumption of scientifically reasonable analysis), we can conclude that samples assigned to these clusters represent very bad tumors that have arrived at an advanced stage.

To make a comparison with benign samples, let's consider now the area delimited by x > -10 and 20 < y < 50, as follows:

```
sdff = dff[(dff.x > -10.0) & (dff.y > 20.0) & (dff.y < 50.0)]
print(sdff[['perimeter_mean', 'area_mean', 'smoothness_mean',
            'concavity_mean', 'symmetry_mean']].describe())
```

The result is shown in the following screenshot:

	perimeter_mean	area_mean	smoothness_mean	concavity_mean	symmetry_mean
count	114.000000	114.000000	114.000000	114.000000	114.000000
mean	64.997719	318.138596	0.095768	0.044920	0.181869
std	6.752474	62.522359	0.014881	0.058654	0.029075
min	43.790000	143.500000	0.052630	0.000000	0.106000
25%	60.437500	275.075000	0.085127	0.012688	0.164000
50%	65.800000	321.600000	0.096720	0.028290	0.179550
75%	70.790000	373.075000	0.104275	0.056798	0.195175
max	75.460000	409.100000	0.163400	0.410800	0.274300

Statistical description of a benign cluster

In this case, the ratio area_mean/perimeter_mean is about 4.89, but area_mean has a larger standard deviation (indeed, its max value is about 410). The concavity_mean is extremely small with respect to the previous one (even with approximately the same standard deviation), while the symmetry_mean is almost equivalent. From this brief analysis, we can deduce that symmetry_mean is not a discriminant feature, while a ratio area_mean/perimeter_mean less than 5.42 (considering the max values) with a concavity_mean less or equal to 0.04 should guarantee a benign result. As concavity_mean can reach a very large max value (larger than the one associated with malignant samples), it's necessary to consider also the other features in order to decide whether its value should be considered as an alarm. However, we can conclude, saying that all samples belonging to these clusters are benign with a negligible error probability. I'd like to repeat that this is more an exercise than a real analysis and, in such situations, the main task of the data scientist is to collect contextual pieces of information that can support the conclusions. Even in the presence of the ground truth, this validation process is always mandatory because the complexity of the underlying causes can lead to completely wrong statements and rules.

Silhouette score

The most common method to assess the performance of a clustering algorithm without knowledge of the ground truth is the **silhouette score**. It provides both a per-sample index and a global graphical representation that shows the level of internal coherence and separation of the clusters. In order to compute the score, we need to introduce two auxiliary measures. The first one is the average intra-cluster distance of a sample $x_i \in K_j$ assuming the cardinality of $|K_j| = n(j)$:

$$a(\bar{x}_i) = \frac{1}{n(j)} \sum_t d(\bar{x}_i, \bar{x}_t) \ \forall \ \bar{x}_t \in K_j$$

For K-means, the distance is assumed to be Euclidean, but there are no specific limitations. Of course, $d(\bullet)$ must be the same distance function employed in the clustering procedure.

Given a sample $x_i \in K_j$, let's denote the nearest cluster as K_c. In this way, we can also define the smallest nearest-cluster distance (as the average nearest-cluster distance):

$$b(\bar{x}_i) = \frac{1}{n(c)} \sum_t d(\bar{x}_i, \bar{x}_t) \ \forall \ \bar{x}_t \in K_c$$

With these two measures, we can define the silhouette score for $x_i \in X$:

$$s(\bar{x}_i) = \frac{b(\bar{x}_i) - a(\bar{x}_i)}{max\ (a(\bar{x}_i), b(\bar{x}_i))}$$

The score $s(\bullet) \in (-1, 1)$. When $s(\bullet) \rightarrow -1$, it means that $b(\bullet) \ll a(\bullet)$, hence the sample $x_i \in K_j$ is closer to the nearest cluster K_c than to the other samples assigned to K_j. This condition indicates a wrong assignment. Conversely, when $s(\bullet) \rightarrow 1$, $b(\bullet) \gg a(\bullet)$, so the sample x_i is much closer to its *neighbors* (belonging to the same cluster) than to any other point assigned to the nearest cluster. Clearly, this is an optimal condition and the reference to employ when fine-tuning an algorithm. However, as this index is not global, it's helpful to introduce silhouette plots, which show the scores achieved by each sample, grouped by cluster and sorted in descending order.

Let's consider silhouette plots for the Breast Cancer Wisconsin dataset for K={2, 4, 6, 8} (the full code is included in the repository):

Chapter 2

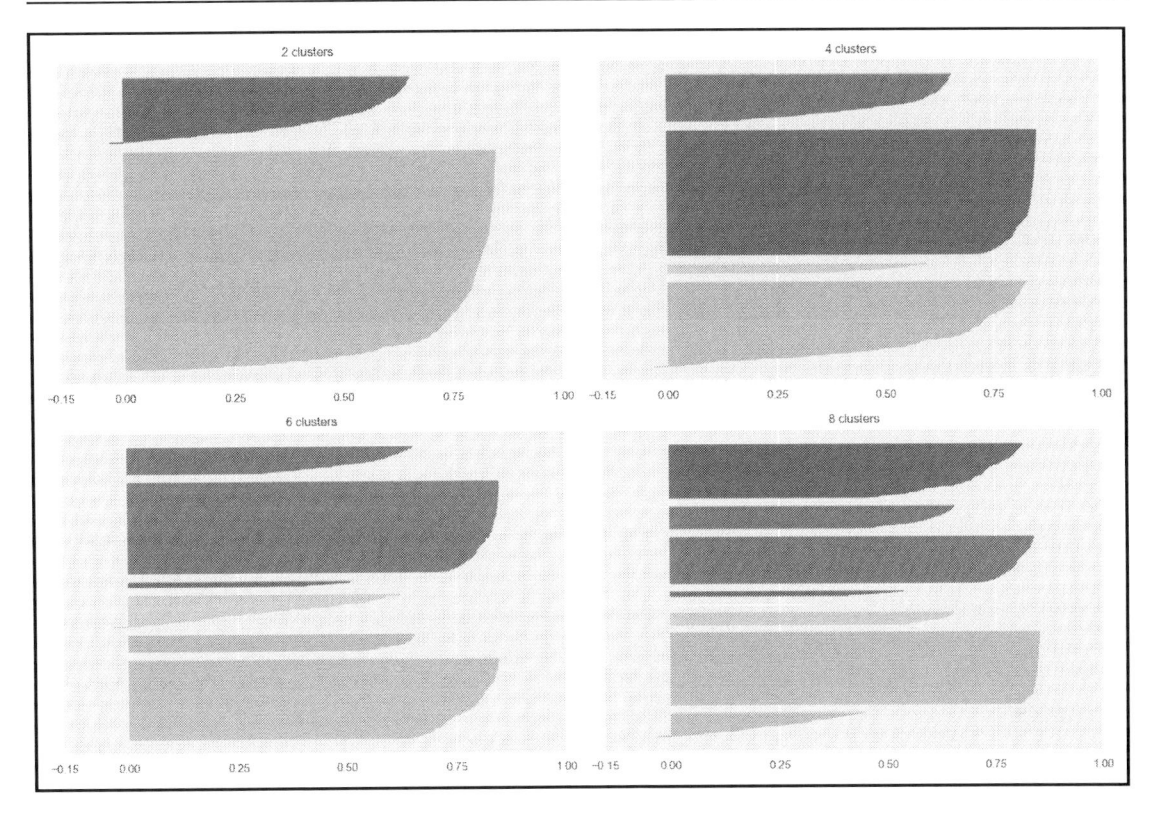

Silhouette plots for the Breast Cancer Wisconsin dataset

The first diagram shows the *natural* clustering with *K=2*. The first silhouette is very sharp, indicating that the average inter-cluster distance has a large variance. Moreover, one cluster has many more assignments than the other one (even if it's less sharp). From the dataset description, we know that the two classes are unbalanced (357 benign versus 212 malignant), hence the asymmetry is partially justified. However, in general, when the datasets are balanced, a good silhouette plot is characterized by homogeneous clusters with a rounded silhouette that should be close to 1.0. In fact, when the shape is similar to a long cigar, it means that the intra-cluster distances are very close to their average (high cohesion) and there's a clear separation between adjacent clusters. For *K=2*, we have reasonable scores, as the first cluster reaches 0.6, while the second one has a peak corresponding to about 0.8. However, while in the latter the majority of samples are characterized by $s(\bullet) >$ *0.75*, in the former one, about half of the samples are below 0.5. This analysis shows that the larger cluster is more homogeneous and it's easier for K-means to assign the samples (that is, in terms of measures, the variance of $x_i \in K_2$ is smaller and, in the high-dimensional space, the ball representing K_2 is more uniform than the one representing K_1).

The other plots show similar scenarios because a very cohesive cluster has been detected together with some sharp ones. That means there is a very consistent width discrepancy. However, increasing K, we obtain slightly more homogeneous clusters because the number of assigned samples tends to become similar. The presence of a very rounded (almost rectangular) cluster with $s(\bullet) > 0.75$ confirms that the dataset contains at least one group of very cohesive samples, whose distances with respect to any other point assigned to other clusters are quite close. We know that the malignant class (even if its cardinality is larger) is more compact, while the benign one spreads over a much wider subspace; hence, we can assume that for all K, the most rounded cluster is made up of malignant samples and all the others can be distinguished according to their sharpness. For example, for K=8, the third cluster is very likely to correspond to the central part of the second cluster in the first plot, while the smaller ones contain samples belonging to isolated regions of the benign subset.

If we don't know the ground truth, we should consider both K=2 and K=8 (or even larger). In fact, in the first case, we are probably losing many fine-grained pieces of information, but we are determining a strong subdivision (assuming that one cluster is not extremely cohesive due to the nature of the problem). On the other side, with K>8, the clusters are obviously smaller, with a moderately higher cohesion and they represent subgroups that share some common features. As we discussed in the previous section, the final choice depends on many factors and these tools can only provide a general indication. Moreover, when the clusters are non-convex or their variance is not uniformly distributed among all features, K-means will always yield suboptimal performances because the resulting clusters will incorporate a large empty space. Without specific directions, the optimal number of clusters is associated with a plot containing homogeneous (with approximately the same width) rounded plots. If the shape remains sharp for any K value, it means that the geometry is not fully compatible with symmetric measures (for example, the clusters are very stretched) and other methods should be taken into account.

Completeness score

This measure (together with all the other ones discussed from now on) is based on knowledge of the ground truth. Before introducing the index, it's helpful to define some common values. If we denote with Y_{true} the set containing the true assignments and with Y_{pred}, the set of predictions (both containing M values and K clusters), we can estimate the following probabilities:

$$\begin{cases} p(y_{true} = k \in K) = \frac{n_{true}(k)}{M} \\ p(y_{pred} = k \in K) = \frac{n_{pred}(k)}{M} \end{cases}$$

In the previous formulas, $n_{true/pred}(k)$ represents the number of true/predicted samples belonging the cluster $k \in K$. At this point, we can compute the entropies of Y_{true} and Y_{pred}:

$$\begin{cases} H(Y_{true}) = -\sum_k \frac{n_{true}(k)}{M} \log\left(\frac{n_{true}(k)}{M}\right) \\ H(Y_{pred}) = -\sum_k \frac{n_{pred}(k)}{M} \log\left(\frac{n_{pred}(k)}{M}\right) \end{cases}$$

Considering the definition of entropy, $H(\bullet)$ is maximized by a uniform distribution, which, in its turn, corresponds to the maximum uncertainty of every assignment. For our purposes, it's also necessary to introduce the conditional entropies (representing the uncertainty of a distribution given the knowledge of another one) of Y_{true} given Y_{pred} and the other way around:

$$\begin{cases} H(Y_{true}|Y_{pred}) = -\sum_i \sum_j \frac{n(i,j)}{M} \log\left(\frac{n(i,j)}{n_{pred}(j)}\right) \\ H(Y_{pred}|Y_{true}) = -\sum_i \sum_j \frac{n(i,j)}{M} \log\left(\frac{n(i,j)}{n_{true}(i)}\right) \end{cases}$$

The function $n(i, j)$ represents, in the first case, the number of samples with true label i assigned to K_j and, in the second case, the number of samples with true label j assigned to K_i.

The completeness score is defined as:

$$c = 1 - \frac{H(Y_{pred}|Y_{true})}{H(Y_{pred})}$$

It's straightforward to understand that when $H(Y_{pred}|Y_{true}) \to 0$, the knowledge of Y_{true} reduces the uncertainty of the predictions and, therefore, $c \to 1$. This is equivalent to saying that all samples with the same true label are assigned to the same cluster. Conversely, when $H(Y_{pred}|Y_{true}) \to H(Y_{pred})$, it means the ground truth doesn't provide any information that reduces the uncertainty of the predictions and $c \to 0$.

Clustering Fundamentals

Of course, a good clustering is characterized by $c \to 1$. In the case of the Breast Cancer Wisconsin dataset, the **completeness score**, computed using the scikit-learn function `completenss_score()`, (which works also with textual labels) and K=2 (the only configuration associated with ground truth), is as follows:

```
import pandas as pd

from sklearn.cluster import KMeans
from sklearn.metrics import completeness_score

km = KMeans(n_clusters=2, max_iter=1000, random_state=1000)
Y_pred = km.fit_predict(cdf)

df_km = pd.DataFrame(Y_pred, columns=['prediction'], index=cdf.index)
kmdff = pd.concat([dff, df_km], axis=1)

print('Completeness: {}'.format(completeness_score(kmdff['diagnosis'],
kmdff['prediction'])))
```

The output of the previous snippet is as follows:

```
Completeness: 0.5168089972809706
```

This result confirms that, for K=2, K-means is not perfectly able to separate the clusters, because, as we have seen, there are some malignant samples that are wrongly assigned to the cluster containing the vast majority of benign samples. However, as c is not extremely small, we can be sure that most of the samples for both classes have been assigned to the different clusters. The reader is invited to check this value using other methods (discussed in Chapter 3, *Advanced Clustering*) and to provide a brief explanation of the different results.

Homogeneity score

The **homogeneity score** is complementary to the previous one and it's based on the assumption that a cluster must contain only samples having the same true label. It is defined as:

$$h = 1 - \frac{H(Y_{true}|Y_{pred})}{H(Y_{true})}$$

Analogously to the completeness score, when $H(Y_{true}|Y_{pred}) \to H(Y_{true})$, it means that the assignments have no impact on the conditional entropy, hence the uncertainty is not reduced after the clustering (for example, every cluster contains samples belonging to all classes) and $h \to 0$. Conversely, when $H(Y_{true}|Y_{pred}) \to 0$, $h \to 1$, because knowledge of the predictions has reduced the uncertainty about the true assignments and the clusters contain almost exclusively samples with the same label. It's important to remember that this score alone is not enough, because it doesn't guarantee that a cluster contains all samples $x_i \in X$ with the same true label. That's why the homogeneity score is always evaluated together with the completeness score.

For the Breast Cancer Wisconsin dataset and K=2, we obtain the following:

```
from sklearn.metrics import homogeneity_score

print('Homogeneity: {}'.format(homogeneity_score(kmdff['diagnosis'],
kmdff['prediction'])))
```

The corresponding output is as follows:

```
Homogeneity: 0.42229071246999117
```

This value (in particular, for K=2) confirms our initial analysis. At least one cluster (the one with the majority of benign samples) is not completely homogeneous, because it contains samples belonging to both classes. However, as the value is not very close to 0, we can be sure that the assignments are partially correct. Considering both values, h and c, we can deduct that K-means is not performing extremely well (probably because of non-convexity), but, at the same time, it's able to separate correctly all those samples whose nearest cluster distance is above a specific threshold. It goes without saying that, with knowledge of the ground truth, we cannot easily accept K-means and we should look for another algorithm that is able to yield both h and $c \to 1$.

A trade-off between homogeneity and completeness using the V-measure

The reader who's familiar with supervised learning should know the concept of F-score (or F-measure), which is the harmonic mean of precision and recall. The same kind of trade-off can be employed also when evaluating clustering results given the ground truth.

Clustering Fundamentals

In fact, in many cases, it's helpful to have a single measure that takes into account both homogeneity and completeness. Such a result can be easily achieved using the **V-measure** (or V-score), which is defined as:

$$V = \frac{2}{\frac{1}{Homogeneity} + \frac{1}{Completeness}} = \frac{2 \cdot Homogeneity \cdot Completeness}{Homogeneity + Completeness}$$

For the Breast Cancer Wisconsin dataset, the V-measure is as follows:

```
from sklearn.metrics import v_measure_score

print('V-Score: {}'.format(v_measure_score(kmdff['diagnosis'],
kmdff['prediction'])))
```

The output of the previous snippet is as follows:

```
V-Score: 0.46479332792160793
```

As expected, the V-Score is an average measure that, in this case, is negatively influenced by a lower homogeneity. Of course, this index doesn't provide any different information, hence it's helpful only to synthesize completeness and homogeneity in a single value. However, with a few simple but tedious mathematical manipulations, it's possible to prove that the V-measure is also symmetric (that is, $V(Y_{pred} | Y_{true}) = V(Y_{true} | Y_{pred})$); therefore, given two independent assignments Y_1 and Y_2, $V(Y_1 | Y_2)$ it is a measure of agreement between them. Such a scenario is not extremely common, because other measures can achieve a better result. However, such a score could be employed, for example, to check whether two algorithms (possibly based on different strategies) tend to produce the same assignments or if they are discordant. In the latter case, even if the ground truth is unknown, the data scientist can understand that one strategy is surely not as effective as the other one and start an exploration process in order to find out the optimal clustering algorithm.

Adjusted Mutual Information (AMI) score

The main goal is of this score is to evaluate the level of agreement between Y_{true} and Y_{pred} without taking into account the permutations. Such an objective can be measured by employing the information theory concept of **Mutual Information** (MI); in our case, it's defined as:

$$MI(Y_{true}; Y_{pred}) = \sum_i \sum_j \frac{n(i,j)}{M} \log\left(\frac{M \cdot n(i,j)}{n_{true}(i) \cdot n_{pred}(j)}\right)$$

The functions are the same as previously defined. When $MI \to 0$, $n(i, j) \to n_{true}(i)n_{pred}(j)$, whose terms are proportional respectively to $p(i, j)$ and $p_{true}(i)p_{pred}(j)$. Hence, this condition is equivalent to saying that Y_{true} and Y_{pred} are statistically independent and there's no agreement. On the other side, with some simple manipulations, we can rewrite MI as:

$$MI(Y_{true}; Y_{pred}) = -H(Y_{pred}|Y_{true}) + H(Y_{pred})$$

Hence, as $H(Y_{pred}|Y_{true}) \leq H(Y_{pred})$, when the knowledge of the ground truth reduces the uncertainty about Y_{pred}, it follows that $H(Y_{pred}|Y_{true}) \to 0$ and the MI is maximized. For our purposes, it's preferable to consider a normalized version (bounded between 0 and 1) that is also adjusted for chance (that is, considering the possibility that a true assignment is due to the chance). The **AMI score**, whose complete derivation is non-trivial and beyond the scope of this book, is defined as:

$$AMI(Y_{true}; Y_{pred}) = \frac{MI(Y_{true}; Y_{pred}) - E[MI(Y_{true}; Y_{pred})]}{mean(H(Y_{true}), H(Y_{pred})) - E[MI(Y_{true}; Y_{pred})]}$$

This value is equal to 0 in the case of the total absence of agreement and equal to 1 when Y_{true} and Y_{pred} completely agree (also in the presence of permutations). For the Breast Cancer Wisconsin dataset and K=2, we obtain the following:

```
from sklearn.metrics import adjusted_mutual_info_score

print('Adj. Mutual info:
{}'.format(adjusted_mutual_info_score(kmdff['diagnosis'],
kmdff['prediction'])))
```

The output is as follows:

```
Adj. Mutual info: 0.42151741598216214
```

The agreement is moderate and compatible with the other measure. Assuming the presence of permutations and the possibility of chance assignments, Y_{true} and Y_{pred} share a medium level of information because, as we have discussed, K-means is able to correctly assign all the samples where the probability of overlap is negligible, while it tends to consider benign many malignant samples that are on the boundary between the two clusters (conversely, it doesn't make wrong assignments for the benign samples). Without any further indication, this index suggests also checking other clustering algorithms that can manage non-convex clusters, because the lack of shared information is mainly due to the impossibility of capturing complex geometries using standard balls (in particular in the subspace where the overlap is more significant).

Adjusted Rand score

The **adjusted Rand score** is a measure of discrepancy between the true label distribution and the predicted one. In order to compute it, it's necessary to define quantities as follows:

- **a**: Representing the number of sample pairs (x_i, x_j) with the same true labels (y_i, y_j) : $y_i = y_j$ and assigned to the same cluster K_c
- **b**: Representing the number of sample pairs (x_i, x_j) with different true labels (y_i, y_j) : $y_i \neq y_j$ and assigned to different clusters K_c and K_d with $c \neq d$

If there are M values, the total number of binary combinations is obtained using the binomial coefficient with $k=2$, therefore, an initial measure of discrepancy is:

$$R = \frac{a+b}{\binom{M}{2}}$$

Obviously, this value can be dominated either by a or b. In both cases, a higher score indicates that the assignments agrees with the ground truth. However, both a and b can be biased by chance assignments. That's why the adjusted Rand score has been introduced. The updated formula is:

$$R_A = \frac{R - E[R]}{max(R) - R}$$

This value is bounded between -1 and 1. When $R_A \to -1$, both a and b are very small and the vast majority of assignments are wrong. On the other side, when $R_A \to 1$, the predicted distribution is very close to the ground truth. For the Breast Cancer Wisconsin dataset and $K=2$, we obtain the following:

```
from sklearn.metrics import adjusted_rand_score

print('Adj. Rand score: {}'.format(adjusted_rand_score(kmdff['diagnosis'],
kmdff['prediction'])))
```

The output of the previous snippet is as follows:

```
Adj. Rand index: 0.49142453622455523
```

This result is better than the other indexes as the value is larger than *-1* (negative extreme). It confirms that the discrepancy between the distributions is not very pronounced and it's mainly due to a limited subset of samples. This score is very reliable and can be used also as a single metric to evaluate the performances of a clustering algorithm. A value close to 0.5 confirms that K-means is unlikely to be the optimal solution, but, at the same time, that the dataset has a geometry that can be almost completely captured by symmetric balls, except for some non-convex regions with high probability of overlap.

Contingency matrix

A very simple and powerful tool that can show the performance of a clustering algorithm when the ground truth is known is the **contingency matrix** C_m. If there are m classes, $C_m \in \Re^{m \times m}$ and each element $C_m(i, j)$ represents the number of samples with $Y_{true} = i$ that have been assigned to the cluster j. Hence, a perfect contingency matrix is diagonal, while the presence of elements in all the other cells indicates a clustering error.

In our case, we obtain the following:

```
from sklearn.metrics.cluster import contingency_matrix

cm = contingency_matrix(kmdff['diagnosis'].apply(lambda x: 0 if x == 'B'
else 1), kmdff['prediction'])
```

The output of the previous snippet can be visualized as a heat map (the variable cm is a (2 × 2) matrix):

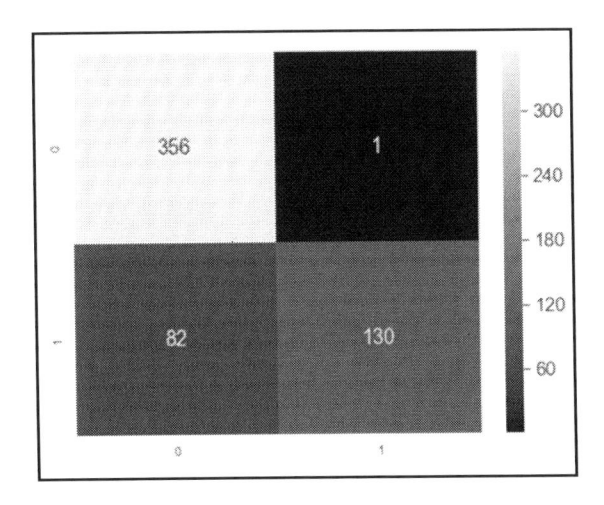

Graphical representation of the contingency matrix

This result shows that almost all benign samples have been correctly clustered, while a moderate percentage of malignant ones have been wrongly assigned to the first cluster. We have already had confirmation using of this other metrics, but, analogously to the confusion matrix in classification tasks, a contingency matrix allows the immediate visualization of which classes are the most difficult to separate, helping the data scientist look for a more effective solution.

K-Nearest Neighbors

K-Nearest Neighbors (KNN) is a method belonging to a category called **instance-based learning**. In this case, there's no parametrized model, but rather a rearrangement of the samples in order to speed up specific queries. In the simplest case (also known as brute-force search), let's say we have a dataset X containing M samples $x_i \in \Re^N$. Given a distance function $d(x_i, x_j)$, it's possible to define the radius neighborhood of a test sample x_i as:

$$\nu(\bar{x}_i) = \{\bar{x}_t : d(\bar{x}_i, \bar{x}_t) \leq R\}$$

The set $\nu(x_i)$ is a ball centered on x_i and including all the samples whose distance is less or equal to R. Alternatively, it's possible to compute only the top k nearest neighbors, which are the k samples closer to x_i (in general, this set is a subset of $\nu(x_i)$, but the opposite condition can also happen when k is very large). The procedure is straightforward but, unfortunately, too expensive from a computational viewpoint. In fact, for each query, it's necessary to compute M^2 N-dimensional distances (that is, assuming N operations per distance, the complexity is $O(NM^2)$), a condition that makes the brute-force approach suffer the curse of dimensionality. For example, with $N=2$ and $M=1,000$, the complexity is $O(2 \cdot 10^6)$, but with $N=1,000$ and $M=10,000$, it becomes $O(10^{11})$. If, for example, each operation requires 1 nanosecond, a query will require 100 seconds, which is beyond a tolerable limit in many real-life cases. Moreover, with 64-bit floating-point values, the pairwise distance matrix will need about 764 MB per computation, which, again, can be an excessive request considering the nature of the task.

For these reasons, KNN concrete implementations use the brute-force search only when M is very small and rely on slightly more complex structures in all other cases. The first alternative approach is based on **kd-trees**, which are a natural extension of binary trees to multi-dimensional datasets.

In the following diagram, there's a representation of a partial kd-tree made up of 3-dimensional vectors:

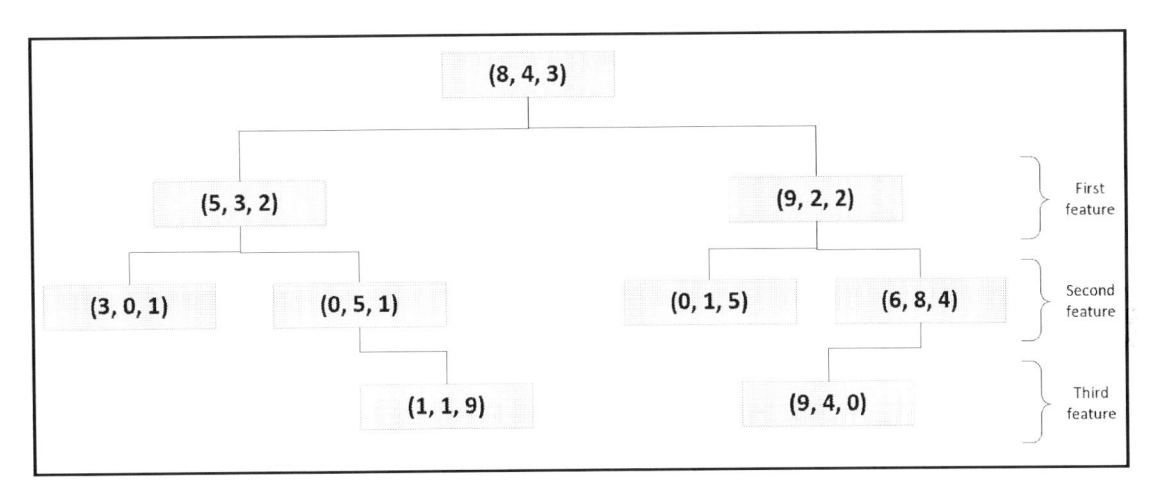

```
                        (8, 4, 3)
                       /         \
            (5, 3, 2)              (9, 2, 2)          } First feature
           /        \              /        \
    (3, 0, 1)   (0, 5, 1)   (0, 1, 5)   (6, 8, 4)     } Second feature
                    |                        |
                (1, 1, 9)                (9, 4, 0)    } Third feature
```

Example of kd-tree with 3-dimensional vectors

The construction of a kd-tree is very simple. Given a root sample $(a_1, a_2, ..., a_N)$, the first split is operated considering the first feature, so that the left branch contains $(b_1 < a_1, ...,$ and so on) and the right one $(c_1 > a_1, ...,$ and so on). The procedure continues with the second feature, the third feature, and so on again until the first feature, and so on until the leaf nodes are reached (the number of samples assigned to a leaf is a hyperparameter subject to tuning. In scikit-learn the parameter is called `leaf_size` and has a default value of 30 samples).

When the dimensionality N is not extremely large, the computational complexity becomes $O(N \log M)$, which is quite a lot better than the brute-force search. For example, with $N=1,000$ and $M=10,000$, the computational complexity becomes $O(4,000) \ll O(10^{11})$. Unfortunately, when N is large, a kd-tree query becomes $O(NM)$, so, considering the previous example, $O(10^7)$, which is better than the brute search but sometimes still too expensive for real-time queries.

The second data structure commonly employed in KNN is the **ball-tree**. In this case, the root node is represented by an R_0-ball, defined exactly as the neighborhood of a sample:

$$\beta_{R_0}(\bar{x}_i) = \{\bar{x}_t : d(\bar{x}_i, \bar{x}_t) \leq R_0\}$$

The first ball is chosen so as to capture all samples. At this point, other smaller balls are nested into β_{R0}, ensuring that each sample will always belong to a single ball. In the following diagram, there's a schematic representation of a simple ball-tree:

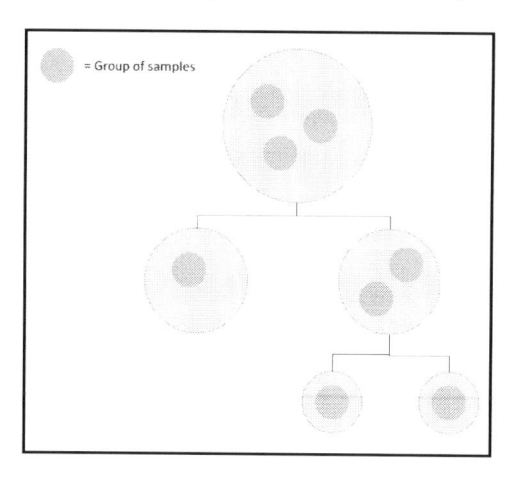

Example of a simple ball-tree

As each ball is fully determined by its center c_j, a query with a test sample x_i requires the computation of distances $d(x_i, c_j)$. Hence, starting from the bottom (where the smallest balls are), a complete scan is performed. If none of the balls contain the sample, the level is increased, until the root node is reached (remember that a sample can belong to a single ball). The computational complexity is now always $O(N \log M)$ thanks to the properties of the balls (that is, given both center and radius, it's possible to check the membership of a sample with a single distance computation). Once the right ball has been determined, the neighbors of a sample x_i require the computation of a limited number of pairwise distances (the value is less than the leaf size, so it's generally negligible if compared to the dimensionality of the dataset).

Of course, these structures are built during the training phase and they are not modified during the production stage. This implies a careful choice of both the minimum radius or the number of samples assigned to a leaf node. In fact, as the queries normally require a number of neighbors k, the optimality is achieved only when $k < |v(x_i)|$. In other words, we'd like to find all neighbors in the same substructure containing x_i. Whenever $k > |v(x_i)|$, the algorithm must check also the adjacent structures and merge the results. Of course, when the leaf size is too large (compared to the total number of samples M), the advantage of these trees vanishes because it's necessary to compute too many pairwise distances in order to answer a query. The right choice of the leaf size must be made considering the production usage of the software.

For example, if a recommendation system needs an initial query with 100 neighbors and a few (for example, 5) subsequent queries with 10 neighbors, a leaf size equal to 10 will optimize the refinement phase, but it has a negative impact on the first query. Conversely, choosing a leaf size equal to 100 will slow down all 10 neighbors queries. A trade-off might be 25, which reduces the burden of the first query but has a moderately negative impact on the computation of the pairwise distances of the refinement queries.

We can now analyze a short example based on the Olivetti faces dataset (provided directly by scikit-learn). It is made up of 400 64 × 64 grayscale images representing portraits of different people. Let's start by loading the dataset as follows:

```
from sklearn.datasets import fetch_olivetti_faces

faces = fetch_olivetti_faces()
X = faces['data']
```

The variable X contains the flattened version of the dataset (400 4,096-dimensional instances already normalized between 0 and 1). At this point, we can train a NearestNeighbor model, assuming default queries with 10 samples (parameter n_neighbors) and a radius equal to 20 (parameter radius). We are keeping the default leaf_size (30) and explicitly setting the Minkowski metric with p=2 (Euclidean distance). The algorithm is based on a ball-tree, but I invite the reader to test both different metrics and kd-tree. We can now create a NearestNeighbors instance and proceed training the model:

```
from sklearn.neighbors import NearestNeighbors

knn = NearestNeighbors(n_neighbors=10, metric='minkowski', p=2,
radius=20.0, algorithm='ball_tree')
knn.fit(X)
```

Once the model is trained, use a noisy test face to find the 10-nearest neighbors, as follows:

```
import numpy as np

i = 20
test_face = X[i] + np.random.normal(0.0, 0.1, size=(X[0].shape[0]))
```

Clustering Fundamentals

The test face is plotted in the following screenshot:

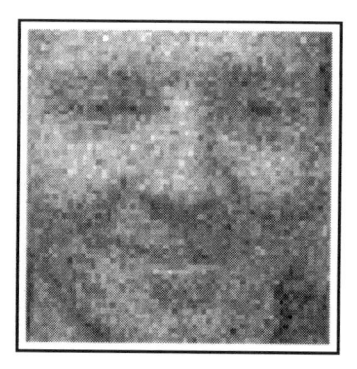

Noisy test face

A query with the default number of neighbors can be performed using the method `kneighbors()` supplying only the test sample (in the case of a different number of neighbors, the function must be called providing also the parameter `n_neighbors`). The function, if the parameter `return_distance=True`, returns a tuple containing `distances, neighbors`, as follows:

```
distances, neighbors = knn.kneighbors(test_face.reshape(1, -1))
```

The result of the query is shown in the following screenshot:

Nearest neighbors of the test sample with their relative distances

The first sample is always the test one (in this case, it is denoised so its distance is not zero). As it's possible to see, even if the distance is a cumulative function, the second and fourth samples refer to the same person, while the others share different anatomical elements. Of course, an Euclidean distance is not the most appropriate way to measure the difference between images, but this example confirms that, to a certain extent, when the pictures are rather similar, a global distance can also provide us with a valuable tool that can be employed to find similar samples.

Chapter 2

Let's now perform a radius query using the method `radius_neighbors()` setting `radius=100`, as follows:

```
import numpy as np

distances, neighbors = knn.radius_neighbors(test_face.reshape(1, -1),
radius=100.0)
sd, sd_arg = np.sort(distances[0]), np.argsort(distances[0])
```

The result containing the first 20 neighbors is shown in the following screenshot:

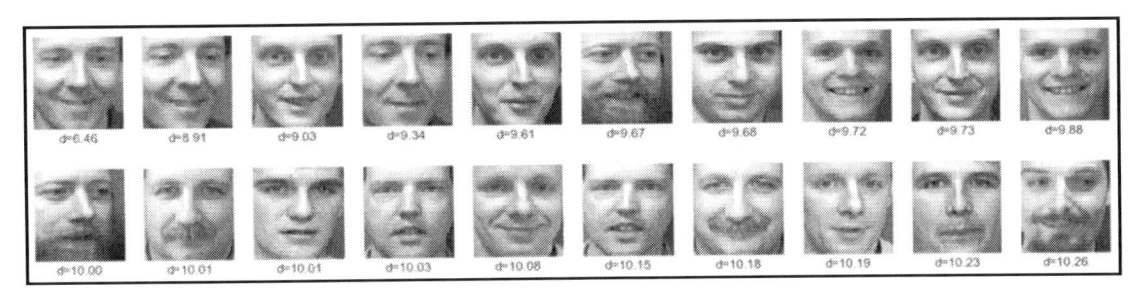

First 50 neighbors using a radius query

It's interesting to notice that the distances don't diverge very quickly (the second sample has d=8.91 and the fifth d=10.26). This is mainly due to two factors: the first one is the global similarity (in terms of geometric elements and tones) among samples and the second one is likely to be connected with the effect of the Euclidean distance on 4,096-dimensional vectors. As explained when talking about the clustering fundamentals, high dimensional samples can suffer a lack of distinguishability (in particular when $p \gg 1$). In this case, the averaging effect of different parts of the pictures can yield results that are totally incompatible with a classification system. In particular, deep learning models tend to avoid this *trap* by using convolutional networks that can learn to detect specific features at different levels. I suggest repeating this example with different metrics, and observing the effect of p on the actual differences shown by the samples of a radius query.

Vector Quantization

Vector Quantization (VQ) is a method that exploits unsupervised learning in order to perform a lossy compression of a sample $x_i \in \Re^N$ (for simplicity, we are supposing the multi-dimensional samples are flattened) or an entire dataset X. The main idea is to find a codebook Q with a number of entries $C \ll N$ and associate each element with an entry $q_i \in Q$. In the case of a single sample, each entry will represent one or more groups of features (for example, it can be the mean), therefore, the process can be described as a transformation T whose general representation is:

$$\bar{x}_i = \left(x_i^{(1)}, x_i^{(2)}, \ldots, x_i^{(N)}\right) \xrightarrow{T} \left(\bar{q}_i, \bar{q}_j, \ldots, \bar{q}_C\right) = \bar{x}_i^q$$

The codebook is defined as $Q = (q_1, q_2, \ldots, q_C)$. Hence, given a synthetic dataset made up of a group of feature aggregates (for example, a group of two consecutive elements), VQ associates a single codebook entry:

$$[(x_1, x_2, \ldots), (x_i, x_j, \ldots), \ldots] \xrightarrow{T} q_i$$

As the input sample is represented using a combination of fixed values that *summarize* the whole group, the process is defined as quantization. Analogously, if the input is a dataset X, the transformation operates with groups of samples, just like any standard clustering procedure. The main difference is the purpose: VQ is employed to represent each cluster with its centroid, thus reducing the variance of the dataset. The process is irreversible. Once the transformation is performed, it's impossible to rebuild the original cluster (the only feasible procedure is based on sampling from a distribution with the same original mean and covariance, but the reconstruction is clearly an approximation).

Let's start by showing an example with a very simple Gaussian dataset, as follows:

```
import numpy as np

nb_samples = 1000
data = np.random.normal(0.0, 1.5, size=(nb_samples, 2))

n_vectors = 16
qv = np.random.normal(0.0, 1.5, size=(n_vectors, 2))
```

Our goal is to represent the dataset with 16 vectors. In the following screenshot, the
diagram shows an example of the initial configuration:

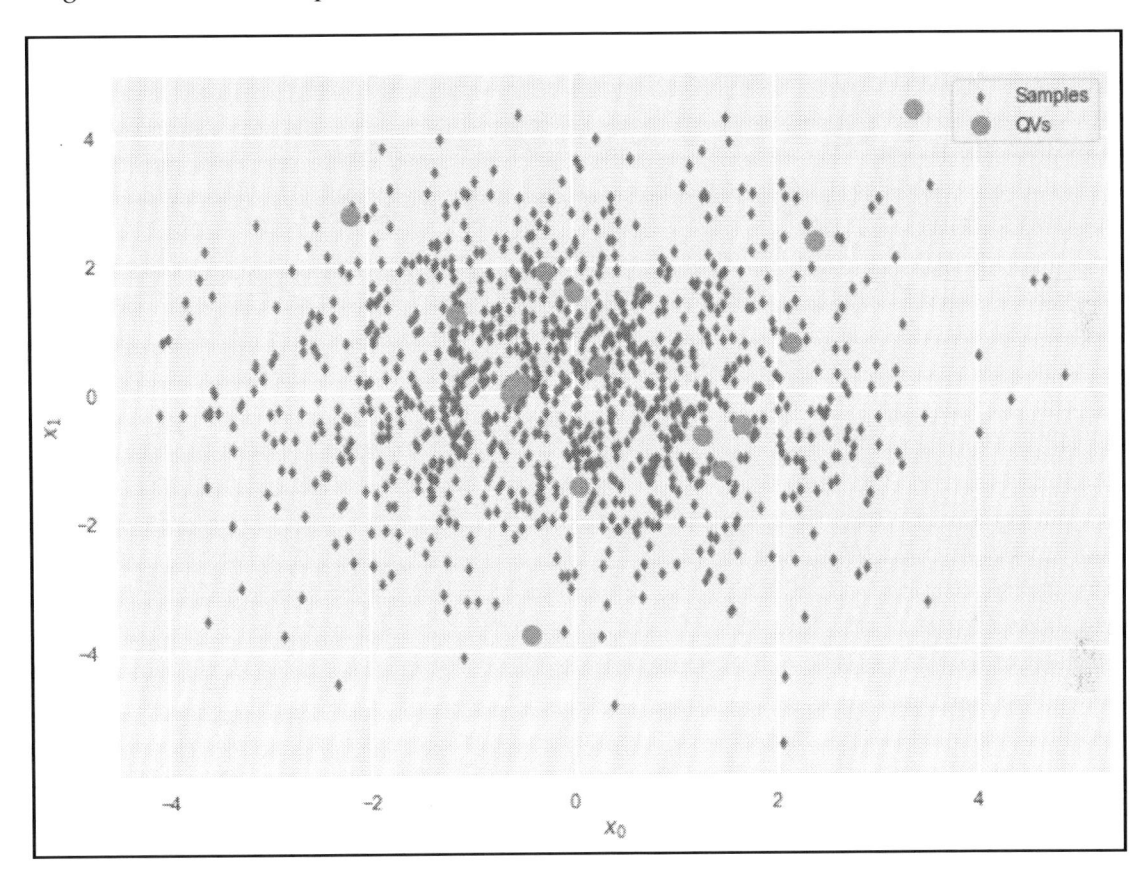

Initial configuration of the vectors for the VQ example

Clustering Fundamentals

As we are working with random numbers, subsequent executions of the same code produce different initial configurations. The procedure iterates over all samples, selecting the nearest quantization vector and reducing its distance by a fixed quantity `delta=0.05`, as follows:

```python
import numpy as np

from scipy.spatial.distance import cdist

delta = 0.05
n_iterations = 1000

for i in range(n_iterations):
    for p in data:
        distances = cdist(qv, np.expand_dims(p, axis=0))
        qvi = np.argmin(distances)
        alpha = p - qv[qvi]
        qv[qvi] += (delta * alpha)

distances = cdist(data, qv)
Y_qv = np.argmin(distances, axis=1)
```

Instead of a fixed for loop, it's also possible to use a while loop that checks whether the quantization vectors have reached their steady state (comparing the norms of vectors computed at time *t* and *t+1*). The result at the end of the process is shown in the following screenshot:

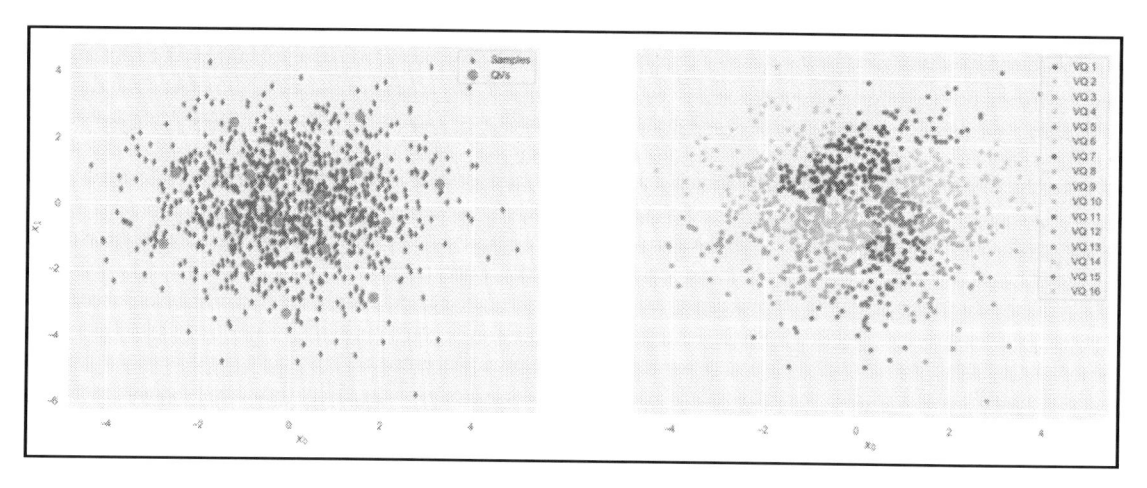

Final configuration of the quantization vectors (left). Influence area of each quantization vector (right)

As expected, the quantization vectors have reached a final configuration where each of them represents a small portion of the dataset (shown in the right plot). At this point, given a point, the nearest vector will represent it. It's interesting to notice that the global variance has not been impacted, but, selecting any subset, the internal variance is instead dramatically reduced. The relative position of the vectors reflects the density of the dataset because *more samples in a region attract more vectors*. In this way, by building a distance matrix, it's possible to obtain a rough density estimation (for example, when the average distance of a vector from its close neighbors is higher, it implies that the underlying region is less dense). We are going to discuss this topic in more detail in `Chapter 6`, *Anomaly Detection*.

Let's now consider an example with a single sample representing a picture of a raccoon. As the process can be very long, the first step is loading the sample RGB image (provided by SciPy) and resizing it to 192 × 256, as follows:

```
from scipy.misc import face
from skimage.transform import resize

picture = resize(face(gray=False), output_shape=(192, 256), mode='reflect')
```

The original picture (already normalized in the range [0, 1]) is shown in the following screenshot:

Sample RGB picture for VQ example

Clustering Fundamentals

We want to perform a VQ with 24 vectors computed using 2 × 2 square regions, (which are represented by flattened vectors containing 2 × 2 × 3 features). However, instead of implementing the procedure from scratch, we are going to employ the K-means algorithm to find the centroids. The first step is collecting all the square regions, as follows:

```
import numpy as np

square_fragment_size = 2
n_fragments = int(picture.shape[0] * picture.shape[1] /
(square_fragment_size**2))

fragments = np.zeros(shape=(n_fragments, square_fragment_size**2 *
picture.shape[2]))
idx = 0

for i in range(0, picture.shape[0], square_fragment_size):
    for j in range(0, picture.shape[1], square_fragment_size):
        fragments[idx] = picture[i:i + square_fragment_size,
                                 j:j + square_fragment_size, :].flatten()
        idx += 1
```

At this point, it's possible to perform K-means clustering with 24 quantization vectors, as follows:

```
from sklearn.cluster import KMeans

n_qvectors = 24

km = KMeans(n_clusters=n_qvectors, random_state=1000)
km.fit(fragments)

qvs = km.predict(fragments)
```

At the end of the training, the variable `qvs` will contain the indexes of the centroids (available through the instance variable `cluster_centers_`) associated with each square region.

The quantized image can now be built using the centroids, as follows:

```
import numpy as np

qv_picture = np.zeros(shape=(192, 256, 3))
idx = 0

for i in range(0, 192, square_fragment_size):
    for j in range(0, 256, square_fragment_size):
        qv_picture[i:i + square_fragment_size,
                   j:j + square_fragment_size, :] = \
            km.cluster_centers_[qvs[idx]].\
                reshape((square_fragment_size, square_fragment_size, 3))
        idx += 1
```

The quantized image is shown in the following screenshot:

Picture quantized with 24 vectors

The result is clearly a lossy compressed version of the original image. Each group can be represented with an index (for example, in our case, it can be an 8-bit integer) pointing to the entry in the codebook (`km.cluster_centers_`). So, if initially there were 192 × 256 × 3 = 1,474,560 8-bit values, after the quantization we have 12,288 8-bit indexes (the number of 2 × 2 × 3 blocks) plus 24 12-dimensional quantization vectors. In order to understand the effect of VQ on the image, it's helpful to plot RGB histograms for the original and processed images as shown in the following histogram:

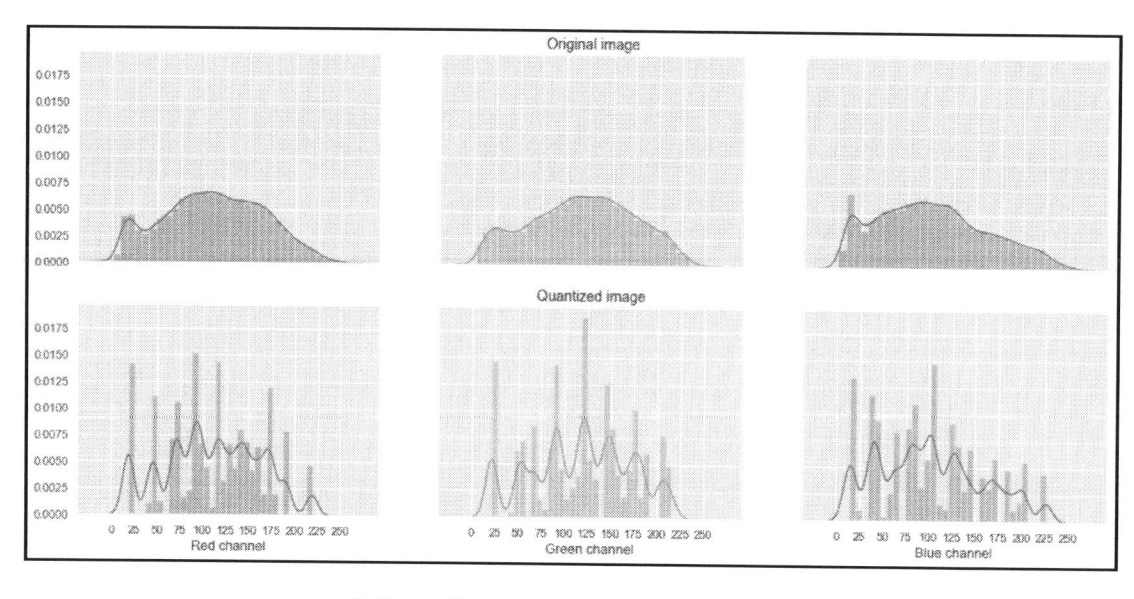

RGB histogram of the original image (top) and quantized version (bottom)

For readers who are not familiar with histograms, we can briefly describe them as having a dataset X and a fixed number of bins. Each bin is assigned to a range (starting from $min(X)$ and ending in $max(X)$) and each range (a, b) is associated with the number of samples such that $a \leq x < b$. The resulting plot is proportional to an approximation of the actual probability distribution that generated X. In our case, on the x-axis, there are all possible values for each pixel per channel (8-bit), while the y-axis represents the estimated frequency (N_x / Total number of pixels).

As it's possible to see, the quantization has reduced the amount of information, but the histograms tend to reproduce the original ones. Increasing the number of quantization vectors has the effect of reducing the approximation, yielding histograms with less significant discrepancies. A complete analysis of this topic is beyond the scope of this book; however, I invite the reader to test the procedure with other images and different numbers of quantization vectors. It's also possible to compare the (co)variance of the original image (or, alternatively, the entropy) with the quantized version and find a threshold that preserves at 80% of the variance. For example, considering only the red channel and approximating the probabilities of every value (0 ÷ 255) with frequency counts, we obtain the following:

```
import numpy as np

hist_original, _ = np.histogram(picture[:, :, 0].flatten() * 255.0,
bins=256)
hist_q, _ = np.histogram(qv_picture[:, :, 0].flatten() * 255.0, bins=256)

p_original = hist_original / np.sum(hist_original)
H_original = -np.sum(p_original * np.log2(p_original + 1e-8))

p_q = hist_q / np.sum(hist_q)
H_q = -np.sum(p_q * np.log2(p_q + 1e-8))

print('Original entropy: {0:.3f} bits - Quantized entropy: {1:.3f}
bits'.format(H_original, H_q))
```

The output of the previous snippet is as follows:

```
Original entropy: 7.726 bits - Quantized entropy: 5.752 bits
```

As the amount of information is proportional to the entropy, we now have confirmation that 24 quantization vectors (with 2 × 2 square blocks) are able to explain about 74% of the original entropy of the red channel (even if the three channels are not independent, a rough approximation of the total entropy can be obtained by summing the three entropies). This method can be efficiently employed to find a trade-off between compression strength and final result quality.

Summary

In this chapter, we explained the fundamental concepts of cluster analysis, starting from the concept of similarity and how to measure it. We discussed the K-means algorithm and its optimized variant called K-means++ and we analyzed the Breast Cancer Wisconsin dataset. Then we discussed the most important evaluation metrics (with or without knowledge of the ground truth) and we have learned which factors can influence performance. The next two topics were KNN, a very famous algorithm that can be employed to find the most similar samples given a query vector, and VQ, a technique that exploits clustering algorithms in order to find a lossy representation of a sample (for example, an image) or a dataset.

In the next chapter, we are going to introduce some of the most important advanced clustering algorithms, showing how they can easily solve non-convex problems.

Questions

1. If two samples have a Minkowski distance ($p=5$) equal to 10, what can you say about their Manhattan distance?
2. The main factor that negatively impacts on the convergence speed of K-means is the dimensionality of the dataset. Is this correct?
3. One of the most important factors that can positively impact on the performance of K-means is the convexity of the clusters. Is this correct?
4. The homogeneity score of a clustering application is equal to 0.99. What does it mean?
5. What is the meaning of an adjusted Rand score equal to -0.5?
6. Considering the previous question, can a different number of clusters yield a better score?
7. An application based on KNN requires on average 100 5-NN base queries per minute. Every minute, 2 50-NN queries are executed (each of them requires 4 seconds with a leaf size=25) and, immediately after them, a 2-second blocking task is performed. Assuming the absence of other delays, how many *basic* queries per minute can be performed with a leaf size=50?
8. A ball-tree structure is not suitable to manage high-dimensional data because it suffers the curse of dimensionality. Is this correct?

9. A dataset is obtained sampling 1,000 samples from 3 bidimensional Gaussian distributions: N([-1.0, 0.0], diag[0.8, 0.2]), N([0.0, 5.0], diag[0.1, 0.1]), and N([-0.8, 0.0], diag[0.6, 0.3]). Which is the most likely number of clusters?
10. Can VQ be employed to compress a text file (for example, building a dictionary with 10,000 words uniformly mapped in the range [0.0, 1.0], splitting the text into tokens, and transforming it into a sequence of floats)?

Further reading

- *On the Surprising Behavior of Distance Metrics in High Dimensional Space*, Aggarwal C. C., Hinneburg A., Keim D. A., ICDT, 2001
- *K-means++: The Advantages of Careful Seeding*, Arthur D., Vassilvitskii S., Proceedings of the Eighteenth Annual ACM-SIAM Symposium on Discrete Algorithms, 2007
- *Visualizing Data using t-SNE*, van der Maaten L., Hinton G., Journal of Machine Learning Research 9, 2008
- *Robust Linear Programming Discrimination of Two Linearly Inseparable Sets*, Bennett K. P., Mangasarian O. L., Optimization Methods and Software 1, 1992
- *Breast cancer diagnosis and prognosis via linear programming*, Mangasarian O. L., Street W.N, Wolberg W. H., Operations Research, 43(4), pages 570-577, July-August 1995
- *V-Measure: A conditional entropy-based external cluster evaluation measure*, Rosenberg A., Hirschberg J., Proceedings of the 2007 Joint Conference on Empirical Methods in Natural Language Processing and Computational Natural Language Learning, 2007

3
Advanced Clustering

In this chapter, we are continuing our exploration of more complex clustering algorithms that can be employed in non-convex tasks (that is, where, for example, K-means fails to obtain both cohesion and separation. A classical example is represented by interlaced geometries). We are also going to show how to apply a density-based algorithm to a complex dataset and how to properly select hyperparameters and evaluate performances according to the desired result. In this way, a data scientist can be ready to face different kinds of problems, excluding the less valuable solutions and focusing only on the most promising ones.

In particular, we are going to discuss the following topics:

- Spectral clustering
- Mean shift
- **Density-based Spatial Clustering of Applications with Noise (DBSCAN)**
- Additional evaluation metrics: Calinski-Harabasz index and cluster instability
- K-medoids
- Online clustering (mini-batch K-means and **Balanced Iterative Reducing and Clustering using Hierarchies (BIRCH)**)

Technical requirements

The code presented in this chapter requires:

- Python 3.5+ (Anaconda distribution: https://www.anaconda.com/distribution/ is highly recommended)
- Libraries:
    - SciPy 0.19+
    - NumPy 1.10+
    - scikit-learn 0.20+
    - pandas 0.22+
    - Matplotlib 2.0+
    - seaborn 0.9+

The dataset can be obtained through UCI. The CSV file can be downloaded from https://archive.ics.uci.edu/ml/datasets/Absenteeism+at+work and doesn't need any preprocessing except for the addition of the column names that will occur during the loading stage.

Examples are available on the Github repository:

https://github.com/PacktPublishing/HandsOn-Unsupervised-Learning-with-Python/Chapter03.

Spectral clustering

One of the most common algorithm families that can manage non-convex clusters is **spectral clustering**. The main idea is to project the dataset X on a space where the clusters can be captured by hyperspheres (for example, using K-means). This result can be achieved in different ways, but, as the goal of the algorithm is to remove the concavities of generic shaped regions, the first step is always the representation of X as a graph $G=\{V, E\}$, where the vertices $V \equiv X$ and the weighted edges represent the proximity of every couple of samples $x_i, x_j \in X$ through the parameter $w_{ij} \geq 0$. The resulting graph can be either complete (fully connected) or it can have edges only between some sample couples (that is, the weight of non-existing weights is set equal to zero). In the following diagram, there's an example of a partial graph:

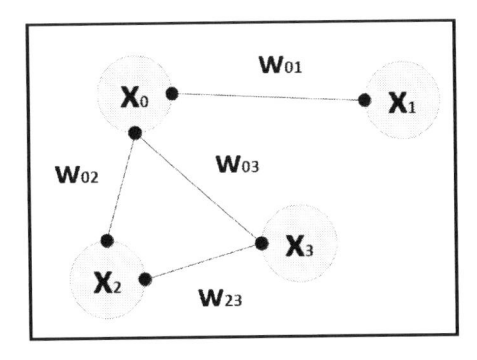

Example of a graph: Point x_0 is the only one that is connected to x_1

There are two main strategies that can be employed to determine the weights w_{ij}: KNN and **Radial Basis Function (RBF)**. The first one is based on the same algorithm discussed in the previous chapter. Considering a number k of neighbors, the dataset is represented as ball-tree or kd-tree and, for each sample x_i, the set $kNN(x_i)$ is computed. At this point, given another sample x_j, the weight is computed as follows:

$$w_{ij} = \begin{cases} 1 & if \ \bar{x}_j \in kNN(\bar{x}_i) \\ 0 & otherwise \end{cases}$$

In this case, the graph doesn't contain any information about the actual distances, and hence, considering the same distance function $d(\bullet)$ employed in KNN, it is preferable to represent w_{ij} as:

$$w_{ij} = \begin{cases} d(\bar{x}_i, \bar{x}_j) & if \ \bar{x}_j \in kNN(\bar{x}_i) \\ 0 & otherwise \end{cases}$$

Advanced Clustering

This method is simple and rather reliable, but the resulting graph is not fully connected. Such a condition can be easily achieved by employing a RBF, defined as follows:

$$w_{ij} = e^{-\gamma \|\bar{x}_i - \bar{x}_j\|^2}$$

In this way, all couples are automatically weighted according to their distance. As the RBF is a Gaussian curve, it is equal to *1* when $x_i = x_j$ and decreases proportionally to the square distance $d(x_i, x_j)$ (represented as the norm of the difference). The parameter γ determines the amplitude of the half-bell curve (in general, the default value is $\gamma=1$). When $\gamma < 1$, the amplitude increases and the other way around. Therefore, $\gamma < 1$ implies a lower sensitivity to the distance, while with $\gamma > 1$, the RBF drops quicker, as shown in the following screenshot:

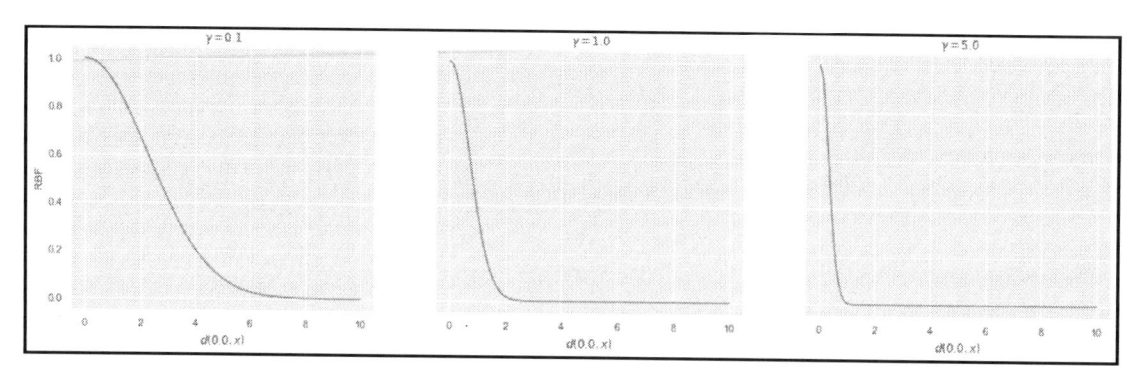

Bidimensional RBFs as functions of the distance between x and 0 computed for $\gamma = 0.1$, 1.0, and 5.0

With $\gamma = 0.1$, $x = 1$ (with respect to 0.0) is weighted about 0.9. This value becomes about 0.5 for $\gamma = 1.0$ and almost zero for $\gamma = 5.0$. Hence, when tuning a spectral clustering model, it's extremely important to consider different values for γ and select the one that yields the best performances (for example, evaluated using the criteria discussed in Chapter 2, *Clustering Fundamentals*). Once the graph has been created, it can be represented using a symmetric **affinity matrix** $W = \{w_{ij}\}$. For KNN W is generally sparse and can be efficiently stored and manipulated with specialized libraries. Instead, with RBF, it is always dense and, if $X \in \Re^{N \times M}$, it needs to store N^2 values.

It's not difficult to prove that the procedure we have analyzed so far is equivalent to a segmentation of X into a number of cohesive regions. In fact, let's consider, for example, a graph G with an affinity matrix obtained with KNN. A connected component C_i is a subgraph where every couple of vertices $x_a, x_b \in C_i$ are connected through a path of vertices belonging to C_i and there are no edges connecting any vertex of C_i with a vertex not belonging to C_i. In other words, a connected component is a cohesive subset $C_i \subseteq G$ that represents an optimal candidate for a cluster selection. In the following diagram, there's an example of a connected component extracted from a graph:

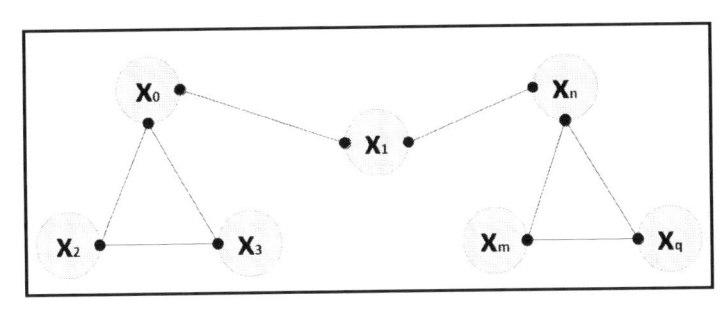

Example of a connected component extracted from a graph

In the original space, the points x_0, x_2, and x_3 are connected to x_n, x_m, and x_q through x_1. This can represent a very simple non-convex geometry such as a half-moon. In fact, in this case, the convexity assumption is no more necessary for an optimal separation because, as we are going to see, these components are extracted and projected onto subspaces with flat geometries (easily manageable by algorithms such as K-means).

This process is more evident when KNN is employed, but, in general, we can say that two regions can be merged when the inter-region distance (for example, the distance between the two closest points) is comparable to the average intra-region distance. One of the most common methods to solve this problem has been proposed by Shi and Malik (in *Normalized Cuts and Image Segmentation, J. Shi and J. Malik, IEEE Transactions on Pattern Analysis and Machine Intelligence, Vol. 22, 08/2000*) and it's called normalized cuts. The whole proof is beyond the scope of this book, but we can discuss the main concepts. Given a graph, it's possible to build the normalized graph Laplacian, defined as:

$$L = I - D^{-1}W \text{ where } D = diag\left(\sum_j w_{ij}\right)$$

Advanced Clustering

The diagonal matrix D is called **degree matrix** and each element d_{ii} is the sum of the weights of the corresponding row. It's possible to prove the following statements:

- After eigendecomposing L (it's easy to compute both eigenvalues and eigenvectors considering the unnormalized graph Laplacian $L_u = D - W$ and solving the equation $L_u v = \lambda D v$), the null eigenvalue is always present with multiplicity p.
- If G is an undirected graph (so $w_{ij} \geq 0 \; \forall \; i, j$), the number of connected components is equal to p (the multiplicity of the null eigenvalue).
- If $A \subseteq \Re^N$ and Θ is a countable subset of A (that is, X is a countable subset because the number of samples is always finite), a vector $v \in \Re^N$ is called the **indicator vector** for Θ if, given $\theta_i \in \Theta$, $v^{(i)} = 1$ if $\theta_i \in A$ and $v^{(i)} = 0$ otherwise. For example, if we have two vectors $a = (1, 0)$ and $b = (0, 0)$ (so, $\Theta = \{a, b\}$) and we consider $A = \{(1, n) \text{ where } n \in [1, 10]\}$, the vector $v = (1, 0)$ is an indicator vector, because $a \in A$ and $b \notin A$.
- The first p eigenvectors of L (corresponding to the null eigenvalue) are indicator vectors for the eigenspaces spanned by each connected component $C_1, C_2, ..., C_p$.

Hence, if the dataset is made up of M samples $x_i \in \Re^N$, and the graph G is associated with an affinity matrix $W^{M \times M}$, Shi and Malik proposed to build a matrix $B \in \Re^{M \times p}$ containing the first p eigenvectors as columns and to cluster the rows using a simpler method such as K-means. In fact, each row represents the projection of a sample onto a p-dimensional subspace where the non-convexities are represented by subregions that can be enclosed into regular balls.

Let's now apply spectral clustering in order to separate a bidimensional sinusoidal dataset generated with the following snippet:

```
import numpy as np

nb_samples = 2000

X0 = np.expand_dims(np.linspace(-2 * np.pi, 2 * np.pi, nb_samples), axis=1)
Y0 = -2.0 - np.cos(2.0 * X0) + np.random.uniform(0.0, 2.0, size=(nb_samples, 1))

X1 = np.expand_dims(np.linspace(-2 * np.pi, 2 * np.pi, nb_samples), axis=1)
Y1 = 2.0 - np.cos(2.0 * X0) + np.random.uniform(0.0, 2.0, size=(nb_samples, 1))

data_0 = np.concatenate([X0, Y0], axis=1)
data_1 = np.concatenate([X1, Y1], axis=1)
data = np.concatenate([data_0, data_1], axis=0)
```

The dataset is shown in the following screenshot:

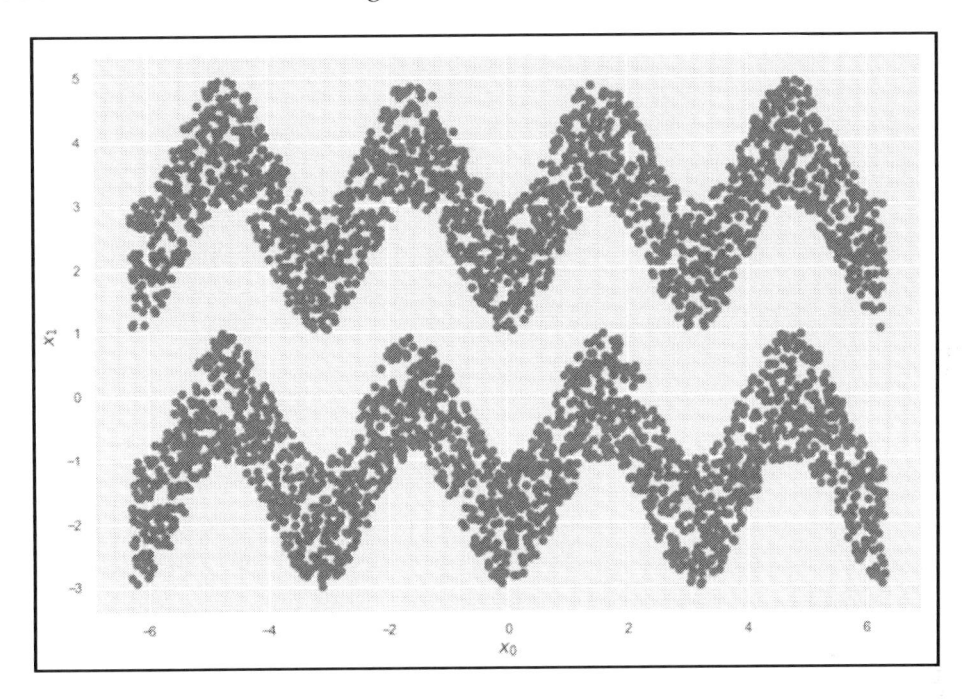

A sinusoidal dataset for the spectral clustering example

We haven't specified any ground truth; however, the goal is to separate the two sinusoids, (which are non-convex). It's easy to check that a ball capturing a sinusoid will also include many samples belonging to the other sinusoidal subset. In order to show the difference between a pure K-means and spectral clustering (scikit-learn implements the Shi-Malik algorithm followed by K-means clustering), we are going to train both models, using for the latter an RBF (affinity parameter) with $\gamma = 2.0$ (gamma parameter). Of course, I invite the reader to also test other values and the KNN affinity. The RBF-based solutions is shown in the following snippet:

```
from sklearn.cluster import SpectralClustering, KMeans

km = KMeans(n_clusters=2, random_state=1000)
sc = SpectralClustering(n_clusters=2, affinity='rbf', gamma=2.0,
random_state=1000)

Y_pred_km = km.fit_predict(data)
Y_pred_sc = sc.fit_predict(data)
```

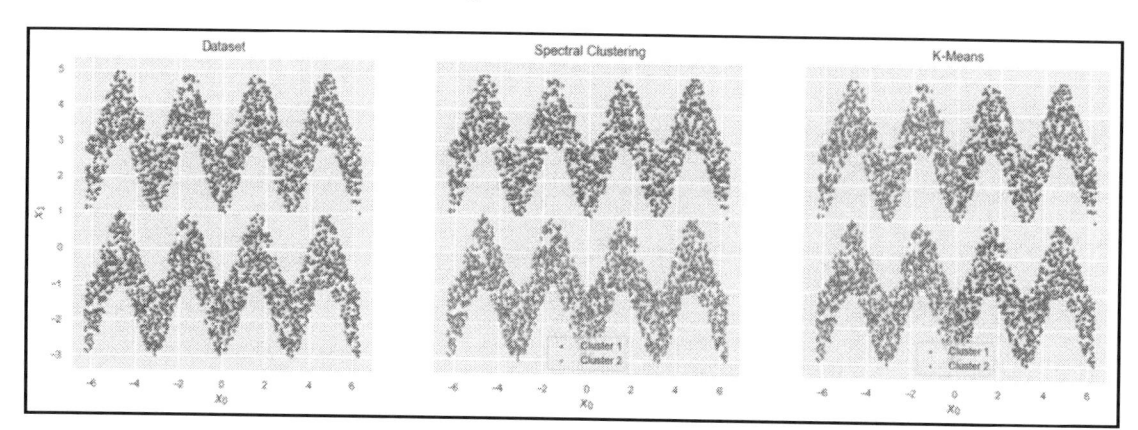

The results are shown in the following screenshot:

Original dataset (left). Spectral clustering result (center). K-means result (right)

As you can see, K-means partitions the dataset with two balls along the x-axis, while spectral clustering succeeds in separating the two sinusoids correctly. This algorithm is very powerful whenever both the number of clusters and the dimensionality of X are not too large (in this case the eigendecomposition of the Laplacian can become very computationally expensive). Moreover, as the algorithm is based on a graph *cutting* procedure, it's perfectly suited when the number of clusters is even.

Mean shift

Let's consider having a dataset $X \in \Re^{M \times N}$ (M N-dimensional samples) drawn from a multivariate data generating process p_{data}. The goal of the **mean shift** algorithm applied to a clustering problem is to find the regions where p_{data} is maximum and associate the samples contained in a surrounding subregion to the same cluster. As p_{data} is a **Probability Density Function (PDF)**, it is reasonable for representing it as the sum of regular PDFs (for example, Gaussians) characterized by a small subset of parameters, such as mean and variance. In this way, a sample can be supposed to be generated by the PDF with the highest probability. We are going to discuss this process also in `Chapter 5`, *Soft Clustering and Gaussian Mixture Models*, and `Chapter 6`, *Anomaly Detection*. For our purposes, it's helpful to restructure the problem as an iterative procedure that updates the position of the mean vectors (centroids) until they reach the maxima. When the centroids have reached their final position, the samples are assigned to each cluster using a standard neighborhood function.

The first step of this algorithm is determining a suitable way to approximate p_{data}. A classical approach, (which will be discussed in Chapter 6, *Anomaly Detection*) is based on the employment of **Parzen windows**. For now, it's enough to say that a Parzen window is a non-negative kernel function $f(\bullet)$ characterized by a parameter called **bandwidth** (for further details, please check the original paper *On Estimation of a Probability Density Function and Mode*, Parzen E., The Annals of Mathematical Statistics. 33, 1962). As the name suggests, the role of such a parameter is to widen or restrict the area where the Parzen window is close to its maximum. Considering an analogy with Gaussian distributions, the bandwidth has the same role as the variance. Hence, small bandwidths will yield functions very peaked around the mean, while larger values are associated with flatter functions. It's not difficult to understand that, in this particular case, the number of clusters is implicitly determined by the bandwidth and the other way around. For this reason, the majority of implementations (such as scikit-learn) employ only a single parameter and compute the other one. Considering that this algorithm has been designed to work with probability distributions, the natural choice is to specify the desired bandwidth or let the implementation detect the optimal one. This process can appear more complex than imposing a specific number of clusters, but, in many real cases and, in particular, when the ground truth is at least partially known, it's easier to test the result of different bandwidths.

The most common choice for mean shift is to approximate the data generating process with the sum of n flat kernels (n is the number of centroids):

$$p_{data} \approx \sum_{i=1}^{n} K_r(\bar{x} - \bar{x}_i) \text{ where } K_r(\bar{x}) = \begin{cases} 1 & if \ \|\bar{x}\| \leq r \\ 0 & otherwise \end{cases}$$

Therefore, after the convergence, each sample is represented by the closest centroid. Unfortunately, this approximation leads to a piece-wise function that is unlikely to represent a real process. Hence, it's preferable to employ a smoothed Parzen window $K(\bullet)$ based on the same underlying kernel:

$$p_{data} \approx \sum_{i=1}^{n} K\left(\frac{\|\bar{x} - \bar{x}_i\|^2}{h^2}\right)$$

Advanced Clustering

$K(\bullet)$ is a function of both the squared distance (such as for a standard ball) and of the bandwidth h. There are many possible candidate functions that can be employed, but, of course, the most obvious is a Gaussian kernel (RBF), where h^2 plays the role of the variance. The resulting approximation is now very smooth, with n peaks corresponding to the centroids (that is, the means). Once the function has been defined, it's possible to compute the optimal position of the centroids $x_1, x_2, ..., x_n$.

Given a centroid and a neighborhood function (for simplicity, we have assumed to work with standard balls B_h with a radius h and $K(x) \neq 0 \; \forall \, x \in B_r$), the corresponding mean shift vector is defined as:

$$\bar{m}(\bar{x}_i) = \frac{\sum_{\bar{x}_h \in B_h(\bar{x}_i)} [K(\bar{x}_h - \bar{x}_i)\bar{x}_h]}{\sum_{\bar{x}_h \in B_h(\bar{x}_i)} K(\bar{x}_h - \bar{x}_i)}$$

As it's possible to see, $m(\bullet)$ is the average of all neighborhood samples weighted with $K(\bullet)$. Obviously, as $K(\bullet)$ is symmetric and works with distances, $m(\bullet)$ will tend to stabilize when x_i reaches the actual mean. The role of the bandwidth is to limit the region around x_i. Now it should be clearer that small values force the algorithm to introduce more centroids in order to assign all samples to a cluster. Conversely, large bandwidths can lead to the *final* configuration with a single cluster. The iterative procedure starts with an initial centroid guess $x_1^{(0)}, x_2^{(0)}, ..., x_n^{(0)}$ and corrects the vectors with the rule:

$$\bar{x}_i^{(t)} = \bar{x}_i^{(t-1)} + \bar{m}\left(\bar{x}_i^{(t-1)}\right) \quad \forall \, i = 1..n$$

The previous formula is straightforward; at every step, the centroid is moved (shifted) closer to $m(\bullet)$. In this way, as $m(\bullet)$ is proportional to the density of the neighborhood computed with respect to x_i, when x_i reaches the position where the probability is maximum, $m(\bullet) \to m_{final}$, no more updates are needed. Of course, the convergence speed is strongly influenced by the number of samples. For very large datasets, the procedure can become very slow because the computation of each mean shift vector requires the pre-computation of the neighborhood. On the other hand, this algorithm is very helpful when the clustering criterion is defined by the density of the data.

As an example, let's now consider a synthetic dataset with 500 bidimensional samples generated by three multivariate Gaussians with diagonal covariance matrices, as follows:

```
import numpy as np

nb_samples = 500

data_1 = np.random.multivariate_normal([-2.0, 0.0], np.diag([1.0, 0.5]), size=(nb_samples,))
data_2 = np.random.multivariate_normal([0.0, 2.0], np.diag([1.5, 1.5]), size=(nb_samples,))
data_3 = np.random.multivariate_normal([2.0, 0.0], np.diag([0.5, 1.0]), size=(nb_samples,))

data = np.concatenate([data_1, data_2, data_3], axis=0)
```

The dataset is shown in the following screenshot:

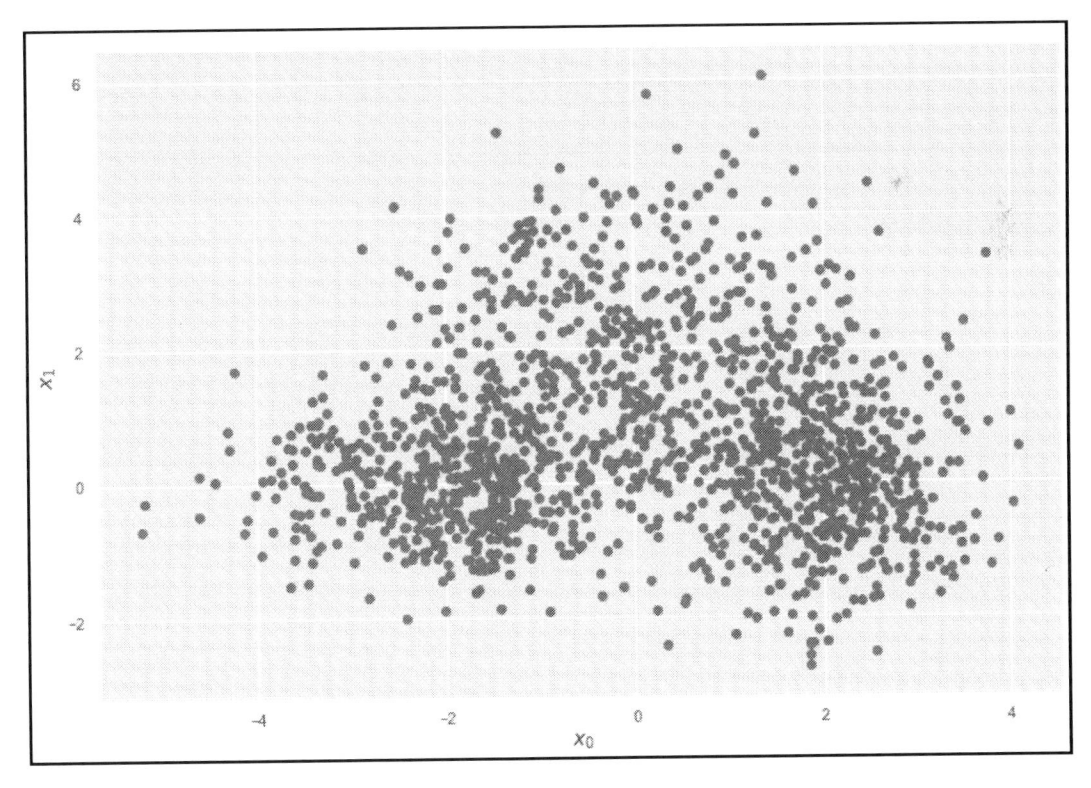

Sample dataset for the mean shift algorithm example

Advanced Clustering

In this case, we know the ground truth, but we want to test different bandwidths and compare the results. As the generating Gaussians are quite close to each other, some *external* regions could be identified as clusters. In order to focus the research on optimal parameters, we can observe that the average variance (considering the asymmetries) is 1, and hence, we can consider the values h=0.9, 1.0, 1.2, and 1.5. At this point, we can instantiate the scikit-learn class MeanShift, passing the h values through the parameter bandwidth, as follows:

```
from sklearn.cluster import MeanShift

mss = []
Y_preds = []
bandwidths = [0.9, 1.0, 1.2, 1.5]

for b in bandwidths:
    ms = MeanShift(bandwidth=b)
    Y_preds.append(ms.fit_predict(data))
    mss.append(ms)
```

The training process automatically selects the number and the initial location of the centroids after a density analysis. Unfortunately, this number is normally larger than the final one (because of local density differences); hence the algorithm will optimize all centroids but, before finishing, a merge procedure is performed to eliminate all those centroids that are too close to other ones (that is, duplicate ones). Scikit-learn provides the parameter bin_seeding that can speed up this research by performing a discretization (binning) of the sample space according to the bandwidth. In this way, it's possible to reduce the number of candidates with a reasonable loss of precision.

The results at the end of the four training processes are shown in the following diagram:

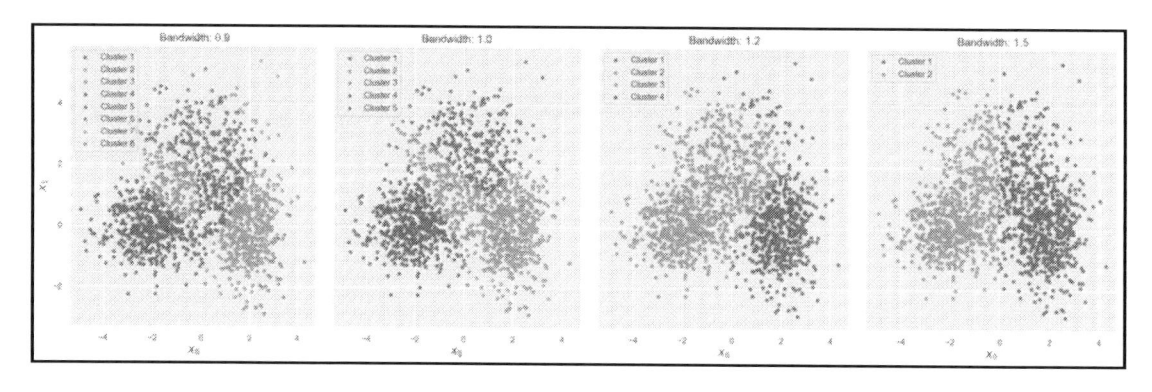

Mean shift clustering results for different bandwidths

As you can see, a small difference in the bandwidth can lead to a different number of clusters. In our case, the optimal value is h=1.2, which produces a result where three distinct regions (plus an extra cluster containing potential outliers) are determined. The centroids of the largest clusters correspond roughly to the actual means, but the shapes of the clusters don't resemble any Gaussian distribution. This is a drawback that can be solved by employing other methods (discussed in Chapter 5, *Soft Clustering and Gaussian Mixture Models*). Mean shift, in fact, works with local neighborhoods and p_{data} is not assumed to belong to a particular distribution. Hence, the final result is a quite accurate segmentation of the dataset into highly dense regions (notice that the maximum separation is no longer a requirement) that can also derive from the superimposition of multiple standard distributions. Without any prior assumption, we cannot expect the result to be very regular, but, comparing this algorithm with a VQ, it's easy to notice that the assignments are based on the idea of finding the optimal representative of every dense blob. For this reason, some points generated by a Gaussian $N(\mu, \Sigma)$ with a low probability are assigned to a different cluster whose centroid is more representative (in terms of distance) than μ.

DBSCAN

DBSCAN is another clustering algorithm based on a density estimation of the dataset. However, contrary to mean shift, there is no direct reference to the data generating process. In this case, in fact, the process *builds the relationships* between samples with a bottom-up analysis, starting from the general assumption that X is made up of high-density regions (blobs) separated by low-density ones. Hence, DBSCAN not only requires the maximum separation constraint, but it enforces such a condition in order to determine the boundaries of the clusters. Moreover, this algorithm doesn't allow specifying the desired number of clusters, which is a consequence of the structure of X, but, analogously to mean shift, it's possible to control the granularity of the process.

In particular, DBSCAN is based on two fundamental parameters: ε, which represents the radius of ball $B_\varepsilon(x_i)$ centered on a sample x_i, and n_{min}, which is the minimum number of samples that must be contained into $B_\varepsilon(x_i)$ in order to consider x_i as a **core point** (that is, a point that can be qualified as an actual member of a cluster). Formally, given a function $N(\cdot)$ that counts the number of samples contained in a set, a sample $x_i \in X$ is called the core point if:

$$N(B_\epsilon(\bar{x}_i)) \geq n_{min}$$

Advanced Clustering

All points $x_j \in B_\varepsilon(x_i)$ are defined as **directly density-reachable** from x_i. Such a condition is the strongest relationship among points because they all belong to the same ball centered on x_i and the total number of samples contained in $B_\varepsilon(x_i)$ is large enough to consider the neighborhood as a dense subregion. Moreover, if there's a sequence $x_i \rightarrow x_{i+1} \rightarrow ... \rightarrow x_j$ where x_{i+1} is directly density-reachable from x_i (for all sequential couples), x_j is as defined as **density-reachable** from x_i. This concept is very intuitive and can be immediately understood by considering the following diagram:

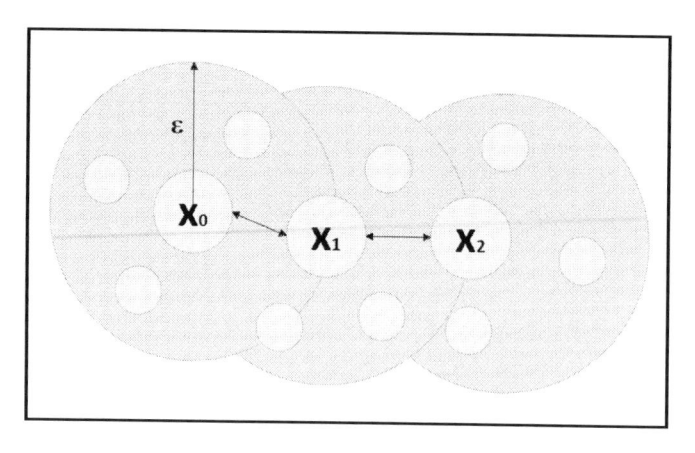

The point x_2 is density-reachable from x_0 if $n_{min} = 4$

If we have set the minimum number of samples equal to four, x_0, x_1, and x_2 are core points and x_1 is directly density-reachable from x_0, and x_2 is directly density-reachable from x_1. Therefore, x_2 is density-reachable from x_0. In other words, it means that it's possible to define a sequence of overlapping dense balls ($N(\bullet) \geq n_{min}$) starting from x_0 and ending on x_2. This concept can be extended to all the other points belonging to the balls by adding a further definition: given a point x_k, the points x_i and x_j are **density-connected** if both x_i and x_j are density-reachable from x_k.

It's important to understand that such a condition is weaker than density-reachability because, in order to guarantee a *dense chain*, it's necessary to consider a third point, which represents a *connector* between two dense subregions. In fact, it's possible to have two density-connected points a and b, with a that is not density-reachable from b (and the other way around). This situation can happen whenever the minimum number of samples conditions is met only moving in a direction (that is, the samples belonging to a ball are not uniformly distributed but tend to accumulate in a small hypervolume).

Therefore, for example, if $N(a) \gg n_{min}$ and $N(a_1) \ll N(a)$, the transition $a \to a_1$ can allow building a ball $B_\varepsilon(a)$ containing also a_1 (together with many other points). However, in the inverse transition $a_1 \to a$, $B_\varepsilon(a_1)$ can't be dense enough to establish a directly density-reachability condition.

Thus, a longer sequence can be *broken* when moving in one of the two directions, with a consequent loss of density-reachability. It should now be clearer that the density-connection between two points x_i and x_j allows us to avoid this problem provided that there's another point that can reach both x_i and x_j.

All couples of density-connected points (x_i, x_j) with $x_i, x_j \in X$ will be assigned to the same cluster C_t. Moreover, if $x_k \in C_t$, all points $x_p \in X$ that are density-reachable from x_k will also belong to the same cluster. A point x_n that is not density-reachable from any other point $x_i \in X$ is defined as a **noise point**. Hence, contrary to other algorithms, DBSCAN outputs n clusters plus an additional set containing all noise points, (which shouldn't necessarily be considered as outliers, but rather as points not belonging to any dense subregion). Of course, as noise points have no labels, their number should be quite low; thus, it's important to tune up the parameters ε and n_{min} with a double objective: maximizing both cohesion and separation and avoiding too many points being marked as noisy. There are no standard rules to achieve such a goal, and hence I recommend testing different values before making the final decision.

Finally, it's important to remember that DBSCAN can work with non-convex geometries and, contrary to mean shift, it assumes the presence of high-density regions surrounded by low-density areas. Moreover, its complexity is strictly related to the KNN approach that is employed (brute-force, ball-trees, or kd-trees). In general, when datasets are not too large, the average performance is about $O(N \log N)$, but it can tend to $O(N^2)$ when N is very large. Another important element to remember is the dimensionality of the samples. As we have already discussed, high-dimensional measures could reduce the discriminability of two points, with a consequent negative impact on the performance of KNN methods. Therefore, DBSCAN should be avoided (or, at least, carefully analyzed) when the dimensionality is very high because the resulting clusters couldn't effectively represent the actual dense regions.

Before showing a concrete example, it's helpful to introduce a further evaluation method that can be employed when the ground truth is unknown.

Calinski-Harabasz score

Let's suppose that a clustering algorithm has been applied to a dataset X containing M samples in order to segment it into n_c clusters C_i represented by a centroid μ_i $\forall\, i = 1..n_c$. We can define the **Within-Cluster Dispersion (WCD)** as follows:

$$WCD(k) = Tr(X_k) \quad where \quad X_k = \sum_{i=1}^{n_c} \sum_{\bar{x} \in C_i} (\bar{x} - \bar{\mu}_i)(\bar{x} - \bar{\mu}_i)^T$$

If x_i is an N-dimensional column vector, $X_k \in \Re^{N \times N}$. It's not difficult to understand that $WCD(k)$ encodes the global information about the *pseudo-variance* of the clusters. If the maximum cohesion condition is met, we expect a limited dispersion around the centroids. On the other hand, $WCD(k)$ can be negatively influenced even by a single cluster containing outliers. Hence, our goal is to minimize $WCD(k)$ in every case. In a similar way, we can define a **Between-Clusters Dispersion (BCD)** as:

$$BCD(k) = Tr(B_k) \quad where \quad B_k = \sum_{i=1}^{n_c} N(C_i)(\bar{\mu}_i - \bar{\mu})(\bar{\mu}_i - \bar{\mu})^T$$

In the previous formula, $N(C_i)$ is the number of elements assigned to the cluster C_i and μ is the global centroid of the whole dataset. Considering the principle of maximum separation, we would like to have dense regions quite far from the global centroid. $BCD(k)$ precisely expresses this principle, hence we need to maximize it in order to achieve better performances.

The **Calinski-Harabasz score** is defined as:

$$CH_k(X, Y_{pred}) = \frac{M - k}{k - 1} \cdot \frac{BCD(k)}{WCD(k)}$$

The explicit dependency on the predicted labels has been introduced because the computation of the centroids is not assumed to be part of the clustering algorithm. The score has no absolute meaning, but rather it's necessary to compare different values in order to understand which solution is better. Clearly, the higher $CH_k(\bullet)$ is, the better the clustering performance because such a condition implies a larger separation and a greater internal cohesion.

Chapter 3

Analysis of the Absenteeism at Work dataset using DBSCAN

The Absenteeism at Work dataset (follow the instructions at the beginning of the chapter to download it) is made up of 740 records containing information regarding employees who took some days off work. There are 20 attributes representing age, service time, education, habits, diseases, disciplinary failures, transportation expense, distance from home to office, and so on (a full description of the fields is available at https://archive.ics.uci.edu/ml/datasets/Absenteeism+at+work). Our goal is to preprocess the data and apply DBSCAN in order to discover dense regions with a specific semantic content.

The first step is loading the CSV file as follows (the placeholder <data_path> must be changed so as to point to the actual location of the file):

```
import pandas as pd

data_path = '<data_path>\Absenteeism_at_work.csv'

df = pd.read_csv(data_path, sep=';', header=0, index_col=0).fillna(0.0)
print(df.count())
```

The output of the previous command is as follows:

```
Reason for absence                 740
Month of absence                   740
Day of the week                    740
Seasons                            740
Transportation expense             740
Distance from Residence to Work    740
Service time                       740
Age                                740
Work load Average/day              740
Hit target                         740
Disciplinary failure               740
Education                          740
Son                                740
Social drinker                     740
Social smoker                      740
Pet                                740
Weight                             740
Height                             740
Body mass index                    740
Absenteeism time in hours          740
dtype: int64
```

Advanced Clustering

Some of these features are categorical and encoded with sequential integers (for example, `Reason for absence`, `Month of absence`, and so on). As these values can affect distances without a precise semantic reason (for example, `Month=12` is larger than `Month=10`, but both months are equivalent in terms of distance), we need to one-hot-encode all these features before proceeding with the next steps (the new features will be appended at the end of the list). In the following snippet, we employ the `get_dummies()` pandas function in order to perform the encoding; then the original columns are removed:

```
import pandas as pd

cdf = pd.get_dummies(df, columns=['Reason for absence', 'Month of absence',
    'Day of the week', 'Seasons', 'Disciplinary failure', 'Education', 'Social
    drinker', 'Social smoker'])

cdf = cdf.drop(labels=['Reason for absence', 'Month of absence', 'Day of
    the week', 'Seasons', 'Disciplinary failure', 'Education', 'Social
    drinker', 'Social smoker']).astype(np.float64)
```

The result of a one-hot encoding normally yields a discrepancy among the means because many features will be constrained to either 0 or 1, while others (for example, age) can have a wider range. For this reason, it's preferable to standardize the means (without impacting the standard deviations, which it's helpful to keep unchanged as they are proportional to the existing information content). This step can be achieved using the `StandardScaler` class setting the parameter `with_std=False`, as follows:

```
from sklearn.preprocessing import StandardScaler

ss = StandardScaler(with_std=False)
sdf = ss.fit_transform(cdf)
```

At this point, as usual, we can employ the t-SNE algorithm to reduce the dimensionality of the dataset (with `n_components=2`) and visualize the structure. The dataframe `dff` will contain the original dataset and the t-SNE coordinates, as follows:

```
from sklearn.manifold import TSNE

tsne = TSNE(n_components=2, perplexity=15, random_state=1000)
data_tsne = tsne.fit_transform(sdf)

df_tsne = pd.DataFrame(data_tsne, columns=['x', 'y'], index=cdf.index)
dff = pd.concat([cdf, df_tsne], axis=1)
```

The resulting plot is shown in the following screenshot:

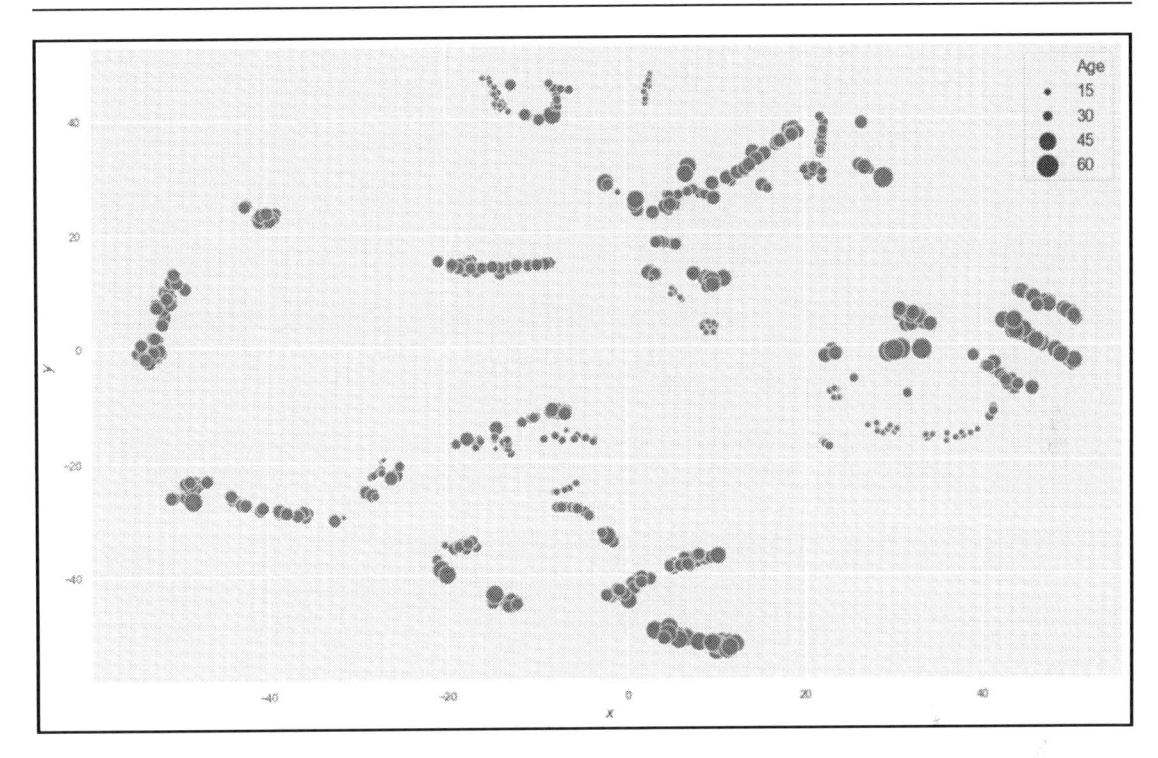

t-SNE bidimensional representation of the Absenteeism at Work dataset

Before any consideration, it's important to repeat that t-SNE yields an optimal low-dimensional representation, but it's always necessary to test the algorithms on the original dataset in order to check whether the neighbors identified by t-SNE correspond to actual agglomerates. In particular, considering the structure of DBSCAN, a ε value can be reasonable considering the t-SNE representation, but when moving to the higher dimensional space, the balls could not capture the same samples anymore. However, the previous plot shows the presence of dense regions surrounded by empty space. Unfortunately, the density is very unlikely to be uniform, (which is one of the suggested requirements of DBSCAN because of the values of both ε and n_{min}, that cannot change), but, in this case, we assume the density to be constant for all the blobs.

Advanced Clustering

In order to find out the best configuration for our purposes, we have plotted the number of clusters, the number of noise points, the silhouette score, and the Calinski-Harabasz score as functions of ε employing a Minkowski metric with $p=2$, $p=4$, $p=8$, and $p=12$, as shown in the following graphs:

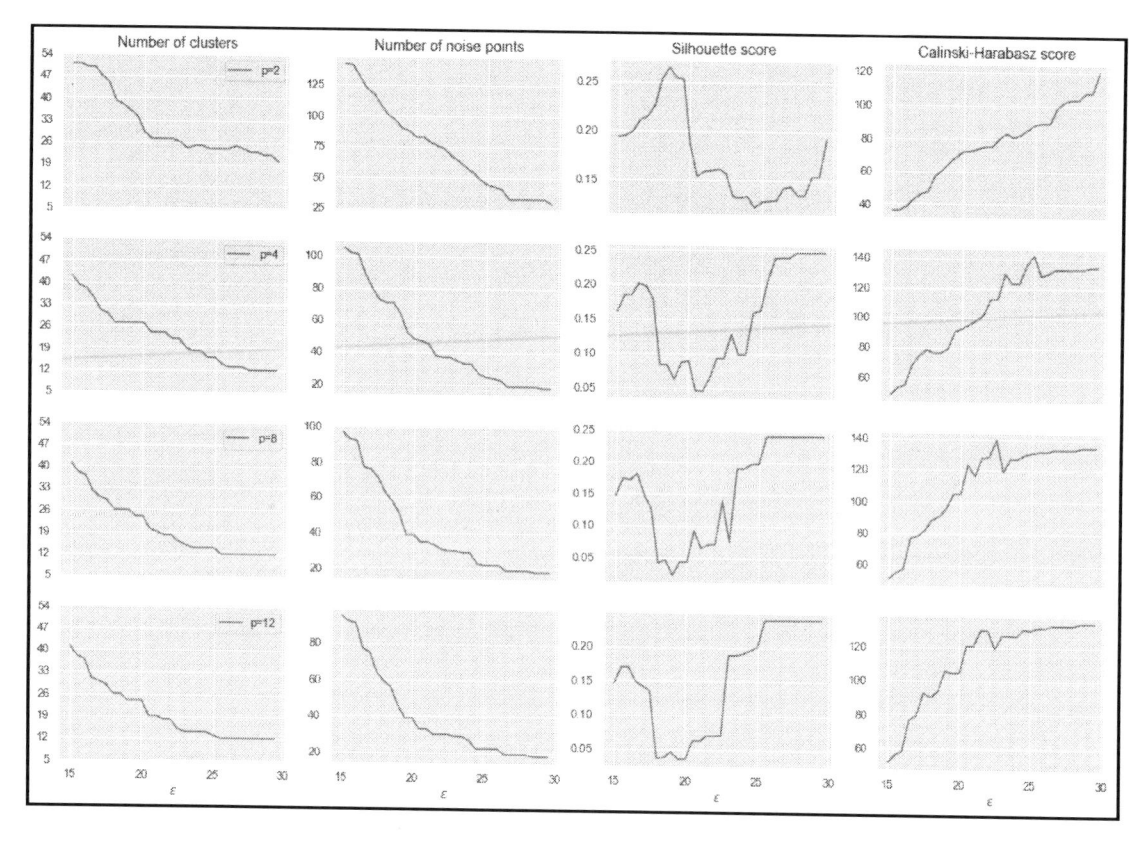

Evaluation metrics as functions of ε

Both silhouette and Calinski-Harabasz are based on the assumption of convex clusters (for example, the dispersion is clearly a measure that assumes a radial distribution of the samples around the centroid), so their expected values in a non-convex case are generally smaller. However, we want to maximize both scores (silhouette → 1 and Calinski-Harabasz → ∞) and, at the same time, avoid a large number of clusters. Considering our initial goal (finding cohesive clusters characterized by a specific set of features), we have chosen ε=25 and a Minkowski metric with $p=12$, which yields a reasonable number of clusters (13) and 22 noise points. In `Chapter 2`, *Clustering Fundamentals*, we have shown that, when $p \to \infty$ (but the effect is visible already for $p > 2$), the distance tends to the largest feature difference.

Hence, such a choice should be always justified by contextual analysis. In this case, we could assume that each (non-)convex blob represents a category dominated by a specific feature (with a secondary contribution of all other ones), therefore *p=12* (leading to 17 clusters) can be a good trade-off for a medium-coarse-grained analysis (considering that there are 20 attributes). Moreover, $\varepsilon=22.5$ is associated with one of the highest Calinski-Harabasz scores, 129.3, and a silhouette score equal to about 0.2. In particular, the latter value indicates that the overall clustering is reasonably correct, but there can be overlaps. As the underlying geometry is very likely to be non-convex, such a result can be acceptable (which it generally isn't in a convex scenario), considering also the Calinski-Harabasz score that has a corresponding peak. Larger values for ε yield slightly higher silhouette scores (less than 0.23), but neither the resulting number of clusters nor the Calinski-Harbasz score is affected by the resulting configurations. It must clear that this choice has not been confirmed by any external evidence and must be validated with a semantic analysis of the results. A configuration with a larger number of clusters and more noisy points could be also acceptable if a fine-grained analysis is needed (so, the reader can *play* with the values and also provide an interpretation of the results). However, the final goal of this example remains the same: segmenting the dataset, so that each cluster contains specific (possibly unique) properties.

We can now instantiate a `DBSCAN` model and train it using the array `sdf`, which contains the normalized features. The configuration is $\varepsilon=25$ (parameter `eps`) and $n_{min}=3$ (parameter `min_samples`), and Minkowski metric (`metric='minkowski'`) with p=12.

We can now perform the following clustering:

```
from sklearn.cluster import DBSCAN
from sklearn.metrics import silhouette_score, calinski_harabaz_score

ds = DBSCAN(eps=25, min_samples=3, metric='minkowski', p=12)
Y_pred = ds.fit_predict(sdf)

print('Number of clusters: {}'.format(np.max(Y_pred) + 1))
print('Number of noise points: {}'.format(np.sum(Y_pred==-1)))

print('Silhouette score: {:.3f}'.format(silhouette_score(dff, Y_pred,
metric='minkowski', p=12)))
print('Calinski-Harabaz score: {:.3f}'.format(calinski_harabaz_score(dff,
Y_pred)))
```

Advanced Clustering

As `DBSCAN` marks noisy points with the label `-1`, the output of the previous snippet is as follows:

```
Number of clusters: 13
Number of noise points: 22

Silhouette score: 0.2
Calinski-Harabaz score: 129.860
```

The resulting plot is shown in the following screenshot:

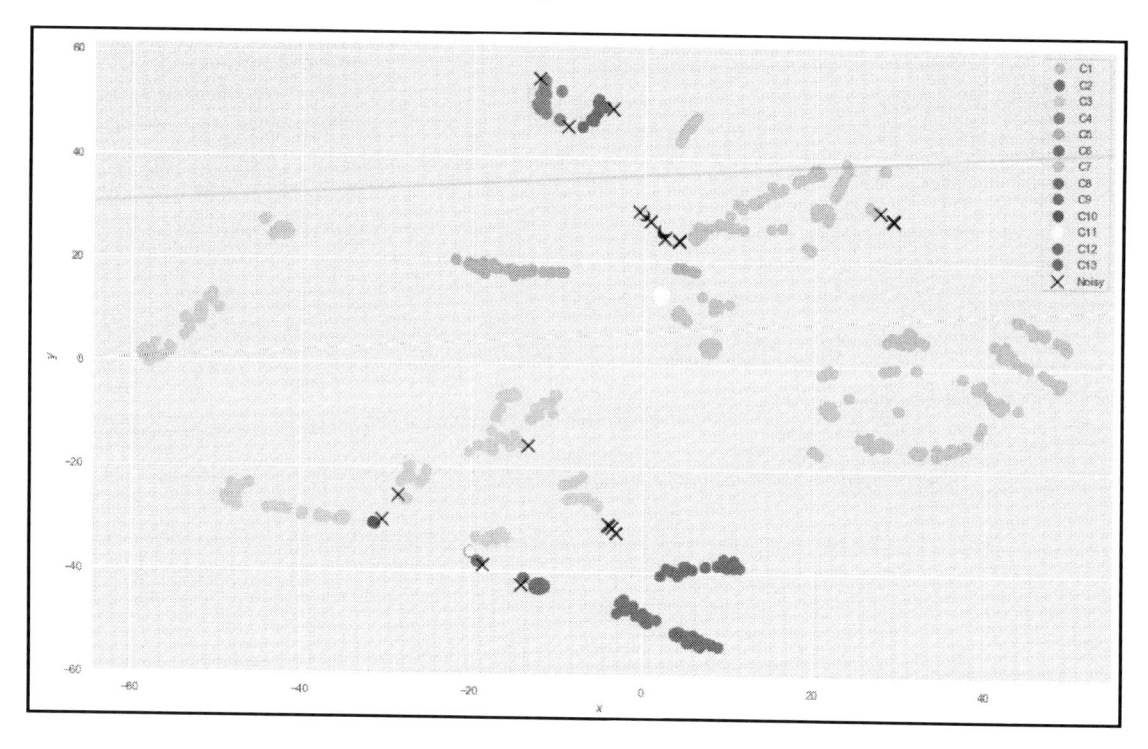

Clustering result for the Absenteeism at Work dataset

As you can see (I suggest running the code in order to have a better visual confirmation), the majority of isolated (even if not cohesive in the t-SNE plot) regions have been successfully detected and the samples have been assigned to the same cluster. We can also observe two fundamental results: the noise points (marked with a cross) are not isolated in the t-SNE representation, and some clusters are partially split. This is not a failure of the algorithm, but a direct consequence of the dimensionality reduction. In the original space, all noise points are really not density-connected to any other sample, but they can appear overlapping or close to some blobs in the t-SNE plot. However, we are interested in the high-density and quasi-cohesive non-convex regions, which, luckily, appear connected also in a bidimensional diagram.

Let's now consider two distinct regions (for simplicity, limiting the analysis to the first 10 attributes after the one-hot encoding). The first one is the bidimensional region x < -45, as follows:

```
sdff = dff[(dff.x < -45.0)]
print(sdff[sdff.columns[0:10]].describe())
```

The print-pretty version of the output is shown in the following screenshot:

	Transportation expense	Distance from Residence to Work	Service time	Age	Work load Average/day	Hit target	Son	Pet	Weight	Height
count	67.0	67.000000	67.000000	67.000000	67.000000	67.000000	67.000000	67.000000	67.000000	67.000000
mean	179.0	50.910448	17.940299	38.223881	251.817418	95.253731	0.014925	0.014925	88.820896	170.074627
std	0.0	0.733017	0.488678	1.832542	10.791695	2.382660	0.122169	0.122169	1.466033	0.610847
min	179.0	45.000000	14.000000	38.000000	230.290000	87.000000	0.000000	0.000000	77.000000	170.000000
25%	179.0	51.000000	18.000000	38.000000	241.476000	93.000000	0.000000	0.000000	89.000000	170.000000
50%	179.0	51.000000	18.000000	38.000000	251.818000	96.000000	0.000000	0.000000	89.000000	170.000000
75%	179.0	51.000000	18.000000	38.000000	264.249000	97.000000	0.000000	0.000000	89.000000	170.000000
max	179.0	51.000000	18.000000	53.000000	271.219000	99.000000	1.000000	1.000000	89.000000	175.000000

Statistical measures corresponding to the subdataset x < -45

Advanced Clustering

Two elements can immediately capture our attention: transportation expenses, (which seem standardized to the value of 179) and the number of sons (that, considering the mean and standard deviation, corresponds to 0 for the large majority of samples). Let's also take into account service time and distance from residence to work, which can help us find a semantic label for the cluster. All the other parameters are less discriminative and we are excluding them in this brief analysis. Therefore, we can suppose that such a subcluster contains people about 40 years old without children, with a large service time, living quite far from the office (I invite the reader to check the overall statistics to confirm this), with standardized transportation expenses (for example, lump sum car expenses).

Let's now compare this result with the region $-20 < x < 20$ and $y < 20$, as follows:

```
sdff = dff[(dff.x > 20.0) & (dff.y > -20.0) & (dff.y < 20.0)]
print(sdff[sdff.columns[0:10]].describe())
```

The corresponding output is as follows:

	Transportation expense	Distance from Residence to Work	Service time	Age	Work load Average/day	Hit target	Son	Pet	Weight	Height
count	165.000000	165.000000	165.000000	165.000000	165.000000	165.000000	165.000000	165.000000	165.000000	165.000000
mean	234.575758	23.212121	11.818182	37.436364	256.334642	94.309091	0.987879	1.436364	78.842424	169.987879
std	8.521244	8.129882	3.616144	8.112991	20.949033	4.166677	0.634264	1.743598	13.169603	4.075489
min	225.000000	11.000000	1.000000	28.000000	205.917000	81.000000	0.000000	0.000000	65.000000	163.000000
25%	225.000000	20.000000	9.000000	28.000000	241.476000	92.000000	1.000000	0.000000	69.000000	167.000000
50%	235.000000	25.000000	13.000000	37.000000	261.306000	95.000000	1.000000	1.000000	69.000000	169.000000
75%	246.000000	26.000000	14.000000	43.000000	268.519000	98.000000	1.000000	2.000000	88.000000	172.000000
max	248.000000	51.000000	16.000000	58.000000	302.585000	99.000000	2.000000	8.000000	106.000000	182.000000

Statistical measures corresponding to the subdataset $-20 < x < -20$ and $y < 20$

In this case, the transportation expenses are larger, while the distance from residence to work is about half that of the previous example (also considering the standard deviation). Moreover, the average number of sons is 1, with a moderate percentage of employees with two children, and the service time is about 12 with a standard deviation of 3.6. We can deduce that this cluster contains all samples of (married) people in the age range (28–58) with a family, living relatively close the office but with larger travel expenses (for example, due to the usage of taxi services). Such employees tend to avoid overtime work, but their average workload is almost identical to the one observed in the previous example. Even if without a formal confirmation, we could suppose that such employees are generally more efficient, while the first set contain productive employees that, however, need more time to achieve their goals (for example, because of the longer travel time).

This isn't clearly an exhaustive analysis, nor a set of objective statements. The goal was to show how it's possible to find the semantic content of a cluster by observing the statistical characteristics of the samples. In a real-life case, all observations must be validated by an expert (for example, an HR manager) in order to understand whether the final part of the analysis (in particular, the definition of a semantic context) is correct or if it's necessary to employ larger numbers of clusters, different metrics, or another algorithm. As an exercise, I invite the reader to analyze all the regions containing a single cluster, in order to complete a big picture and to test the prediction of artificial samples corresponding to different categories (for example, very young people, employees with three children, and so on).

Cluster instability as a performance metric

Cluster instability is a method proposed by Von Luxburg (in *Cluster stability: an overview, Von Luxburg U., arXiv 1007:1075v1, 2010*) that can measure the goodness of an algorithm with respect to a specific dataset. It can be employed for different purposes (for example, tuning hyperparameters or finding the optimal number of clusters) and it's relatively easy to compute. The method is based on the idea that a clustering result meeting the requirements of maximum cohesion and separation should also be robust to noisy perturbations of the dataset. In other words, if dataset X has been segmented into cluster set C, a derived dataset X_n (based on small perturbations of the features) should be mapped to the same cluster set. If this condition is not met, there are generally two possibilities: the noise perturbations are too strong or the algorithm is too sensitive to small variations and, therefore, is not very stable. Hence, we define a set of k perturbed (or subsampled) versions of the original dataset X:

$$X_n = \left\{ X_n^{(1)}, X_n^{(2)}, \ldots, X_n^{(k)} \right\}$$

If we apply an algorithm A that produces the same number of clusters n_c, we can define a distance metric $d(\bullet)$ between $A(X_i)$ and $A(X_j)$, which measures the number of discordant assignments (that is, $A(X_i)$ and can be represented as a vectorial function that returns the assignments corresponding to each point. Hence, $d(\bullet)$ can simply count the numbers of different labels, assuming that the algorithm, if necessary, is seeded in the same way and the datasets are obviously not shuffled. The instability of an algorithm (with respect to a k noisy variations of X) is defined as:

$$I(A) = Avg_{\tilde{X}_n^{(i),(j)} \in X_n} \left(d\left(A(X_n^{(i)}), A(X_n^{(j)}) \right) \right)$$

So, the instability is the average distance between the clustering results of couples of noisy variations. Of course, this value is not absolute, so the rule that it is possible to derive is: select the configuration that yields the smallest instability. It's also important to say that such a method is not comparable to the other ones previously discussed because it's based on other hyperparameters (the number of noisy variations, noise mean and variance, subsampling ratio, and so on) and so it can produce different results also when A and X are fixed. In particular, the magnitude of the noise can dramatically change the instability, therefore it's necessary to evaluate the mean and covariance matrix of X before deciding, for example, the μ and Σ of Gaussian noise. In our example (based on the DBSCAN clustering in the Absenteeism at Work dataset), we have created 20 perturbed versions starting from an additive noise term $n_i \sim N(E[X], Cov(X)/4)$ and applying a multiplicative mask sampled from a uniform distribution $U(0, 1)$. In this way, some noise terms are randomly canceled out or reduced, as seen in the following code:

```
import numpy as np

data = sdf.copy()

n_perturbed = 20
n_data = []

data_mean = np.mean(data, axis=0)
data_cov = np.cov(data.T) / 4.0

for i in range(n_perturbed):
    gaussian_noise = np.random.multivariate_normal(data_mean, data_cov, size=(data.shape[0], ))
    noise = gaussian_noise * np.random.uniform(0.0, 1.0, size=(data.shape[0], data.shape[1]))
    n_data.append(data.copy() + noise)
```

In this case, we want to compute the instability as a function of ε, but it's possible to repeat the example with any other algorithm and hyperparameter. Moreover, we are employing the normalized Hamming distance, which is proportional to the number of discordant assignments between two clustering results, as follows:

```
from sklearn.cluster import DBSCAN
from sklearn.metrics.pairwise import pairwise_distances

instabilities = []

for eps in np.arange(5.0, 31.0, 1.5):
    Yn = []
    for nd in n_data:
        ds = DBSCAN(eps=eps, min_samples=3, metric='minkowski', p=12)
```

```
            Yn.append(ds.fit_predict(nd))
        distances = []
        for i in range(len(Yn)-1):
            for j in range(i, len(Yn)):
                d = pairwise_distances(Yn[i].reshape(-1, 1), Yn[j].reshape(-1,
    1), 'hamming')
                distances.append(d[0, 0])
        instability = (2.0 * np.sum(distances)) / float(n_perturbed ** 2)
        instabilities.append(instability)
```

The result is shown in the following plot:

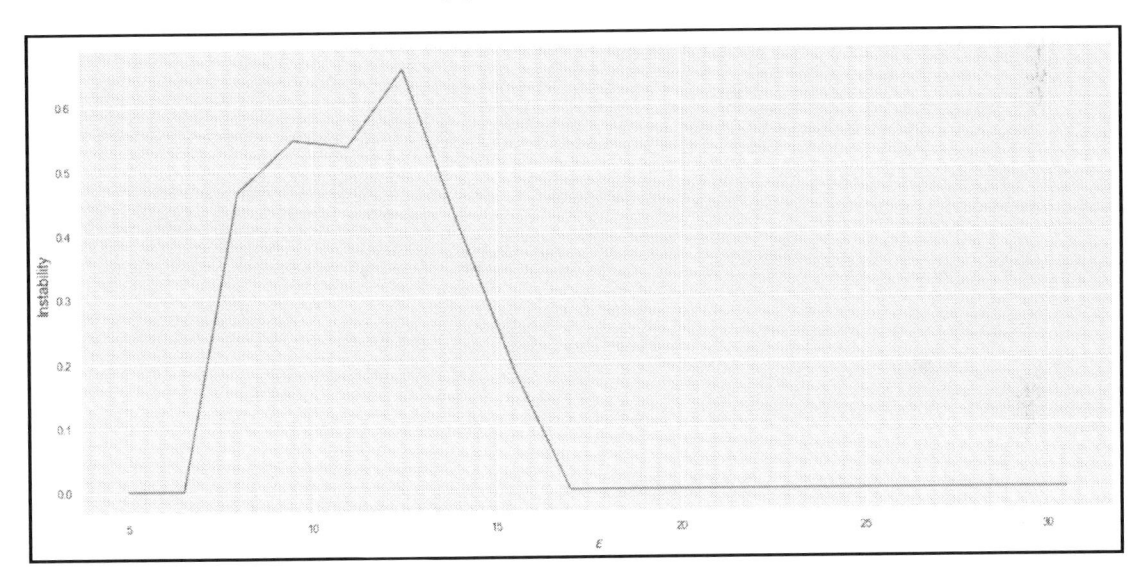

Cluster instability of DBSCAN applied to the Absenteeism at Work dataset as a function of ε

The value is null for about $\varepsilon < 7$. Such a result is due to the large number of clusters and noisy samples generated by the algorithm. As the samples are spread in different regions, small perturbations cannot alter the assignments. For $7 < \varepsilon < 17$, we observe a positive slope reaching a maximum corresponding to about $\varepsilon = 12.5$, followed by a negative slope reaching the final value of 0. In this case, the clusters are becoming larger and include more and more samples; however, when ε is still too small, the *density-reachability chains* are easily broken by small perturbations (that is, a sample can overcome the boundaries of a ball and so it is excluded from a cluster). As a result, the samples are often assigned to different clusters after the application of additive noise. This phenomenon reaches its maximum for $\varepsilon = 12.5$, then it begins to become less significant.

In fact, when ε is large enough, the union of the balls is able to *wrap* an entire cluster, leaving *enough free space* for small perturbations. Of course, after a threshold depending on the dataset, only a single cluster will be produced and, if the noise is not too strong, any perturbated version will yield the same assignments. In our specific case, ε = 25 guarantees high stability, which is also confirmed by the t-SNE plot. Generally speaking, this method can be employed with all algorithms and geometries, but I suggest a thorough analysis of X before deciding how to create the perturbed versions. A wrong decision, in fact, can compromise the results, yielding a large/small instability that is not indicative of bad/good performances. In particular, when clusters have different variances (for example, in Gaussian mixtures), an additive noise term can have a negligible effect on some samples, while it can completely alter the structure of the remaining ones. In these cases, this method is weaker than other approaches and should be applied using, for example, subsampling together with Gaussian noise with a very small variance (in general, less than the smallest cluster (co-)variance). On the other hand, subsampling can obviously be very dangerous with density-based algorithms where a small cluster could become a set of isolated noisy points because of the loss of reachability. I invite the reader to test this method also with K-means, in order to find the optimal number of clusters, (which is normally associated with the minimum instability).

K-medoids

In the previous chapter, we have shown that K-means is generally a good choice when the geometry of the clusters is convex. However, this algorithm has two main limitations: the metric is always Euclidean, and it's not very robust to outliers. The first element is obvious, while the second one is a direct consequence of the nature of the centroids. In fact, K-means chooses centroids as actual means that cannot be part of the dataset. Hence, when a cluster has some outliers, the mean is influenced and moved proportionally toward them. The following diagram shows an example where the presence of a few outliers forces the centroid to reach a position outside the dense region:

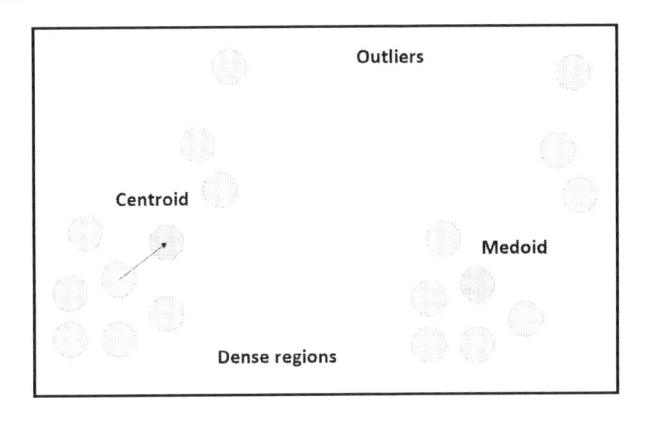

Example of centroid selection (left) and medoid selection (right)

K-medoids was proposed (in *Clustering by means of Medoids, Kaufman L., Rousseeuw P.J., in Statistical Data Analysis Based on the L1–Norm and Related Methods, North-Holland, 1987*) initially to mitigate the lack of robustness to outliers (in the original paper, the algorithm has been designed to work only with a Manhattan metric), but different versions were later designed to allow the usage of any metric (in particular, arbitrary Minkowski metrics). The main difference with K-means is in the choice of the centroids, which, in this case, are exemplary samples (called **medoids**) that always belong to the dataset. The algorithm itself is very similar to a standard K-means and alternates the definition of the medoids $\mu_i = x_i \in X$ (as the elements that minimize the average or total distance from all the other samples assigned to a cluster C_i) with the reassignment of the samples to the cluster with the closest medoid.

It's easy to understand that outliers don't have a high weight anymore because, contrary to standard centroids, the probability that they are chosen as medoids is close to zero. On the other hand, K-medoids is less performant when a cluster is made up of a dense blob surrounded by *far* samples that cannot be classified as outliers. In such a case, the algorithm can wrongly assign these samples because it's not able to generate a *virtual ball* that can capture them (remember that the radius is implicitly defined by the mutual position of the centroids/medoids). Hence, while K-means can move the centroid to a non-dense region in order to also capture far points, K-medoids isn't likely to behave in this way when the dense blob contains many points.

Moreover, K-medoids tends to *aggregate* very overlapping blobs whose density has two peaks, while K-means generally splits the overall region into two parts according to the position of the means. This behavior is generally accepted if the assumption of a convex geometry holds, but it can be a limitation in other scenarios (we are going to show this effect in the example).

The last fundamental difference is the metric distance. As there are no limitations, K-medoids can be more or less *aggressive*. As we discussed at the beginning of Chapter 2, *Clustering Fundamentals*, the longest distance is provided by the Manhattan metric (which evaluates every component different in the same way), while when p increases (in a generic Minkowski metric), the maximum difference between components becomes dominant. K-means is based on the most common compromise (the Euclidean distance), but there are some particular cases when a larger p can lead to better performances (the effect is more evident when comparing $p=1$ with $p>1$). For example, if $c_1=(0, 0)$, $c_2=(2, 1)$, and $x=(0.55, 1.25)$, the Manhattan distances $d_1(x, c_1)$ and $d_1(x, c_2)$ are respectively 1.8 and 1.7, while the Euclidean distances are 1.37 and 1.47. Therefore, with $p=1$, the point is assigned to the second cluster, while with $p=2$ it's assigned to the first one.

In general, it's not easy to predict the right value p, but it's always possible to test several configurations using methods such as the silhouette and adjusted Rand scores and to select the one that yields a better segmentation (that is, maximum cohesion and separation or a higher adjusted Rand score). In our example, we are going to generate a dataset containing also the ground truth, hence we can easily evaluate performances using the latter option. Therefore, we are going to use the function make_blobs to generate 1000 samples split into 8 blobs in box delimited by [-5.0, 5.0], as follows:

```
from sklearn.datasets import make_blobs

nb_samples = 1000
nb_clusters = 8

X, Y = make_blobs(n_samples=nb_samples, n_features=2, centers=nb_clusters,
          cluster_std=1.2, center_box=[-5.0, 5.0],
random_state=1000)
```

The resulting dataset presents some strong overlaps (shown in the final plot), so we don't expect to obtain high-level results using symmetric methods, but we're interested in comparing the assignments made by both K-means and K-medoids.

Let's start evaluating the adjusted Rand score reached by K-means, as follows:

```
from sklearn.cluster import KMeans
from sklearn.metrics import adjusted_rand_score

km = KMeans(n_clusters=nb_clusters, random_state=1000)
C_km = km.fit_predict(X)

print('Adjusted Rand score K-Means: {}'.format(adjusted_rand_score(Y,
C_km)))
```

The output of the previous block is as follows:

```
Adjusted Rand score K-Means: 0.4589907163792297
```

This value is enough to understand that K-means is making many wrong assignments, in particular, in overlapping regions. As the dataset is very difficult to cluster using this kind of method, we are not considering this result as a real indicator, but only as a measure that can be compared with the K-medoids score. Let's now implement this algorithm using a Minkowski metric with p = 7 (the reader is invited to change this value and check the results), as follows:

```
import numpy as np

C = np.random.randint(0, nb_clusters, size=(X.shape[0], ), dtype=np.int32)
mu_idxs = np.zeros(shape=(nb_clusters, X.shape[1]))

metric = 'minkowski'
p = 7
tolerance = 0.001

mu_copy = np.ones_like(mu_idxs)
```

The array C contains the assignments, while mu_idxs will contain the medoids. As the amount of space needed to store whole medoids is generally quite small, we have preferred this method instead of storing only indexes. The optimization algorithm is as follows:

```
import numpy as np

from scipy.spatial.distance import pdist, cdist, squareform
from sklearn.metrics import adjusted_rand_score

while np.linalg.norm(mu_idxs - mu_copy) > tolerance:
    for i in range(nb_clusters):
        Di = squareform(pdist(X[C==i], metric=metric, p=p))
        SDi = np.sum(Di, axis=1)
        mu_copy[i] = mu_idxs[i].copy()
```

```
            idx = np.argmin(SDi)
            mu_idxs[i] = X[C==i][idx].copy()

    C = np.argmin(cdist(X, mu_idxs, metric=metric, p=p), axis=1)

print('Adjusted Rand score K-Medoids: {}'.format(adjusted_rand_score(Y,
C)))
```

The behavior is very simple. At each iteration, we compute the pairwise distance between all elements belonging to a cluster (this is actually the most expensive part), then we select the medoids that minimize the sum `SDi`. After a cycle, we assign the samples by minimizing their distance from the medoids. The operations are repeated until the norm variation of the medoids becomes smaller than a predefined threshold. The adjusted Rand score is as follows:

```
Adjusted Rand score K-Medoids: 0.4761670824763849
```

> The final adjusted Rand score is influenced by the random initialization of the algorithm (hence, the previous result can slightly change when running the code). In real applications, I suggest employing a double stopping criterion based on the maximum number of iterations together with a small tolerance.

Therefore, even if the overlappings have not been resolved, the performances are slightly better than that of K-means. The ground truth, K-means, and K-medoids results are shown in the following screenshot:

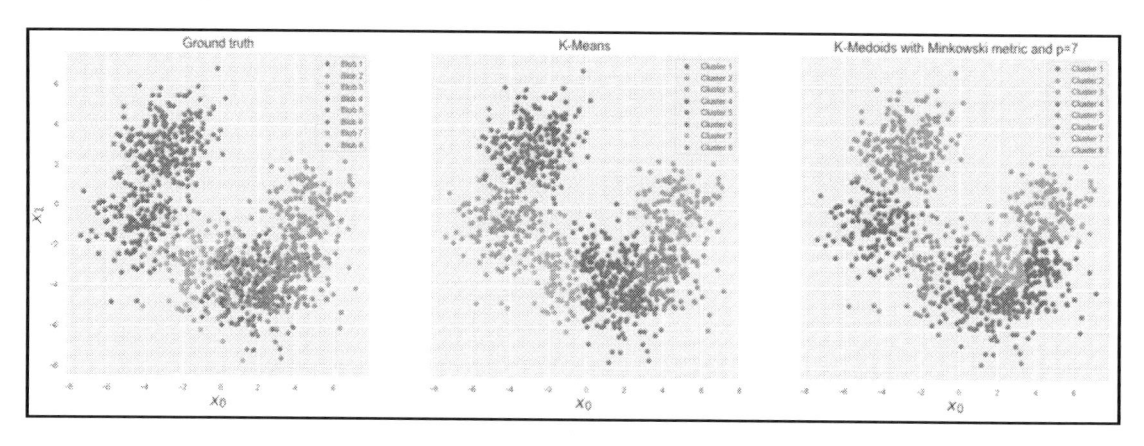

Ground truth (left), K-means (center), and K-medoids (right)

As you can see, the ground truth contains two overlapped regions that are extremely difficult to cluster. In this particular example, we are not interested in solving this problem, but rather in showing the different behavior of the two methods. If we consider the first two blobs (top-left), K-means splits the overall region into two parts, while K-medoids assigns all the elements to the same cluster. Without knowing the ground truth, the latter result is probably more coherent than the first one. In fact, observing the first plot, it's possible to notice that the density difference is not so strong as to fully justify the split, (which can, however, be reasonable in some contexts). As the region is quite dense and separated from its neighbor, a single cluster is likely to be the expected result. Moreover, it's almost impossible to distinguish samples in terms of dissimilarities (most samples close to the separation line are wrongly assigned), so K-medoids is *less aggressive* than K-means and shows a better compromise. Conversely, the second overlapped region (bottom-right) is managed almost in the same way by both algorithms. This is due to the fact that K-means places the centroids in positions very near to some actual samples. In the two cases, the algorithms needed to create an almost horizontal separation between 0 and 4, because it's otherwise impossible to segment the regions. Such a behavior is common to all methods based on standard balls and, in this particular case, it's a normal consequence of the extremely complex geometry (many adjacent points have different labels). Hence, we can conclude by saying that K-medoids is more robust to outliers and sometimes performs better than K-means by avoiding undesired separations. On the other hand, the two algorithms (in particular, when the same metric is employed) are equivalent when working in very dense regions without outliers. As an exercise, I invite the reader to employ other metrics (including the cosine distance) and to compare the results.

Online clustering

Sometimes a dataset is too large to fit in memory, or the samples are streamed through a channel and received at different time steps. In this cases, none of the algorithms previously discussed can be employed because they assume to access to the whole dataset since the first steps. For this reasons, some online alternatives have been proposed and they are currently implemented in many real-life processes.

Mini-batch K-means

This algorithm is an extension of standard K-means but, as centroids cannot be computed with all samples, it's necessary to include an additional step that is responsible for reassigning the samples when an existing cluster is no longer valid. In particular, instead of computing global means, **mini-batch K-means** works with streaming averages. Once a batch is received, the algorithm computes a partial mean and determines the position of the centroids. However, not all clusters will have the same number of assignments, so the algorithm must decide whether to wait or to reassign the samples.

This concept can be immediately understood by considering a very inefficient streaming process that starts sending all samples belonging to a semi-space and including only a few points belonging to the complementary semi-space. As the number of clusters is fixed, the algorithm will start optimizing the centroids while considering only a subregion. Let's suppose that a centroid has been placed at the center of a ball surrounding the few samples belonging to the complementary subspace. If more and more batches continue to add points to the dense region, the algorithm can reasonably decide to drop the isolated centroid and reassign the samples. However, if the process starts to send points belonging to the complementary semi-space, the algorithm must be ready to assign them to the most appropriate clusters (that is, it must place other centroids in the empty region).

This method is normally based on a parameter called **reassignment ratio** α. When α is small, the algorithm will wait for a longer time before reassigning the samples, while larger values accelerate this process. Of course, we want to avoid both extreme situations. In other words, we need to avoid a too static algorithm that needs many samples before making a decision and, at the same time, a too fast-changing algorithm that reassigns the samples after each batch. In general, the first case yields suboptimal solutions with a lower computational cost, while the latter can become very similar to a standard K-means re-applied to the streamed dataset after each batch. Considering this scenario, which is often related to real-time processes, we are normally not interested in extremely accurate solutions that require a high computational cost, but rather in good approximations that are improved while new data is collected.

However, the choice of the reassignment ratio must be evaluated considering every single context, including a reasonable prevision of the streaming process (for example, is it purely random? Are the samples independent? Are some samples more frequent during a certain time-frame?). Also, the amount of data that must be clustered (that is, the batch size, which is an extremely important factor), and, of course, the hardware that can be provisioned. In general, it's possible to prove that mini-batch K-means yields results comparable to standard K-means with lower memory requirements and higher computational complexity when the batch size is not too small (but this is often not a controllable hyperparameter because it depends on external resources) and the reassignment ratio is chosen accordingly.

When instead the batches are uniformly sampled from the true data generating process, the reassignment ratio becomes a less important parameter and its impact is lower. In fact, in these cases, the batch size is normally the main influencing factor for a good result. If it is large enough, the algorithm is immediately able to determine the most likely positions of the centroids and subsequent batches can't alter this configuration dramatically (so reducing the need for continuous reassignments). Of course, in an online scenario, it's quite difficult to determine the structure of the data generating process, hence it's normally possible only to suppose that a batch, if not too small, contains enough representatives of each distinctive region. The main task of the data scientist is to validate this hypothesis by collecting enough samples to execute a complete K-means and comparing the performance with a mini-batch version. It's not surprising to observe scenarios where the smaller batch sizes yield better final results (with the same reassignment ratio). This phenomenon can be understood by considering that this algorithm doesn't reassign the samples immediately; therefore, sometimes, a larger batch can lead to a wrong configuration that, however, has more representatives, so the probability of reassignment is lower (that is, the algorithm is faster but less accurate). Conversely, in the same situation, a smaller batch can force the algorithm to perform more iterations because of the frequent reassignments, with a (consequently more accurate) final configuration. As it's not easy to define a generic rule of thumb, the general suggestion is to check different values before making a decision.

BIRCH

This algorithm (whose name stands for **Balanced Iterative Reducing and Clustering using Hierarchies**) has slightly more complex dynamics than mini-batch K-means and the final part employs a method (**hierarchical clustering**) that we are going to present in Chapter 4, *Hierarchical Clustering in Action*. However, for our purposes, the most important part concerns the data preparation phase, which is based on a particular tree structure called **Clustering** or **Characteristic-Feature Tree (CF-Tree)**. Given a dataset X, every node of the tree is made up of a tuple of three elements:

$$CF_k = \left(N_k, \sum_j \bar{x}_j, \sum_j \|\bar{x}_j\|^2 \right)$$

Advanced Clustering

The characteristic elements are respectively the number of sample of belonging to a node, the sum of all samples, and the sum of squared norms. The reason behind this choice will be immediately clear, but let's now focus our attention on the structure of the tree and how new elements are inserted while trying to balance the height. In the following diagram, there's a generic representation of a CF-Tree where all terminal nodes are the actual subclusters that must be merged in order to obtain the desired number of clusters:

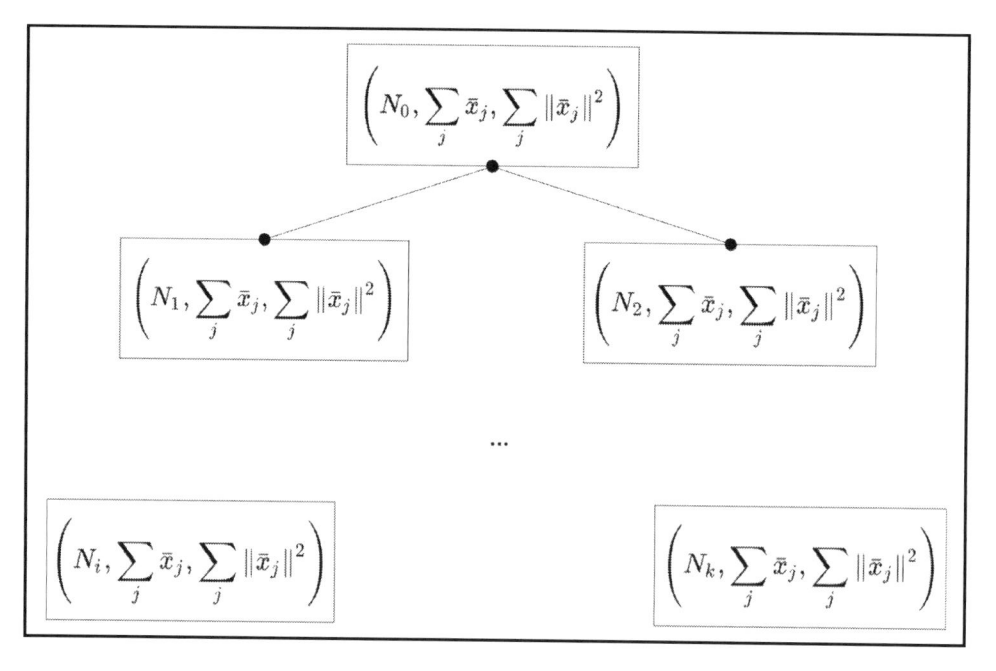

$$\left(N_0, \sum_j \bar{x}_j, \sum_j \|\bar{x}_j\|^2\right)$$

$$\left(N_1, \sum_j \bar{x}_j, \sum_j \|\bar{x}_j\|^2\right) \qquad \left(N_2, \sum_j \bar{x}_j, \sum_j \|\bar{x}_j\|^2\right)$$

...

$$\left(N_i, \sum_j \bar{x}_j, \sum_j \|\bar{x}_j\|^2\right) \qquad \left(N_k, \sum_j \bar{x}_j, \sum_j \|\bar{x}_j\|^2\right)$$

Example of a simple CF-Tree with a binary repartition

In the previous diagram, the dots represent pointers to child nodes. Thus, every non-terminal node is stored together with the pointers to all its children (CF_i, p_i), while terminal nodes are pure CFs. In order to discuss the insert strategy, two more elements must be taken into account. The first one is called the **branching factor** B, while the second is a **threshold** T. Moreover, each non-terminal node can contain at most B tuples. This strategy has been designed to maximize the performance in a streaming process, which relies only on the main memory, by reducing the amount of data that is stored as well as the number of calculations.

Let's now consider a new sample x_i that needs to be inserted. It's quite easy to understand that the centroid of a $CF_j = (n_j, a_j, b_j)$ is simply $\mu_j = a_j / n_j$; therefore, x_i is propagated along the tree since it reaches the terminal CF (subcluster) where the distance $d(x_i, \mu_j)$ is the minimum. At that point, the CF is updated incrementally:

$$\left(N_j, \sum_p \bar{x}_p, \sum_p \|\bar{x}_p\|^2 \right) \to \left(N_j + 1, \left(\sum_p \bar{x}_p \right) + \bar{x}_i, \left(\sum_p \|\bar{x}_p\|^2 \right) + \|\bar{x}_i\|^2 \right)$$

However, without a control, the tree can easily become unbalanced, with a consequent performance loss. Therefore, the algorithm performs an additional step. Once the CF has been determined, the updated radius r_j is computed and, whether or not $r_j > T$ and the number of CFs are greater than the branching factor, a new block is allocated and the original CF is kept unchanged. As this new block is almost completely empty (except for x_i), BIRCH performs an additional step checking the dissimilarities between all subclusters (this concept will be clearer in Chapter 4, *Hierarchical Clustering in Action*; however, the reader can think about the average distance between the points belonging to two different subclusters). The most dissimilar couple is split into two parts and one of them is moved into the new block. Such a choice guarantees a high compactness of the subclusters and speeds up the final step. In fact, the algorithm involved in the actual clustering phase needs to merge the subclusters until the total number is reduced to the desired value; hence, it's easier to carry out this operation if the total dissimilarity has been previously minimized because the *segments* can be immediately identified as contiguous and merged. This phase will not be discussed in detail in this chapter, but it's not difficult to imagine. All terminal CFs are sequentially merged into larger blocks until a single cluster is determined (even if it's possible to stop the process when the number matches the desired number of clusters). Therefore, this method, contrary to mini-batch K-means, can easily manage large numbers of clusters n_c, whereas it's not very effective when n_c is small. In fact, as we're going to see in the example, its accuracy is often less than that achievable with mini-batch k-means and its optimal usage requires an accurate choice of both branching factor and threshold. As the main purpose of this algorithm is to work in online scenarios, B and T could become ineffective after processing some batches (while mini-batch K-means is generally able to correct the clustering after a few iterations), yielding suboptimal results. Therefore, the main use case for BIRCH is an online procedure that requires a very fine-grained segmentation, while it's generally preferable to select mini-batch K-means as an initial option in all other cases.

Comparison between mini-batch K-means and BIRCH

In this example, we want to compare the performances of both algorithms with a bidimensional dataset containing 2,000 samples split into 8 blobs (as the purpose is analytic, we are also using the ground truth), as follows:

```
from sklearn.datasets import make_blobs

nb_clusters = 8
nb_samples = 2000

X, Y = make_blobs(n_samples=nb_samples, n_features=2, centers=nb_clusters,
            cluster_std=0.25, center_box=[-1.5, 1.5], shuffle=True,
random_state=100)
```

The dataset (which is already shuffled to remove any inter-correlation in the streaming process) is shown in the following screenshot:

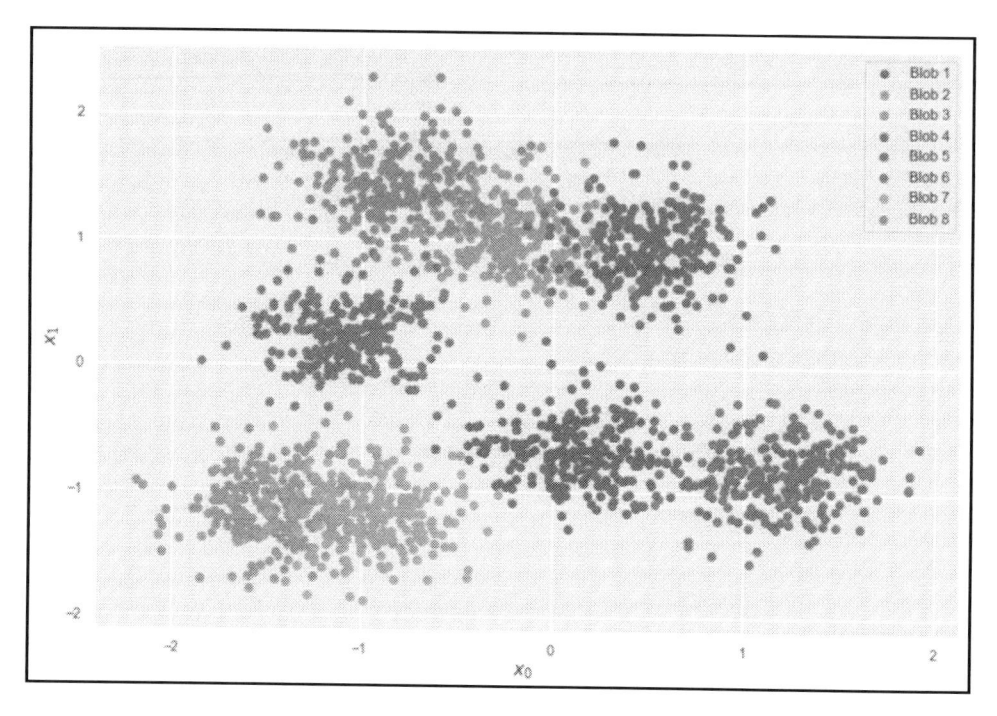

Bidimensional dataset for a comparison between mini-batch K-means and BIRCH

Before performing online clustering, it's helpful to evaluate the adjusted Rand score of a standard K-means, as follows:

```
from sklearn.cluster import KMeans

km = KMeans(n_clusters=nb_clusters, random_state=1000)
Y_pred_km = km.fit_predict(X)

print('Adjusted Rand score: {}'.format(adjusted_rand_score(Y, Y_pred_km)))
```

The output of the previous block is as follows:

```
Adjusted Rand score: 0.8232109771787882
```

Considering the structure of the dataset (there are no concavities), we can reasonably assume that this value represents a benchmark for the online processes. We can now instantiate the classes `MiniBatchKMeans` and `Birch`, with the parameters respectively equal to `reassignment_ratio=0.001`, `threshold=0.2`, and `branching_factor=350`. These values have been chosen after research but I invite the reader to repeat the example with different configurations, comparing the results. In both cases, we are assuming a batch size equal to 50 samples, as follows:

```
from sklearn.cluster import MiniBatchKMeans, Birch

batch_size = 50

mbkm = MiniBatchKMeans(n_clusters=nb_clusters, batch_size=batch_size,
reassignment_ratio=0.001, random_state=1000)
birch = Birch(n_clusters=nb_clusters, threshold=0.2, branching_factor=350)
```

The goal of the example is now to employ the method `partial_fit()` to train both models incrementally and to evaluate the adjusted Rand score considering the whole amount of data processed till every step, as follows:

```
from sklearn.metrics import adjusted_rand_score

scores_mbkm = []
scores_birch = []

for i in range(0, nb_samples, batch_size):
    X_batch, Y_batch = X[i:i+batch_size], Y[i:i+batch_size]
    mbkm.partial_fit(X_batch)
    birch.partial_fit(X_batch)
    scores_mbkm.append(adjusted_rand_score(Y[:i+batch_size],
mbkm.predict(X[:i+batch_size])))
    scores_birch.append(adjusted_rand_score(Y[:i+batch_size],
birch.predict(X[:i+batch_size])))
```

Advanced Clustering

```
print('Adjusted Rand score Mini-Batch K-Means: 
{}'.format(adjusted_rand_score(Y, Y_pred_mbkm)))
print('Adjusted Rand score BIRCH: {}'.format(adjusted_rand_score(Y, 
Y_pred_birch)))
```

The output of the previous snippet contains the adjusted Rand scores for the whole dataset:

```
Adjusted Rand score Mini-Batch K-Means: 0.814244790452388
Adjusted Rand score BIRCH: 0.767304858161472
```

As expected, mini-batch K-means almost reaches the benchmark when all samples have been processed, while the BIRCH performance is slightly worse. To better understand the behavior, let's consider a plot of the incremental scores as functions of the batches, as shown in the following graph:

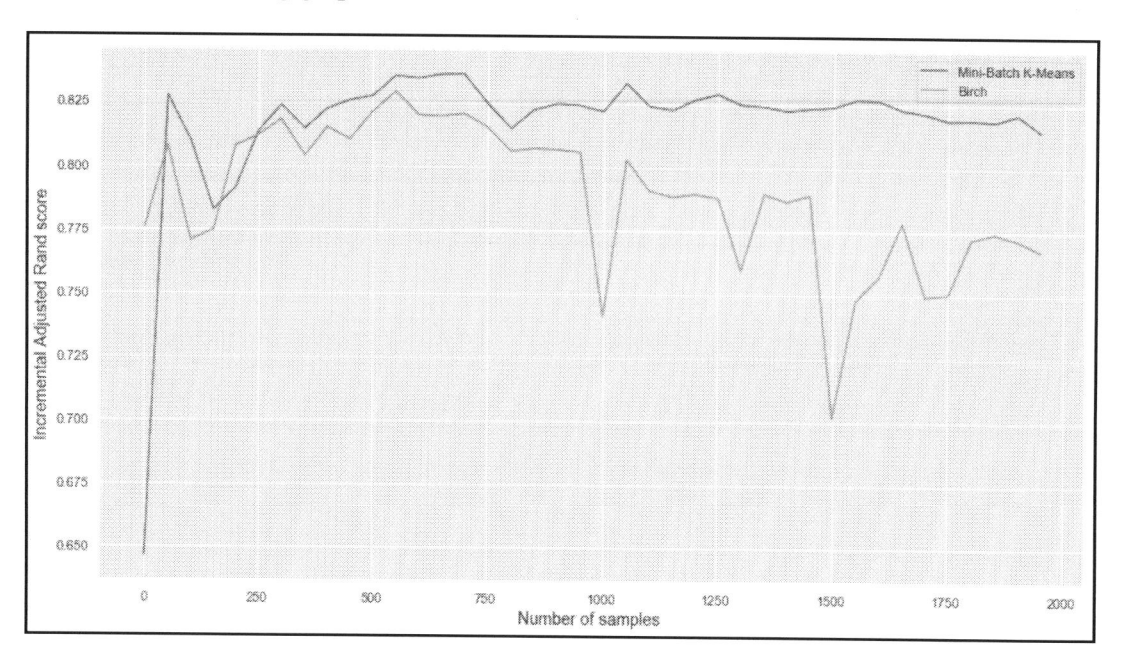

Incremental adjusted Rand scores as functions of the batches (number of samples)

As you can see, mini-batch K-means reaches the maximum very soon and all subsequent oscillations are due to reassignments. Conversely, BIRCH performance is always worse with a negative trend. The main reason for such a discrepancy is due to the different strategies. In fact, mini-batch K-means can correct the initial guess for the centroids after a few batches and the reassignments don't alter the configuration dramatically. On the other hand, the number of merges performed by BIRCH is influenced by the number of samples.

In the beginning, the performance is not very dissimilar because the number of subclusters in the CF-Tree is not very large (so, the aggregation is more *coherent*), but after a few batches, BIRCH has to aggregate more and more subclusters in order to obtain the desired final number of clusters. Such a condition, together with the increasing number of streamed samples, drives the algorithm to rearrange the tree, very often with a consequent loss of stability. Moreover, the dataset has some overlaps that can be more easily managed by a symmetric method (the centroids can, in fact, reach their final positions in this case, even if the assignments are wrong), while a hierarchical method (such as the one employed by BIRCH) is more able to find all subregions but can be more prone to errors when merging the subclusters with a minimum separation or, even worse, an overlap. However, this example confirms that mini-batch K-means is generally preferable as a first option and BIRCH should be selected only when the performance doesn't meet expectations (with a careful choice of its parameters). I invite the reader to repeat the example with a larger number of desired clusters (for example, `nb_clusters=20` and `center_box=[-10.5, 10.5]`). It will be possible to see how in this case (keeping all the other parameters unchanged) the reassignments performed by mini-batch K-means slow down the convergence with a worse final adjusted Rand score, while BIRCH immediately reaches the optimal value (almost equal to the one achieved by a standard K-means) and it's not influenced by the number of samples anymore.

Summary

In this chapter, we have presented some of the most important clustering algorithms that can be employed to solve non-convex problems. Spectral clustering is a very popular technique that performs a projection of the dataset onto a new space where concave geometries become convex and a standard algorithm such as K-means can easily segment the data.

Conversely, mean shift and DBSCAN analyze the density of the dataset and try to split it so that all dense and connected regions are merged together to make up the clusters. In particular, DBSCAN is very efficient in very irregular contexts because it's based on local nearest neighbors sets that are concatenated until the separation overcomes a predefined threshold. In this way, the algorithm can solve many specific clustering problems with the only drawback being that it also yields a set of noise points that cannot be automatically assigned to an existing cluster. In the example based on the Absenteeism at Work dataset, we have shown how to select hyperparameters so as to obtain the desired number of clusters with a minimum number of noise points and an acceptable silhouette or Calinski-Harabasz score.

In the last part, we have analyzed K-medoids as an alternative to K-means, which is also more robust to outliers. The algorithm cannot be employed to solve non-convex problems, but it's sometimes more efficient than K-means because, instead of selecting actual means as centroids, it relies only on the dataset and cluster centers (called medoids) are exemplary samples. Moreover, this algorithm is not strictly bound to the Euclidean metric, therefore, it can fully exploit the potential of alternative distance functions. The final topic concerns two online clustering algorithms (mini-batch K-means and BIRCH), which can be employed when the dataset is too large to fit into memory or when the data is streamed during a long time frame.

In the next chapter, we are going to analyze a very important family of clustering algorithms that can output a complete hierarchy, allowing us to observe the complete aggregation process, and select the most helpful and coherent final configuration.

Questions

1. Is a half-moon-shaped dataset a convex cluster?
2. A bidimensional dataset is made up of two half-moons. The second one is fully contained in the concavity of the first one. Which kind of kernel can easily allow the separation of the two clusters (using spectral clustering)?
3. After applying the DBSCAN algorithm with $\varepsilon=1.0$, we discover that there are too many noisy points. What should we expect with $\varepsilon=0.1$?
4. K-medoids is based on the Euclidean metric. Is this correct?
5. DBSCAN is very sensitive to the geometry of the dataset. Is this correct?
6. A dataset contains 10,000,000 samples and can be easily clustered using a large machine using K-means. Can we, instead, use a smaller machine and mini-batch K-means?
7. A cluster has a standard deviation equal to 1.0. After applying a noise $N(0, 0.005)$, 80% of the original assignments are changed. Can we say that such a cluster configuration is generally stable?

Further reading

- *Normalized Cuts and Image Segmentation, J. Shi and J. Malik, IEEE Transactions on Pattern Analysis and Machine Intelligence, Vol. 22, 08/2000*
- *A Tutorial on Spectral Clustering, Von Luxburg U., 2007*
- *Functions and Graphs Vol. 2, Gelfand I. M., Glagoleva E. G., Shnol E. E., The MIT Press, 1969*
- *On Estimation of a Probability Density Function and Mode, Parzen E., The Annals of Mathematical Statistics, 33, 1962*
- *Application of a neuro fuzzy network in prediction of absenteeism at work, Martiniano A., Ferreira R. P., Sassi R. J., Affonso C., in Information Systems and Technologies (CISTI), 7th Iberian Conference on (pp. 1-4). IEEE, 2012*
- *A Density-Based Algorithm for Discovering Clusters in Large Spatial Databases with Noise, Ester M., Kriegel H. P., Sander J., Xu X., Proceedings of the 2nd International Conference on Knowledge Discovery and Data Mining, Portland, OR, AAAI Press, 1996*
- *Machine Learning Algorithms, Second Edition, Bonaccorso G., Packt Publishing, 2018*
- *Cluster stability: an overview, Von Luxburg U., arXiv 1007:1075v1, 2010*
- *Clustering by means of Medoids, Kaufman L., Rousseeuw P.J., in Statistical Data Analysis Based on the L1–Norm and Related Methods, North-Holland, 1987*

Hierarchical Clustering in Action

In this chapter, we are going to discuss the concept of hierarchical clustering, which is a powerful and widespread technique for generating a complete hierarchy of clustering configurations, starting with either a single cluster equivalent to the dataset (the divisive approach) or a number of clusters equal to the number of samples (the agglomerative approach). This method is particularly helpful when it's necessary to analyze the whole grouping process at once in order to understand, for example, how smaller clusters are merged into larger ones.

In particular, we will discuss the following topics:

- Hierarchical clustering strategies (divisive and agglomerative)
- Distance metrics and linkage methods
- Dendrograms and their interpretation
- Agglomerative clustering
- Cophenetic correlation as a performance measure
- Connectivity constraints

Technical requirements

The code presented in this chapter requires the following:

- Python 3.5+ (Anaconda distribution (https://www.anaconda.com/distribution/) is highly recommended)
- Libraries:
    - SciPy 0.19+
    - NumPy 1.10+
    - scikit-learn 0.20+
    - pandas 0.22+
    - Matplotlib 2.0+
    - seaborn 0.9+

The dataset can be obtained from the UCI machine learning repository. The CSV file can be downloaded from https://archive.ics.uci.edu/ml/datasets/water+treatment+plant and doesn't need any preprocessing, except for the addition of the column names, which will occur during the loading stage.

The examples are available on the GitHub repository: https://github.com/PacktPublishing/HandsOn-Unsupervised-Learning-with-Python/Chapter04.

Cluster hierarchies

In the previous chapters, we analyzed clustering algorithms, where the output is a single segmentation based either on a predefined number of clusters or the result of a parameter set and a precise underlying geometry. On the other hand, **hierarchical clustering** generates a sequence of clustering configurations that can be arranged in the structure of a tree. In particular, let's suppose that we have a dataset, X, containing n samples:

$$X = \{\bar{x}_1, \bar{x}_2, \ldots, \bar{x}_n\} \quad where \quad \bar{x}_i \in \mathbb{R}^m$$

An **agglomerative** approach starts by assigning each sample to a cluster, C_i, and proceeds by merging two clusters at each step until a single final cluster (corresponding to X) has been produced:

$$(C_1, C_2, \ldots, C_n) \Rightarrow (C_1, C_2, \ldots, C_{i-1}, C_{i+1}, \ldots, C_{j-1}, C_{j+1}, C_k, \ldots, C_{n-1}) \ldots \Rightarrow \ldots (X)$$

In the preceding example, the clusters C_i and C_j are merged into C_k; hence, we obtain *n-1* clusters in the second step. The process continues until the two remaining clusters are merged into a single block containing the whole dataset. Conversely, a **divisive** approach (initially proposed by Kaufman and Roussew, with an algorithm called DIANA) operates in the opposite direction, starting from X and ending with a segmentation where each cluster contains a single sample:

$$(X) \Rightarrow (C_i, C_j) \Rightarrow (C_i, C_{j+1}, C_{j+2}) \dots \Rightarrow \dots (C_0, C_1, \dots, C_n)$$

In both cases, the result is in the form of a hierarchy, where each level is obtained by performing a merger or a splitting operation on the previous level. Complexity is the primary difference between the two approaches as it's higher for divisive clustering. In fact, the merging/splitting decision is made by considering all possible combinations and by selecting the most appropriate one (according to a specific criterion). For example, while comparing the first steps, it's evident that it's easier to find out the most suitable couple of samples (in the agglomerative scenario) than finding the optimal split of X, considering all possible combinations (in the divisive scenario), which requires an exponential complexity.

As the final results are almost the same, while the computational complexity of the divisive algorithm is much higher, generally, there are no particular reasons for preferring such an approach. Therefore, in this book, we are going to discuss only agglomerative clustering (assuming that all concepts are immediately applicable to a divisive algorithm). I encourage you to always think about the entire hierarchy, even if the majority of implementations (for example, scikit-learn) are required to specify the desired number of clusters. In a real application, in fact, it's preferable to stop the process once the goal has been reached instead of computing the entire tree. However, this step is an essential part of the analysis stage (in particular, when the number of clusters is not well defined) and we will demonstrate how to visualize the tree and make the most reasonable decision for each specific problem.

Agglomerative clustering

As seen in other algorithms, in order to perform aggregations, we need to define a distance metric first, which represents the dissimilarity between samples. We have already analyzed many of them but, in this context, it's helpful to start considering the generic **Minkowski distance** (parametrized with *p*):

$$d_p(\bar{x}_i, \bar{x}_j) = \left(\sum_k \left| \bar{x}_i^{(k)} - \bar{x}_j^{(k)} \right|^p \right)^{\frac{1}{p}}$$

Two particular cases correspond to p=2 and p=1. In the former case, when p=2, we obtain the standard **Euclidean distance** (equivalent to the L_2 norm):

$$d_2(\bar{x}_i, \bar{x}_j) = \sqrt{\sum_k \left(\bar{x}_i^{(k)} - \bar{x}_j^{(k)}\right)^2} = \|\bar{x}_i - \bar{x}_j\|_2$$

When p=1, we obtain the **Manhattan** or **city block** distance (equivalent to the L_1 norm):

$$d_1(\bar{x}_i, \bar{x}_j) = \sum_k \left|\bar{x}_i^{(k)} - \bar{x}_j^{(k)}\right| = \|\bar{x}_i - \bar{x}_j\|_1$$

The main differences between these distances were discussed in Chapter 2, *Clustering Fundamentals*. In this chapter, it's useful to introduce the **cosine** distance, which is not a proper distance metric (from a mathematical point of view), but it is very helpful when the discrimination between samples must depend only on the angle they form:

$$d_c(\bar{x}_i, \bar{x}_j) = 1 - \frac{\bar{x}_i \cdot \bar{x}_j}{\|\bar{x}_i\|_2 \|\bar{x}_j\|_2} = 1 - \frac{\|\bar{x}_i\|_2 \|\bar{x}_j\|_2 \cos(\bar{x}_i \hat{\bar{x}}_j)}{\|\bar{x}_i\|_2 \|\bar{x}_j\|_2} = 1 - \cos(\bar{x}_i \hat{\bar{x}}_j)$$

The applications of the cosine distance are very particular (for example, **Natural Language Processing (NLP)**), and, therefore, it's not a common choice. However, I encourage you to check its properties with some sample vectors (for example, (0, 1), (1, 0), and (0.5, 0.5), because it can solve many real-life problems (for example, in word2vec, the similarity of two words can be easily evaluated by checking their cosine similarity). Once a distance metric has been defined, it's helpful to define a **proximity matrix**, *P*:

$$P_{ij} = [d(\bar{x}_i, \bar{x}_j)]$$

P is symmetric and all the diagonal elements are null. For this reason, some applications (such as SciPy's pdist function) yield a condensed matrix, P_c, which is a vector containing only the upper triangular part of the matrix so that the ij^{th} element of P_c corresponds to $d(x_i, x_j)$.

The next step is defining a merging strategy, which, in this case, is called **linkage**. The goal of a linkage method is to find out the clusters that must be merged into a single one at each level of the hierarchy. Therefore, it must work with generic sample sets, which represent the clusters. In this case, let's suppose that we are analyzing a couple of clusters (C_a, C_b) and we need to find which index, *a* or *b*, corresponds to the couple that will be merged.

Single and complete linkages

The simplest approaches are called **single** and **complete linkages** and they are defined as follows:

$$L_{single}(a, b) = min\{d(\bar{x}_i, \bar{x}_j) \ \forall \ \bar{x}_i \in C_a \ and \ \bar{x}_j \in C_b\} \ \forall \ C_a, C_b$$

The single linkage method selects the couple containing the closest couple of samples (each of them belonging to a different cluster). This process is shown in the following diagram, where **C1** and **C2** are selected for merging:

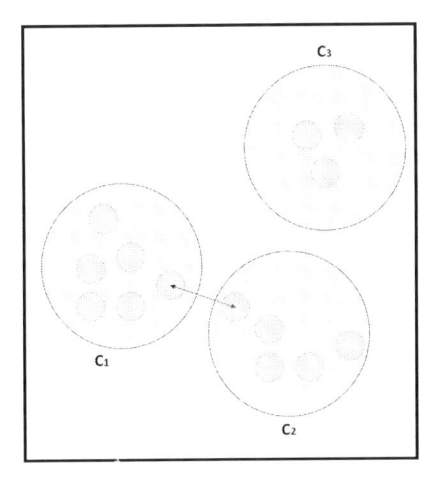

Example of single linkage. C_1 and C_2 are selected to be merged

The primary drawback of this method is the possibility of having small clusters together with very large ones. As we are going to see in the next section, single linkage can keep *outliers* isolated until there are very high dissimilarity levels. In order to avoid or mitigate this problem, the average, and Ward's methods can be used.

Conversely, complete linkage is defined as:

$$L_{complete}(a, b) = max\{d(\bar{x}_i, \bar{x}_j) \ \forall \ \bar{x}_i \in C_a \ and \ \bar{x}_j \in C_b\} \ \forall \ C_a, C_b$$

Hierarchical Clustering in Action

The goal of this linkage method is to minimize the distance between the furthest samples belonging to the merged clusters. In the following diagram, there's an example of complete linkage, where C_1 and C_3 have been selected:

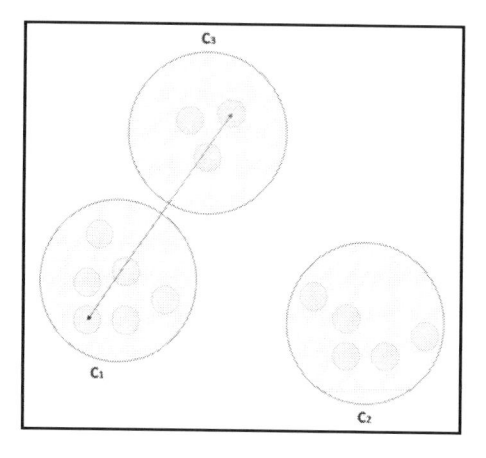

Example of complete linkage. C_1 and C_3 are selected for merging

The algorithm selects C_1 and C_3 in order to increase the internal cohesion. In fact, it's easy to understand that complete linkage results in the maximization of cluster density, considering all possible combinations. In the example shown in the previous diagram, if the desired number of clusters is two, merging C_1 and C_2 or C_2 and C_3 would yield a final configuration with less cohesion, which is generally an undesired outcome.

Average linkage

Another common method is called **average linkage** (or **Unweighted Pair Group Method with Arithmetic Mean (UPGMA)**). It is defined as follows:

$$L_{average}(a, b) = \frac{1}{|C_a||C_b|} \sum_{\bar{x}_i \in C_a} \sum_{\bar{x}_j \in C_b} d(\bar{x}_i, \bar{x}_j) \ \forall \ C_a, C_b$$

The idea is quite similar to complete linkage, but, in this case, the average of each cluster is taken into account and the goal is to minimize the average inter-cluster distance, considering all possible pairs (C_a, C_b). The following diagram shows an example of average linkage:

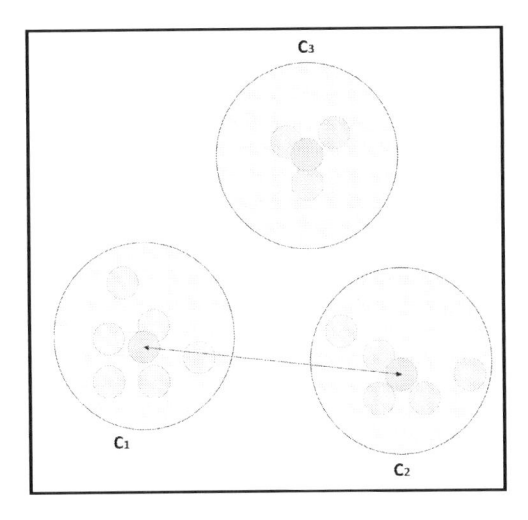

Example of average linkage. C_1 and C_2 are selected for merging. The highlighted points are the averages.

Average linkage is particularly helpful in bioinformatics applications (which is the main context in which hierarchical clustering has been defined). The mathematical explanation of its properties is non-trivial and I encourage you to check out the original paper (*A Statistical Method for Evaluating Systematic Relationships*, Sokal R., Michener C., *University of Kansas Science Bulletin, 38, 1958*) for further details.

Ward's linkage

The last method we are going to discuss is called **Ward's linkage** (named after its author and originally proposed in *Hierarchical Grouping to Optimize an Objective Function*, Ward Jr J. H., *Journal of the American Statistical Association. 58(301), 1963*). It's based on the Euclidean distance and the formal definition is as follows:

$$L_{Ward}(a,b) = \sum_{\bar{x}_i \in C_a} \sum_{\bar{x}_j \in C_b} \|\bar{x}_i - \bar{x}_j\|_2^2 \quad \forall\, C_a, C_b$$

At every level, all clusters are taken into account and two of them are selected with the goal of minimizing the sum of the squared distances. The process itself is not very different from average linkage and it's possible to prove that the merging process leads to a reduction in the variance of the clusters (that is, increasing their internal cohesion). Moreover, Ward's linkage tends to produce clusters containing approximately the same number of samples (that is, compared with single linkage, Ward's method avoids the presence of small clusters together with very large ones, as discussed in the next section). Ward's linkage is a popular default choice, but, in order to make the right choice in every specific context, it's necessary to introduce the concept of the dendrogram.

Analyzing a dendrogram

A **dendrogram** is a tree data structure that allows us to represent the entire clustering hierarchy produced by either an agglomerative or divisive algorithm. The idea is to put the samples on the x axis and the dissimilarity level on the y axis. Whenever two clusters are merged, the dendrogram shows a connection corresponding to the dissimilarity level at which it occurred. Hence, in an agglomerative scenario, a dendrogram always starts with all samples considered as clusters and moves upward (the direction is purely conventional) until a single cluster is defined.

For didactic purposes, it's preferable to show the dendrogram corresponding to a very small dataset, X, but all the concepts that we are going to discuss can be applied to any situation. However, with larger datasets, it will often be necessary to apply some truncations in order to visualize the entire structure in a more compact form.

Let's consider a small dataset, X, made up of 12 bidimensional samples generated by 4 Gaussian distributions with mean vectors in the range (-1, 1) × (-1, 1):

```
from sklearn.datasets import make_blobs

nb_samples = 12
nb_centers = 4

X, Y = make_blobs(n_samples=nb_samples, n_features=2, center_box=[-1, 1],
                  centers=nb_centers, random_state=1000)
```

The dataset (with the labels) is shown in the following screenshot:

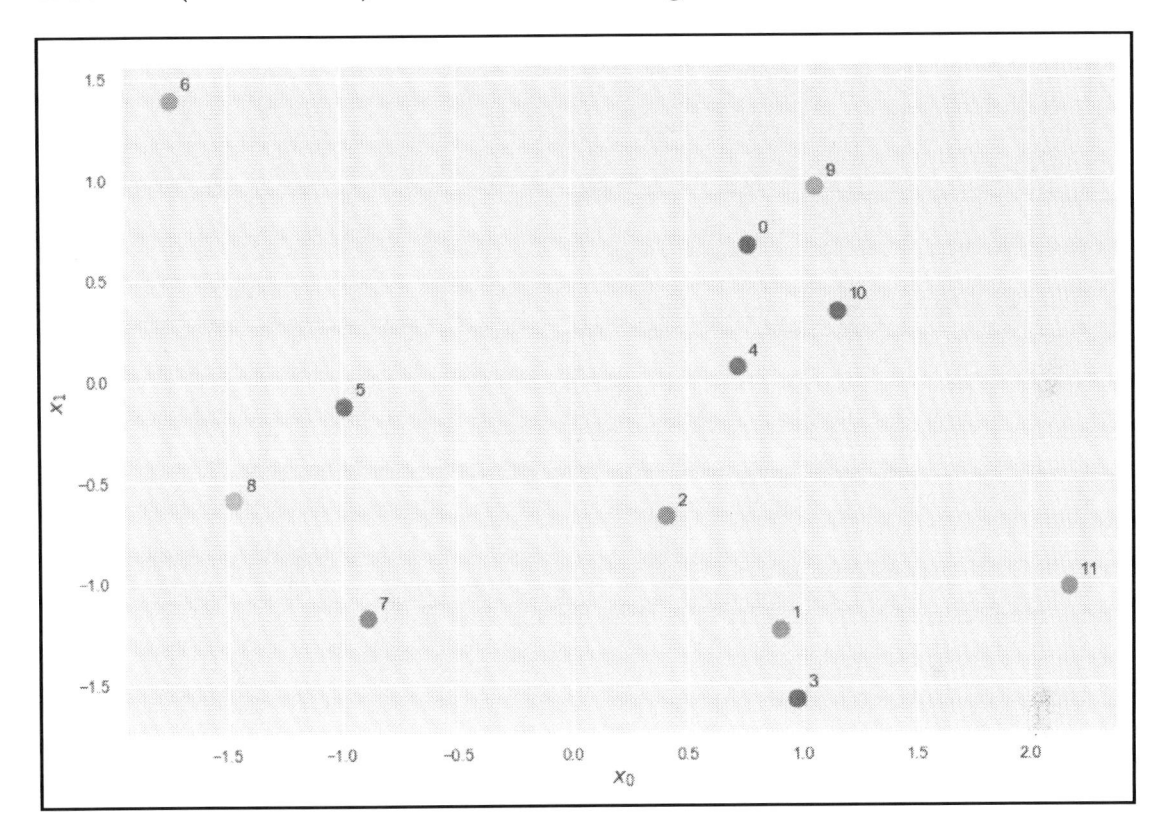

Dataset employed for dendrogram analysis

Hierarchical Clustering in Action

In order to generate a dendrogram (using SciPy), we first need to create a linkage matrix. In this case, we have chosen a Euclidean metric with Ward's linkage (but, as usual, I encourage you to perform the analysis with different configurations):

```
from scipy.spatial.distance import pdist
from scipy.cluster.hierarchy import linkage

dm = pdist(X, metric='euclidean')
Z = linkage(dm, method='ward')
```

The dm array is a condensed pairwise distance matrix, while Z is the linkage matrix produced by Ward's method (the linkage() function requires the method parameter, which accepts, among others, the values single, complete, average, and ward). At this point, we can generate and plot the dendrogram (the dendrogram() function can automatically plot the diagram using a default or supplied Matplotlib axis object):

```
import matplotlib.pyplot as plt

from scipy.cluster.hierarchy import dendrogram

fig, ax = plt.subplots(figsize=(12, 8))

d = dendrogram(Z, show_leaf_counts=True, leaf_font_size=14, ax=ax)

ax.set_xlabel('Samples', fontsize=14)
ax.set_yticks(np.arange(0, 6, 0.25))

plt.show()
```

The diagram is displayed in the following screenshot:

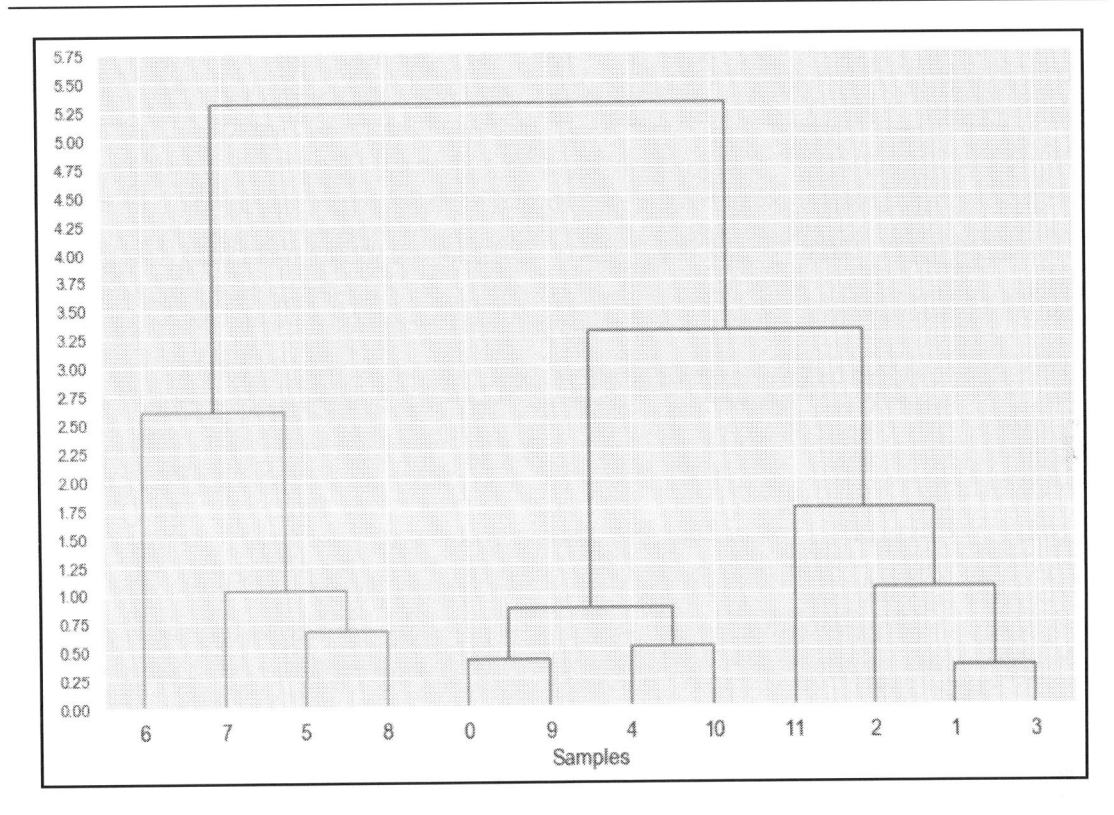

Dendrogram corresponding to Ward's linkage applied to the dataset

As explained in the preceding screenshot, the *x* axis represents the samples intended to minimize the risk of cross-connections, while the *y* axis shows the dissimilarity level. Let's now analyze the diagram from the bottom. The initial state corresponds to all samples considered as independent clusters (so the dissimilarity is null). Moving upward, we start to observe the first mergers. In particular, when the dissimilarity is about 0.35, samples **1** and **3** are merged.

The second step happens with a dissimilarity of slightly below 0.5, when the samples **0** and **9** are also merged. The process goes on until a dissimilarity of about 5.25, when a single cluster is created. Let's now dissect the dendrogram horizontally when the dissimilarity is equal to 1.25. Looking at the underlying connections, we discover that the clustering structure is: {6}, {7, 5, 8}, {0, 9, 4, 10}, {11}, {2, 1, 3}.

Hierarchical Clustering in Action

Therefore, we have five clusters, with two of them made up of a single sample. It's not surprising to observe that samples **6** and **11** are the last ones to be merged. In fact, they are much further apart than all the other ones. In the following screenshot, four different levels are shown (only the clusters containing more than one sample are marked with a circle):

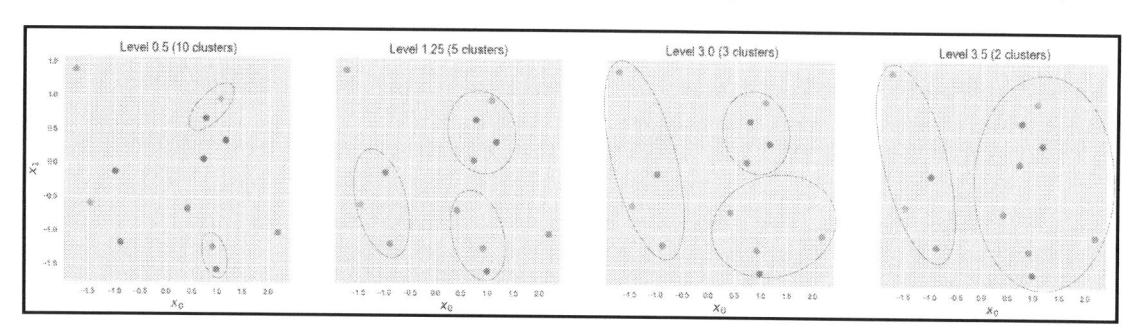

Clusters generated by cutting the dendrogram at different levels (Ward's linkage)

As is easy to understand, the agglomeration starts by selecting the most similar clusters/samples and proceeds by adding the *nearest neighbors*, until the root of the tree has been reached. In our case, at a dissimilarity level equal to 2.0, three well-defined clusters have been detected. The left one is also kept in the next cut, while the two right ones (which are clearly closer) are selected for merging in order to yield a single cluster. The process itself is straightforward and doesn't need particular explanations; however, there are two important considerations.

The first one is inherent to the dendrogram structure itself. Contrary to other methods, hierarchical clustering allows observing an entire clustering tree, and such a feature is extremely helpful when it's necessary to show how the process evolves by increasing the dissimilarity level. For example, a product recommender application could not provide any information about the desired number of clusters representing the users, but executive management might be interested in understanding how the merging process is structured and evolves.

In fact, observing how clusters are merged allows deep insight into the underlying geometry and it's also possible to discover which clusters could potentially be considered as parts of larger ones. In our example, at level 0.5, we have the small cluster {**1**, **3**}. The question of "what samples can be added to this cluster by increasing the dissimilarity?" can be answered immediately with {**2**}. Of course, in this case, this is a trivial problem that can be solved by looking at the data plot, but with high-dimensional datasets, it can become more difficult without the support of a dendrogram.

Chapter 4

The second advantage of dendrograms is the possibility to compare the behavior of different linkage methods. Using Ward's method, the first mergers happen at quite low dissimilarity levels, but there's a large gap between **five clusters** and **three clusters**. This is a consequence of both the geometry and the merging strategy. What happens, for example, if we employ a single linkage (which is intrinsically very different)? The corresponding dendrogram is shown in the following screenshot:

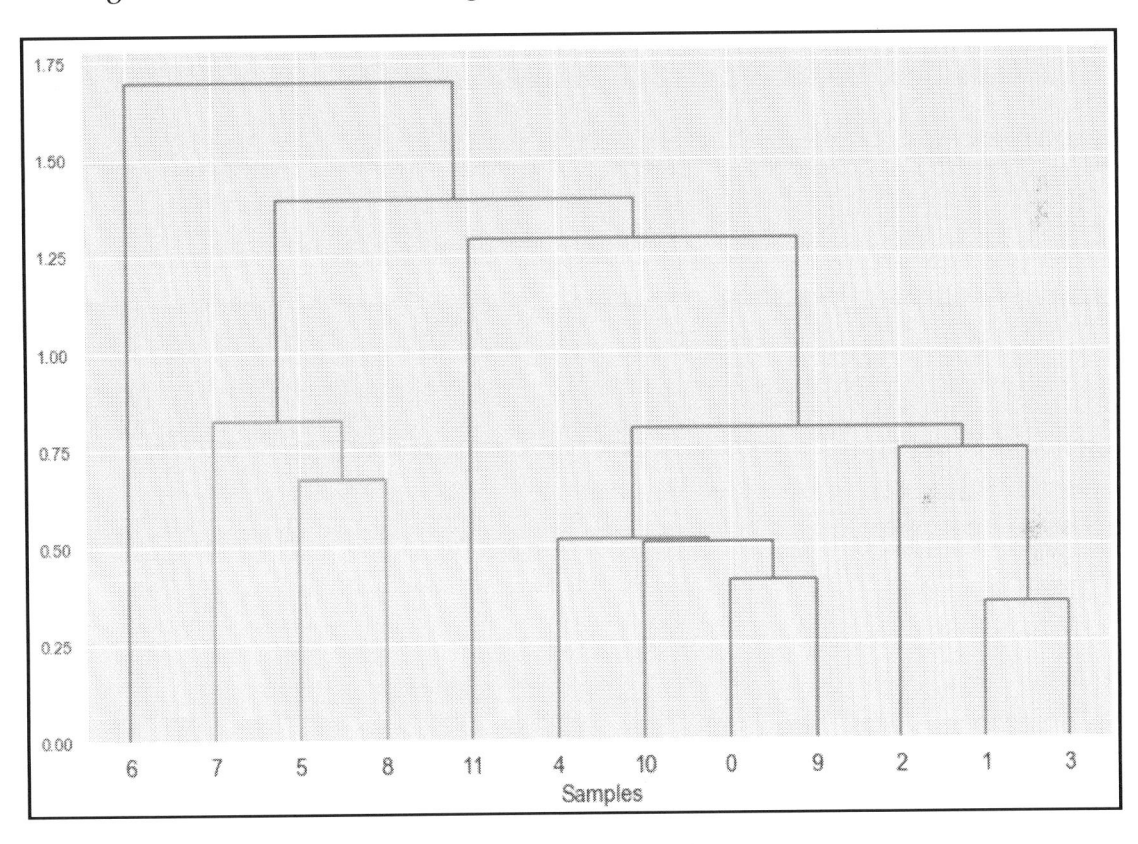

Dendrogram corresponding to single linkage applied to the dataset

Hierarchical Clustering in Action

The conclusion is that the dendrogram is asymmetric and the clusters are generally merged with a single sample or with small agglomerates. Starting from the right, we can see that samples {11} and {6} were merged very late. Moreover, sample {6} (which could be an outlier) is merged at the highest dissimilarity, when the final single cluster must be produced. The process can be better understood with the following screenshot:

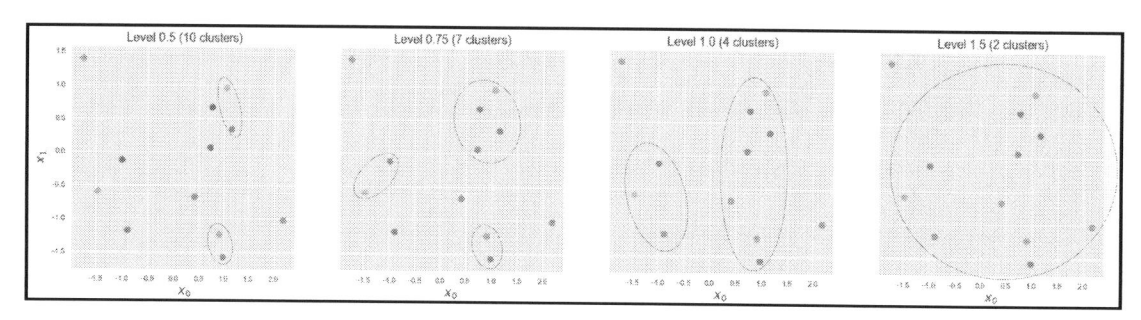

Clusters generated by cutting the dendrogram at different levels (single linkage)

As you can see from the screenshot, while Ward's method generates two clusters containing all samples, a single linkage aggregates the largest blocks at **Level 1.0** by keeping the potential outliers outside. Therefore, the dendrogram also allows defining aggregation semantics, which can be very helpful in a psychometric and sociological context. While Ward's linkage proceeds in a way that is very similar to other symmetric algorithms, single linkage has a step-wise fashion that shows an underlying preference for clusters built incrementally, resulting in the avoidance of large gaps in the dissimilarity.

Finally, it's interesting to note that, while Ward's linkage yields a potential optimal number of clusters (three) by cutting the dendrogram at **Level 3.0**, single linkage never reaches such a configuration (because cluster {6} is merged only in the final step). This effect is strictly related to the double principle of maximum separation and maximum cohesion. Ward's linkage tends to find the most cohesive and separated clusters very quickly. It allows cutting the dendrogram when the dissimilarity gap overcomes a predefined threshold (and, of course, when the desired number of clusters has been reached), while other linkages require a different approach and, sometimes, yield undesirable final configurations.

Considering the nature of the problem, I always encourage you to test the behavior of all linkage methods and to find out the most appropriate method for some sample scenarios (for example, the segmentation of the population of a country according to education level, occupancy, and income). This is the best approach to increase awareness and to improve the ability to provide a semantic interpretation of the processes (which is a fundamental goal of any clustering procedure).

Cophenetic correlation as a performance metric

Hierarchical clustering performance can be evaluated by using any of the methods presented in the previous chapters. However, in this particular case, a specific measure (that doesn't require the ground truth) can be employed. Given a proximity matrix, P, and a linkage, L, a couple of samples, x_i and $x_j \in X$, are always assigned to the same cluster at a certain hierarchical level. Of course, it's important to remember that in the agglomerative scenario, we start with n different clusters and we end up with a single cluster equivalent to X. Moreover, as two merged clusters become a single one, two samples belonging to a cluster will always continue to belong to the same *enlarged* cluster until the end of the process.

Considering the first dendrogram shown in the previous section, samples {1} and {3} are immediately merged; then sample {2} is added, followed by {11}. At this point, the whole cluster is merged with another block (containing samples {0}, {9}, {4}, and {10}). On the last level, the remaining samples are merged in order to form a single final cluster. Hence, naming the dissimilarity levels $DL_0, DL_1, ...,$ and DL_k, samples {1} and {3} start belonging to the same cluster at DL_1, while, for example, {2} and {1} are found in the same cluster at DL_6.

At this point, we can define DL_{ij} as the dissimilarity level at which x_i and x_j belong to the same cluster for the first time and the **cophenetic matrix** denoted as CP in the following ($n \times n$) matrix:

$$CP_{ij} = [DL_{ij}]$$

In other words, the CP_{ij} element is the smallest dissimilarity needed to observe x_i and x_j in the same cluster. It's possible to prove that CP_{ij} is a distance metric between x_i and x_j; therefore, CP is analogous to P and it has the same properties of the proximity matrix (for example, all diagonal elements are null). In particular, we are interested in their correlation (normalized in the range -1 and 1). Such a value (**cophenetic correlation coefficient (CPC)**) indicates the level of agreement between P and CP and can be easily computed, as displayed in the following equation.

Hierarchical Clustering in Action

As both P and CP are (n × n) symmetric matrices with null diagonal elements, it's possible to consider only the lower triangular part (excluding the diagonal and indicated as Tril(•)), containing n(n-1)/2 values. Therefore, the average values are as follows:

$$\hat{P} = \frac{2}{n(n-1)} \sum_{(i,j) \in Tril(P)} P(i,j) \quad \text{and} \quad \hat{CP} = \frac{2}{n(n-1)} \sum_{(i,j) \in Tril(CP)} CP(i,j)$$

The normalized sum of squares values are as follows:

$$SP = \frac{2}{n(n-1)} \sum_{(i,j) \in Tril(P)} P(i,j)^2 - \hat{P}^2 \quad \text{and} \quad SCP = \frac{2}{n(n-1)} \sum_{(i,j) \in Tril(CP)} CP(i,j)^2 - \hat{CP}^2$$

Hence, the normalized cophenetic correlation is simply equal to the following:

$$CPC = \frac{\frac{2}{n(n-1)} \sum_{(i,j) \in Tril(P \text{ or } CP)} P(i,j) \cdot CP(i,j) - \hat{P} \cdot \hat{CP}}{\sqrt{SP \cdot SCP}}$$

The preceding equation is based on the assumption that if three samples, x_i, x_j, and x_p, have distances such as $d(x_i, x_j) < d(x_i, x_p)$, it is reasonable to expect that x_i and x_j will be merged in the same cluster before x_i and x_p (that is, the dissimilarity level corresponding to the merger of x_i and x_j is lower than the one corresponding to the merger of x_i and x_p). Therefore, CPC → 1 indicates that linkage generates an optimal hierarchy, which reflects the underlying geometry. On the other hand, CPC → -1 indicates a complete disagreement and a potential clustering result that is not coherent with the geometry. It goes without saying that, given a problem, our goal is to find a metric and linkage that maximizes the CPC.

Considering the example described in Chapter 3, *Advanced Clustering*, we can compute the cophenetic matrices and the CPCs corresponding to different linkages (assuming the Euclidean distance) using the SciPy function, cophenet. This function requires the linkage matrix as the first argument and the proximity matrix as the second one, and returns both the cophenetic matrix and the CPC (the dm variable is the condensed proximity matrix previously computed):

```
from scipy.cluster.hierarchy import linkage, cophenet

cpc, cp = cophenet(linkage(dm, method='ward'), dm)
print('CPC Ward\'s linkage: {:.3f}'.format(cpc))

cpc, cp = cophenet(linkage(dm, method='single'), dm)
print('CPC Single linkage: {:.3f}'.format(cpc))
```

```
cpc, cp = cophenet(linkage(dm, method='complete'), dm)
print('CPC Complete linkage: {:.3f}'.format(cpc))

cpc, cp = cophenet(linkage(dm, method='average'), dm)
print('CPC Average linkage: {:.3f}'.format(cpc))
```

The output of this snippet is shown here:

```
CPC Ward's linkage: 0.775
CPC Single linkage: 0.771
CPC Complete linkage: 0.779
CPC Average linkage: 0.794
```

These values are very close and indicate that all linkages yield quite good results (even if they are not optimal because of the presence of the two outliers). However, if we need to select a method, the average linkage is the most accurate and should be preferred to the other linkages if there are no specific reasons for skipping it.

The cophenetic correlation is an evaluation metric peculiar to hierarchical clustering and it generally provides reliable outcomes. However, when the geometries are more complex, the CPC value could be misleading and result in sub-optimal configurations. For this reason, I always suggest using other metrics as well (for example, the silhouette score or the adjusted Rand score) in order to double-check performance and make the most appropriate choices.

Agglomerative clustering on the Water Treatment Plant dataset

Let's now consider a more detailed problem on a larger dataset (the instructions to download it are provided in the *Technical requirements* section at the beginning of the chapter) containing 527 samples with 38 chemical and physical variables describing the status of water treatment plants. As the same authors (Bejar, Cortes, and Poch) stated, the domain is poorly-structured and careful analysis is needed. At the same time, our goal is to find the optimal clustering with an agnostic approach; in other words, we won't consider the semantic labeling process (which needs a domain expert) but only the geometrical structure of the dataset and the relations discovered by the agglomerative algorithm.

Hierarchical Clustering in Action

Once downloaded, the CSV file (called water-treatment.data) can be loaded using pandas (of course, the term <DATA_PATH> must be changed in order to point to the exact location of the file). The first column is an index related to the specific plant, while all the other values are numeric and can be converted to float64. The missing values are indicated with the '?' character and, as we don't have any other pieces of information, they are set with the mean of each attribute:

```
import pandas as pd

data_path = '<DATA_PATH>/water-treatment.data'

df = pd.read_csv(data_path, header=None, index_col=0,
na_values='?').astype(np.float64)
df.fillna(df.mean(), inplace=True)
```

As the single variables have very different magnitudes (I invite the reader to check this statement using the describe function on the DataFrame), it's preferable to normalize them in the range (-1, 1), preserving the original variance:

```
from sklearn.preprocessing import StandardScaler

ss = StandardScaler(with_std=False)
sdf = ss.fit_transform(df)
```

At this point, as usual, we can employ the t-SNE algorithm to project the dataset onto a bidimensional space:

```
from sklearn.manifold import TSNE

tsne = TSNE(n_components=2, perplexity=10, random_state=1000)
data_tsne = tsne.fit_transform(sdf)

df_tsne = pd.DataFrame(data_tsne, columns=['x', 'y'], index=df.index)
dff = pd.concat([df, df_tsne], axis=1)
```

The resulting plot is shown in the following screenshot:

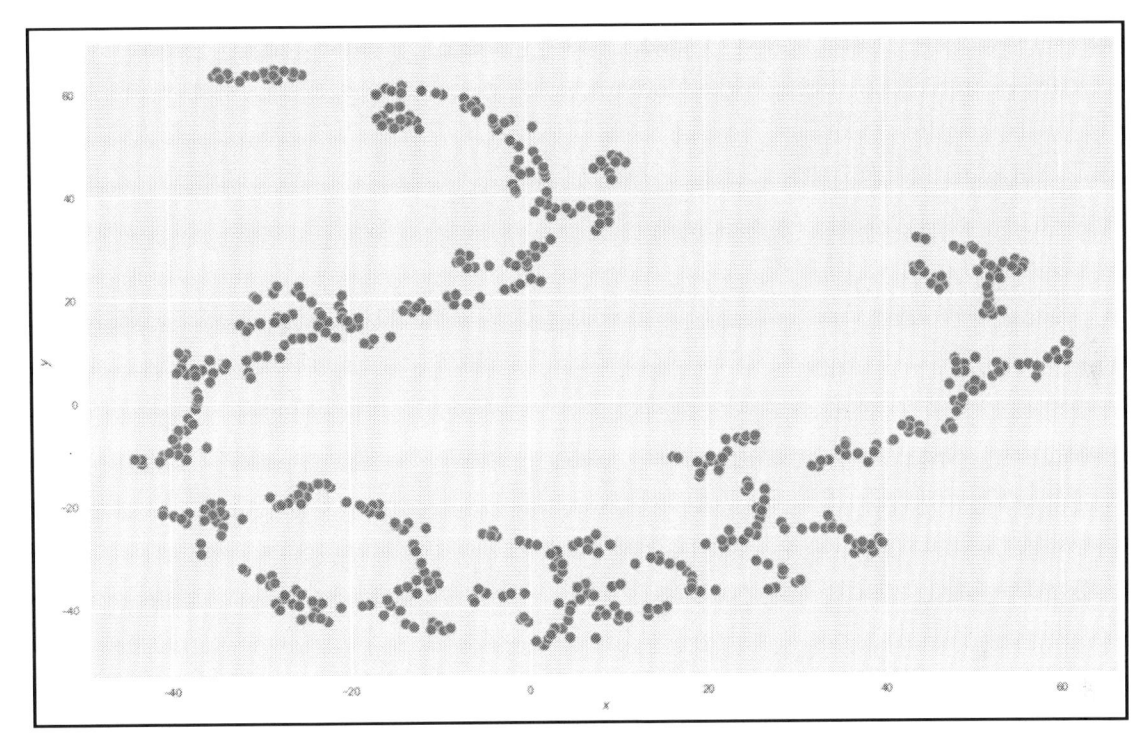

t-SNE plot of the Water Treatment Plant dataset

The plot shows a potential non-convex geometry with many small *islands* (dense regions) separated by empty spaces. However, without any domain information, it's not so easy to decide which blobs can be considered parts of the same cluster. The only *pseudo-constraint* that we can decide to impose (considering that all plants operate in a similar way) is to have a moderate or small final number of clusters. Therefore, assuming the Euclidean distance and using the scikit-learn `AgglomerativeClustering` class, we can compute both the cophenetic correlation and silhouette score for all linkages and 4, 6, 8, and 10 number of clusters:

```
import numpy as np

from sklearn.cluster import AgglomerativeClustering
from sklearn.metrics import silhouette_score

from scipy.spatial.distance import pdist
from scipy.cluster.hierarchy import linkage, cophenet
```

Hierarchical Clustering in Action

```
nb_clusters = [4, 6, 8, 10]
linkages = ['single', 'complete', 'ward', 'average']

cpcs = np.zeros(shape=(len(linkages), len(nb_clusters)))
silhouette_scores = np.zeros(shape=(len(linkages), len(nb_clusters)))

for i, l in enumerate(linkages):
    for j, nbc in enumerate(nb_clusters):
        dm = pdist(sdf, metric='minkowski', p=2)
        Z = linkage(dm, method=l)
        cpc, _ = cophenet(Z, dm)
        cpcs[i, j] = cpc

        ag = AgglomerativeClustering(n_clusters=nbc, affinity='euclidean', linkage=l)
        Y_pred = ag.fit_predict(sdf)
        sls = silhouette_score(sdf, Y_pred, random_state=1000)
        silhouette_scores[i, j] = sls
```

The corresponding plots are shown in the following screenshot:

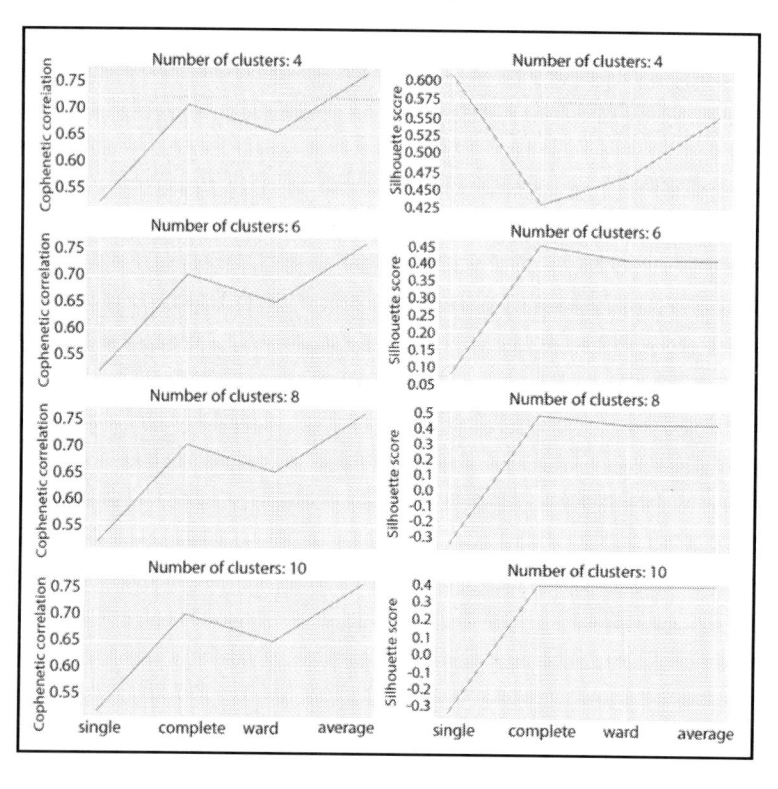

Cophenetic correlation (left) and silhouette score (right) for a different number of clusters and four linkage methods

The first element to consider is that the cophenetic correlation is reasonably acceptable for complete and average linkage, while it's too low for single linkage. Considering the silhouette scores, the maximum value (about 0.6) is achieved with single linkage and four clusters. This result indicates that four regions can be separated with a medium or high level of internal cohesion, even if the hierarchical algorithm yields a sub-optimal configuration.

As explained in the previous section, cophenetic correlation can sometimes be misleading and, in this case, we can conclude that, if the theoretical number of potential clusters is four, using single linkage is the best choice. However, all the other diagrams show a maximum corresponding to complete linkage (and a minimum for the single one). Hence, the first question to answer is: do we need even clusters? In this example, let's assume that many plants operate in a very standard way (with differences being shared by many samples), but there can also be some particular cases (improper *outliers*) that can exhibit very different behavior.

Such a hypothesis is realistic in many contexts and can be due to innovative or experimental processes, a lack of resources, internal problems during the measurements, and so on. A domain expert can confirm or reject our assumption, but, as this is a generic example, we can decide to keep eight clusters with complete linkage (with a silhouette score of about 0.5). This value indicates the presence of overlaps, but, considering the dimensionality of the dataset and the non-convexity, it can be acceptable in many real-life cases.

At this point, we can also analyze the dendrogram truncated to 80 leaves (this is possible by setting the `trucate_mode='lastp'` parameter and `p=80`), so as to avoid intervals that are too small and hard to distinguish (however, you can remove this constraint and increase the resolution):

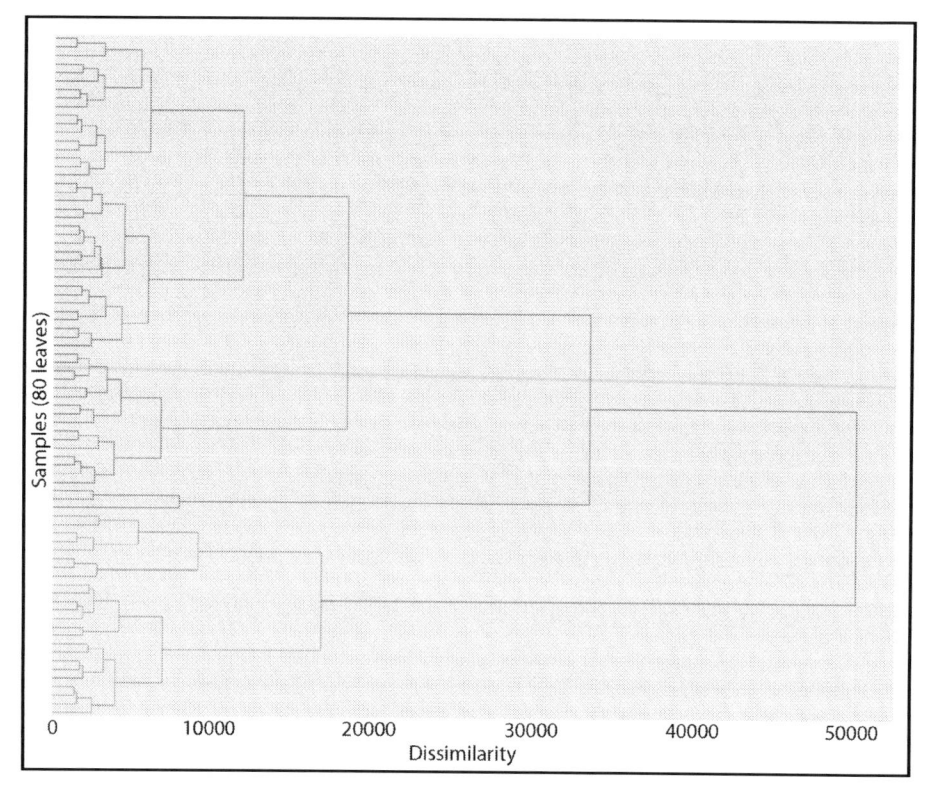

Dendrogram of the Water Treatment Plant dataset with the Euclidean metric and complete linkage

As we can see, the agglomeration process is not homogeneous. In the beginning of the process, the dissimilarity increases quite slowly, but after a value corresponding approximately to 10,000, the jumps become larger. Looking at the t-SNE plot, it's possible to understand that the effect of non-convexities has a stronger impact on very large clusters because the density decreases and, implicitly, the dissimilarity grows. It's straightforward that very small numbers of clusters (for example, 1, 2, or 3) are characterized by very high internal dissimilarities and pretty low cohesion.

Moreover, the dendrogram shows that there are two main uneven aggregations at a level of about 17,000, so we can deduce that coarse-grained analysis highlights the presence of a dominant behavior (looking at the plot from the top) and a secondary one, employed by a smaller number of plants. In particular, the smaller group is very stable, because it will be merged to a final single cluster at a dissimilarity level of about 50,000. Hence, we should expect the presence of pseudo-outliers that are grouped into more isolated regions (this is also confirmed by the t-SNE plot).

Cutting at a level in the range of 4,000 ÷ 6,000 (corresponding to about eight clusters), the larger block is denser than the smaller ones. In other words, the outlier clusters will contain much fewer samples than the other clusters. This is not surprising because, as discussed in the *Analyzing a dendogram* section dedicated to dendrograms, the furthest clusters are normally merged quite late in complete linkage.

At this point, we can finally perform clustering and check the result. Scikit-learn's implementation doesn't compute the whole dendrogram, but rather it stops the process when the desired number of clusters has been reached (unless the `compute_full_tree` parameter is not `True`):

```
import pandas as pd

from sklearn.cluster import AgglomerativeClustering

ag = AgglomerativeClustering(n_clusters=8, affinity='euclidean',
linkage='complete')
Y_pred = ag.fit_predict(sdf)

df_pred = pd.Series(Y_pred, name='Cluster', index=df.index)
pdff = pd.concat([dff, df_pred], axis=1)
```

Hierarchical Clustering in Action

The final plot is shown in the following screenshot:

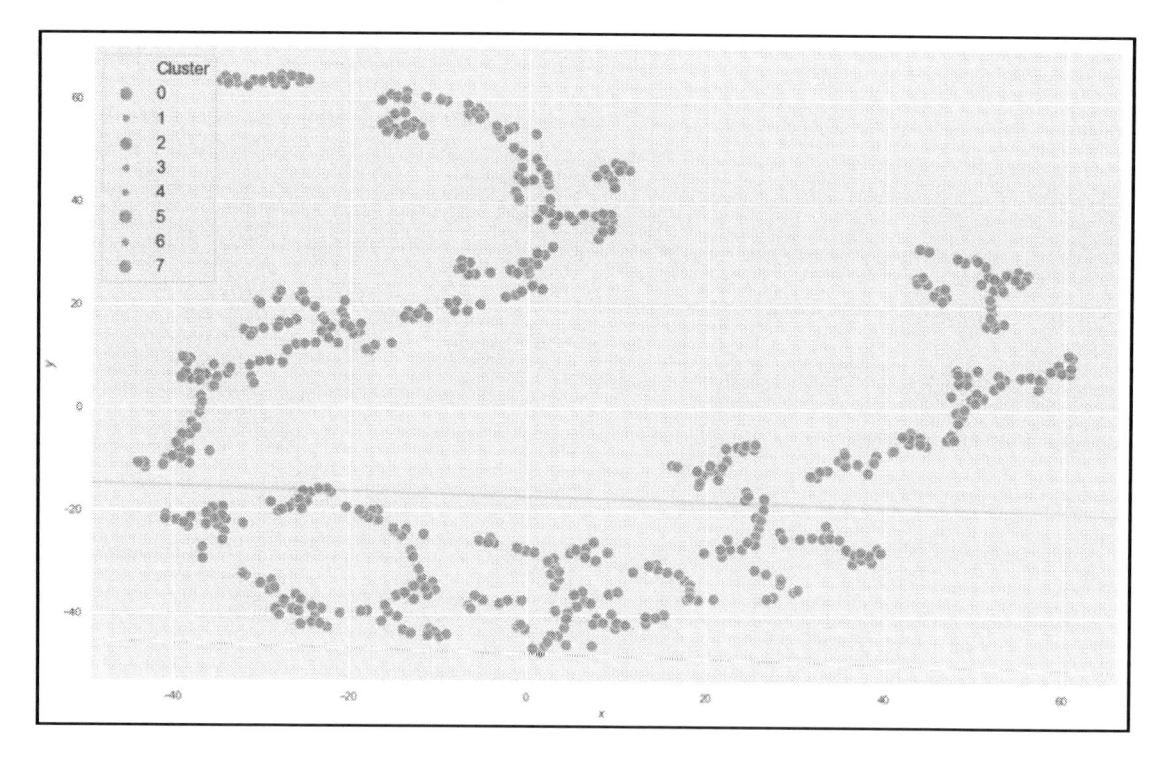

Clustering result of the Water Treatment Plant dataset (eight clusters)

As expected, the clusters are uneven, but they are quite coherent with the geometry. Moreover, isolated clusters (for example, in the region $x \in (-40, -20)$ and $y > 60$) are very small and they are very likely to contain true outliers, whose behavior is very different from the majority of the other samples. We are not going to analyze the semantics, because the problem is very specific. However, it's reasonable to think that the large cluster in the region $x \in (-40, 40)$ and $y \in (-40, -10)$, even though non-convex, represents a suitable baseline. Conversely, the other large blocks (at the extremes of this cluster) correspond to plants with specific properties or behaviors, which are diffused enough to be considered standard alternative practices. Of course, as mentioned at the beginning, this is an agnostic analysis, which should be helpful for understanding how to work with hierarchical clustering.

Chapter 4

As a final step, we want to cut the dendrogram at a dissimilarity level of about 35,000 (corresponding to two clusters). The result is shown in the following screenshot:

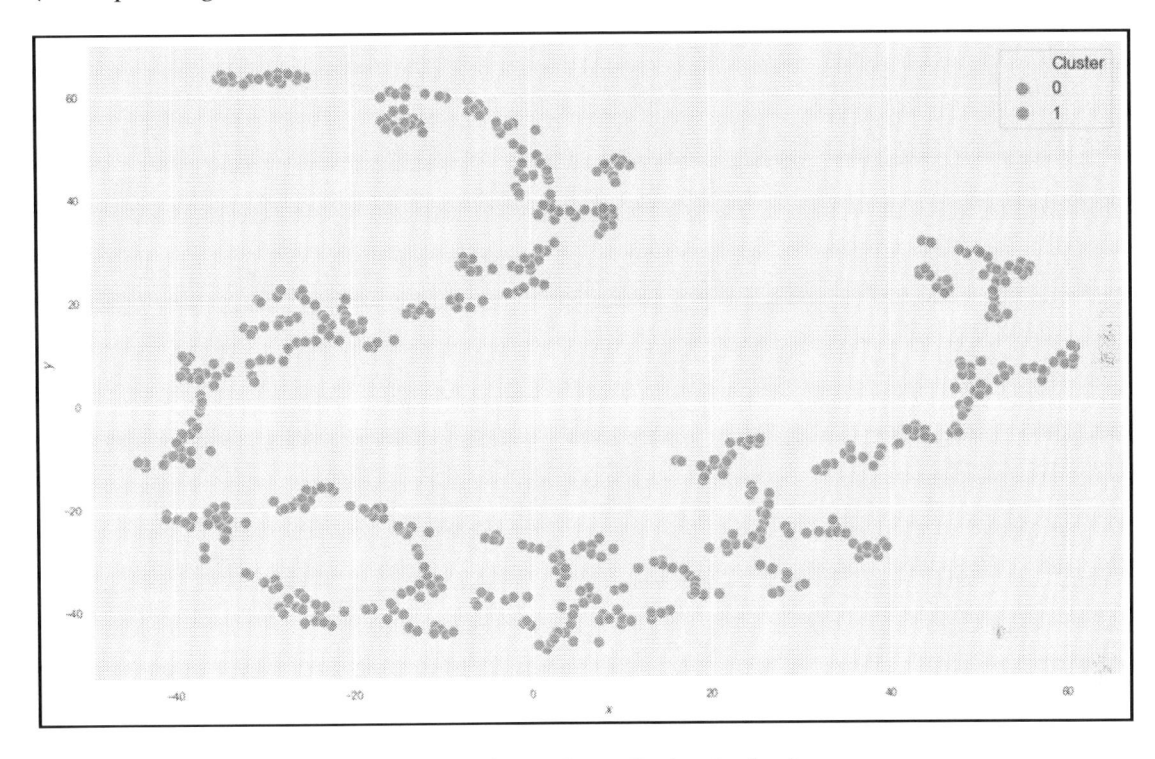

Clustering result of the Water Treatment Plant dataset (two clusters)

At this level, the dendrogram shows a large percentage of samples belonging to a cluster and a remaining smaller block. Now we know that such a secondary region corresponds to $x \in (-40, 10)$ and $y > 20$. Again, the result is not surprising, because the t-SNE plot shows that these samples are the only ones with $y > 20 \div 25$ (while the larger cluster, even with a vast empty region, covers almost all of the range).

Therefore, we could state that such samples represent very different plants with *extreme* behaviors and, if a new sample is assigned to that cluster, it is probably a non-standard plant (assuming that a standard plant has a behavior similar to the majority of its peers). As an exercise, I encourage you to test other amounts of clusters and different linkages (in particular, single linkage, which is very peculiar), and try to validate or reject some samples, prior hypotheses (it's not necessary for them to be physically acceptable).

Connectivity constraints

An important feature of agglomerative hierarchical clustering is the possibility to include connectivity constraints to force the merging of specific samples. This kind of prior knowledge is very common in contexts where there are strong relationships between neighbors or when we know that some samples must belong to the same cluster because of their intrinsic properties. To achieve this goal, we need to use a **connectivity matrix,** $A \in \{0, 1\}^{n \times n}$:

$$A_{ij} = \begin{cases} [1] & if\ \bar{x}_i\ and\ \bar{x}_j\ are\ connected \\ [0] & otherwise \end{cases}$$

In general, A is the adjacency matrix induced by a graph of the dataset; however, the only important requirement is the absence of isolated samples (without connections), because they cannot be merged in any way. The connectivity matrix is applied during the initial merging stages and forces the algorithm to aggregate the specified samples. As the following agglomerations don't impact on connectivity (two merged samples or clusters will remain merged until the end of the process), the constraints are always enforced.

In order to understand this process, let's consider a sample dataset containing 50 bidimensional points drawn from 8 bivariate Gaussian distributions:

```
from sklearn.datasets import make_blobs

nb_samples = 50
nb_centers = 8

X, Y = make_blobs(n_samples=nb_samples, n_features=2, center_box=[-1, 1],
centers=nb_centers, random_state=1000)
```

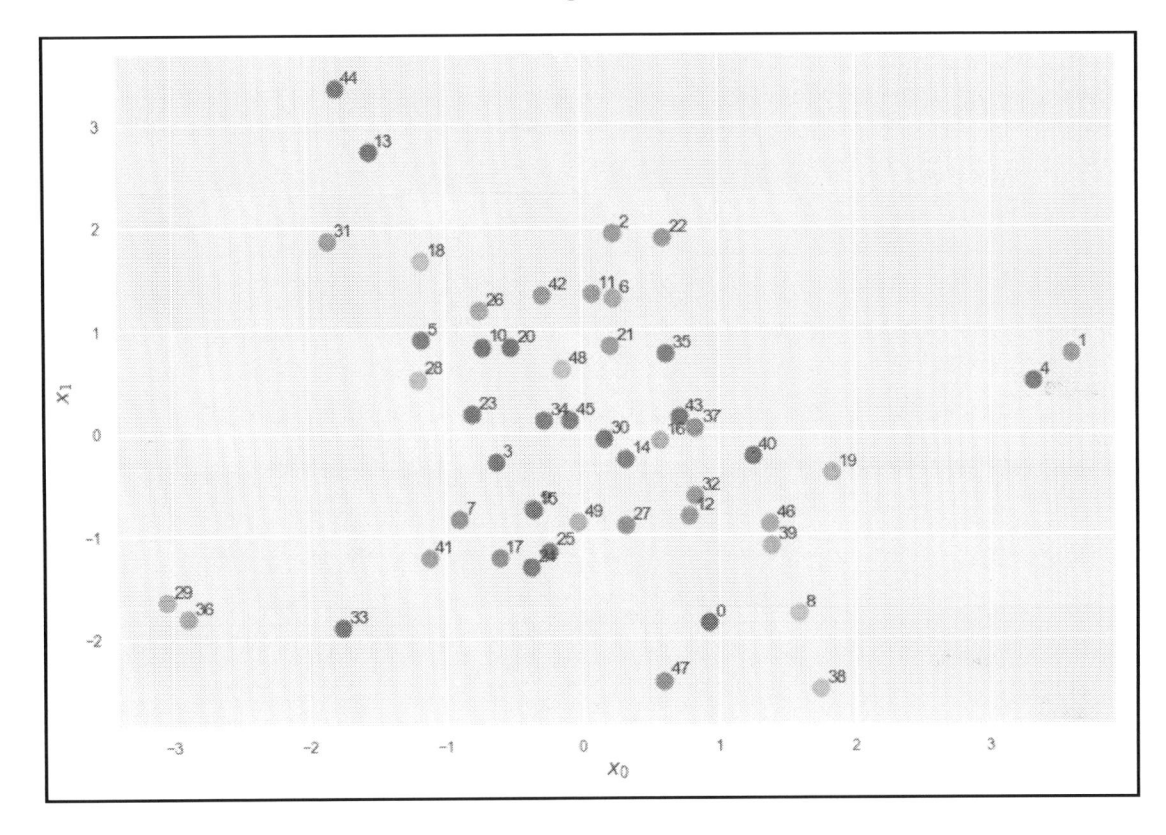

The labeled dataset is shown in the following screenshot:

Dataset for connectivity constraints example

Looking at the plot, we see that samples **18** and **31** ($x_0 \in$ *(-2, -1)* and $x_1 \in$ *(1, 2)*) are quite close; however, we don't want them to be merged because sample **18** has many more neighbors in the large central blob, while point **31** is partially isolated and should be considered an autonomous cluster. We also want sample **33** to form a single cluster. These requirements will force the algorithm to merge clusters not respecting the underlying geometry anymore (in terms of Gaussian distributions), but rather the prior knowledge.

Hierarchical Clustering in Action

In order to check how clustering works, let's now compute the dendrogram (truncated to 20 leaves) using the Euclidean distance and average linkage:

```
from scipy.spatial.distance import pdist
from scipy.cluster.hierarchy import linkage, dendrogram

dm = pdist(X, metric='euclidean')
Z = linkage(dm, method='average')

fig, ax = plt.subplots(figsize=(20, 10))

d = dendrogram(Z, orientation='right', truncate_mode='lastp', p=20, ax=ax)

ax.set_xlabel('Dissimilarity', fontsize=18)
ax.set_ylabel('Samples', fontsize=18)
```

The dendrogram (right-to-left) is shown in the following screenshot:

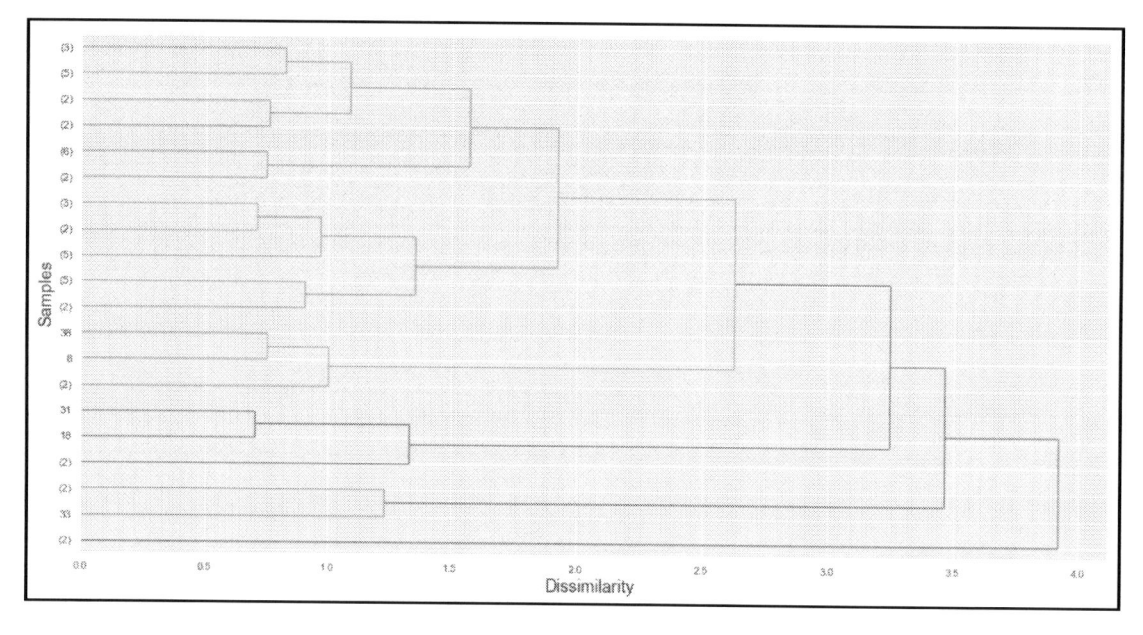

Dendrogram for the connectivity constraints example with the Euclidean distance and average linkage

As expected, samples **18** and **31** are immediately merged and then aggregated with another cluster containing 2 samples (when the number is between parentheses, it means that it's a composite block containing more samples), which are likely to be **44** and **13**. Sample 33 is merged too, so it won't remain in an isolated cluster. As confirmation, let's perform clustering with `n_clusters=8`:

```
from sklearn.cluster import AgglomerativeClustering

ag = AgglomerativeClustering(n_clusters=8, affinity='euclidean',
linkage='average')
Y_pred = ag.fit_predict(X)
```

The plot of the clustered dataset is shown in the following screenshot:

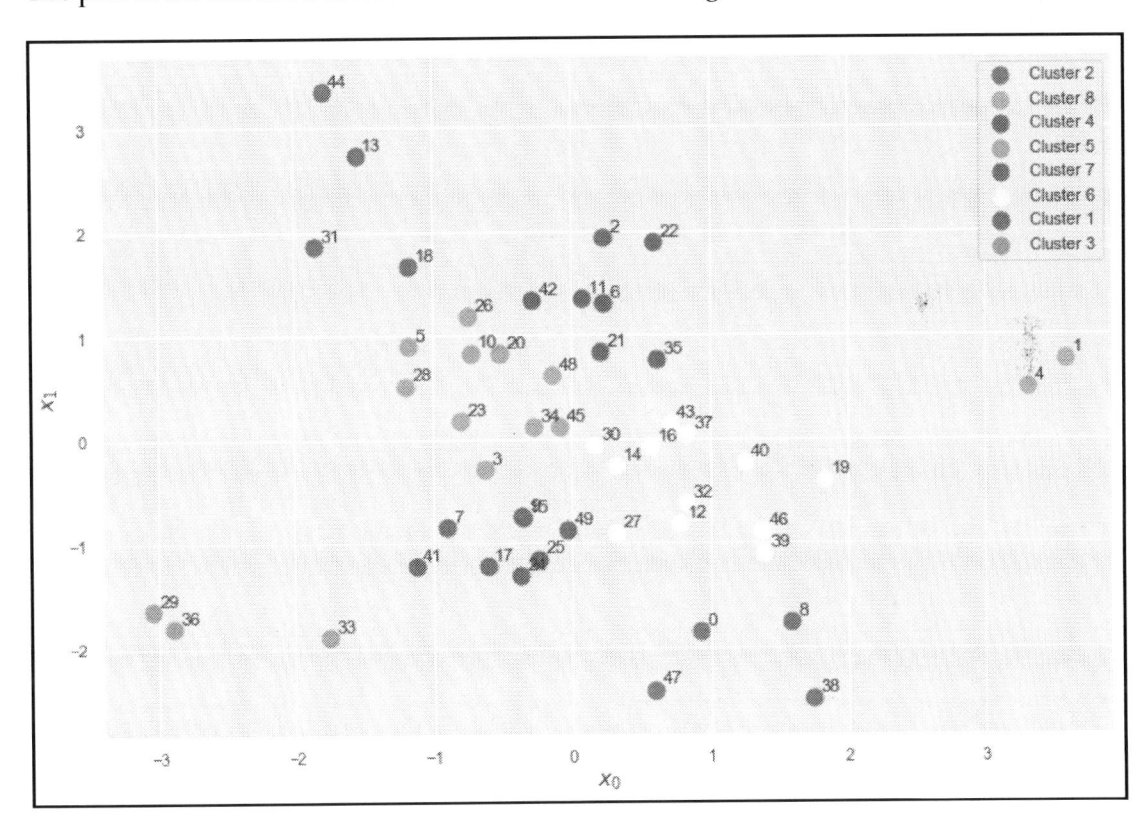

Dataset clustered using the Euclidean distance and average linkage

The result confirms the previous analysis. Without constraints, average linkage yields reasonable partitioning that is compatible with the ground truth (eight Gaussian distributions). In order to split the large central blob and keep the required number of clusters, the algorithm is obliged to also merge the isolated samples, even if the dendrogram confirms that they are merged at the end, at the highest dissimilarity levels.

In order to impose our constraints, we can observe that a connectivity matrix based on the first two nearest neighbors is very likely to force the aggregation of all samples belonging to the denser regions (considering that the neighbors are closer) and end up keeping the isolated points in autonomous clusters. The reason for this hypothetical behavior is based on the goal of average linkage (to minimize the inter-cluster average distance). So, after imposing the constraints, the algorithm is more prone to aggregating close clusters with other neighbors (remember that A has null values but in the positions corresponding to the two nearest neighbors) and to leaving the farthest points unmerged until the dissimilarity level is large enough (yielding very uneven clusters).

In order to check whether our assumption is true, let's generate a connectivity matrix using the scikit-learn, kneighbors_graph() function, with n_neighbors=2 and recluster the dataset, setting the connectivity constraint:

```
from sklearn.cluster import AgglomerativeClustering
from sklearn.neighbors import kneighbors_graph

cma = kneighbors_graph(X, n_neighbors=2)

ag = AgglomerativeClustering(n_clusters=8, affinity='euclidean',
linkage='average', connectivity=cma)
Y_pred = ag.fit_predict(X)
```

The graphical output of the previous snippet is shown in the following screenshot:

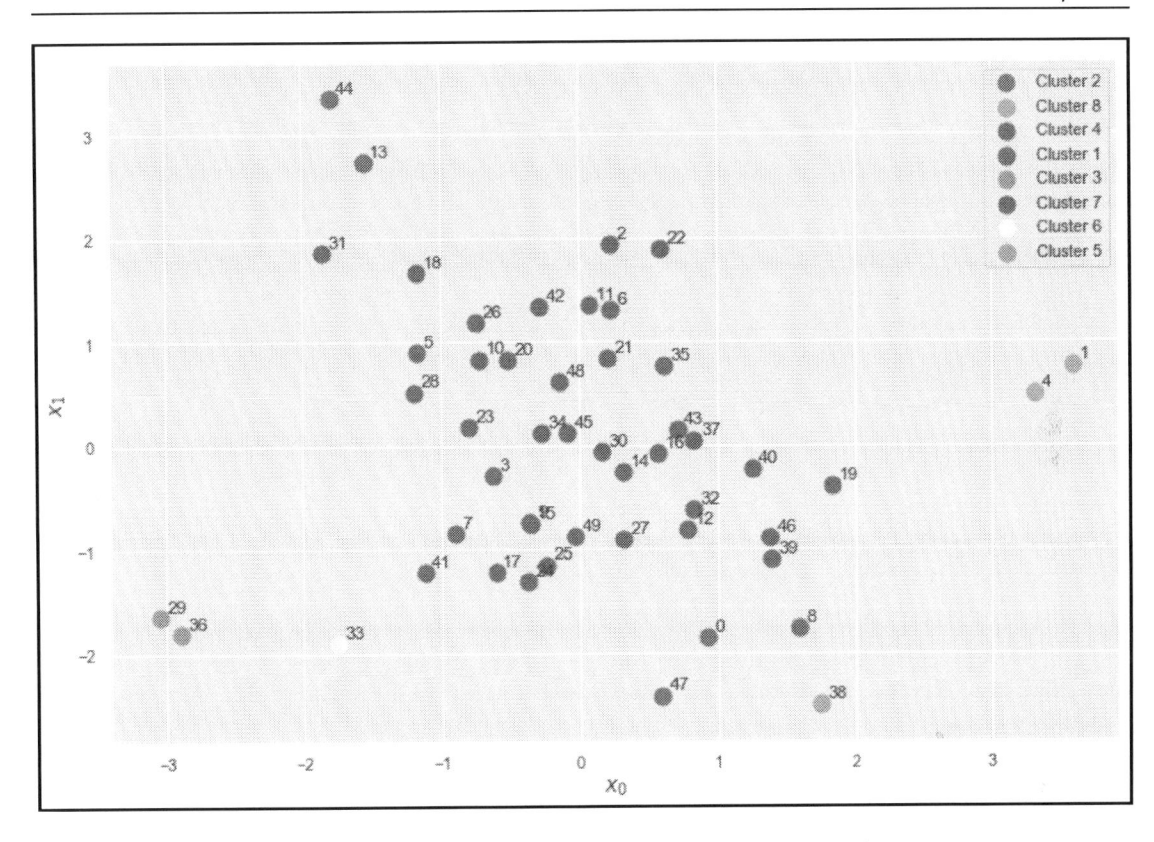

Dataset clustered using the Euclidean distance and average linkage using connectivity constraints

As expected, sample **18** has been assigned to the large central cluster, while points **31** and **33** are now isolated. Of course, as the process is hierarchical, it's easier to impose the connectivity constraints than the separation ones. In fact, while single samples can easily be merged during the initial stages, their exclusion before the final merge cannot be easily guaranteed using all linkages.

When complex constraints are required (given a distance and a linkage), it is often necessary to tune both the connectivity matrix and the desired number of clusters. Of course, if the desired result is achieved with a specific number of clusters, it will be also accomplished with larger values until a dissimilarity lower-bound (that is, the merging process reduces the number of clusters; hence, if the dissimilarity is large enough, all existing constraints will remain valid). For example, if three samples are constrained to belong to the same cluster, we cannot generally expect this result after the initial merging stages.

However, if the merging of all three samples happens at a certain dissimilarity level (for example, 2.0 corresponding to 30 clusters), it will also remain valid for $n < 30$ clusters and for all the configuration with $DL > 2.0$. Therefore, if we start with 5 clusters, we can easily increase this number while taking care to have a dissimilarity level that is larger than the one corresponding to the last merger imposed by the constraints. I encourage you to test this method with other datasets, and try to define prior constraints that can be easily verified after the clustering process.

Summary

In this chapter, we have presented the hierarchical clustering approach, focusing on the different strategies that can be employed (divisive and agglomerative strategies). We also discussed methods that are used to discover which clusters can be merged or split (linkages). In particular, given a distance metric, we analyzed the behavior of four linkage methods: single, complete, average, and Ward's method.

We have shown how to build a dendrogram and how to analyze it in order to understand the entire hierarchical process using different linkage methods. A specific performance measure, called cophenetic correlation, was introduced to evaluate the performance of a hierarchical algorithm without the knowledge of the ground truth.

We analyzed a larger dataset (Water Treatment Plant dataset), defining some hypotheses and validating them using all the tools previously discussed. Toward the end of the chapter, we discussed the concept of connectivity constraints, which allow the introduction of prior knowledge into the process using a connectivity matrix.

In the next chapter, we are going to introduce the concept of soft clustering, focusing on a fuzzy algorithm and two very important Gaussian mixture models.

Questions

1. What's the difference between agglomerative and divisive approaches?
2. Given two clusters a: [(-1, -1), (0, 0)] and b: [(1, 1), (1, 0)], what are the single and complete linkages considering the Euclidean distance?
3. A dendrogram represents the different linkage results for a given dataset. Is this correct?
4. In agglomerative clustering, the bottom (initial part) of a dendrogram contains a single cluster. Is this correct?
5. What's the meaning of the y axis of a dendrogram in agglomerative clustering?
6. The dissimilarity decreases while merging smaller clusters. Is this correct?
7. An element, $C(i, j)$, of the cophenetic matrix reports the dissimilarity level at which two corresponding elements, x_i and x_j, appear in the same cluster for the first time. Is this correct?
8. What's the main purpose of connectivity constraints?

Further reading

- *A Statistical Method for Evaluating Systematic Relationships, Sokal R., Michener C., University of Kansas Science Bulletin, 38, 1958*
- *Hierarchical Grouping to Optimize an Objective Function, Ward Jr J. H., Journal of the American Statistical Association. 58(301), 1963*
- *LINNEO+: A Classification Methodology for Ill-structured Domains, Bejar J., Cortes U., Poch M., Research report RT-93-10-R. Dept. Llenguatges i Sistemes Informatics, Barcelona, 1993*
- *Machine Learning Algorithms, Second Edition, Bonaccorso G., Packt Publishing, 2018*

5
Soft Clustering and Gaussian Mixture Models

In this chapter, we will discuss the concept of soft clustering, which allows us to obtain a membership degree for each sample of a dataset with respect to a defined cluster configuration. That is, considering a range from 0% to 100%, we want to know to what extent x_i belong to a cluster. The extreme values are 0, which means that x_i is completely outside the domain of the cluster and 1 (100%), indicating that x_i is fully assigned to a single cluster. All intermediate values imply a partial domain of two or more different clusters. Therefore, in contrast with hard clustering, here, we are interested in determining not a fixed assignment, but a vector with the same properties of a probability distribution (or a probability itself). Such an approach allows having better control over borderline samples and helps us in finding out a suitable approximation of the generative process from which the dataset is supposed to be drawn.

In particular, we will discuss the following topics:

- Fuzzy C-means
- Gaussian mixtures
- AIC and BIC as performance metrics
- Bayesian Gaussian mixtures (a brief introduction)
- Generative (semi-supervised) Gaussian mixtures

Technical requirements

The code that will be presented in this chapter will require the following:

- Python 3.5+ (`Anaconda distribution` is highly recommended)
- The following libraries:
    - SciPy 0.19+
    - NumPy 1.10+
    - scikit-learn 0.20+
    - Scikit-fuzzy 0.2
    - pandas 0.22+
    - Matplotlib 2.0+
    - seaborn 0.9+

The examples are available in the GitHub repository at `https://github.com/PacktPublishing/HandsOn-Unsupervised-Learning-with-Python/tree/master/Chapter05`.

Soft clustering

All of the algorithms that were analyzed in `Chapter 4`, *Hierarchical Clustering in Action*, belong to the family of hard clustering methods. This means that a given sample is always assigned to a single cluster. On the other hand, soft clustering is aimed at associating each sample, x_i with a vector, generally representing the probability that x_i belongs to every cluster:

$$c(\bar{x}_i) = (p(\bar{x}_i \in C_1), p(\bar{x}_i \in C_2), \dots, p(\bar{x}_i \in C_k))$$

Alternatively, the output can be interpreted as a membership vector:

$$c(\bar{x}_i) = (w_{i1}, w_{i2}, \dots, w_{ik}) \quad with \quad \sum_j w_{ij} = 1$$

Formally, there are no differences between the two versions, but normally, the latter is employed when the algorithm is not explicitly based on a probability distribution. However, for our purposes, we always associate $c(x_i)$ with a probability. In this way, the reader is incentivized to think about the data-generating process that has been used to obtain the dataset. A clear example is the interpretation of such vectors as the probabilities associated with the specific contributions that make up the approximations of the data-generating process, p_{data}. For example, employing a probabilistic mixture, we can decide to approximate p_{data} as follows:

$$p_{data}(\bar{x}_i) \approx p(\bar{x}_i) = \sum_j w_j p_j(\bar{x}_i)$$

Hence, the process is split into a weighted sum of (independent) components, and the output is the probability of x_i for each of them. Of course, we normally expect to have a dominant component responsible for every sample, but with this approach, we have a major awareness of all of the boundary points, subject to small perturbations, that could be assigned to different clusters. For this reason, soft clustering is very helpful when the output can be fed into another model (for example, a neural network) that can take advantage of the whole probability vector. For example, a recommender can first segment the users employing a soft clustering algorithm, and then process the vectors, in order to find more complex relationships based on explicit feedback. A common scenario involves the corrections made through the answers to questions like, "Is this result relevant to you?" Or, "Do you want to see more results like these ones?" As the answers are provided directly by the users, they can be employed in supervised or reinforcement learning models whose input is based on soft automatic segmentation (for example, based on the purchase history or detailed page views). In this way, borderline users can easily be managed by changing the effects of the original assignments (which can be completely insignificant due to the large contributions provided by different clusters), while the recommendations for other users with a strong membership (for example, a probability that is close to 1) can be slightly modified to improve their returns.

We can now start our discussion of Fuzzy c-means, which is a very flexible algorithm that extends the concepts discussed for k-means to soft clustering scenarios.

Fuzzy c-means

The first algorithm that we will propose is a variation of k-means that's based on soft assignments. The name **Fuzzy c-means** derives from the concept of a fuzzy set, which is an extension of classical binary sets (that is, in this case, a sample can belong to a single cluster) to sets based on the superimposition of different subsets representing different regions of the whole set. For example, a set based on the age of some users can have the degrees `young`, `adult`, and `senior`, associated with three different (and partially overlapping) age ranges: 18-35, 28-60, and >50. So, for example, a 30-year-old user is both `young` and `adult`, to different degrees (and, indeed, is a borderline user, considering the boundaries). For further details about these kinds of sets and all of the related operations, I suggest the book *Concepts and Fuzzy Logic*, Belohlavek R., Klir G. J. (edited by), The MIT Press, 2011. For our purposes, we can imagine the dataset, X, containing m samples, partitioned into k overlapping clusters, so that each sample is always associated with every cluster, according to a membership degree, w_{ij} (which is a value bound between 0 and 1). If $w_{ij} = 0$, it means that x_i is completely outside of cluster C_j, while, conversely, $w_{ij} = 1$ indicates a hard assignment to cluster C_j. All intermediate values represent partial membership. Of course, for obvious reasons, the sum of all of the membership degrees of a sample must be normalized to 1 (like a probability distribution). In this way, a sample always belongs to the union of all clusters, and splitting a cluster into two or more sub-clusters always yields a coherent result, in terms of membership.

The algorithm is based on the optimization of generalized inertia, S_f:

$$S_f = \sum_{j=1}^{k} \sum_{\bar{x}_i \in C_j} w_{ij}^m \left\| \bar{x}_i - \bar{\mu}_j \right\|^2$$

In the previous formula, μ_j is the centroid of cluster C_j, while m ($m > 1$) is a reweighting exponential coefficient. When $m \approx 1$, the weights are not affected. With larger values, such as $w_{ij} \in (0, 1)$, their importance is proportionally reduced. Such a coefficient can be selected to compare the results of different values and the level of desired fuzziness. In fact, after each iteration (exactly equivalent to k-means), the weights are updated using the following formula:

$$w_{ij} = \frac{1}{\sum_p \left(\frac{\left\| \bar{x}_i - \bar{\mu}_j \right\|}{\left\| \bar{x}_i - \bar{\mu}_p \right\|} \right)^{\frac{2}{m-1}}}$$

If x_i is close to the centroids, μ_j, the sum becomes close to 0, and the weight is incremented (of course, in order to avoid numeric instabilities, a small constant is added to the denominator so it can never be equal to 0). When $m \gg 1$, the exponent becomes close to 0, and all of the terms in the sum tend to 1. This means that the preference for a specific cluster is weakened and $w_{ij} \approx 1/k$ corresponds to a uniform distribution. Hence, a larger m implies flatter partitioning, without a clear difference between different assignments (unless the sample is extremely close to a centroid), while when $m \approx 1$, a single, dominant weight will be almost equal to 1, and the other ones will be close to 0 (that is, the assignment is hard).

Centroids are updated in a way analogous to k-means (in other words, with the goal of maximizing both separation and internal cohesion):

$$\bar{\mu}_j = \frac{\sum_j w_{ij}^m \bar{x}_i}{\sum_j w_{ij}^m}$$

The process is repeated until the centroids and the weights become stable. After the convergence, it's possible to evaluate the results with a specific measure, called normalized **Dunn's Partitioning Coefficient**, defined as follows:

$$P_C = \frac{w_C - \frac{1}{k}}{1 - \frac{1}{k}} \quad \text{where} \quad w_C = \frac{1}{m}\sum_i\sum_j w_{ij}^2$$

Such a coefficient is bound between 0 and 1. When $P_C \approx 0$, it means that $w_C \approx 1/k$, which implies a flat distribution and a high fuzziness level. On the other hand, when $P_C \approx 1$, then $w_C \approx 1$, indicating almost hard assignments. All of the other values are proportional to the level of fuzziness. Therefore, given a task, the data scientist can immediately evaluate how the algorithm is performing, according to the desired result. In some cases, hard assignments are preferable, and hence, P_C can be considered a check to perform before switching, for example, to standard k-means. In fact, when $P_C \approx 1$ (and such a result is the expected one), it doesn't make sense to use Fuzzy c-means anymore. Conversely, a value less than 1 (for example, $P_C = 0.5$) informs us of the possibility of having very unstable, hard assignments, due to the presence of many borderline samples.

Now, let's apply the Fuzzy c-means algorithm to the reduced MNIST dataset, provided by scikit-learn. The algorithm is provided by the Scikit-Fuzzy library, which implements all of the most important fuzzy logic models. The first step is loading and normalizing the samples, as follows:

```
from sklearn.datasets import load_digits

digits = load_digits()
X = digits['data'] / 255.0
Y = digits['target']
```

The X array contains 1,797 flattened samples, $x \in \Re^{64}$, corresponding to grayscale 8×8 images (whose values are normalized between 0 and 1). We want to analyze the behavior of different *m* coefficients (5 uniform values between 1.05 and 1.5) and check the weights of a sample (in our case, we are going to use X[0]). Hence, we are calling the Scikit-Fuzzy cmeans function, setting c=10 (the number of clusters) and the two convergence parameters, error=1e-6 and maxiter=20000. Moreover, for reproducibility reasons, we will also set a standard random seed=1000. The input array is expected to contain the samples as columns; therefore, we need to transpose it, as follows:

```
from skfuzzy.cluster import cmeans

Ws = []
pcs = []

for m in np.linspace(1.05, 1.5, 5):
    fc, W, _, _, _, _, pc = cmeans(X.T, c=10, m=m, error=1e-6, maxiter=20000, seed=1000)
    Ws.append(W)
    pcs.append(pc)
```

The previous snippet performs different types of clustering and appends the corresponding weight matrices, W, and the partition coefficients, pc, to two lists. Before analyzing a specific configuration, it's helpful to show the final weights (corresponding to each of the digits) for a test sample (representing the digit 0):

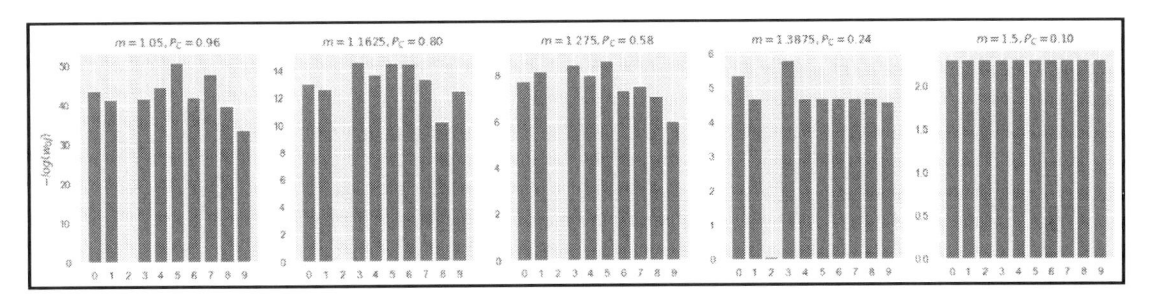

Weights (in an inverse logarithmic scale) for the sample X[0], corresponding to different m values

As extreme values tend to be very different, we have chosen to use an inverse logarithmic scale (that is, $-log(w_{0j})$ instead of w_{0j}). When $m = 1.05$, P_C is about 0.96, and all of the weights (except the one corresponding to C_2) are very small (remember that if $-log(w) = 30$, then $w = e^{-30}$). Such a configuration clearly shows very hard clustering with a dominant component (C_2). The subsequent three plots in the previous figure keep showing dominance, but, while m increases (and P_C decreases), the difference between the dominant and the secondary components becomes smaller and smaller. This effect confirms an increasing fuzziness that reaches its maximum for $m > 1.38$. In fact, when $m = 1.5$, even if $P_C \approx 0.1$, all of the weights are almost identical, and the test sample cannot easily be assigned to a dominant cluster. As we discussed before, we now know that an algorithm like k-means can easily find hard partitioning, because on average, the samples corresponding to different digits are quite different from each other, and the Euclidean distance is enough to assign them to the right centroid. In this example, we want to maintain moderate fuzziness; therefore, we have chosen $m = 1.2$ (corresponding to $P_C \approx 0.73$):

```
fc, W, _, _, _, _, pc = cmeans(X.T, c=10, m=1.2, error=1e-6, maxiter=20000, seed=1000)
Mu = fc.reshape((10, 8, 8))
```

The Mu array contains the centroids, which are shown in the following diagram:

Centroids corresponding to m = 1.2 and $P_C \approx 0.73$

Soft Clustering and Gaussian Mixture Models

As you can see, all of the different digits have been selected, and, as expected, the third cluster (indicated by C_2) corresponds to the digit 0. Now, let's check the weights corresponding to X[0] (also, W is transposed, so they are stored in W[:, 0]):

```
print(W[:, 0])
```

The output is as follows:

```
[2.68474857e-05 9.14566391e-06 9.99579876e-01 7.56684450e-06
 1.52365944e-05 7.26653414e-06 3.66562441e-05 2.09198951e-05
 2.52320741e-04 4.41638611e-05]
```

Even if the assignments are not particularly hard, the dominance of cluster C_2 is evident. The second potential assignment is C_8, corresponding to the digit 9 (with a ratio of about 4,000). Such a result is absolutely coherent with the shapes of the digits, and, considering the difference between the maximum weight and the second one, it's clear that most of the samples will be hardly assigned (that is, as in k-means), even with $P_c \approx 0.75$. In order to check the performance of hard assignments (obtained using the argmax function on the weight matrix), and considering that we know the ground truth, we can employ the adjusted_rand_score, as follows:

```
from sklearn.metrics import adjusted_rand_score

Y_pred = np.argmax(W.T, axis=1)

print(adjusted_rand_score(Y, Y_pred))
```

The output of the previous snippet is as follows:

```
0.6574291419247339
```

Such a value confirms that the majority of samples have been successfully hard assigned. As a supplementary exercise, let's find the sample whose weights have the smallest standard deviation:

```
im = np.argmin(np.std(W.T, axis=1))

print(im)
print(Y[im])
print(W[:, im])
```

The output is as follows:

```
414
8
[0.09956437 0.05777962 0.19350572 0.01874303 0.15952518 0.04650815
 0.05909216 0.12910096 0.17526108 0.06091973]
```

The sample, *X[414]*, represents a digit (8), and it's shown in the following screenshot:

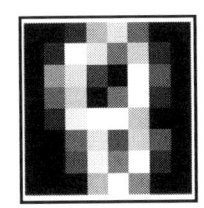

Plot of the sample, X[414], corresponding to the weight vector with the smallest standard deviation

In this case, there are three dominant clusters: C_8, C_4, and C_7 (in descending order). Unfortunately, none of them correspond to the digit 8, which is associated with C_5. It's not difficult to understand that such an error is mainly due to the malformation of the lower part of the digit, which yields a result more similar to a 9 (such a misclassification could also happen for a human being). However, the low standard deviation and the absence of a clearly dominant component should inform us that a decision cannot easily be made, and the sample has features belonging to three main clusters. A more complex supervised model could easily avoid this error, but the result is not so negative, considering that we are performing an unsupervised analysis, and we are only using the ground truth for evaluation purposes. I suggest you test the results using other *m* values, and try to find out some potential composition rules (that is, most of the 8 digits are softly assigned to C_i and C_j, so we can suppose that the corresponding centroids encode part of the common features shared, for example, by all 8 and 9 digits).

We can now discuss the concept of Gaussian mixture, which is a very widely used way to model the distribution of datasets characterized by dense blobs surrounded by low-density regions.

Gaussian mixture

Gaussian mixture is one of the most well-known soft clustering approaches, with dozens of specific applications. It can be considered the father of k-means, because the way it works is very similar; but, contrary to that algorithm, given a sample $x_i \in X$ and k clusters (which are represented as Gaussian distributions), it provides a probability vector, $[p(x_i \in C_1), ..., p(x_i \in C_k)]$.

In a more general way, if the dataset, X, has been sampled from a data-generating process, p_{data}, a Gaussian mixture model is based on the following assumption:

$$p_{data}(\bar{x}_i) \approx p(\bar{x}_i) = \sum_{j=1}^{k} p(N=j) N(\bar{x}_i | \bar{\mu}_j, \Sigma_j) = \sum_{j=1}^{k} w_j N(\bar{x}_i | \bar{\mu}_j, \Sigma_j)$$

In other words, the data-generating process is approximated by the weighted sum of multivariate Gaussian distributions. The probability density function of such a distribution is as follows:

$$N(\bar{x}_i; \bar{\mu}_j, \Sigma_j) = \frac{1}{\sqrt{2\pi \det \Sigma_j}} e^{-\frac{1}{2}(\bar{x}_i - \bar{\mu}_j)^T \Sigma_j^{-1} (\bar{x}_i - \bar{\mu}_j)}$$

The influence of each component of every multivariate Gaussian depends on the structure of the covariance matrix. The following diagram shows the three main possibilities for a bivariate Gaussian distribution (the results can easily be extended to n-dimensional spaces):

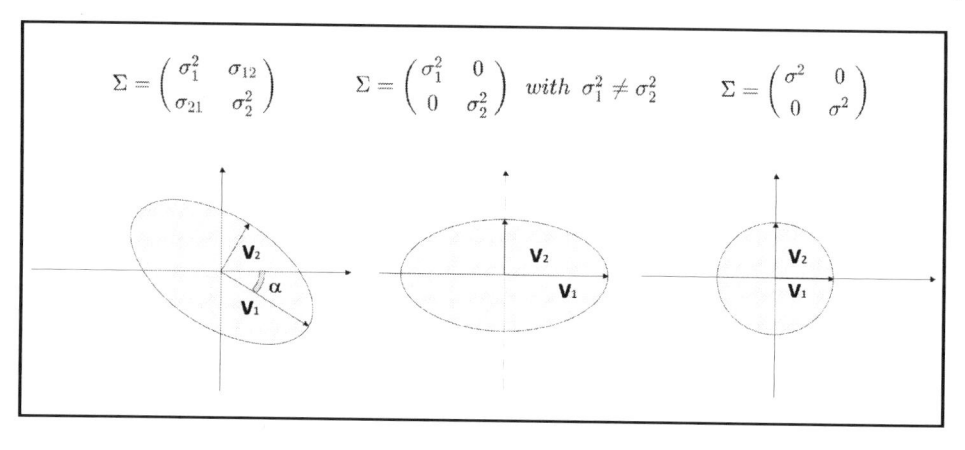

Full covariance matrix (left); diagonal covariance (center); circular/spherical covariance (right)

From now on, we will always be considering the case of full covariance matrices, which allow the achievement of maximum expressivity. It's easy to understand that when such distributions are completely symmetric (that is, the covariance matrices are circular/spherical), the shapes of the pseudo-clusters are the same as k-means (of course, in a Gaussian mixture, a cluster has no boundaries, but it's always possible to cut the Gaussian after a fixed number of standard deviations). Conversely, when the covariance matrices are not diagonal or with different variances, the influence is no longer symmetric (for example, in the case of bivariate, a component can show a larger variance than the other one). In both cases, Gaussian mixture allows us to compute actual probabilities, instead of measuring the distance between a sample, x_i, and a mean vector, μ_j, (as in k-means). An example of a univariate mixture is shown in the following diagram:

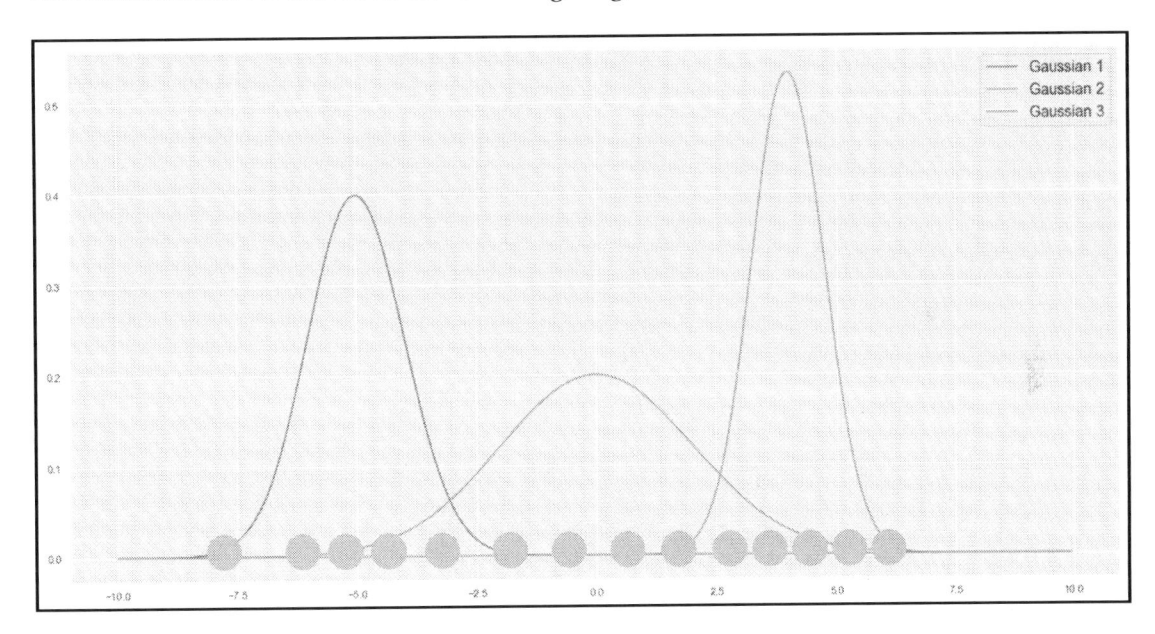

Example of a univariate Gaussian mixture

In this case, each sample always has a non-null probability under each Gaussian, whose influence is determined by its mean and covariance matrix. For example, the point corresponding to the *x*-position, 2.5, can belong to both the central Gaussian and to the right-hand one (while the left-hand one has minimum influence). As was explained at the beginning of the chapter, any soft clustering algorithm can be turned into a hard clustering one by selecting the component with the maximum influence (`argmax`).

You will immediately understand that, in this specific case and with diagonal covariance matrices, `argmax` provides an additional piece of information (which is completely discarded by k-means) that can be employed in further processing steps (that is, a recommender application can extract the main features of all clusters and reweight them, according to the relative probabilities).

EM algorithm for Gaussian mixtures

The complete algorithm (which is fully described in *Mastering Machine Learning Algorithms*, by Bonaccorso G., Packt Publishing, 2018) is a little more complex than k-means, and it requires deeper mathematical knowledge. As the scope of this book is more practical, we are only discussing the main steps, without providing formal evidence.

Let's start by considering a dataset, X, containing n samples:

$$X = \{\bar{x}_1, \bar{x}_2, \ldots, \bar{x}_n\} \text{ where } \bar{x}_i \in \mathbb{R}^m$$

Given k distributions, we need to find the weights, w_j, and the parameters of each Gaussian (μ_j, Σ_j), with the following condition:

$$\sum_{j=1}^{k} w_j = 1$$

This last condition is necessary to maintain consistency with the laws of probability. If we group all of the parameters into a single set, $\theta_j = (w_j, \mu_j, \Sigma_j)$, we can define the probability of sample x_i under the jth Gaussian, as follows:

$$p(\bar{x}_i, j | \theta_j)$$

In a similar way, we can introduce a Bernoulli distribution, $z_{ij} = p(j|x_i, \theta_j) \sim B(p)$, which is the probability that the jth Gaussian has generated sample x_i. In other words, given a sample, x_i, z_{ij} will be equal to 1, with the probability $p(j|x_i, \theta_j)$, and 0 otherwise.

At this point, we can compute the joint log-likelihood for the whole dataset, as follows:

$$L(\theta; X, Z) = \log \left(\prod_{i=1}^{n} \prod_{j=1}^{k} p(\bar{x}_i, j|\theta_j)^{z_{ij}} \right) = \sum_{i=1}^{n} \sum_{j=1}^{k} z_{ij} \log p(\bar{x}_i, j|\theta_j)$$

In the previous formula, we exploited the exponential-indicator notation, which relies on the fact that z_{ij} can only be 0 or 1. Hence, when $z_{ij} = 0$, it means that sample x_i has not been generated by the jth Gaussian, and the corresponding term in the product becomes 1 (that is, $x^0 = 1$). Conversely, when $z_{ij} = 1$, the term is equal to the joint probability of x_i and the jth Gaussian. Therefore, the joint log-likelihood is the joint probability that the whole dataset has been generated by the model, assuming that every $x_i \in X$ is **independent and identically distributed** (IID). The problem to solve is a **Maximum Likelihood Estimation** (MLE), or, in other words, finding the parameters that maximize $L(\theta; X, Z)$. However, the variables, z_{ij}, are not observed (or latent), so it's impossible to maximize the likelihood directly, because we don't know their values.

The most efficient way to address this problem is to employ the EM algorithm (proposed by Dempster, Laird, and Rubin in Dempster A. P., Laird N. M., and Rubin D. B., *Maximum Likelihood from Incomplete Data via the EM Algorithm, Journal of the Royal Statistical Society*, Series B. 39 (1), 1977). A full explanation is beyond the scope of this book, but we want to provide the main steps. The first thing to do is to employ the chain rule of probabilities, in order to transform the previous expression into a sum of conditional probabilities (which can easily be managed):

$$L(\theta; X, Z) = \sum_{i=1}^{n} \sum_{j=1}^{k} z_{ij} \log p(\bar{x}_i, j|\theta_j) = \sum_{i=1}^{n} \sum_{j=1}^{k} z_{ij} \log p(\bar{x}_i|j, \theta_j) + z_{ij} \log p(j|\theta_j)$$

The two probabilities are now straightforward. The term $p(x_i|j, \theta_j)$ is the probability of x_i under the jth Gaussian, while $p(j|\theta_j)$ is simply the probability of the jth Gaussian, which is equivalent to the weight, w_j. In order to get rid of latent variables, the EM algorithm proceeds in an iterative way, made up of two steps. The first one (called **Expectation step**, or **E-step**) is the computation of a proxy for the likelihood without the latent variables. If we indicate the whole set of parameters as θ, and the same set computed at iteration t as θ_t, we can compute the following function:

$$Q(\theta|\theta_t) = E_{Z|X,\theta_t}[L(\theta; X, Z)]$$

$Q(\theta|\theta_t)$ is the expected value of the joint log-likelihood, with respect to the variables, z_{ij}, and conditioned to the dataset, X, and the parameter set at the iteration, t. This operation has the effect of removing latent variables (which are summed, or integrated out) and yielding an approximation of the actual log-likelihood. As is easy to imagine, the second step (called **Maximization-step**, or **M-step**) has the goal of maximizing $Q(\theta|\theta_t)$, generating a new parameter set, θ_{t+1}. The procedure is repeated until the parameters become stable and it's possible to prove that the final parameter set corresponds to the MLE. Skipping all of the intermediate steps and assuming that the optimal parameter set is θ_f, the final results are as follows:

$$\bar{\mu}_j = \frac{\sum_{i=1}^n p(j|\bar{x}_i, \theta_f)\bar{x}_i}{\sum_{i=1}^n p(j|\bar{x}_i, \theta_f)} \qquad \Sigma_j = \frac{\sum_{i=1}^n p(j|\bar{x}_i, \theta_f)\left[(\bar{x}_i - \bar{\mu}_j)(\bar{x}_i - \bar{\mu}_j)^T\right]}{\sum_{i=1}^n p(j|\bar{x}_i, \theta_f)} \qquad w_j = \frac{p(j|\bar{x}_i, \theta_f)}{n}$$

For clarity, the probability, $p(j|x_i, \theta_f)$, can be computed by using Bayes' theorem:

$$p(j|\bar{x}_i, \theta_f) \propto w_j p(\bar{x}_i|j, \theta_f) \quad where \quad p(\bar{x}_i|j, \theta_f) = \frac{1}{\sqrt{2\pi \det \Sigma_{j_f}}} e^{-\frac{1}{2}(\bar{x}_i - \bar{\mu}_{j_f})^T \Sigma_{j_f}^{-1}(\bar{x}_i - \bar{\mu}_{j_f})}$$

The proportionality can be removed by normalizing all of the terms so that their sum is equal to 1 (meeting the requirements of a probability distribution).

Now, let's consider a practical example by using scikit-learn. As the goal is purely didactic, we have used a bidimensional dataset that can easily be visualized:

```
from sklearn.datasets import make_blobs

nb_samples = 300
nb_centers = 2

X, Y = make_blobs(n_samples=nb_samples, n_features=2, center_box=[-1, 1],
centers=nb_centers, cluster_std=[1.0, 0.6], random_state=1000)
```

The dataset has been generated by sampling from two Gaussian distributions with different standard deviations (1.0 and 0.6), and it is shown in the following screenshot:

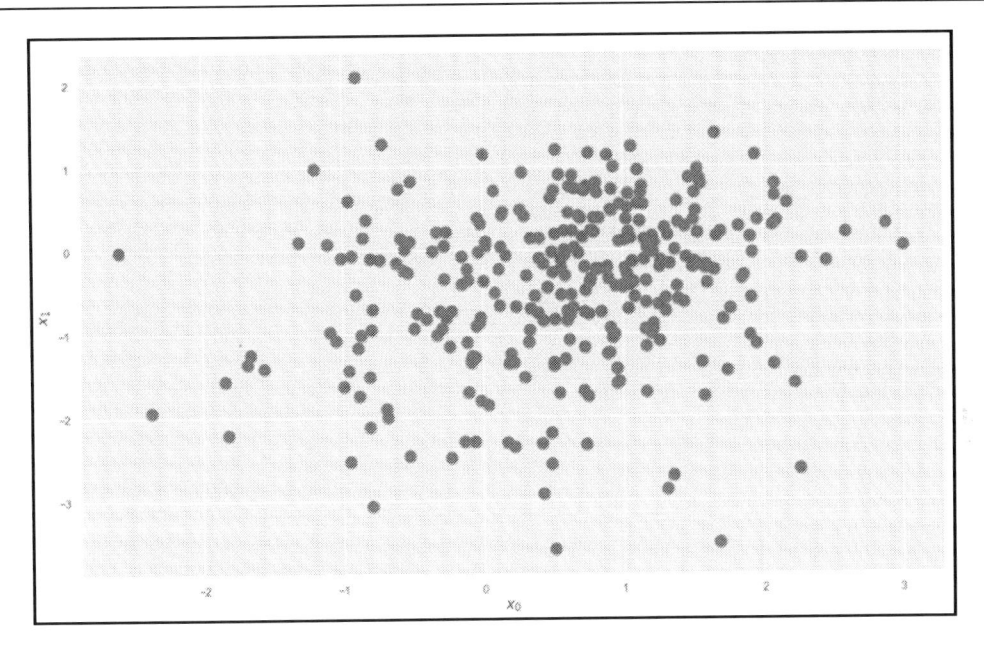

Dataset for the Gaussian mixture example

Our goal is to employ both a Gaussian mixture model and k-means, and compare the final results. As we expect two components, the approximation of the data-generating process is as follows:

$$p_{data}(\bar{x}) \approx w_1 N(\bar{x}; \bar{\mu}_1, \Sigma_1) + w_2 N(\bar{x}; \bar{\mu}_2, \Sigma_2)$$

We can now train a `GaussianMixture` instance with `n_components=2`. The default covariance type is a full one, but it's possible to change this option by setting the `covariance_type` parameter. The allowed values are `full`, `diag`, `spherical`, and `tied` (which forces the algorithm to use a shared single covariance matrix for all Gaussians):

```
from sklearn.mixture import GaussianMixture

gm = GaussianMixture(n_components=2, random_state=1000)
gm.fit(X)
Y_pred = gm.fit_predict(X)

print('Means: \n{}'.format(gm.means_))
print('Covariance matrices: \n{}'.format(gm.covariances_))
print('Weights: \n{}'.format(gm.weights_))
```

The output of the previous snippet is as follows:

```
Means:
[[-0.02171304 -1.03295837]
 [ 0.97121896 -0.01679101]]

Covariance matrices:
[[[ 0.86794212 -0.18290731]
  [-0.18290731  1.06858097]]

 [[ 0.44075382  0.02378036]
  [ 0.02378036  0.37802115]]]

Weights:
[0.39683899 0.60316101]
```

Hence, the MLE yielded two components, with a slightly dominant one (that is, $w_2 = 0.6$). In order to know the orientation of the axes of the Gaussians, we need to compute the normalized eigenvectors of the covariance matrices (this concept will be explained fully in Chapter 7, *Dimensionality Reduction and Component Analysis*):

```
import numpy as np

c1 = gm.covariances_[0]
c2 = gm.covariances_[1]

w1, v1 = np.linalg.eigh(c1)
w2, v2 = np.linalg.eigh(c2)

nv1 = v1 / np.linalg.norm(v1)
nv2 = v2 / np.linalg.norm(v2)

print('Eigenvalues 1: \n{}'.format(w1))
print('Eigenvectors 1: \n{}'.format(nv1))

print('Eigenvalues 2: \n{}'.format(w2))
print('Eigenvectors 2: \n{}'.format(nv2))
```

The output is as follows:

```
Eigenvalues 1:
[0.75964929 1.17687379]
Eigenvectors 1:
[[-0.608459   -0.36024664]
 [-0.36024664  0.608459  ]]

Eigenvalues 2:
[0.37002567 0.4487493 ]
Eigenvectors 2:
[[ 0.22534853 -0.6702373 ]
 [-0.6702373  -0.22534853]]
```

In both bivariate Gaussians (which, once truncated and observed from the top, can be imagined as ellipses), the major component is the second one (that is, the second column, corresponding to the largest eigenvalues). The eccentricities of the ellipses are determined by the ratio between the eigenvalues. If such a ratio is equal to 1, the shapes are circles, and the Gaussians are perfectly symmetric; otherwise, they are stretched along an axis. The angles (in degrees) between the major components and the x-axis are as follows:

```
import numpy as np

a1 = np.arccos(np.dot(nv1[:, 1], [1.0, 0.0]) / np.linalg.norm(nv1[:, 1])) * 180.0 / np.pi
a2 = np.arccos(np.dot(nv2[:, 1], [1.0, 0.0]) / np.linalg.norm(nv2[:, 1])) * 180.0 / np.pi
```

The previous formulas are based on the dot product between the major component, v_1, and the x-versor, e_0 (that is, $[1, 0]$):

$$\bar{v}_1 \cdot \bar{e}_0 = \|\bar{v}_1\| \|\bar{e}_0\| \cos \alpha_1 \Rightarrow \alpha_1 = \arccos \frac{\bar{v}_1 \cdot \bar{e}_0}{\|\bar{v}_1\| \|\bar{e}_0\|}$$

Before showing the final results, it will be helpful to cluster the dataset using k-means:

```
from sklearn.cluster import KMeans

km = KMeans(n_clusters=2, random_state=1000)
km.fit(X)
Y_pred_km = km.predict(X)
```

Soft Clustering and Gaussian Mixture Models

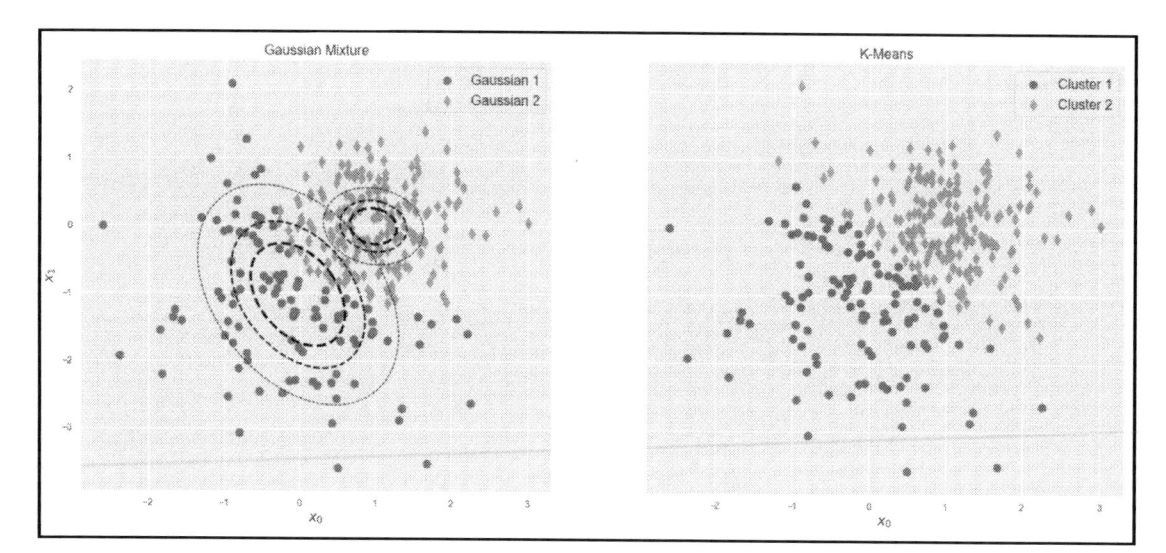

The clustering results are shown in the following screenshot:

Gaussian mixture result (left) with the shapes of three horizontal sections; k-means result (right)

As expected, both algorithms yield very similar results, and the main discrepancies are due to the non-symmetry of the Gaussians. In particular, the pseudo-cluster corresponding to the bottom-left part of the dataset has a larger variance in both directions, and the corresponding Gaussian is the dominant one. In order to check the behavior of the mixture, let's compute the probabilities of three sample points ((0, -2); (1, -1)—a borderline sample; and (1, 0)), using the `predict_proba()` method:

```
print('P([0, -2]=G1) = {:.3f} and P([0, -2]=G2) =
{:.3f}'.format(*list(gm.predict_proba([[0.0, -2.0]]).squeeze())))
print('P([1, -1]=G1) = {:.3f} and P([1, -1]=G2) =
{:.3f}'.format(*list(gm.predict_proba([[1.0, -1.0]]).squeeze())))
print('P([1, 0]=G1) = {:.3f} and P([1, 0]=G2) =
{:.3f}'.format(*list(gm.predict_proba([[1.0, 0.0]]).squeeze())))
```

The output of the previous block is as follows:

```
P([0, -2]=G1) = 0.987 and P([0, -2]=G2) = 0.013
P([1, -1]=G1) = 0.354 and P([1, -1]=G2) = 0.646
P([1, 0]=G1) = 0.068 and P([1, 0]=G2) = 0.932
```

I invite the reader to repeat the example by using the other covariance types, and to then compare all of the hard assignments with k-means.

Assessing the performance of a Gaussian mixture with AIC and BIC

As a Gaussian mixture is a probabilistic model, finding the optimal number of components requires an approach different from the methods analyzed in the previous chapters. One of the most widely used techniques is the **Akaike Information Criterion** (**AIC**), which is based on information theory (presented for the first time in Akaike H., *A new look at the statistical model identification, IEEE Transactions on Automatic Control*, 19 (6)). If a probabilistic model has n_p parameters (that is, single values that must be learned) and achieves the maximum negative log-likelihood, L_{opt}, the AIC is defined as follows:

$$AIC(n_p, L_{opt}) = 2n_p - 2L_{opt}$$

Such a method has two important implications. The first one is about the value itself; the smaller the AIC, the higher the score. In fact, considering Occam's razor principle, the goal of a model is to achieve the optimal likelihood with the smallest number of parameters. The second implication is strictly related to information theory (we are not discussing the details, which are mathematically-heavy), and, in particular, to the information loss between a data-generating process and a generic probabilistic model. It's possible to prove that the asymptotic minimization of the AIC (that is, when the number of samples tends toward infinity) is equivalent to the minimization of the information loss. Considering several Gaussian mixtures based on a different number of components (n_p is the sum of all weights, means, and covariance parameters), the configuration with the smallest AIC corresponds to the model that reproduces the data-generating process with the highest accuracy. The main limitation of AIC concerns small datasets. In such cases, AIC tends to reach its minimum for a large number of parameters, which is in contrast with Occam's razor principle. However, in the majority of real-life cases, AIC provides a helpful relative measure that can help data scientists to exclude many configurations and to only analyze the most promising ones.

When it's necessary to force the number of parameters to remain quite low, it's possible to employ the **Bayesian Information Criterion** (**BIC**), which is defined as follows:

$$BIC(n, n_p, L_{opt}) = log(n)n_p - 2L_{opt}$$

In the previous formula, *n* is the number of samples (for example, for *n = 1000* and using the natural logarithm, the penalty is about 6.9); hence, the BIC is almost equivalent to the AIC, with a stronger penalty for the number of parameters. However, even if the BIC tends to select smaller models, the results are generally less reliable than the AIC. The main advantage of the BIC is that when $n \to \infty$, the Kullback-Leibler divergence between the data-generating process, p_{data}, and the model, p_m (with the smallest BIC), tends to be 0:

$$D_{KL}(p_m \| p_{data}) = \sum_{i=1}^{n} p_m(\bar{x}_i) \log \frac{p_m(\bar{x}_i)}{p_{data}(\bar{x}_i)} \to 0 \Rightarrow p_m(\bar{x}) \to p_{data}(\bar{x})$$

As the Kullback-Leibler divergence is null when two distributions are identical, the previous condition implies that the BIC tends to select, asymptotically, the model that reproduces exactly the data-generating process.

Now, let's consider the previous example, checking both AIC and BIC for a different number of components. Scikit-learn incorporates these measures as methods (`aic()` and `bic()`) of the `GaussianMixture` class. Moreover, we also want to compute the final log-likelihood achieved by each model. This can be achieved by multiplying the value obtained through the `score()` method (which is the average per-sample log-likelihood, times the number of samples), as follows:

```
from sklearn.mixture import GaussianMixture

n_max_components = 20

aics = []
bics = []
log_likelihoods = []

for n in range(1, n_max_components + 1):
 gm = GaussianMixture(n_components=n, random_state=1000)
 gm.fit(X)
 aics.append(gm.aic(X))
 bics.append(gm.bic(X))
 log_likelihoods.append(gm.score(X) * nb_samples)
```

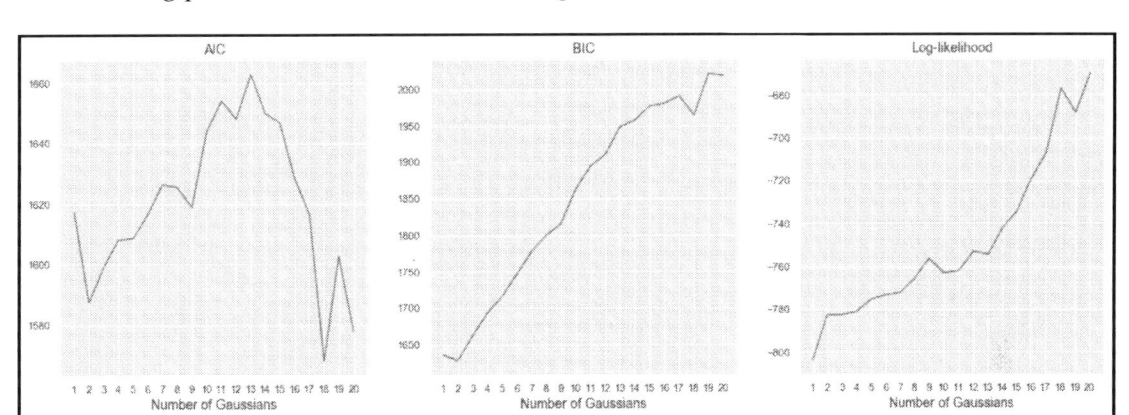

The resulting plots are shown in the following screenshot:

AICs, BICs, and log-likelihoods for Gaussian mixtures with the number of components in the range (1, 20)

In this case, we know that the dataset has been generated by two Gaussian distributions, but let's suppose that we do not have this piece of information. Both AIC and BIC have a (local) minimum of $n_c = 2$. However, while BIC keeps on getting larger and larger, AIC has its pseudo-global minimum of $n_c = 18$. Hence, if we trust the AIC, we should select 18 components, which is the equivalent of hyper-segmenting the dataset with many Gaussians, with a small variance. On the other hand, the difference between $n_c = 2$ and $n_c = 18$ is not very large when compared to the other values, so we can also prefer the former configuration, considering that it's much simpler. Such a choice is confirmed by the BIC. In fact, even if there's also a local minimum corresponding to $n_c = 18$, its value is quite a lot larger than the BIC achieved for $n_c = 2$. As we explained before, this behavior is due to the sample-size extra penalty imposed by the BIC. As each bivariate Gaussian requires one variable for the weight, two variables for the mean, and four variables for the covariance matrix, for $n_c = 2$, we get $n_p = 2(1 + 2 + 4) = 14$, and for $n_c = 18$, we get $n_p = 18(1 + 2 + 4) = 126$. As there are 300 samples, the BIC is penalized with $log(300) \approx 5.7$, which leads to a BIC increase of about 350. As the log-likelihood increases when n_c becomes larger (because, in an extreme scenario, each point can be considered to be generated by a single Gaussian with null variance, equivalent to a Dirac's delta), the number of parameters plays a major role in the model selection process.

Without any extra penalty, a bigger model is very likely to be selected as the best choice, but in a clustering process, we also need to enforce the maximum separation principle, too. Such a condition is partially related to fewer components, and hence, the BIC should become the optimal method. In general, I suggest comparing both criteria, trying to find the n_c that corresponds to the maximum agreement between AIC and BIC. Moreover, basic background knowledge should be also taken into account, because many data-generating processes have well-defined behaviors, and it's possible to restrict the range of potential components by excluding all of those values that are not realistic. I invite the reader to repeat the previous example with $n_c = 18$, plotting all of the Gaussians and comparing the probabilities of some specific points.

Component selection using Bayesian Gaussian mixture

A Bayesian Gaussian mixture model is an extension of a standard Gaussian mixture based on variational framework. This topic is quite advanced, and it requires a thorough mathematical description, which is beyond the scope of this book (you can find it in Nasios N. and Bors A. G., *Variational Learning for Gaussian Mixture Models, IEEE Transactions On Systems, Man, and Cybernetics*, 36/ 4, 08/2006). However, before we discuss the main properties, it will be helpful to understand the main concepts and the differences. Let's suppose that we have a dataset, X, and a probabilistic model parameterized with the vector θ. In the previous sections, you saw that the probability, $p(X|\theta)$, is the likelihood, $L(\theta|X)$, and its maximization leads to a model that generates X with the largest probability. However, we are not imposing any constraints on the parameters, and their final values depend exclusively on X. If we introduce Bayes' theorem, we get the following:

$$p(\bar{\theta}|X) = \alpha p(X|\bar{\theta})p(\bar{\theta})$$

The left-hand side is the posterior probability of the parameters, given the dataset, and we know that it is proportional to the likelihood times the prior probability of the parameters. In a standard MLE, we only work with $p(X|\theta)$, but, of course, we could also include a piece of prior knowledge about θ (in terms of a probability distribution) and maximize $p(\theta|X)$ or a proportional proxy function. However, in general, $p(\theta|X)$ is intractable and the previous $p(\theta)$ is often very difficult to define, because there's not enough knowledge about the highly probable regions. For this reason, it's preferable to model the parameters as probability distributions parametrized with η (the set of all specific parameters, such as means, coefficients, and so on) and introduce a **variational posterior**, $q(\theta|X; \eta)$ that approximates the real distribution.

Such a tool is a key element of a technique called **Variational Bayesian Inference** (you can find further details in the aforementioned paper), which allows us to easily find the optimal parameters without the need to work with the actual $p(\theta|X)$. In particular, in a Gaussian mixture, there are three different sets of parameters, and each of them is modeled with an appropriate distribution. In this context, we prefer not to discuss the details of these choices, but it's useful to understand the rationale.

In the Bayesian framework, given a likelihood, $p(X|\theta)$, a probability density function, $p(\theta)$, belonging to the same family of the posterior, $p(\theta|X)$, is called the **conjugate prior**. In this case, the procedure is obviously simplified, because the effect of the likelihood is limited to the modification of the parameters of the previous. For this reason, as the likelihood is normal, in order to model the means, we can employ normal distribution (which is the conjugate prior with respect to the mean), and for the covariance matrices, we can use the Wishart distribution (which is the conjugate prior with respect to the inverse of the covariance matrix). In this discussion, it's not necessary to be familiar with all these distributions (except the normal distributions), but it's helpful to remember that they are conjugate priors, so, given an initial guess about the parameters, the role of the likelihood is to adjust them, in order to maximize their joint probability, given the dataset.

As the weights of the mixture are normalized so that their sum must always be equal to 1, and we want to auto-select only a subset of a larger number of components, we can use the Dirichlet distribution, which has the helpful property of being sparse. In other words, given a set of weights w_1, w_2, ..., and w_n, the Dirichlet distribution tends to keep the probability of the majority of the weights quite low, while a smaller subgroup of non-null weights determines the major contribution. An alternative is provided by the Dirichlet process, which is a particular stochastic process that generates probability distributions. In both cases, the goal is to tune up a single parameter (called a **weight concentration parameter**) that increases or decreases the probability of having sparse distributions (or, simply, the sparsity of a Dirichlet distribution).

Scikit-learn implements a Bayesian Gaussian mixture (through the `BayesianGaussianMixture` class) that can be based on both the Dirichlet process and the distribution. In this example, we are going to keep the default value (`process`) and check the behaviors of different concentration values (the `weight_concentration_prior` parameter). It's also possible to tune up the mean of the Gaussian for the means and the degrees of freedom of the Wishart for inverse covariances. However, without any specific prior knowledge, it is quite difficult to set these values (we are supposing that we do not know where the means are likely to be located or the structures of the covariance matrices), and hence, it's preferable to keep the values derived from the structure of the problem. Therefore, the means (Gaussian) will be equal to the mean of X (the displacement can be controlled with the `mean_precision_prior` parameter; a value < 1.0 tends to move the single means toward the mean of X, while larger values increase the displacement), and the number of degrees of freedom (Wishart) is set equal to the number of features (the dimensionality of X). In many cases, these parameters are automatically tuned by the learning process, and there's no need to change their initial values.

Instead, `weight_concentration_prior` can be tuned, in order to increase or decrease the number of active components (that is, whose weights are not close to zero or are much lower than the other ones).

In this example, we will generate 500 bidimensional samples, using 5 partially overlapped Gaussian distributions (in particular, 3 of them share a very large overlapping region):

```
from sklearn.datasets import make_blobs

nb_samples = 500
nb_centers = 5

X, Y = make_blobs(n_samples=nb_samples, n_features=2, center_box=[-5, 5],
                  centers=nb_centers, random_state=1000)
```

Let's start with a large weight concentration parameter (1000) and the maximum number of components equal to 5. In this case, we expect to find a large number (possibly 5) of active components, because the Dirichlet process is not able to achieve a high level of sparsity:

```
from sklearn.mixture import BayesianGaussianMixture

gm = BayesianGaussianMixture(n_components=5, weight_concentration_prior=1000,
                             max_iter=10000, random_state=1000)
gm.fit(X)

print('Weights: {}'.format(gm.weights_))
```

The output of the previous snippet is as follows:

```
Weights: [0.19483693 0.20173229 0.19828598 0.19711226 0.20803253]
```

As expected, all of the components have approximately the same weight. In order to get further confirmation, we can check how many samples are hardly assigned (through the `argmax` function) to each of them, as follows:

```
Y_pred = gm.fit_predict(X)

print((Y_pred == 0).sum())
print((Y_pred == 1).sum())
print((Y_pred == 2).sum())
print((Y_pred == 3).sum())
print((Y_pred == 4).sum())
```

The output is as follows:

```
96
102
97
98
107
```

Soft Clustering and Gaussian Mixture Models

Therefore, on average, all of the Gaussians are generating the same number of points. The final configuration is shown in the following screenshot:

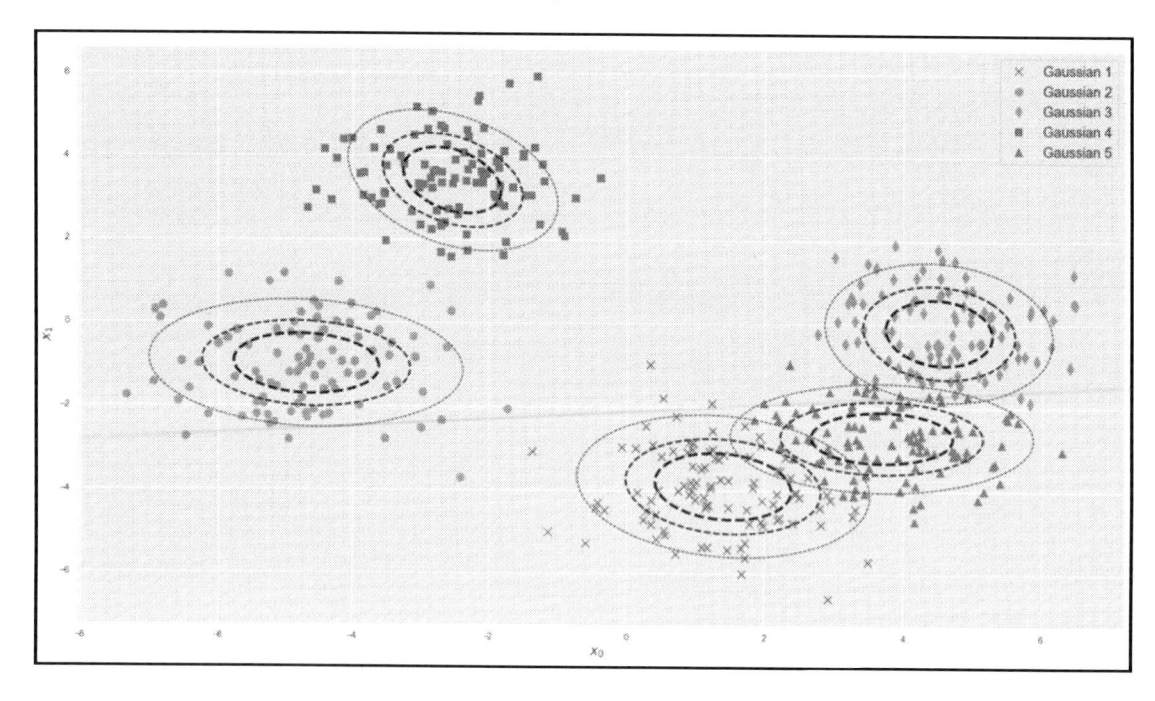

Final configuration, with five active components

This model is generally acceptable; however, let's suppose we know that the number of underlying causes (that is, the generating Gaussian distributions) is likely to be 4, instead of 5. The first thing that we can try is to keep the original maximum number of components and reduce the weight concentration parameter (that is, 0.1). If the approximation can successfully generate X using fewer Gaussian distributions, we should find a null weight:

```
gm = BayesianGaussianMixture(n_components=5,
weight_concentration_prior=0.1,
                              max_iter=10000, random_state=1000)

gm.fit(X)

print('Weights: {}'.format(gm.weights_))
```

The output is now as follows:

```
Weights: [3.07496936e-01 2.02264778e-01 2.94642240e-01 1.95417680e-01
 1.78366038e-04]
```

As is possible to see, the fifth Gaussian has a weight much smaller than the other ones, and it can be completely discarded (I invite you to check whether a few samples have been hardly assigned to it). The new configuration, with four active components, is shown in the following screenshot:

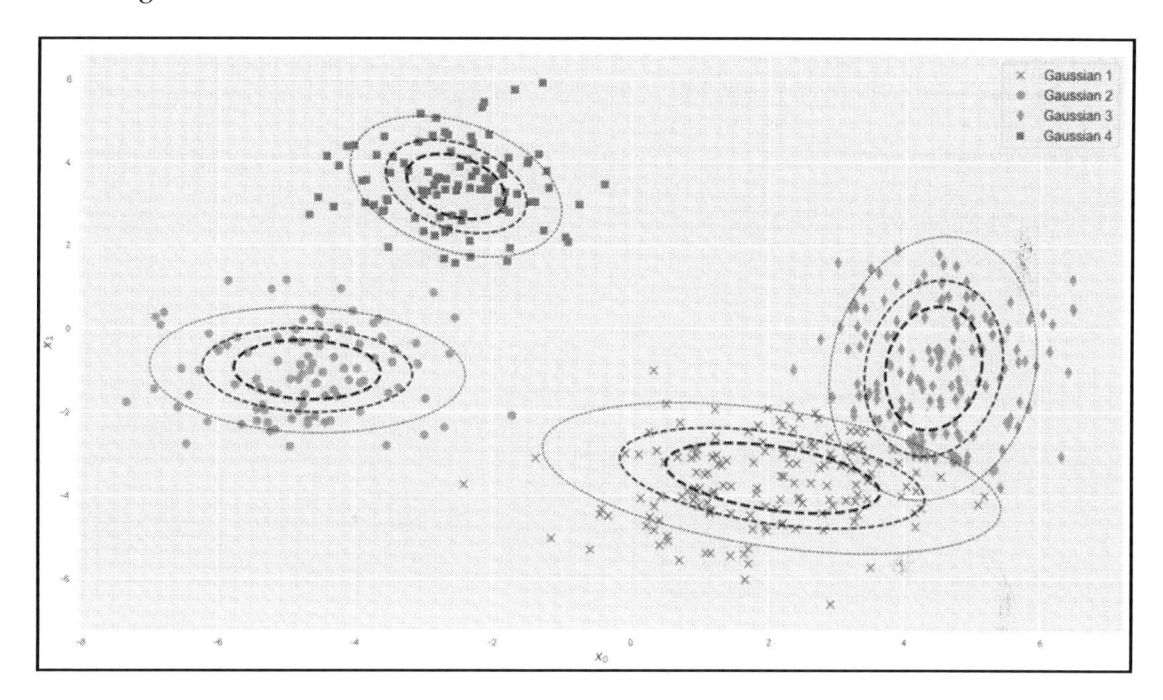

Final configuration, with four active components

As is possible to see, the model has performed the automatic selection of the number of components, and it has split the larger right blob into two parts, which are almost orthogonal. This result remains unchanged, even if the model is trained with a larger number of initial components (for example, 10). As an exercise, I suggest repeating the example with other values, checking the difference between the weights. Bayesian Gaussian mixtures are very powerful because of their ability to avoid overfitting. In fact, while a standard Gaussian mixture will use all of the components by reducing their covariances, if necessary (so as to cover a dense area), these models exploit the properties of the Dirichlet process/distribution, in order to avoid the activation of too many components. For example, it's possible to have good insight into the potential data-generating process by checking the minimum number of components achievable by the model. Without any other prior knowledge, such a value is a good candidate for the final configuration, because a smaller number of components will yield a lower final likelihood, too. Of course, it's possible to use AIC/BIC together with this method, in order to have another form of confirmation. However, the main difference with a standard Gaussian mixture is the possibility of including prior information, coming from an expert (for example, the structure of the causes in terms of means and covariance). For this reason, I invite you to repeat the example by changing the value of `mean_precision_prior`. For example, it's possible to set the `mean_prior` parameter to a value different from the mean of X and adjust `mean_precision_prior`, so as to force the model to achieve a different segmentation based on some prior knowledge (that is, all of the samples in a region should be generated by a specific component).

Generative Gaussian mixture

A Gaussian mixture model is primarily a generative one. This means that the goal of the training process is to optimize the parameters, in order to maximize the likelihood that the model has generated the dataset. If the assumptions are correct and X has been sampled from a specific data-generating process, the final approximation must be able to generate all of the other potential samples. In other words, we are assuming that $x_i \in X$ is IDD, and $x_i \sim p_{data}$; hence, when the optimal approximation, $p \approx p_{data}$, has been found, all of the samples, x_j, whose probability under p is high are also very likely to be generated by p_{data}.

In this example, we want to employ a Gaussian mixture model in a semi-supervised scenario. This means that we have a dataset containing both labeled and unlabeled samples, and we want to exploit the labeled samples as ground truth and find out the optimal mixture that can generate the whole dataset. Such a condition is very common when it's very difficult and expensive to label a very large dataset. In order to overcome this problem, it's possible to label a uniformly sampled subset and train a generative model that is able to generate the remaining samples with the largest possible likelihood.

We are going to employ the updated formulas for weights, means, and covariance matrices that were discussed in the main section with a simple procedure, as follows:

- All of the labeled samples are considered ground truth; so, if there are k classes, we also need to define *k* components and assign each class to one of them. Hence, if x_i is a generic sample labeled with $y_i = \{1, 2, ..., k\}$, the corresponding probability vector will be $p(x_i) = (0, 0, ..., 1, 0, ..., 0)$, where the 1 corresponds to the Gaussian associated with the y_i class. In other words, we are trusting the labeled samples and forcing a single Gaussian to generate the subset with the same label.
- All of the unlabeled samples are treated in the standard way, and the probability vectors are determined by multiplying the weights by the probabilities under each Gaussian.

Let's start by generating a dataset containing 500 bidimensional samples (100 labeled, with the remaining ones unlabeled), with the true labels, 0 and 1, and an unlabeled mark equal to -1:

```
from sklearn.datasets import make_blobs

nb_samples = 500
nb_unlabeled = 400

X, Y = make_blobs(n_samples=nb_samples, n_features=2, centers=2,
cluster_std=1.5, random_state=100)

unlabeled_idx = np.random.choice(np.arange(0, nb_samples, 1),
replace=False, size=nb_unlabeled)
Y[unlabeled_idx] = -1
```

At this point, we can initialize the Gaussian parameters (the weights are chosen to be equal, and the covariance matrices must positive semidefinite. If a reader is not familiar with this concept, we can say that a symmetric square matrix $A \in \Re^{n \times n}$ is positive semi-definite if:

$$\bar{x}^T A \bar{x} \geqslant 0 \quad \forall \ \bar{x} \neq (0) \in \mathbb{R}^n$$

Moreover, all eigenvalues are non-negative and the eigenvectors generate an orthonormal basis (this concept will be very helpful when talking about PCA in Chapter 7, *Dimensionality Reduction and Component Analysis*).

Soft Clustering and Gaussian Mixture Models

If the covariance matrices are chosen randomly, in order to be positive semi-definite, it's necessary to multiply each of them by its transpose):

```
import numpy as np

m1 = np.array([-2.0, -2.5])
c1 = np.array([[1.0, 1.0],
               [1.0, 2.0]])
q1 = 0.5

m2 = np.array([1.0, 3.0])
c2 = np.array([[2.0, -1.0],
               [-1.0, 3.5]])
q2 = 0.5
```

The dataset and the initial Gaussians are shown in the following screenshot:

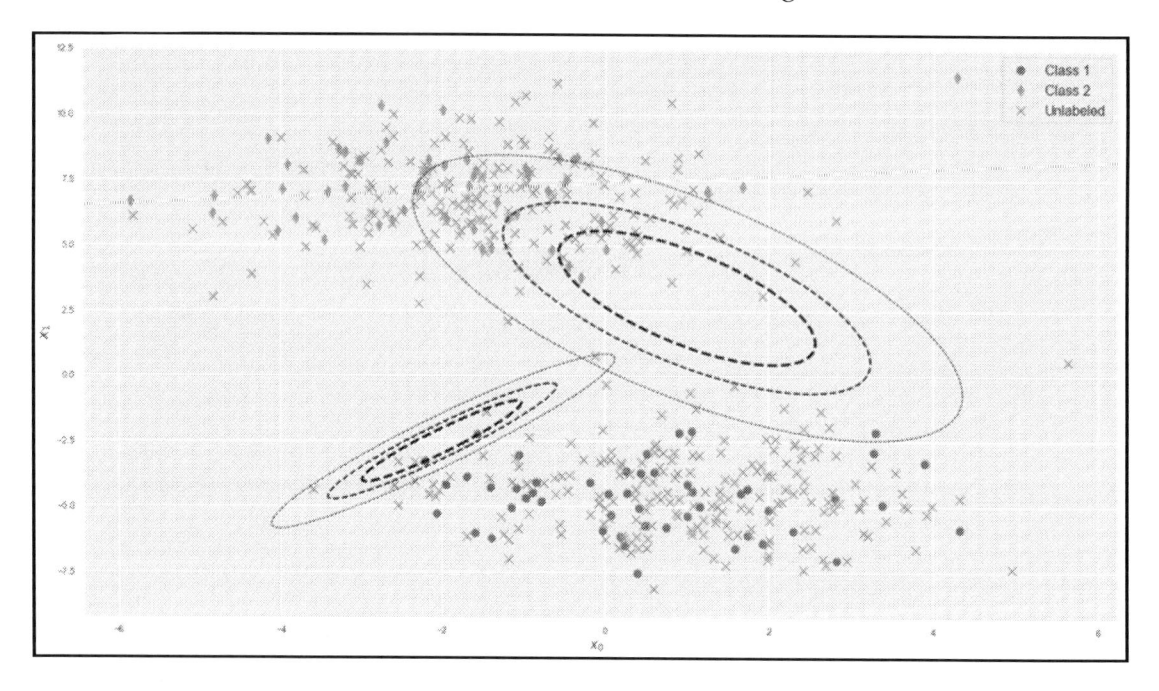

Dataset (the unlabeled samples are marked with an x) and initial configuration

Now, we can perform a few iterations (in our case, 10), following the rule that was previously defined (of course, it's also possible to check the stability of the parameters, in order to stop the iterations). The probabilities under each Gaussian are computed using the SciPy `multivariate_normal` class:

```
from scipy.stats import multivariate_normal

nb_iterations = 10

for i in range(nb_iterations):
    Pij = np.zeros((nb_samples, 2))
    for i in range(nb_samples):
        if Y[i] == -1:
            p1 = multivariate_normal.pdf(X[i], m1, c1, allow_singular=True) * q1
            p2 = multivariate_normal.pdf(X[i], m2, c2, allow_singular=True) * q2
            Pij[i] = [p1, p2] / (p1 + p2)
        else:
            Pij[i, :] = [1.0, 0.0] if Y[i] == 0 else [0.0, 1.0]

    n = np.sum(Pij, axis=0)
    m = np.sum(np.dot(Pij.T, X), axis=0)
    m1 = np.dot(Pij[:, 0], X) / n[0]
    m2 = np.dot(Pij[:, 1], X) / n[1]
    q1 = n[0] / float(nb_samples)
    q2 = n[1] / float(nb_samples)
    c1 = np.zeros((2, 2))
    c2 = np.zeros((2, 2))
    for t in range(nb_samples):
        c1 += Pij[t, 0] * np.outer(X[t] - m1, X[t] - m1)
        c2 += Pij[t, 1] * np.outer(X[t] - m2, X[t] - m2)
    c1 /= n[0]
    c2 /= n[1]
```

The Gaussian mixture parameters at the end of the process are as follows:

```
print('Gaussian 1:')
print(q1)
print(m1)
print(c1)

print('\nGaussian 2:')
print(q2)
print(m2)
print(c2)
```

Soft Clustering and Gaussian Mixture Models

The output of the previous snippet is as follows:

```
Gaussian 1:
0.4995415573662937
[ 0.93814626  -4.4946583 ]
[[ 2.53042319  -0.10952365]
 [-0.10952365   2.26275963]]

Gaussian 2:
0.5004584426337063
[-1.52501526   6.7917029 ]
[[ 2.46061144  -0.08267972]
 [-0.08267972   2.54805208]]
```

As expected, due to the symmetry of the dataset, the weights remained almost unchanged, while the means and covariance matrices were updated, in order to maximize the likelihood. The final plot is shown in the following screenshot:

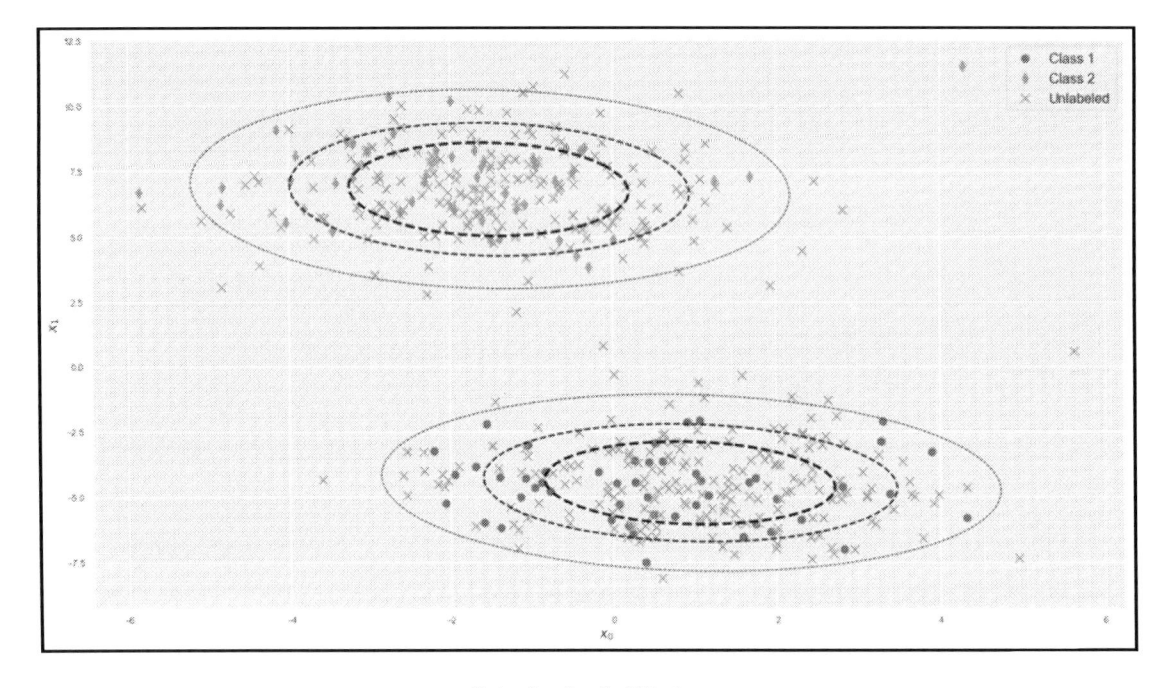

Final configuration, after 10 iterations

As is possible to see, both Gaussians have been successfully optimized, and they are able to generate the whole dataset, starting from a few labeled samples that play the role of **trusted guides**. Such a method is very powerful, because it allows us to include some prior knowledge in the model without any modification. However, as the labeled samples have a fixed probability equal to 1, this method is not extremely robust in terms of outliers. If a sample has not been generated by the data-generating process or is affected by noise, the model can be led to misplace the Gaussians. However, this case should normally be disregarded, because any prior knowledge, when included in the estimation, always has to be pre-evaluated, in order to check whether it's reliable. Such a step is necessary, to avoid the risk of forcing the model to learn only a part of the original data-generating process. Conversely, when the labeled samples are truly representative of the underlying process, their inclusion reduces the error and speeds up convergence. I invite the reader to repeat the example after introducing some noisy points (for example, (-20, -10)), and to compare the probabilities of a few unlabeled test samples.

Summary

In this chapter, we presented some of the most common soft clustering approaches, focusing on their properties and features. Fuzzy c-means is an extension of the classic k-means algorithm, based on the concept of a fuzzy set. A cluster is not considered a mutually exclusive partition, but rather a flexible set that can overlap some of the other clusters. All of the samples are always assigned to all of the clusters, but a weight vector determines the membership level with respect to each of them. Contiguous clusters can define partially overlapped properties; hence, a given sample can have a not-null weight for two or more clusters. The magnitude determines how much it belongs to every segment.

Gaussian mixture is a generative process that is based on the assumption that it's possible to approximate a real data-generating process with a weighted sum of Gaussian distributions. The model is trained, in order to maximize the likelihood, given a predefined number of components. We discussed how to use AIC and BIC as performance measures, in order to find out the optimal number of Gaussian distributions. We also briefly introduced the concept of Bayesian Gaussian mixture, and we looked at how the inclusion of prior knowledge can help in auto-selecting a small subset of active components. In the last part, we discussed the concept of semi-supervised Gaussian mixture, showing how it's possible to use some labeled samples as guides, in order to optimize the training process with a larger number of unlabeled points.

In the next chapter, we will discuss the concept of kernel density estimation and its applications in the field of anomaly detection.

Questions

1. What's the main difference between soft and hard clustering?
2. Fuzzy c-means can easily deal with non-convex clusters. Is this statement correct?
3. Which is the main assumption of a Gaussian mixture?
4. Suppose that two models achieve the same optimal log-likelihood; however, the first one has an AIC that is double the second one. What does this mean?
5. Considering the previous question, which model would we prefer?
6. Why would we want to employ the Dirichlet distribution as the prior for the weights of a Bayesian Gaussian mixture?
7. Suppose that we have a dataset containing 1,000 labeled samples, whose values have been certified by an expert. We collect 5,000 samples from the same sources, but we don't want to pay for extra labeling. What can we do in order to incorporate them into our model?

Further reading

- *Theoretical Neuroscience, Dayan P., Abbott L. F., The MIT Press, 2005*
- *Maximum Likelihood from Incomplete Data via the EM Algorithm, Journal of the Royal Statistical Society, Dempster A. P., Laird N. M., and Rubin D. B., Series B. 39 (1), 1977*
- *A new look at the statistical model identification, Akaike H., IEEE Transactions on Automatic Control, 19 (6)*
- *Variational Learning for Gaussian Mixture Models, Nasios N. and Bors A. G., IEEE Transactions on Systems, Man, and Cybernetics, 36/ 4, 08/2006*
- *Belohlavek R., Klir G. J. (edited by), Concepts and Fuzzy Logic, The MIT Press, 2011*
- *Chapelle O., Schölkopf B., and Zien A. (edited by), Semi-Supervised Learning, The MIT Press, 2010*
- *Mastering Machine Learning Algorithms, Bonaccorso G., Packt Publishing, 2018*
- *Machine Learning Algorithms, Second Edition, Bonaccorso G., Packt Publishing, 2018*

6
Anomaly Detection

In this chapter, we are going to discuss a practical application of unsupervised learning. Our goal is to train models that are either able to reproduce the probability density function of a specific data-generating process or to identify whether a given new sample is an inlier or an outlier. Generally speaking, we can say that the specific goal we want to pursue is finding anomalies, which are often samples that are very unlikely under the model (that is, given a probability distribution $p(x) \ll \lambda$ where λ is a predefined threshold) or quite far from the centroid of the main distribution.

In particular, the chapter will comprise of the following topics:

- A brief introduction to probability density functions and their basic properties
- Histograms and their limitations
- **Kernel density estimation (KDE)**
- Bandwidth selection criteria
- Univariate example of anomaly detection
- Examples of anomaly detection with HTTP attacks, using the KDD Cup 99 dataset
- One-class support vector machines
- Anomaly detection with Isolation Forests

Technical requirements

The code presented in this chapter requires:

- Python 3.5+ (Anaconda distribution (https://www.anaconda.com/distribution/) is highly recommended)
- Libraries:
    - SciPy 0.19+
    - NumPy 1.10+
    - scikit-learn 0.20+
    - pandas 0.22+
    - Matplotlib 2.0+
    - seaborn 0.9+

The examples are available on the GitHub repository at https://github.com/PacktPublishing/HandsOn-Unsupervised-Learning-with-Python/tree/master/Chapter06.

Probability density functions

In all previous chapters, we have always supposed that our datasets were drawn from an implicit data-generating process p_{data} and all the algorithms assumed $x_i \in X$ as **independent and identically distributed** (IID) and uniformly sampled. We were supposing that X represented p_{data} with enough accuracy so that an algorithm could learn to generalize with limited initial knowledge. In this chapter, instead, we are interested in directly modeling p_{data} without any specific restriction (for example, a Gaussian mixture model achieves this goal by imposing a constraint on the structure of the distributions). Before discussing some very powerful approaches, it's helpful to briefly recap the properties of a generic continuous probability density function $p(x)$ defined on a measurable subset $X \subseteq \Re n$ (to avoid confusion, we are going to indicate the density function with $p(x)$ and the actual probability with $P(x)$):

$$\int_X p(x)dx = 1 \quad and \quad P(x \in C) = \int_{C \subseteq X} p(x)dx$$

For example, a univariate Gaussian distribution is fully characterized by mean μ and variance σ^2:

$$p(x) = \frac{1}{\sqrt{2\pi\sigma^2}} e^{-\frac{(x-\mu)^2}{2\sigma^2}}$$

Hence, the probability that $x \in (a, b)$ is as follows:

$$P(a \leqslant x \leqslant b) = \int_a^b \frac{1}{\sqrt{2\pi\sigma^2}} e^{-\frac{(x-\mu)^2}{2\sigma^2}} dx$$

Even if the absolute probability of an event in a continuous space (for example, a Gaussian) is null (because the integral has the same extremes), the probability density function provides a very helpful measure of understanding how much a sample is more likely than another one. For example: considering a Gaussian distribution $N(0, 1)$, the density $p(1) = 0.4$, while it decreases to about 0.05 for $x = 2$. It means that 1 is $0.4 / 0.05 = 8$ times more likely than 2. In the same way, we can set an acceptance threshold α and define all the samples x_i whose $p(x_i) < \alpha$ as anomalies (for example, in our case, $\alpha = 0.01$). This choice is a crucial step in the anomaly detection process, and, as we are going to discuss, it must include also the potential outliers which, however, are still regular samples.

In many cases, the feature vectors are modeled with multi-dimensional random variables. For example: a dataset $X \subseteq \Re^3$ can be represented with a joint probability density function $p(x, y, z)$. In the general case, the actual probability requires a triple integral:

$$P(a \leqslant x \leqslant b, c \leqslant y \leqslant d, e \leqslant z \leqslant f) = \int_a^b \int_c^d \int_e^f p(x, y, z) dx dy dz$$

It's easy to understand that any algorithm using such a joint probability will be negatively impacted by the complexity. A strong simplification can be obtained by assuming the statistical independence of the single components:

$$p(x, y, z) = p(x)p(y)p(z)$$

The reader who is unfamiliar with this concept can imagine a population of students before an exam. The features modeled with random variables are hours of study (x) and the number of completed lessons (y) and we want to find out the probability of success given these factors $p(Success|x, y)$ (such an example is based on the conditional probability, but the main concept is always the same). We can suppose that a student that has completed all the lessons needs to study less at home; however, such a choice implies a dependence (and a correlation) between the two factors, which cannot be evaluated alone anymore. Conversely, we can decide to simplify the procedure by assuming the absence of any correlation and work with the marginal probabilities of success given the number of completed lessons and hours of homework. It's important to remember that the independence among features is different than the independence of samples subsequently drawn from a distribution. When we say that a dataset is made up of IID samples, we mean that the probability $p(x_i|x_{i-1}, x_{i-2}, ..., p_1) = p(x_i)$ for each sample. In words, we assume the absence of correlation among samples. Such a condition is easier to achieve because it's often enough to shuffle the dataset to remove any residual correlation. Instead, the correlation among features is a peculiar property of the data-generating process and cannot be removed. Therefore, in some cases, we assume the independence because we know that its effect is negligible and the final result is not heavily affected, while, in other cases, we are going to train models based on the whole multi-dimensional feature vectors. We can now define the concept of anomaly that will be employed in the remaining sections.

Anomalies as outliers or novelties

The main topic of this chapter is the automatic detection of anomalies without any supervision. As the models are not based on feedback provided by labeled samples, we can only rely on the properties of the whole dataset to find out the similarities and highlight the dissimilarities. In particular, we start from a very simple but effective assumption: common events are *normal*, while unlikely events are generally treated as **anomalies**. Of course, this definition implies that the process we are monitoring is working properly and the majority of outcomes are considered as valid. For example: a silicon-processing factory has to cut a wafer into equal chunks. We know that each of them is 0.2 × 0.2 inches (about 0.5 × 0.5 cm) with a standard deviation of 0.001 in for each side. This measure has been determined after 1,000,000 processing steps. Are we authorized to consider a 0.25 × 0.25 inches chip as an anomaly? Of course, we are. In fact, let's suppose that the length of each side is modeled as a Gaussian distribution (a very reasonable choice) with $\mu = 0.2$ and $\sigma = 0.001$; after three standard deviations, the probability drops to almost zero. Hence, for example: $P(side > 0.23) \approx 0$ and a chip with such dimensions must clearly be considered as an anomaly.

Obviously, this is an extremely easy example that doesn't need any model. However, in real-life cases, the structure of the densities can be very complex, with several high-probability regions surrounded by low-probability ones. That's why more generic approaches must be employed to model the whole sample space.

Of course, the semantics of anomalies cannot be standardized, and it always depends on the specific problem that is being analyzed. For this reason, a common way to define the concept of anomalies is to make a distinction between **outliers** and **novelties**. The former are samples included in the dataset, even if the distance between them and the other samples is larger than the average. Therefore, an **outlier detection** process is aimed at finding out such *strange* samples (for example: considering the previous example, a 0.25 × 0.25 inches chip is clearly an outlier if included in the dataset). Instead, the goal of **novelty detection** is slightly different, because, in this case, we assume to work with a dataset containing only *normal* samples; hence, given a new one, we are interested in understanding whether we can consider it as drawn from the original data-generating process or as an outlier (for example: a novice technician asks us this question: is a 0.25 × 0.25 inches chip an outlier? If we have collected a dataset of *normal* chips, we can use our model to answer the question.

Another way to describe such a scenario is by considering the samples as a series of values that can be affected by variable noise: $y(t) = x(t) + n(t)$. When $||n(t)|| \ll ||x(t)||$, the samples can be classified as *clean*: $y(t) \approx x(t)$. Conversely, when $||n(t)|| \approx ||x(t)||$ (or even greater), they are outliers, which cannot be representatives of the true underlying process p_{data}. As the average magnitude of the noise is normally quite smaller than the signal, the probability that $P(||n(t)|| \approx ||x(t)||)$ is close to zero. Therefore, we can imagine the anomalies as normal samples affected by an abnormal external noise. The real main difference between the management of an anomaly and a noisy sample is often about the ability to detect the true anomalies and to label the samples accordingly. In fact, while noisy signals are definitely corrupted and the goal is then to minimize the impact of the noise, anomalies can be very frequently identified by human beings and marked correctly. However, as already discussed, in this chapter, we are interested in finding out discovery methods that don't rely on existing labels. Moreover, to avoid confusion, we are always referring to anomalies, defining each time the content of the dataset (only inliers or inliers and outliers) and the goal of our analysis. In the next section, we will briefly discuss the expected structure of the datasets.

Structure of the dataset

In standard supervised (and often also unsupervised) tasks, the dataset is expected to be balanced. In other words, the number of samples belonging to each class should be almost the same. In the tasks we are going to discuss in this chapter, instead, we assume to have very unbalanced datasets X (containing N samples):

- $N_{outliers} \ll N$, if there is an outlier detection (that is, the dataset is partially *dirt;*, therefore, we need to find out a way to filter all outliers out)
- $N_{outliers} = 0$ (or, more realistically, $P(N_{outliers} > 0) \to 0$), if there is a novelty detection (that is, we can generally trust the existing samples and focus our attention on the new ones)

The reason for these criteria is quite obvious: let's consider the example previously discussed. If the anomaly rate observed after 1,000,000 processing steps is equal to 0.2%, there are 2,000 anomalies, which can be a reasonable value for a working process. If such a number is much larger, it means that there should be a more serious problem in the system, which is beyond the role of a data scientist. Therefore, in such cases, we expect a dataset containing a large number of correct samples and a very smaller number of anomalies (or even zero). In many cases, the rule of thumb is to reflect the underlying data-generating process, and, hence, if an expert can confirm, for example, to have 0.2% anomalies, the ratio should be *1000÷2* to find out a realistic probability density function. In such a case, in fact, it's more important to find out the factors that determine the distinguishability of the outliers. On the other side, if we are requested to perform only a novelty detection (for example: to distinguish between valid and malicious network requests), the dataset must be validated in order not to contain anomalies, but, at the same time, to reflect the true data-generating process responsible for all possible valid samples.

In fact, if the population of the correct samples is exhaustive, any large deviation from the high-probability region can be enough to trigger an alarm. Conversely, a limited region of the true data-generating process could drive to false positive results (that is, valid samples that haven't been included in the training set and are wrongly identified as outliers). In the worst case, a very noisy subset could also determine false negatives if the features are altered (that is, outliers that are wrongly identified as valid samples). In the majority of real-life cases, however, the most important factors are the number of samples and the context from where they are collected. It goes without saying that any model must be trained with the same kind of elements that are going to be tested. For example: if a measure inside a chemical plant is taken using a low precision instrument, tests collected with a high-precision one could be not representative of the population (while, of course, they are much more reliable than the dataset). Therefore, before performing an analysis, I strongly suggest double-checking the nature of the data, and also asking whether all the test samples have been drawn from the same data-generating process.

We can now introduce the concept of **histograms**, which is the easiest way to estimate the distribution of a dataset containing observations.

Histograms

The simplest way to find out an approximation of the probability density function is based on a frequency count. If we have a dataset X containing m samples $x_i \in \Re$ (for simplicity, we are considering only univariate distributions, but the process is exactly equivalent for multidimensional samples), we can define m and M as follows:

$$m = min(X) \text{ and } M = max(X)$$

The interval (m, M) can be split into a fixed number b of bins (which can have either the same or different widths denoted as $w(b_j)$ so that $n_p(b_j)$ corresponds to the number of samples included into the bin b_j. At this point, given a test sample x_t, it's easy to understand that the approximation of the probability can be easily obtained by detecting the bin containing x_t and using the following formula:

$$p(x) \approx \frac{1}{m} \frac{n_p(b_t)}{w(b_t)}$$

Before analyzing the pros and cons of this approach, let's consider a simple example based on the distribution of the ages of people subdivided into 10 different classes:

```
import numpy as np

nb_samples = [1000, 800, 500, 380, 280, 150, 120, 100, 50, 30]

ages = []

for n in nb_samples:
    i = np.random.uniform(10, 80, size=2)
    a = np.random.uniform(i[0], i[1], size=n).astype(np.int32)
    ages.append(a)
ages = np.concatenate(ages)
```

> The dataset can be reproduced only using the random seed `1000` (that is, setting `np.random.seed(1000)`).

Anomaly Detection

The `ages` array contains all the samples, and we want to create a histogram to have an initial insight into the distribution. We are going to employ the NumPy `np.histrogram()` function, which provides all the necessary tools. The first problem to solve is finding out the optimal number of bins. This can be easy for standard distributions, but it can become extremely hard when there is no prior knowledge about the probability density. The reason is straightforward: as we need to approximate a continuous function with a stepwise one, the width of the bins determines the final accuracy. For example: if the density is flat (for example: a uniform distribution), a few bins are enough to achieve a good result. Conversely, when there are peaks, it's helpful to place more (shorter) bins in the areas when the first derivative of the function is large and a smaller number when the derivative is close to zero (indicating a flat region). As we are going to discuss, this process becomes easier using more sophisticated techniques, while histograms are generally based on more rough computations of the optimal number of bins. In particular, NumPy allows setting the `bins='auto'` parameter, which forces the algorithm to auto-select the number according to a well-defined statistical method (based on the Freedman Diaconis Estimator and the Sturges formula):

$$n_{bins} = max\left(1 + log_2 m, \frac{2IQR}{\sqrt[3]{m}}\right)$$

In the preceding formula, **interquartile range (IQR)** corresponds to the difference between the 75th and 25th percentiles. As we don't have a clear idea about the distribution, we prefer to rely on the automatic selection, as shown in the following snippet:

```
import numpy as np

h, e = np.histogram(ages, bins='auto')

print('Histograms counts: {}'.format(h))
print('Bin edges: {}'.format(e))
```

The output of the previous snippet is as follows:

```
Histograms counts: [177   86  122  165  236  266  262  173  269  258  241  116  458  257
 311    1    1    5   6]
Bin edges: [16.         18.73684211 21.47368421 24.21052632 26.94736842
 29.68421053
 32.42105263 35.15789474 37.89473684 40.63157895 43.36842105 46.10526316
 48.84210526 51.57894737 54.31578947 57.05263158 59.78947368 62.52631579
 65.26315789 68.        ]
```

Therefore, the algorithm has defined 19 bins and it has output both the frequency counts and the edges (that is, the minimum value is `16`, while the maximum is `68`). We can now show a plot of the histogram:

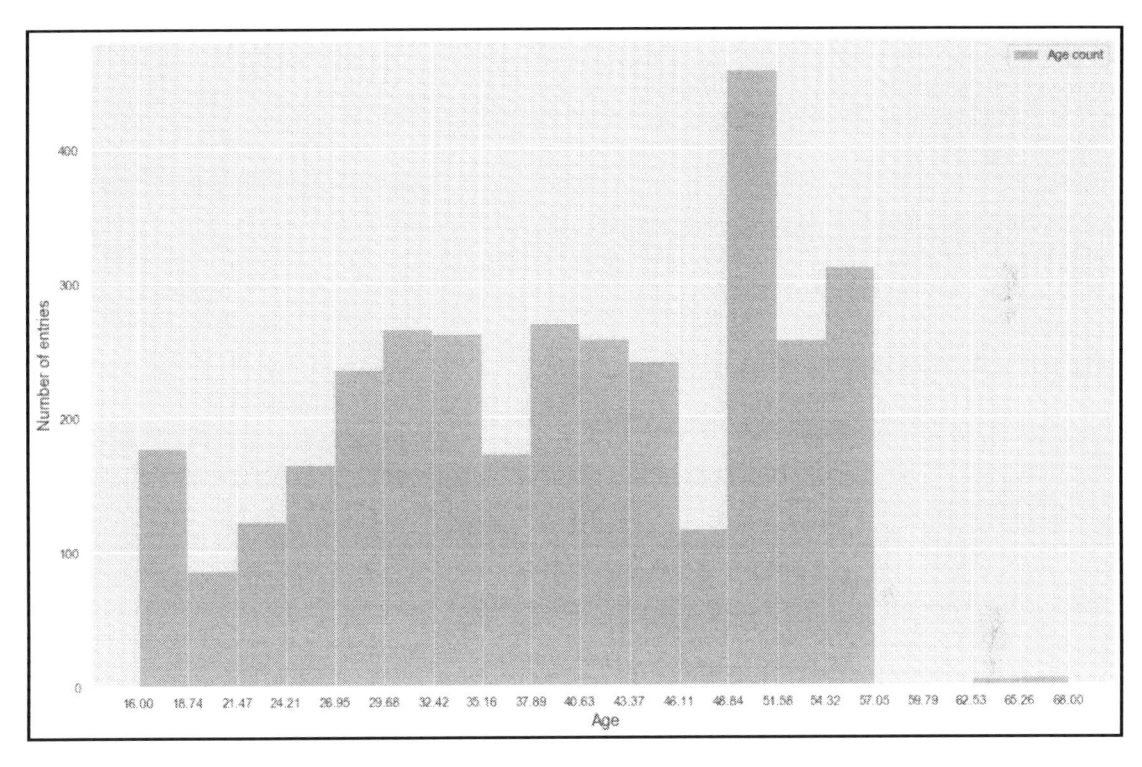

Histogram of the test distribution

The plot confirms that the distribution is quite irregular, and some regions have peaks surrounded by flatter areas. As explained before, a histogram is helpful when the queries are based on the probability of a sample to belong to a specific bin. In this case, for example, we could be interested in determining the probability that a person has an age between **48.84** and **51.58** (that corresponds to the 12th bin starting from **0**). As all the bins have the same width, we can simply approximate such a value with the ratio between $n_p(b_{12})$ (`h[12]`) and m (`ages.shape[0]`):

```
d = e[1] - e[0]
p50 = float(h[12]) / float(ages.shape[0])

print('P(48.84 < x < 51.58) = {:.2f} ({:.2f}%)'.format(p50, p50 * 100.0))
```

The output is as follows:

```
P(48.84 < x < 51.58) = 0.13 (13.43%)
```

Hence, the approximation of the probability is about 13.5%, which is also confirmed by the structure of the histogram. However, the reader should have clearly understood that such a method has clear limitations. The first and most obvious is about the number and the widths of the bins. A small number, in fact, yields rough results that can't take into account the fast oscillations. On the other hand, a very large number drives to a *holed* histogram, because most of the bins will have no samples. Therefore, a more solid approach is needed, considering all possible dynamics that van be encountered in real-life cases. This is what we are going to discuss in the next section.

Kernel density estimation (KDE)

The solution to the problem of the discontinuity of histograms can be effectively addressed with a simple method. Given a sample $x_i \in X$, it's possible to consider a hypervolume (normally a hypercube or a hypersphere), assuming that we are working with multivariate distributions, whose center is x_j. The extension of such a region is defined through a constant h called **bandwidth** (the name has been chosen to support the meaning of a limited area where the value is positive). However, instead of simply counting the number of samples belonging to the hypervolume, we now approximate this value using a smooth kernel function $K(x_j; h)$ with some important features:

$$K(\bar{x}; h) \text{ is positive with } K(\bar{x}; h) = K(-\bar{x}; h)$$

Moreover, for statistical and practical reasons, it's also necessary to enforce the following integral constraints (for simplicity, they are shown only for a univariate case, but the extension is straightforward):

$$\int_{-\infty}^{\infty} K(x; h)dx = 1, \quad \int_{-\infty}^{\infty} x^2 K(x; h)dx = 1, \quad \int_{-\infty}^{\infty} x^t K(x; h)dx < \infty \text{ if } t \in [0, \infty)$$

Before discussing the technique called **kernel density estimation** (KDE), it's helpful to show some common choices for $K(\bullet)$.

Gaussian kernel

This is one of the most employed kernels, whose structure is as follows:

$$K(\bar{x}; h) = \frac{1}{\sqrt[n]{2\pi h^2}} e^{-\frac{\bar{x}^T \bar{x}}{2h^2}}$$

The graphical representation is shown in the following screenshot:

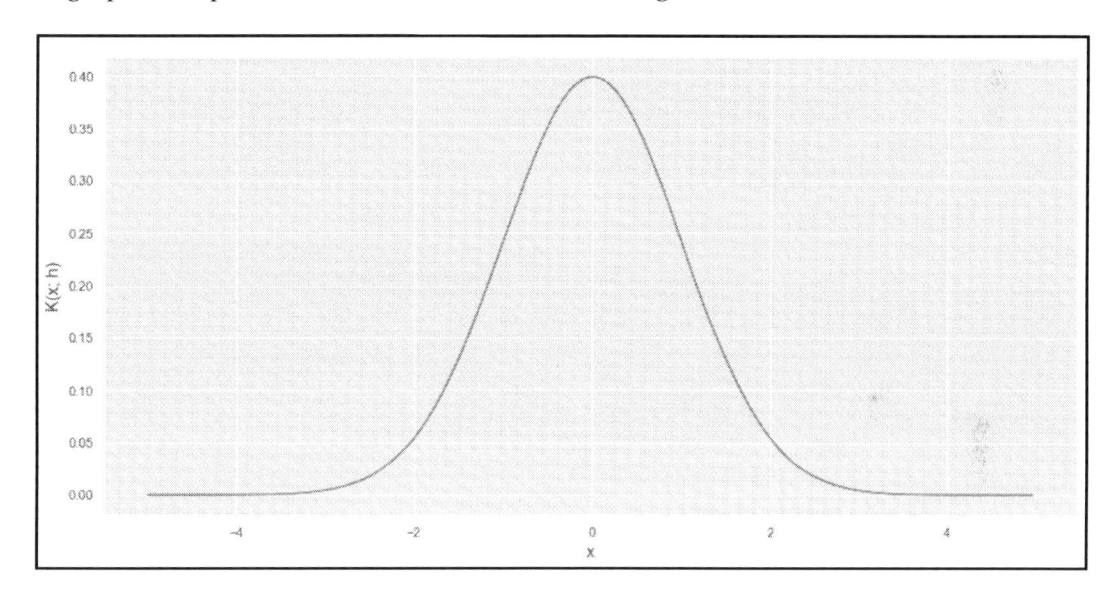

Gaussian kernel

Given its regularity, a Gaussian kernel is a common choice for many density estimation tasks. However, as the method doesn't allow the mixing of different kernels, the choice must consider all the properties. From statistics, we know that a Gaussian distribution can be considered as an average reference for the kurtosis (which is proportional to the peak and to the heaviness of the tails). To maximize the selectiveness of the kernel, we need to reduce the bandwidth. This means that even the smallest oscillations will alter the density and that the result is a very irregular estimation. On the other hand, when h is large (that is, the variance of the Gaussian), the approximation becomes very smooth and can lose the ability to capture all the peaks. For this reason, together with the selection of the most appropriate bandwidth, it's helpful to also consider other kernels that can naturally simplify the process.

Epanechnikov kernel

This kernel has been proposed to minimize the mean squared error, and it has also the property to be very regular (indeed, it can be imagined as inverted parabola). The formula is as follows:

$$K(x; h) = \epsilon\left(1 - \frac{x^2}{h^2}\right) \quad for \quad |x| < 1$$

The constant ϵ has been introduced to normalize the kernel and meet all requirements (in an analogous way, it's possible to extend the kernel in range (-h, h) so as to be more consistent with the other functions). A graphical representation is shown in the following screenshot:

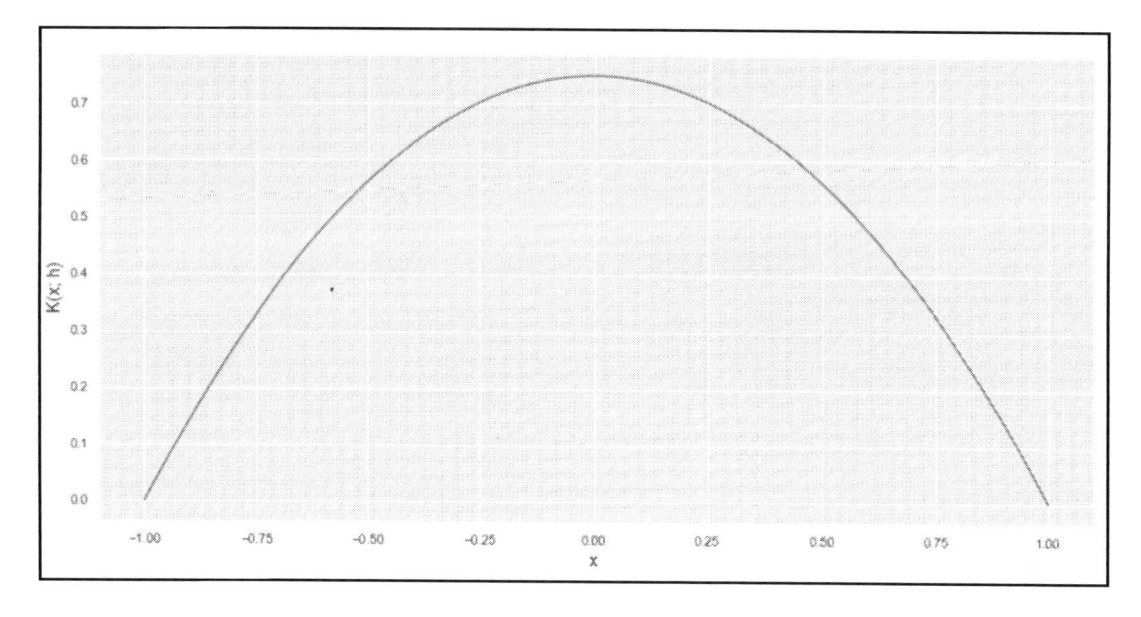

Epanechnikov kernel

The kernel can become very peaked when $h \to 0$. However, given its mathematical structure, it will always remain very regular; therefore, in the majority of cases, there's no need to use it as a replacement of the Gaussian kernel (even if the latter has a slightly larger mean square error). Moreover, as the function is discontinuous at $x = \pm h$ ($K(x; h) = 0$ for $|x| > h$), it can cause rapid drops in the density estimation, in particular at the boundaries, where, for example, a Gaussian function decreases very gently.

Exponential kernel

A very peaked kernel is the exponential one, whose generic expression is as follows:

$$K(x; h) = \epsilon e^{-\frac{|x|}{h}}$$

Contrary to the Gaussian one, this kernel has very heavy tails and a sharp peak. A plot is shown in the following screenshot:

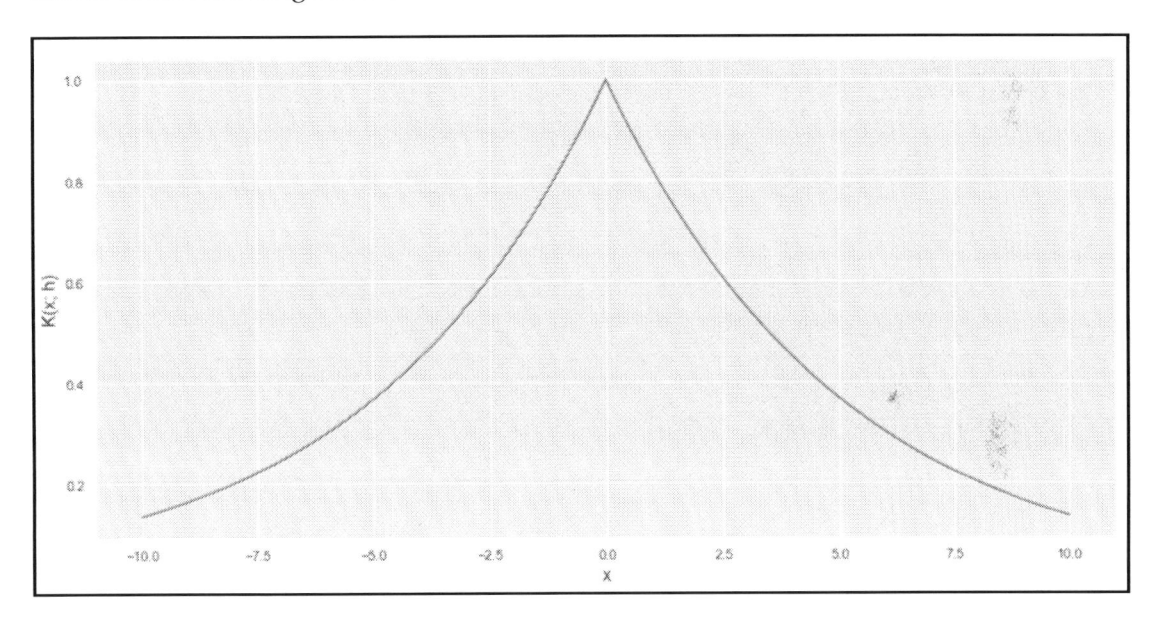

Exponential kernel

As it's possible to see, such a function is suitable to model very irregular distributions with a density highly concentrated around some specific points. On the other hand, the error can become very high when the data-generating process is quite regular with smooth surfaces. A good theoretical measure that can be employed to assess the performances of a kernel (and a bandwidth) is the **mean integrated square error (MISE)**, defined as follows:

$$MISE(K) = E\left[\int_{-\infty}^{\infty} (p_K(x) - p(x))^2 dx\right]$$

Anomaly Detection

In the previous formula, $p_K(x)$ is the estimated density, while $p(x)$ is the actual one. Unfortunately, $p(x)$ is unknown (otherwise, we don't need any estimation); therefore, such a method can only be used for theoretical evaluations (for example: the optimality of the Epanechnikov kernel). However, it's easy to understand that the MISE will be larger whenever the kernel is not able to stay close to the actual surface. As the exponential one jumps to a peak very abruptly, it can be suitable only in specific situations. In all the other cases, its behavior leads to larger MISEs, and other kernel are hence preferable.

Uniform (or Tophat) kernel

This is the simplest and less smooth kernel function, and its usage resembles the standard procedure of building a histogram. It is equal to the following:

$$K(x; h) = \frac{1}{2h} \quad for \quad |x| < h$$

Clearly, it is a step that is constant in the range delimited by the bandwidth, and it's helpful only when the estimation doesn't need to be smooth.

Estimating the density

Once a kernel function has been selected, it's possible to build a complete approximation of a probability density function using a k-nearest neighbors approach. In fact, given a dataset X (for simplicity, $X \in \Re^m$, so the values are real numbers), it's easy to create, for example, a ball-tree (as discussed in Chapter 2, *Clustering Fundamentals*) to partition the data in an efficient way. When the data structure is ready, it's possible to obtain all the neighbors of query point x_j inside a radius defined by the bandwidth. Let's assume that such a set is $X_j = \{x_1, ..., x_t\}$ and the number of points is N_j. The estimation of the probability density is obtained as follows:

$$p_K(x_j) = \frac{1}{N_j h} \sum_t K\left(\frac{x_j - x_t}{h}; h\right)$$

It's not difficult to prove that, if the bandwidth is chosen appropriately (as a function of the number of samples contained in the neighborhood), p_K converges in probability to the actual $p(x)$. In other words, if the granularity is large enough, the absolute error between the approximation and the true density converges to zero. The building process of $p_K(x_j)$ is shown in the following diagram:

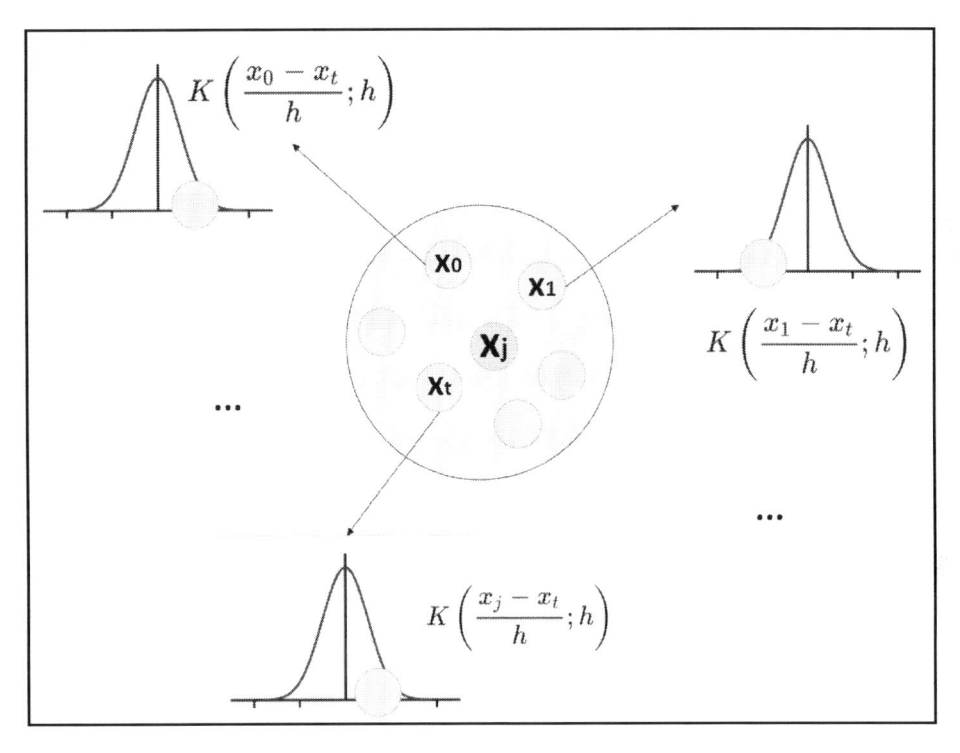

Density estimation of x_j. The Kernel functions are evaluated in each point belonging to the neighborhood of x_j

At this point, it's natural to ask why not to use the entire dataset for each query instead of a k-NN approach? The answer is very simple, and it's based on the assumptions that the value of the density function computed at x_j can be easily interpolated using the local behavior (that is, for a multivariate distribution, a ball centered in x_j) and the *far points* have no influence on the estimation. Therefore, we can limit the computation to a smaller subset of X, avoiding including contributions that are close to zero.

Anomaly Detection

Before discussing how to determine the optimal bandwidth, let's show the density estimation (using scikit-learn) for the previously defined dataset. As we don't have any specific prior knowledge, we are going to employ a Gaussian kernel with different bandwidths (0.1, 0.5, and 1.5). All the other parameters are kept to their default values; however, the `KernelDensity` class allows setting the metric (default is `metric='euclidean'`), the data structure (default is `algorithm='auto'`, which performs an auto-selection between ball-tree and kd-tree according to the dimensionality), and both the absolute and relative tolerances (respectively, 0 and 10^{-8}). In many cases, it's not necessary to change the default values; however, for very large datasets with specific features, it can be helpful, for example, to change the `leaf_size` parameter to improve the performances (as discussed in Chapter 2, *Clustering Fundamentals*). Moreover, the default metric cannot be adequate for all tasks (for example: the standard documentation shows an example based on the Haversine distance, which can be employed when working with latitude and longitude). Other cases are the ones where, instead of balls, it's preferable to work with hypercubes (this is the case with the Manhattan distance).

Let's start by instantiating the classes and fitting the models:

```
from sklearn.neighbors import KernelDensity

kd_01 = KernelDensity(kernel='gaussian', bandwidth=0.1)
kd_05 = KernelDensity(kernel='gaussian', bandwidth=0.5)
kd_15 = KernelDensity(kernel='gaussian', bandwidth=1.5)

kd_01.fit(ages.reshape(-1, 1))
kd_05.fit(ages.reshape(-1, 1))
kd_15.fit(ages.reshape(-1, 1))
```

At this point, it's possible to invoke the `score_samples()` method to get the log-density estimation for a set of data points (in our case, we are considering the range (10, 70) with 0.05 increments). As the values are $log(p)$, it's necessary to compute $e^{log(p)}$ to get the actual probabilities.

Chapter 6

The resulting plots are shown in the following screenshot:

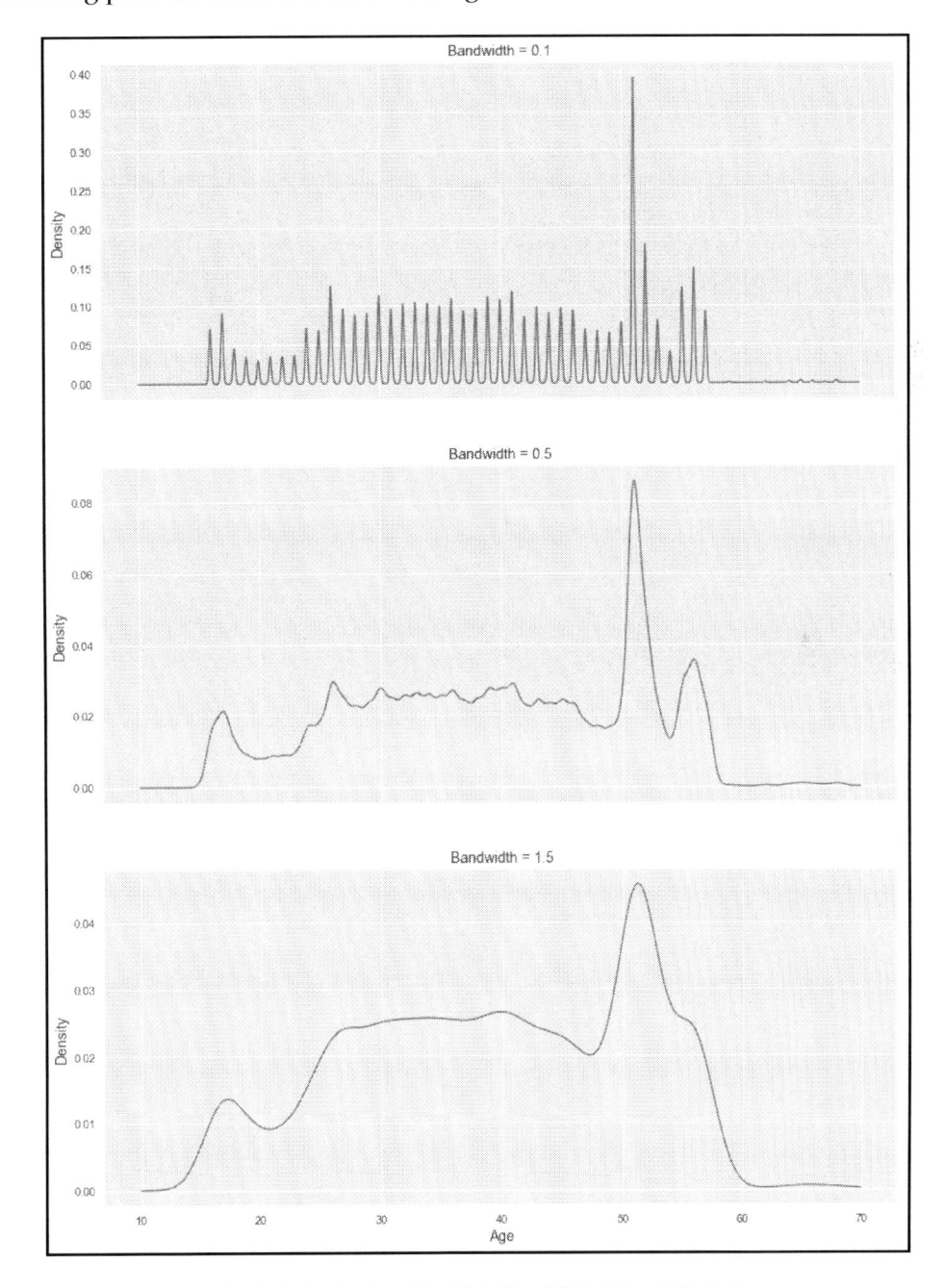

Gaussian density estimations with bandwidths: 0.1 (top), 0.5 (middle), and 1.5 (bottom)

Anomaly Detection

As it's possible to notice, when the bandwidth is very small (0.1), the density has strong oscillations due to the lack of samples for specific sub-ranges. When $h = 0.5$, the contour (as the dataset is univariate) becomes more stable, but there are still some residual fast-variations induced by the internal variance of the neighbors. Such behavior is almost completely removed when h becomes larger (1.5, in our case). An obvious question is this: How is it possible to determine the most appropriate bandwidth? Of course, the most natural choice is the value of h that minimizes the MISE, but, as discussed, this method can only be employed when the true probability density is known. However, there are a couple of empiric criteria that have been confirmed to be very reliable. Given a complete dataset $X \in \Re^m$, the first one is based on the following formula:

$$h = 1.06 \cdot std(X) \cdot m^{-0.2}$$

In our case, we obtain the following:

```
import numpy as np

N = float(ages.shape[0])
h = 1.06 * np.std(ages) * np.power(N, -0.2)

print('h = {:.3f}'.format(h))
```

The output is as follows:

```
h = 2.415
```

Therefore, the suggestion is to increase the bandwidth even more than that in our last experiment. The second method is thus based on the inter-quartile range (IQR = Q3 - Q1 or, equivalently, 75th percentile - 25th percentile), and it's more robust to very strong internal variations:

$$h = 0.9 \cdot min\left(std(X), \frac{IQR}{1.34}\right) \cdot m^{-0.2}$$

The computation is as follows:

```
import numpy as np

IQR = np.percentile(ages, 75) - np.percentile(ages, 25)
h = 0.9 * np.min([np.std(ages), IQR / 1.34]) * np.power(N, -0.2)

print('h = {:.3f}'.format(h))
```

The output now is this:

```
h = 2.051
```

This value is rather smaller than the previous one, indicating that $p_K(x)$ can be more accurate with smaller hypervolumes. As a rule of thumb, I suggest selecting the method with the smallest bandwidth, even if the second one generally provides the best results in different contexts. Let's now re-perform the estimation, using $h = 2.0$ and the Gaussian, Epanechnikov, and Exponential kernels (we are excluding the uniform one because the final result is equivalent to a histogram):

```
from sklearn.neighbors import KernelDensity

kd_gaussian = KernelDensity(kernel='gaussian', bandwidth=2.0)
kd_epanechnikov = KernelDensity(kernel='epanechnikov', bandwidth=2.0)
kd_exponential = KernelDensity(kernel='exponential', bandwidth=2.0)

kd_gaussian.fit(ages.reshape(-1, 1))
kd_epanechnikov.fit(ages.reshape(-1, 1))
kd_exponential.fit(ages.reshape(-1, 1))
```

Anomaly Detection

The graphical output is shown in the following screenshot:

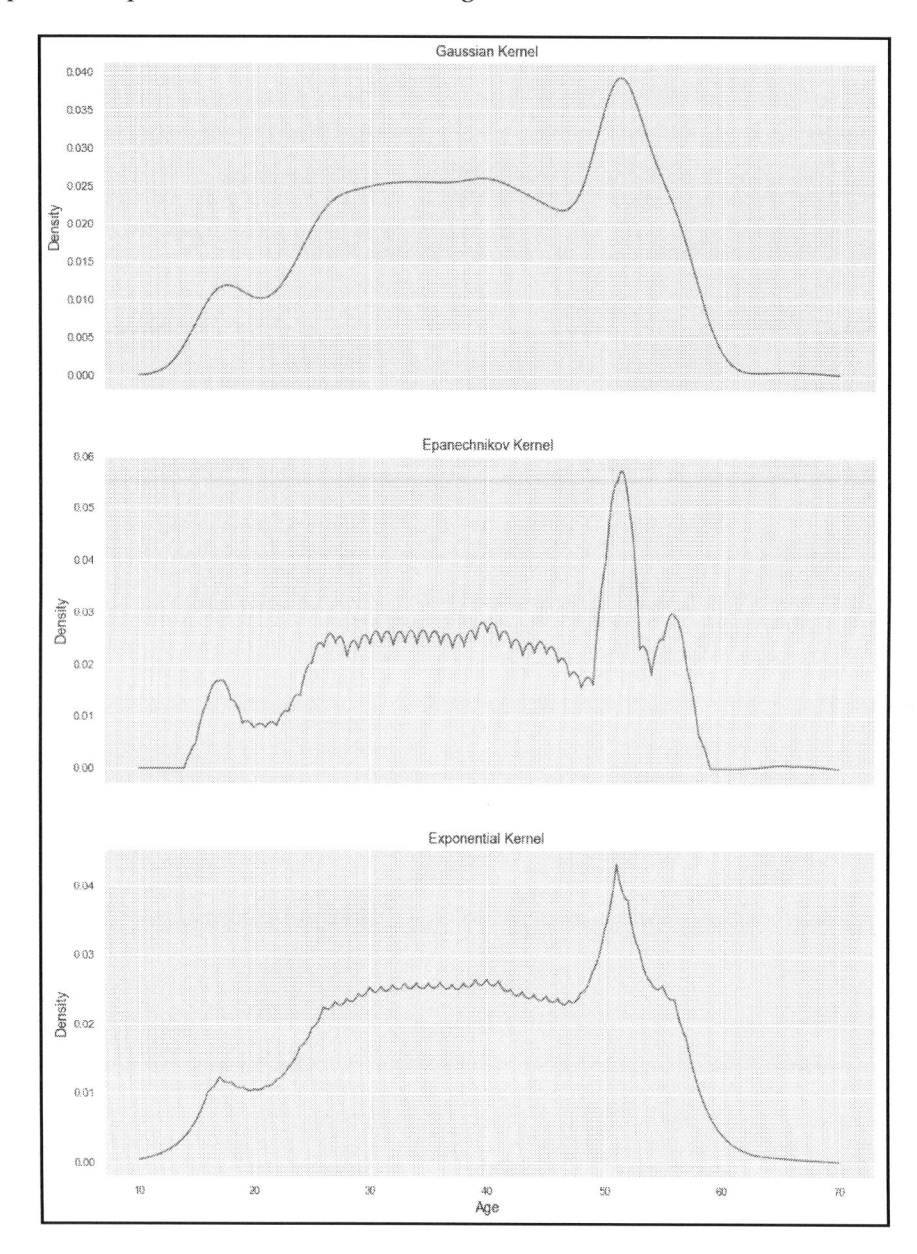

Density estimations with bandwidths equal to 2.0 and Gaussian kernel (top), Epanechnikov kernel (middle), and Exponential kernel (bottom)

As expected, both Epanechnikov and Exponential kernels are more oscillating than the Gaussian one (because they tend to be more peaked when h is small); however, it's evident that the central plot is surely the most accurate (in terms of MISE). A similar result has been previously achieved with a Gaussian kernel and $h = 0.5$, but, in that case, the oscillations were extremely irregular. As explained, the Epanechnikov kernel has a very strong discontinuous trend when the value reaches the boundaries of the bandwidth. This phenomenon can be immediately understood by looking at the extremes of the estimation, which drops almost vertically to zero. Conversely, the Gaussian estimation with $h = 2$ seems to be very smooth, and it doesn't capture the variation between 50 and 60 years. The same happens for the Exponential kernel, which also shows its peculiar behavior: very spiky extremes. In the following example, we are going to employ the Epanechnikov kernel; however, I invite the reader to check the results also for the Gaussian one with different bandwidths. This choice has a precise rationale (that cannot be discarded without a solid reason): we are considering the dataset as exhaustive, and we want to penalize all the samples that overcome the natural extremes. In all other scenarios, a very small residual probability can be preferred; however, such a choice must be made considering every specific goal.

Anomaly detection

Let's now apply the Epanechnikov density estimation to perform an example of anomaly detection. According to the structure of the probability density, we have decided to impose a cut-off at $p(x) < 0.005$. Such a condition is displayed in the following screenshot:

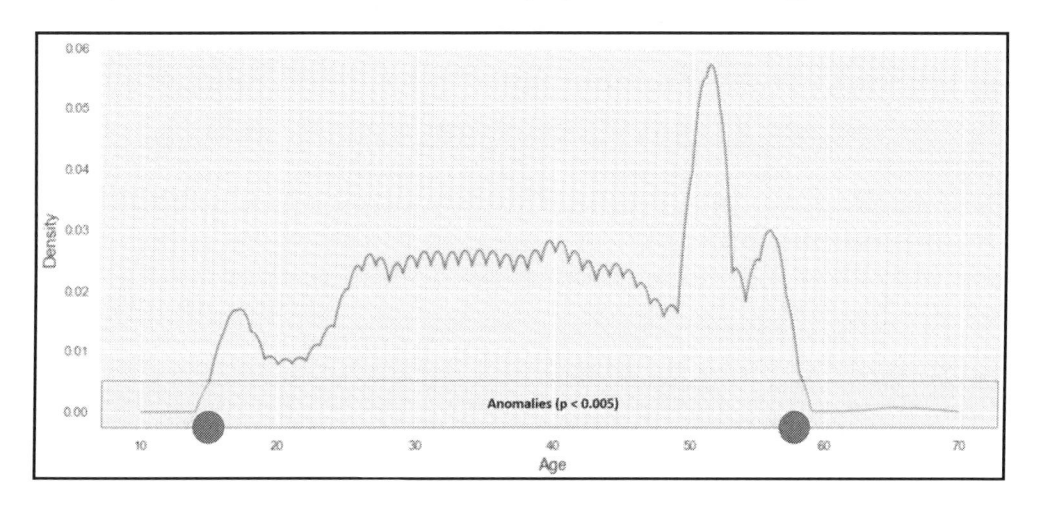

Epanechnikov density estimation with anomaly cut-off

Anomaly Detection

The red dots indicate the age limits for a sample to be classified as an anomaly. Let's compute the probability densities for some test points:

```
import numpy as np

test_data = np.array([12, 15, 18, 20, 25, 30, 40, 50, 55, 60, 65, 70, 75,
80, 85, 90]).reshape(-1, 1)

test_densities_epanechnikov =
np.exp(kd_epanechnikov.score_samples(test_data))
test_densities_gaussian = np.exp(kd_gaussian.score_samples(test_data))

for age, density in zip(np.squeeze(test_data),
test_densities_epanechnikov):
    print('p(Age = {:d}) = {:.7f} ({})'.format(age, density, 'Anomaly' if
density < 0.005 else 'Normal'))
```

The output of the previous snippet is this:

```
p(Age = 12) = 0.0000000 (Anomaly)
p(Age = 15) = 0.0049487 (Anomaly)
p(Age = 18) = 0.0131965 (Normal)
p(Age = 20) = 0.0078079 (Normal)
p(Age = 25) = 0.0202346 (Normal)
p(Age = 30) = 0.0238636 (Normal)
p(Age = 40) = 0.0262830 (Normal)
p(Age = 50) = 0.0396169 (Normal)
p(Age = 55) = 0.0249084 (Normal)
p(Age = 60) = 0.0000825 (Anomaly)
p(Age = 65) = 0.0006598 (Anomaly)
p(Age = 70) = 0.0000000 (Anomaly)
p(Age = 75) = 0.0000000 (Anomaly)
p(Age = 80) = 0.0000000 (Anomaly)
p(Age = 85) = 0.0000000 (Anomaly)
p(Age = 90) = 0.0000000 (Anomaly)
```

As it's possible to see, the abrupt drop of the function has created a sort of vertical separation. A person aged 15 is almost at the boundary ($p(15) \approx 0.0049$), while the behavior is even more drastic for the upper bound. The cut-off is about 58 years, but a sample aged 60 is about 10 times less likely than a one aged 57 (this is also confirmed by the initial histogram). As this is only a didactic example, it's very easy to detect the anomalies; however, even a slightly more complex distribution could create a few problems without a standardized algorithm. In particular, in this specific case, which is a simple univariate distribution, the anomalies are generally located in the tails.

Therefore, we are assuming that given the overall density estimation $p_K(x)$:

$$p_K(x_a) \leqslant p_K(x_n) \ \forall \ x_a \in Anomalies \subseteq X \ and \ x_n \in X$$

Such a behavior is not generally true when considering a dataset containing all the samples (both normal ones and anomalies), and the data scientist must be careful when deciding the thresholds. Even if it can be obvious, it's a good idea to learn the normal distribution by removing all anomalies from the dataset so as to flatten ($p_K(x) \to 0$) the regions where the anomalies are located. In this way, the previous criterion remains valid, and it's easy to compare different densities to make a distinction.

Before moving on to the next example, I suggest modifying the initial distribution by creating artificial holes and setting different thresholds for the detection. Moreover, I invite the reader to generate a bivariate distribution (for example: based on the sum of some Gaussians) based, for example, on age and height and create a simple model that is able to detect all people whose parameters are very unlikely.

Anomaly detection with the KDD Cup 99 dataset

This example is based on the KDD Cup 99 dataset, which collects a long series of normal and malicious internet activities. In particular, we are going to focus on the subset of HTTP requests, which has four attributes: duration, source bytes, destination bytes, and behavior (which is more a classification element, but it's helpful for us to have immediate access to some specific attacks). As the original values were very small numbers around zero, all versions (included the scikit-learn one) renormalize the variables, using the formula $log(x + 0.1)$ (hence, it must be applied when simulating the anomaly detection with new samples). Of course, the inverse transformation is as follows:

$$y = log(x + 0.1) \implies x = e^y - 0.1$$

Let's start by loading and preparing the dataset using the scikit-learn built-in function `fetch_kddcup99()` and selecting `percent10=True` to limit the data to 10% of the original collection (which is very large). Of course, I invite the reader to test also with the whole dataset and the full parameter list (which contains 34 numerical values).

Anomaly Detection

In this case, we are also selecting `subset='http'`, which has been already prepared to contain a very larger number of normal connections and a few specific attacks (as in a standard periodical log):

```
from sklearn.datasets import fetch_kddcup99

kddcup99 = fetch_kddcup99(subset='http', percent10=True, random_state=1000)

X = kddcup99['data'].astype(np.float64)
Y = kddcup99['target']

print('Statuses: {}'.format(np.unique(Y)))
print('Normal samples: {}'.format(X[Y == b'normal.'].shape[0]))
print('Anomalies: {}'.format(X[Y != b'normal.'].shape[0]))
```

The output is as follows:

```
Statuses: [b'back.' b'ipsweep.' b'normal.' b'phf.' b'satan.'] Normal samples: 56516 Anomalies: 2209
```

Therefore, there are four types of attacks (whose details are not important in this context) with 2209 malicious samples and 56516 normal connections. To perform a density estimation, we are going to consider the three components as independent random variables (which is not completely true, but it can be a reasonable starting point) for some preliminary consideration, but the final estimation is based on the full joint distribution. As we want to determine an optimal bandwidth, let's perform a basic statistical analysis:

```
import numpy as np

means = np.mean(X, axis=0)
stds = np.std(X, axis=0)
IQRs = np.percentile(X, 75, axis=0) - np.percentile(X, 25, axis=0)
```

The output of the previous snippet is as follows:

```
Means: [-2.26381954  5.73573107  7.53879208]
Standard devations: [0.49261436 1.06024947 1.32979463]
IQRs: [0.         0.34871118 1.99673381]
```

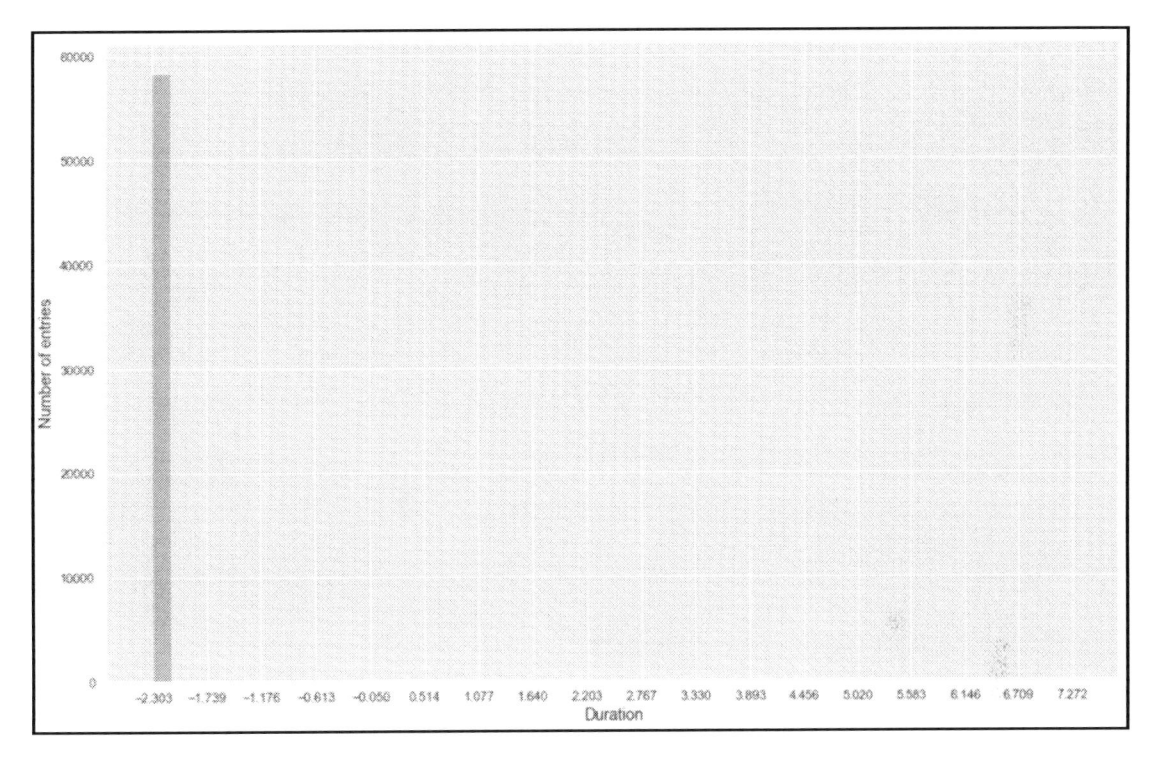

The IQR for the duration (first component) is null; therefore, the majority of values are equal. Let's plot a histogram to confirm this:

Histogram for the first component (duration)

As expected, such a component is not very significant, because only a small percentage of the samples have different values. Therefore, in this example, we are going to skip it and work only with source and destination bytes. Let's now compute the bandwidth as explained previously:

```
import numpy as np

N = float(X.shape[0])

h0 = 0.9 * np.min([stds[0], IQRs[0] / 1.34]) * np.power(N, -0.2)
h1 = 0.9 * np.min([stds[1], IQRs[1] / 1.34]) * np.power(N, -0.2)
h2 = 0.9 * np.min([stds[2], IQRs[2] / 1.34]) * np.power(N, -0.2)

print('h0 = {:.3f}, h1 = {:.3f}, h2 = {:.3f}'.format(h0, h1, h2))
```

Anomaly Detection

The output is as follows:

```
h0 = 0.000, h1 = 0.026, h2 = 0.133
```

Excluding the first value, we need to choose between `h1` and `h2`. As the magnitude of the values is not large and we want to be quite selective, we are going to set *h = 0.025* and employ a Gaussian kernel, which provides a good smoothness. The split output (obtained using the seaborn visualization library, which includes an internal KDE module) containing also the first component is shown in the following screenshot:

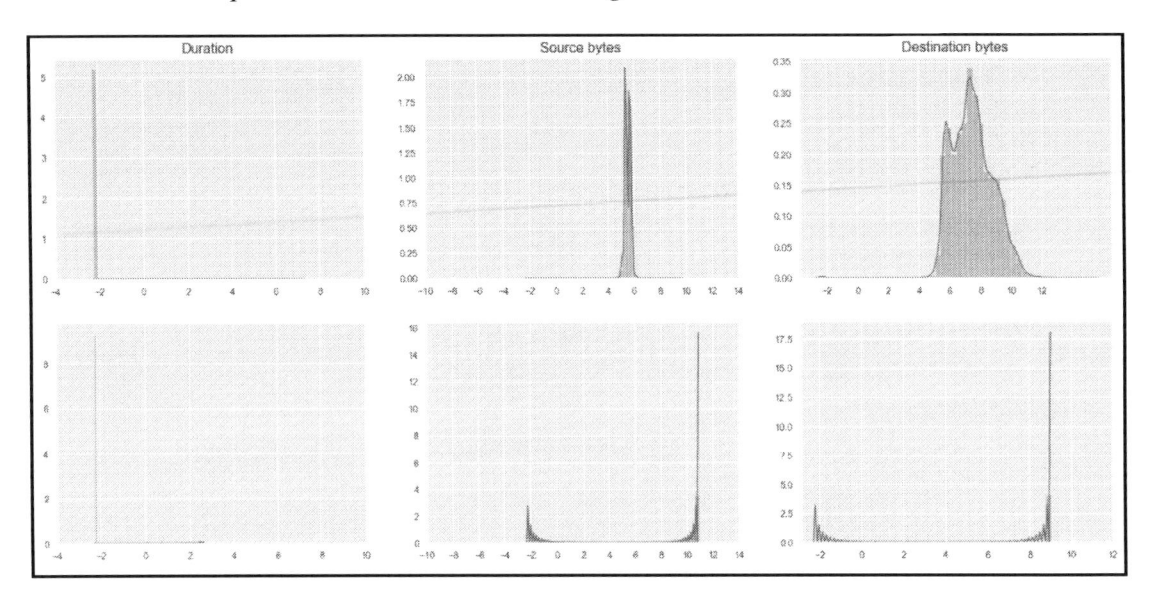

Density estimations for normal connections (upper line) and malicious attacks (lower line)

The first line shows the densities for normal connections, while the lower ones are malicious attacks. As expected, the first component (duration) is almost identical in both cases, and it can be discarded. Conversely, both source and destination bytes exhibit very different behaviors. Without considering the logarithmic transformation, normal connections send on average of **5** bytes with a very low variance that extends the potential range to the interval (**4, 6**). The responses have a larger variance, with values between **4** and **10** and a very low density starting from **10**. Conversely, both source and destination bytes for malicious attacks are characterized by two peaks: a shorter one corresponding to **-2** and a taller one corresponding, respectively, to about **11** and **9** (with a minimum overlap with the normal regions). Even without considering the full joint probability density, it's not difficult to understand that the majority of attacks send more input data and receive longer responses (while the connection duration is not strongly affected).

We can now train the estimator by selecting only the normal samples (that is, corresponding to `Y == b'normal.'`):

```
from sklearn.neighbors import KernelDensity

X = X[:, 1:]

kd = KernelDensity(kernel='gaussian', bandwidth=0.025)
kd.fit(X[Y == b'normal.'])
```

Let's compute the densities for both normal and anomaly samples:

```
Yn = np.exp(kd.score_samples(X[Y == b'normal.']))
Ya = np.exp(kd.score_samples(X[Y != b'normal.']))

print('Mean normal: {:.5f} - Std: {:.5f}'.format(np.mean(Yn), np.std(Yn)))
print('Mean anomalies: {:.5f} - Std: {:.5f}'.format(np.mean(Ya), np.std(Ya)))
```

The output is as follows:

```
Mean normal: 0.39588 - Std: 0.25755
Mean anomalies: 0.00008 - Std: 0.00374
```

It's clear that we can expect an anomaly when, for example, $p_K(x) < 0.05$ (considering three standard deviations) for an anomaly, we get $p_K(x) \in (0, 0.01)$), while the median of `Yn` is about 0.35. This means that at least half of the samples have $p_K(x) > 0.35$. However, after a simple count check, we obtain this:

```
print(np.sum(Yn < 0.05))
print(np.sum(Yn < 0.03))
print(np.sum(Yn < 0.02))
print(np.sum(Yn < 0.015))
```

The output is as follows:

```
3147
1778
1037
702
```

Anomaly Detection

As there are 56,516 normal samples, we can decide to pick two thresholds (to consider also the anomaly outliers):

- **Normal connection**: $p_K(x) > 0.03$
- **Medium alert**: 0.03 (which involves 3.1% of normal samples that can be identified as false positives)
- **High alert**: 0.015 (in this case, only 1.2% of normal samples can trigger the alarm)

Moreover, with the second alert, we catch this:

```
print(np.sum(Ya < 0.015))
```

The output is as follows:

```
2208
```

Hence, only an anomaly sample has $p_K(x) > 0.015$ (there are 2,209 vectors), which confirms that such a choice is reasonable. The previous results are also confirmed by the histogram of the densities:

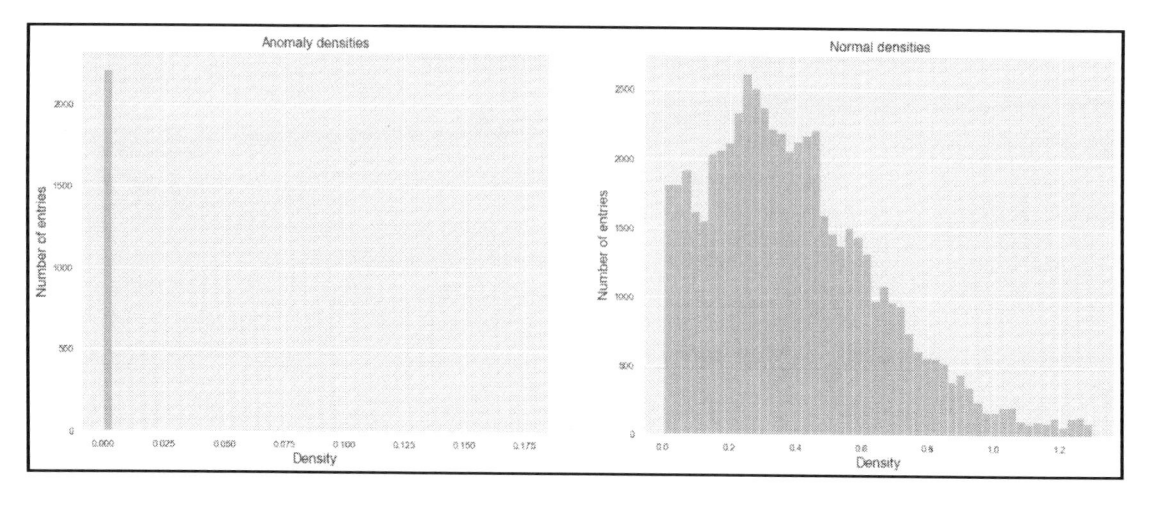

Histogram of anomaly (left) and normal (right) densities

The right tail of the normal distribution is not alarming because the anomalies are highly concentrated on the left side. In this area, there are also the majority of anomalies and it's, and therefore, the most critical. The reason is strictly related to the specific domain (where input and output bytes can be very similar for different kinds of requests) and, in a more stable solution, it's necessary to consider further parameters (for example: the complete KDD Cup 99 dataset). However, for didactic purposes, we can define a simple function (based on the thresholds previously defined) to check the status of a connection according to the amount of source and destination bytes (not logarithmic):

```
import numpy as np

def is_anomaly(kd, source, destination, medium_thr=0.03, high_thr=0.015):
    xs = np.log(source + 0.1)
    xd = np.log(destination + 0.1)
    data = np.array([[xs, xd]])
    density = np.exp(kd.score_samples(data))[0]
    if density >= medium_thr:
        return density, 'Normal connection'
    elif density >= high_thr:
        return density, 'Medium risk'
    else:
        return density, 'High risk'
```

We can now test the function with three different examples:

```
print('p = {:.2f} - {}'.format(*is_anomaly(kd, 200, 1100)))
print('p = {:.2f} - {}'.format(*is_anomaly(kd, 360, 200)))
print('p = {:.2f} - {}'.format(*is_anomaly(kd, 800, 1800)))
```

The output is as follows:

```
p = 0.30 - Normal connection
p = 0.02 - Medium risk
p = 0.00000 - High risk
```

Anomaly Detection

For a general overview, it's also possible to consider a bivariate plot of the source and destination bytes densities:

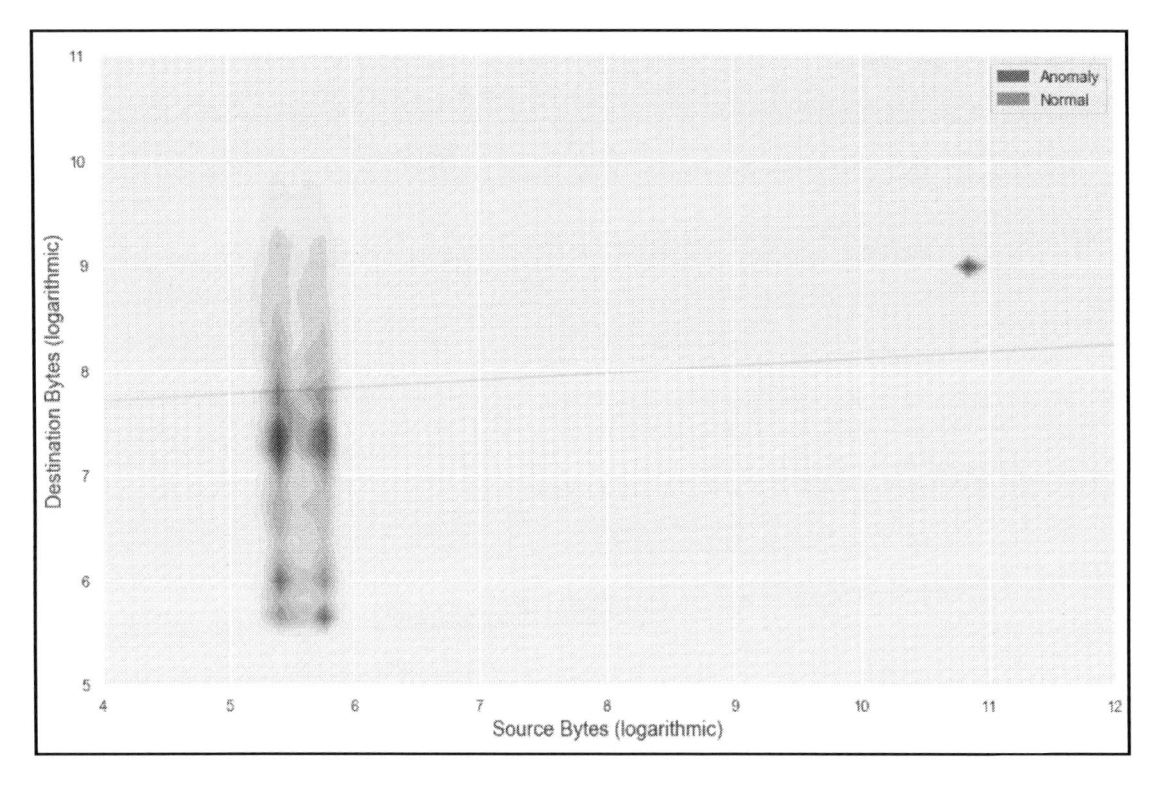

Bivariate plot of the source and destination bytes densities

The preceding screenshot confirms that, while the attacks involve normally a larger amount of input bytes, the responses are very similar to normal ones, even if they occupy an extreme part of the region. As an exercise, I invite the reader to train a model with the whole KDD Cup 99 dataset and find out the optimal thresholds to detect very dangerous and medium-risk attacks.

One-class support vector machines

The concept of one-class **support vector machines** (**SVMs**) has been proposed by Schölkopf B, Platt J C, Shawe-Taylor J C, Smola A J, and Williamson R C, in the article *Estimating the Support of a High-Dimensional Distribution, Neural Computation, 13/7, 2001* as a method to classify the novelties either as samples drawn from the true data-generating process or as outliers. Let's start with the goal we want to achieve: finding an unsupervised model that, given a sample x_i, can yield a binary output y_i (conventionally, SVMs outcomes are bipolar: -1 and +1), so that, if x_i is inlier $y_i = +1$ and, conversely, $y_i = -1$ if x_i is an outlier (more correctly, the authors, in the aforementioned paper, assume that the outcome is *1* for the majority of inliers, which constitute the training set). At a first glance, it can seem a classical supervised problem; however, it isn't because it doesn't require a labeled dataset. In fact, given a dataset X containing *m* samples $x_i \in \Re^n$, the model will be trained using a single fixed class, with the goal to find a separating hyperplane that maximizes the distance between X and the origin. To start with, let's consider a simple linear case, as shown in the following diagram:

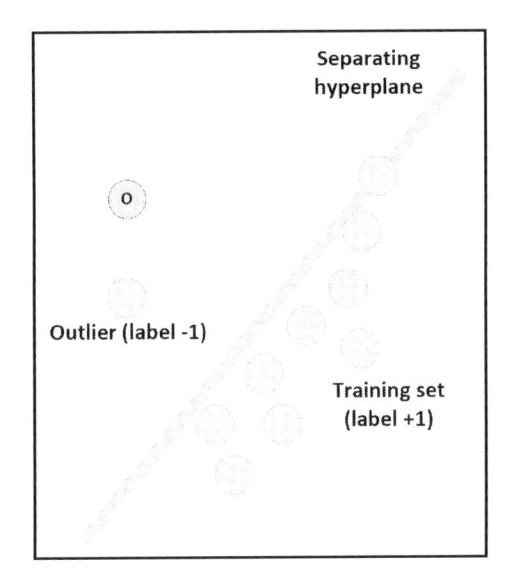

Linear one-class SVM scenario: the training set is separated from the origin with the largest margin

Anomaly Detection

The model is trained to find out the parameters of the hyperplane that maximize the distance from the origin. All the samples on one side of the hyperplane are expected to be inliers and the output label is +1, while all the remaining ones are considered as outliers and the output label is -1. This criterion seems effective, but it works only for linearly separable datasets. Standard SVMs address this problem by projecting the dataset (through the function $\varphi(\bullet)$) on to a feature space D where it acquires such a property:

$$\phi(\bar{x}_i) : X \rightarrow D$$

In particular, considering the mathematical nature of the problem, the projection becomes computationally lightweight if a kernel is chosen. In other words, we want to employ a function that has the following property:

$$K(\bar{x}_i, \bar{x}_j) = \phi(\bar{x}_i)^T \cdot \phi(\bar{x}_j)$$

The existence of the projecting function $\varphi(\bullet)$ is guaranteed to exist under a condition (called the Mercer's condition) that is quite easy to obtain (that is, in a real subspace, the kernel must be positive semi-definite). The reason for such a choice is strictly related to the process involved in the solution of the problem (a more detailed explanation can be found in *Machine Learning Algorithms Second Edition, Bonaccorso G, Packt Publishing*, 2018). However, the reader who is not familiar with SVMs should not be worried, because we are not going to discuss too many mathematical details. The most important thing to remember is that a generic projection that doesn't support any kernel leads to a dramatic increase in the computational complexity (in particular, for large datasets).

One of the most common choice for $K(\bullet, \bullet)$ is the Radial Basis Function (already analyzed in `Chapter 3`, *Advanced Clustering*):

$$K(\bar{x}_i, \bar{x}_j) = e^{-\gamma \|\bar{x}_i - \bar{x}_j\|^2}$$

Another helpful kernel is the polynomial one:

$$K(\bar{x}_i, \bar{x}_j) = \left(a + b\bar{x}_i^T \cdot \bar{x}_j\right)^c$$

In this case, the exponent c defines the degree of the polynomial function, which is proportional to the dimensionality of the feature space. However, the choice of both the kernel and its hyperparameters is context-dependent, and there are no general rules that are always valid. Hence, for every problem, preliminary analysis and often also a grid search are needed to make the most appropriate choice. Once a kernel has been selected, the problem can be expressed in the following way:

$$\begin{cases} min_{\bar{w},\xi,\rho} \left[\frac{1}{2} \|\bar{w}\|^2 + \frac{1}{m\nu} \sum_{i=1}^{n} \xi_i - \rho \right] \\ subject\ to\ \bar{w} \cdot \phi(\bar{x}_i) \geq \rho - \xi_i \quad \forall \bar{x}_i \in X\ and\ \xi_i \geq 0 \end{cases}$$

Without a complete discussion (which is beyond the scope of this book), we can focus our attention on a few important elements. First of all, the decision function is as follows:

$$y_i = sign\left(\bar{w} \cdot \phi(\bar{x}_i) - \rho\right)$$

The mathematical process involved in the solution allows us to simplify the following expression, but, for our purposes, it's preferable to keep the original one. If a reader has a basic knowledge of supervised learning, they can easily understand that the dot product between the weight vector and the projection of a sample x_i allows determining the position of x_i with respect to the separating hyperplane. In fact, the dot product is non-negative if the angle between the two vectors is less than 90° ($\pi/2$). It's equal to zero when the angle is exactly 90° (that is, the vectors are orthogonal) and it's negative when such an angle is between 90° and 180°. This process is shown in the following diagram:

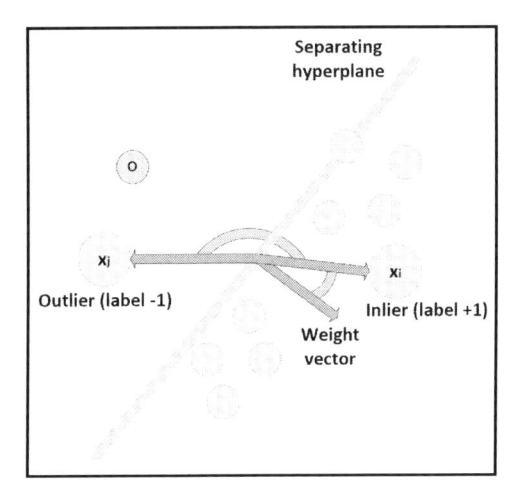

Decision process in SVM

Anomaly Detection

The weight vector is orthogonal to the separating hyperplane. The sample x_i is identified as an inlier because the dot product is positive and greater than the threshold ϱ. Conversely, x_j is marked as an outlier because the sign of the decision function is negative. The terms ξ_i ($\xi_i \geq 0$) are called slack variables and are introduced to allow a more flexible boundary between outliers and inliers. In fact, if those variables are all equal to zero (and, for simplicity, also $\varrho=1$), the condition imposed on the optimization problem becomes this:

$$\bar{w} \cdot \phi(\bar{x}_i) \geq 1 \ \forall \ \bar{x}_i \in X$$

This implies that all training samples must be considered as inliers and, consequently, the separating hyperplane must be selected so that all x_i are on the same side. However, the usage of slack variables allows greater flexibility by defining a soft boundary. Each training sample is associated with a variable ξ_i and, of course, the problem imposes their minimization. However, through this trick, a few boundary samples can also lie on the opposite side of the hyperplane (close enough to it) even if they continue to be identified as inliers. The last element to consider is one of the most important in this context and concerns the hyperparameter $v \in (0, 1)$. In the aforementioned paper, the authors proved that whenever $\varrho \neq 0$, v can be interpreted as an upper bound of the fraction of training samples, which are actually outliers. At the beginning of the chapter, we have stated that in a novelty detection problem the dataset must be clean. Unfortunately, this is not always true; therefore, the conjoint usage of v and the slack variables allows us to also cope with datasets containing a small fraction of outliers. In terms of probability, if X has been drawn from a data-generating process that is partially corrupted by noise, v is the probability to find an outlier in X.

Let's now analyze a bidimensional example based on a dataset of students identified with a tuple (age, height). We are going to generate 2,000 inliers drawn from a bivariate Gaussian distribution and 200 test points uniformly sampled:

```
import numpy as np

nb_samples = 2000
nb_test_samples = 200

X = np.empty(shape=(nb_samples + nb_test_samples, 2))

X[:nb_samples] = np.random.multivariate_normal([15, 160], np.diag([1.5, 10]), size=nb_samples)
X[nb_samples:, 0] = np.random.uniform(11, 19, size=nb_test_samples)
X[nb_samples:, 1] = np.random.uniform(120, 210, size=nb_test_samples)
```

As the scales are different, it's preferable to normalize the dataset before training the model:

```
from sklearn.preprocessing import StandardScaler

ss = StandardScaler()
Xs = ss.fit_transform(X)
```

A plot of the normalized dataset is shown in the following screenshot:

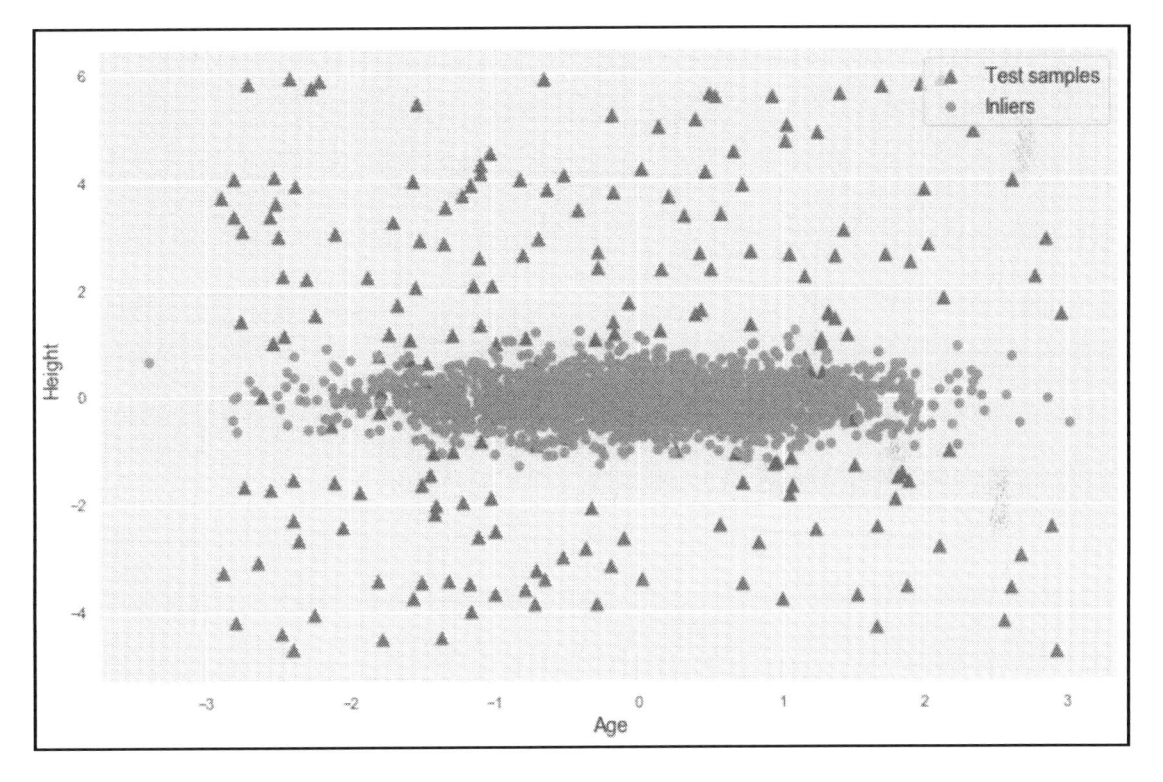

Dataset for the one-class SVM example

The main blob is mainly made up of inliers and a part of the test samples lie in the same highly-dense region; therefore, we can reasonably suppose to have about 20% of outliers in the dataset containing all the samples (therefore, $v=0.2$). Of course, such a choice is based on an assumption of ours and, in any real-life scenario, the value for v must always reflect the actual percentage of expected outliers in the dataset. When this piece of information is not available, it's preferable to start from a larger value (for example, $v=0.5$) and to proceed by decreasing it until the optimal configuration has been found (that is, the probability of misclassification is minimum).

Anomaly Detection

It's also important to remember that the training process can sometimes find a sub-optimal solution; therefore, a few inliers could be marked as outliers. In these cases, the best strategy is to test the effect of different kernels and, for example, when working with polynomial ones, increasing their complexity until the optimal solution (which does not necessarily exclude all errors) has been found.

Let's now initialize an instance of the scikit-learn `OneClassSVM` class using an RBF kernel (which is particularly suitable for Gaussian data-generating processes) and train the model:

```
from sklearn.svm import OneClassSVM

ocsvm = OneClassSVM(kernel='rbf', gamma='scale', nu=0.2)
Ys = ocsvm.fit_predict(Xs)
```

We have chosen the recommended value `gamma='scale'`, which is based on the following formula:

$$\gamma = \frac{1}{n \cdot std(X)}$$

Such a choice is very often the best starting point and can be changed (increased or decreased depending on whether the result is not acceptable). In our case, as the dataset is bidimensional ($n=2$) and normalized ($std(X) = 1$), $\gamma = 0.5$, which corresponds to a unit-variance Gaussian distribution (hence, we should expect it to be the most appropriate choice). At this point, we can plot the results by highlighting the outliers:

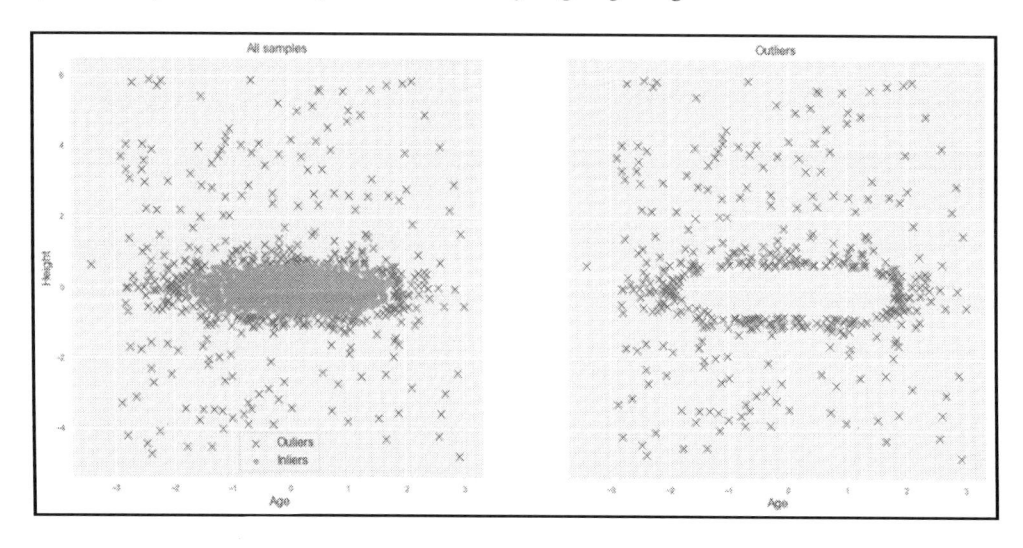

Classification result (left). Outliers from the test set (right)

As it's possible to see in the left diagram, the model has successfully identified the higher-density part of the dataset and it has also marked as outliers some samples in the outer region of the dense blob. They correspond to values with a low probability under the bivariate Gaussian and, in our case, we have assumed that they are noisy samples that should be filtered out. In the right diagram, it's possible to see only the outlier region, which, of course, is the complement of the high-density blob. We can conclude by saying that the one-class SVM, even if a little bit prone to overfit, is able to help us in identifying the novelties with a very small error probability. This is also due to the structure of the dataset (that, however, is quite common in many situations), which can be easily managed using RBF kernels. Unfortunately, with high-dimensional data, this simplicity is often lost and a more thorough hyperparameter search is necessary to minimize the error rate.

Anomaly detection with Isolation Forests

A very powerful anomaly detection method has been proposed by Liu F T, Ting K M, and Zhou Z, in the article *Isolation Forest, ICDM 2008, Eighth IEEE International Conference on Data Mining,* 2008) and it's based on the general framework of ensemble learning. As this topic is very wide and mainly covered in supervised machine-learning books, we invite the reader to check one of the suggested resources if necessary. In this context, instead, we are going to describe the model without a very strong reference to all the underlying theory.

Let's start by saying that a forest is a set of independent models called **decision trees**. As the name suggests, more than algorithms, they are a very practical way to partition a dataset. Starting from the root, for each node, a feature and a threshold are selected and the samples are split into two subsets (this is not true for non-binary trees, but in general, all trees involved is these models are binary), as shown in the following diagram:

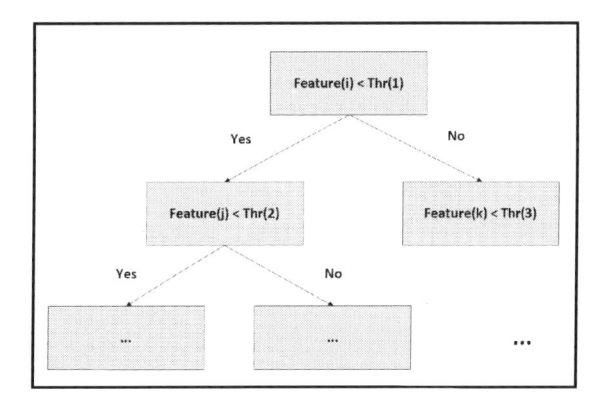

Generic structure of a binary decision tree

Anomaly Detection

In supervised tasks, the selection tuple (feature, threshold) is chosen according to specific criteria that minimize the impurity of the children. This means that the goal is normally to split a node so that the resulting subsets contain the majority of samples belonging to a single class. Of course, as easily understandable, the process ends either when all the leaves are pure or when a maximum depth has been reached. In this specific context, instead, we start from a very particular (but empirically proven) assumption: If the trees belonging to an **Isolation Forest** are grown selecting every time random features and a random threshold, the average length of the path from the root to the leaf containing any inlier is longer than the one required to isolate an outlier. The reason for this assumption can be easily understood by considering a bidimensional example, as shown by the authors:

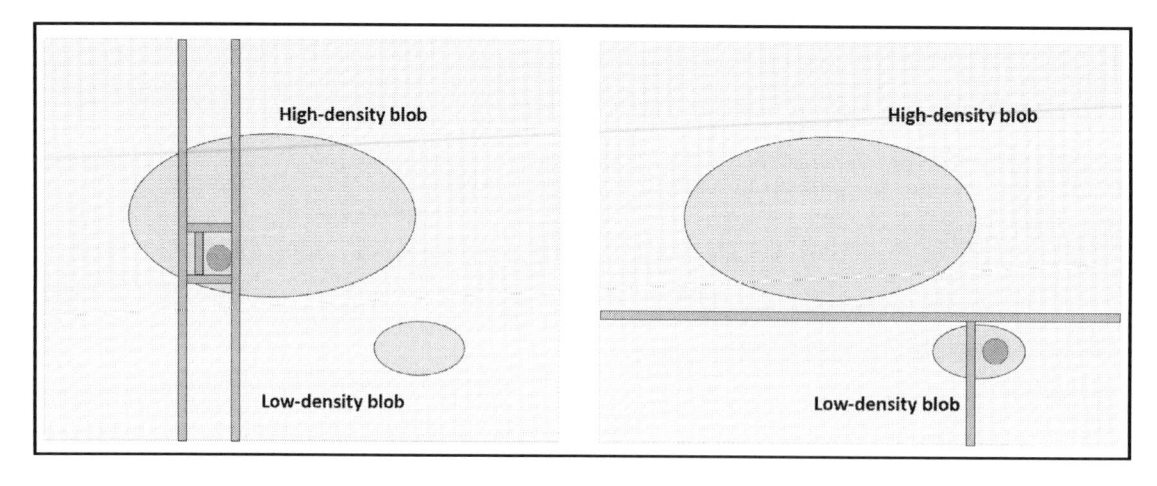

Bidimensional random partitioning. On the left, an inlier is isolated. On the right, an outlier belonging to a low-density region is detected

As it's possible to observe, inliers normally belong to high-density regions that require more partition to isolate the sample. Conversely, outliers that lie in low-density regions can be detected with less partitioning steps because the granularity that is required is proportional to the density of the blobs. Therefore, an isolation forest is built with the goal to measure the average path length for all the inliers and compare it to the one required by new samples. When such a length is shorter, the probability of being an outlier increases. The anomaly score proposed by the authors is based on an exponential function:

$$s(\bar{x}_i, m) = e^{-\frac{avg(h(\bar{x}_i))}{c(m)}}$$

In the previous formula, m is the number of samples belonging to the training set X, $avg(h(x_i))$ is the average path length of sample x_i considering all the trees, and $c(m)$ is a normalization term that depends only on m. The sample x_i is identified as an anomaly when $s(x_i, m) \to 1$. Consequently, as $s(\bullet)$ is bounded between 0 and 1, if we consider a threshold at 0.5, normal samples are associated with values $s(x_i, m) \ll 0.5$.

Let's now consider the wine dataset, which contains 178 samples $x_i \in \Re^{13}$, where each feature is a specific chemical property (for example, alcohol, malic acid, ash, and so forth) and train an isolation forest to detect whether a new wine can be considered as an inlier (so, for example, a variant of an existing brand) or an outlier, because its chemical properties are incompatible with every existing sample. The first step consists of loading and normalizing the dataset:

```
import numpy as np

from sklearn.datasets import load_wine
from sklearn.preprocessing import StandardScaler

wine = load_wine()
X = wine['data'].astype(np.float64)

ss = StandardScaler()
X = ss.fit_transform(X)
```

We can now instantiate an `IsolationForest` class and set the most important hyperparameters. The first one is `n_estimators=150`, which informs the model to train 150 trees. The other fundamental parameter (analogous to v in one-class SVMs) is called `contamination` and its value indicates the expected percentage of outliers in the training set. As we trust the dataset, we have chosen a value equal to 0.01 (1%) to address the presence of a negligible number of strange samples. The `behaviour='new'` parameter has been inserted for compatibility reasons (check the official documentation for further information) and `random_state=1000` guarantees the reproducibility of the experiment. Once the class has been initialized, the model can be trained:

```
from sklearn.ensemble import IsolationForest

isf = IsolationForest(n_estimators=150, behaviour='new',
contamination=0.01, random_state=1000)
Y_pred = isf.fit_predict(X)

print('Outliers in the training set: {}'.format(np.sum(Y_pred == -1)))
```

Anomaly Detection

The output of the previous snippet is:

```
2
```

Hence, the isolation forest has successfully identified 176 out of 178 inliers. We can accept this result, but, as usual, I recommend to tune up the parameters in order to obtain a model that is compatible with every specific situation. At this point, we can generate a few noisy samples:

```
import numpy as np

X_test_1 = np.mean(X) + np.random.normal(0.0, 1.0, size=(50, 13))
X_test_2 = np.mean(X) + np.random.normal(0.0, 2.0, size=(50, 13))
X_test = np.concatenate([X_test_1, X_test_2], axis=0)
```

The test set is split into two blocks. The first array, `X_test_1`, contains samples with a relatively low noise level ($\sigma=1$), while the second one, `X_test_2`, contains more noisy samples ($\sigma=2$). Therefore, we expect a lower number of outliers in the first group and a larger number in the second one. The array `X_test` is the ordered concatenation of the two test sets. Let's now predict the status. As the values are bipolar and we want to distinguish them from the training results, we are going to multiply the prediction times 2 (that is, -1 indicates outliers in the training set, 1 inliers in the training set, -2 outliers in the test set, and 2 inliers in the test set):

```
Y_test = isf.predict(X_test) * 2

Xf = np.concatenate([X, X_test], axis=0)
Yf = np.concatenate([Y_pred, Y_test], axis=0)

print(Yf[::-1])
```

The output is as follows:

```
[ 2  2 -2 -2 -2 -2 -2  2  2  2 -2 -2 -2 -2 -2 -2 -2 -2 -2 -2 -2 -2  2 -2  2  2
 -2 -2 -2  2 -2 -2 -2 -2  2  2 -2 -2 -2 -2 -2 -2  2  2 -2  2 -2 -2  2 -2  2  2  2  2  2  2
  2  2  2  2  2  2  2  2  2  2  2  2  2  2  2  2  2  2  2  2  2  2  2  2  2  2  2  2 -2  2
  2  2  2  2  2  1  1  1  1  1  1  1  1  1  1  1  1  1  1  1  1  1  1  1  1  1  1  1  1  1
  1  1  1  1  1  1  1  1  1  1  1  1  1  1  1  1  1  1  1  1  1 -1  1  1  1  1  1  1  1  1 -1  1
  1  1  1  1  1  1  1  1  1  1  1  1  1  1  1  1  1  1  1  1  1  1  1  1  1  1  1  1  1  1
  1  1  1  1  1  1  1  1  1  1  1  1  1  1  1  1  1  1  1  1  1  1  1  1  1  1  1  1  1  1
  1  1  1  1  1  1  1  1  1  1  1  1  1  1  1  1  1  1  1  1  1  1  1  1  1  1  1  1  1]
```

As the order is preserved and inverted, we can see that the majority of samples belonging to X_test_2 (high variance) are classified as anomalies, while the majority of low variance samples are identified as inliers. To have further visual confirmation, we can perform a t-SNE dimensionality reduction, considering that the final result is the bidimensional distribution whose Kullback-Leibler divergence with the original (13-dimensional) one is the lowest. This means the interpretability of the resulting dimensions is very low and the diagram can be employed only to understand which regions of the bidimensional space are more likely to be occupied by inliers:

```
from sklearn.manifold import TSNE

tsne = TSNE(n_components=2, perplexity=5, n_iter=5000, random_state=1000)
X_tsne = tsne.fit_transform(Xf)
```

The resulting plot is shown in the following graph:

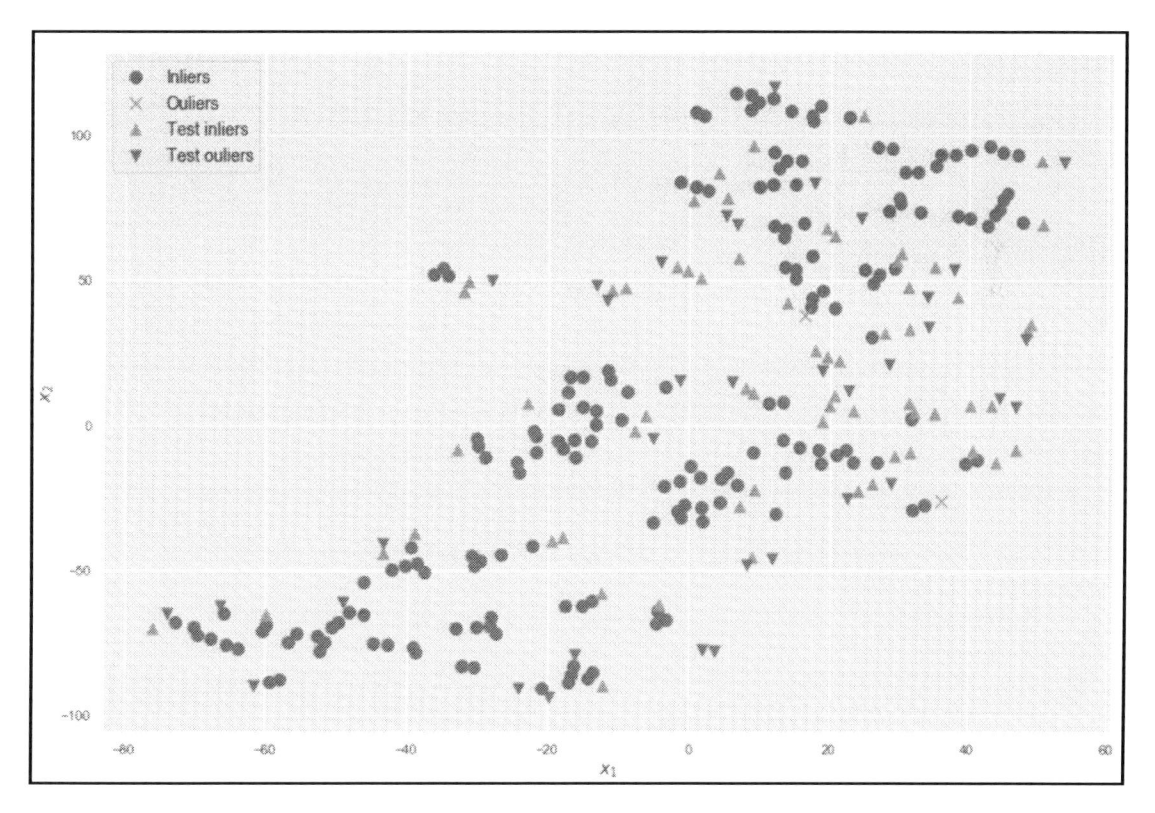

t-SNE plot for the novelty detection with the wine dataset

As it's possible to see, many samples close to training inliers are inliers themselves and, in general, almost all far test samples are outliers. However, it's very difficult to draw more conclusions because of the strong dimensionality reduction. However, we know that when the noise is small enough, the probability of finding inliers is large (which is a reasonable outcome). As an exercise, I invite the reader to check the single chemical properties (available at `https://scikit-learn.org/stable/datasets/index.html#wine-dataset`) and, for each of them or for groups, find out which is the threshold that transforms an inlier into an outlier (for example, answering this question: what is the maximum amount of alcohol compatible with the training set?).

Summary

In this chapter, we have discussed the properties of the probability density functions and how they can be employed to compute actual probabilities and relative likelihoods. We have seen how to create a histogram, which is the simplest method to represent the frequency of values after grouping them into predefined bins. As histograms have some important limitations (they are very discontinuous and it's difficult to find out the optimal bin size), we have introduced the concept of kernel density estimation, which is a slightly more sophisticated way to estimate a density using smooth functions.

We have analyzed the properties of the most common kernels (Gaussian, Epanechnikov, Exponential, and Uniform) and two empirical methods that can be employed to find out the best bandwidth for each dataset. Using such a technique, we have tried to solve a very simple univariate problem based on a synthetic dataset. We have analyzed the HTTP subset of the KDD Cup 99 dataset, which contains the log records of several normal and malicious network connections. And we have used the KDE technique to create a simple anomaly detection system based on two thresholds, and we have also explained which factors must be taken into account when working with these kinds of problems.

In the last part, we have analyzed two common methods that can be employed to perform novelty detection. One-class SVMs exploit the power of kernels to project complex datasets on to a feature space where they can be linearly separable. The next step is based on the assumption that all training sets (except a small percentage) are inliers and, therefore, they belong to the same class. The model is trained with the goal of maximizing the separation between the inliers and the origin of the feature space and an outcome is based on the position of the sample with respect to the separating hyperplane. Isolation Forests, instead, are ensemble models based on the assumption that the path from the root to a sample in randomly trained decision trees is on average shorter for outliers.

Therefore, after training the forest, an anomaly score can be computed considering the average path length for a given new sample. When such a score is close to 1, we can conclude that the probability of an anomaly is also very large. Conversely, very small score values indicate that the novelties are instead potential inliers.

In the next chapter, we are going to discuss the most common techniques of dimensionality reduction and dictionary learning, which are extremely helpful when it's necessary to manage datasets with a large number of features.

Questions

1. The probability that a person is 1.70 m tall is $p(Tall) = 0.75$, while the probability that tomorrow it's going to rain is $P(Rain) = 0.2$. What is the probability $P(Tall, Rain)$? (that is, the probability that a person is 1.70 m tall and tomorrow it's going to rain).
2. Given a dataset X, we build an histogram with 1,000 bins and we find that many of them are empty. Why does this happen?
3. A histogram contains three bins with, respectively 20, 30, and 25 samples. The first bin has a range $0 < x < 2$, the second $2 < x < 4$, and the third $4 < x < 6$. What is the approximate probability that $P(x) > 2$?
4. Given a normal distribution $N(0, 1)$, can a sample x with $p(x) = 0.35$ be considered as an anomaly?
5. A dataset X with 500 samples has $std(X) = 2.5$ and $IQR(X) = 3.0$. What is the optimal bandwidth?
6. An expert told us that a distribution is extremely peaked around two values and the density abruptly drops 0.2 standard deviations from the mean of the peaks. Which kind of kernel is the most appropriate?
7. Given a sample x (collected from a streaming population of 10,000 samples), we are not sure if it's an anomaly or a novelty because $p(x) = 0.0005$. After another 10,000 observations, we retrain the model and x keeps having $p(x) < 0.001$. Can we conclude that x is an anomaly?

Further reading

- *Epanechnikov V A, Non-parametric estimation of a multivariate probability density, Theory of Probability and its Applications,* 14, 1969

- *Parzen E, On Estimation of a Probability Density Function and Mode, The Annals of Mathematical Statistics,* 1962

- *Sheather S J, The performance of six popular bandwidth selection methods on some real data sets (with discussion), Computational Statistics,* 7, 1992

- *Schölkopf B, Platt J C, Shawe-Taylor J C, Smola A J, Williamson R C, Estimating the support of a high-dimensional distribution, Neural Computation,* 13/7, 2001

- *Liu F T, Ting K M, Zhou Z, Isolation forest, ICDM 2008, Eighth IEEE International Conference on Data Mining,* 2008

- *Dayan P, Abbott L F, Theoretical Neuroscience, The MIT Press,* 2005

- *Machine Learning Algorithms Second Edition, Bonaccorso G., Packt Publishing,* 2018

7
Dimensionality Reduction and Component Analysis

In this chapter, we will introduce and discuss some very important techniques that can be employed to perform both dimensionality reduction and component extraction. In the former case, the goal is to transform a high-dimensional dataset into a lower-dimensional one, to try to minimize the amount of information loss. The latter is a process that's needed to find a dictionary of atoms that can be mixed up, in order to build samples.

In particular, we will discuss the following topics:

- **Principal Component Analysis (PCA)**
- **Singular Value Decomposition (SVD)** and whitening
- Kernel PCA
- Sparse PCA and dictionary learning
- Factor analysis
- **Independent Component Analysis (ICA)**
- **Non-Negative Matrix Factorization (NNMF)**
- **Latent Dirichlet Allocation (LDA)**

Technical requirements

The code that will be presented in this chapter will require the following:

- Python 3.5+ (the Anaconda distribution (https://www.anaconda.com/distribution/) is highly recommended)
- The following libraries:
    - SciPy 0.19+
    - NumPy 1.10+
    - scikit-learn 0.20+
    - pandas 0.22+
    - Matplotlib 2.0+
    - seaborn 0.9+

The examples are available in the GitHub repository, at https://github.com/PacktPublishing/HandsOn-Unsupervised-Learning-with-Python/tree/master/Chapter07.

Principal Component Analysis (PCA)

One of the most common ways to reduce the dimensionality of a dataset is based on the analysis of the sample covariance matrix. In general, we know that the information content of a random variable is proportional to its variance. For example, given a multivariate Gaussian, the entropy, which is the mathematical expression that we employ to measure the information, is as follows:

$$H = \frac{1}{2} \log \left(\det \left(2\pi e \Sigma \right) \right)$$

In the previous formula, Σ is the covariance matrix. If we assume (without loss of generality) that Σ is diagonal, it's easy to understand that the entropy is larger (proportionally) than the variance of each single component, σ_i^2. This is not surprising, because a random variable with a low variance is concentrated around the mean, and the probability of surprises is low. On the other hand, when σ^2 becomes larger and larger, the potential outcomes increase along with the uncertainty, which is directly proportional to the amount of information.

Of course, the influence of the components is generally different; therefore, the goal of **Principal Component Analysis (PCA)** is to find a linear transformation of the samples that can project them onto a lower-dimensional subspace, so as to preserve the largest possible amount of the initial variance. In practice, let's consider a dataset, $X \in \Re^{m \times n}$:

$$X = \{\bar{x}_1, \bar{x}_2, \ldots, \bar{x}_m\} \ where \ \bar{x}_i \in \mathbb{R}^n$$

The linear transformation that we want to find is a new dataset, as follows:

$$Z = \{\bar{z}_1, \bar{z}_2, \ldots, \bar{z}_n\} \ where \ \bar{z}_i = A^T \bar{x}_i$$

After applying such a transformation, we expect to have the following:

$$\begin{cases} dim(\bar{z}_i) < (\ll) dim(\bar{x}_i) \ \forall \ i \\ H(z) \approx H(x) \end{cases}$$

Let's start to consider the sample covariance matrix (for our purposes, we can also employ biased estimation); for simplicity, we will also assume X has a zero mean:

$$\Sigma_s = \frac{1}{m} X^T X \in \mathbb{R}^{n \times n}$$

Such a matrix is symmetric and positive semi-definite (it doesn't matter if you are not familiar with these concepts, but they are very important to justify the following steps), so its eigenvectors constitute an orthonormal basis. As a quick recap, if A is a square matrix, a vector, v_i, is called an eigenvector associated to the eigenvalue, λ_i, if the following is true:

$$A\bar{x}_i = \lambda_i \bar{x}_i$$

In other words, an eigenvector is transformed into an expanded or contracted version of itself (no rotations can occur). It's not difficult (but all of the mathematical details will be omitted) to prove that the eigenvectors of the covariance matrix define the directions of the covariance components (that is, the directions where the dataset has a specific covariance component). The reason is, however, quite simple; in fact, after the transformation, the new covariance matrix (of the transformed dataset, Z) is uncorrelated (that is, it's diagonal) because the new axes are aligned with the covariance components. This implies that a versor (for example, $v_0 = (1, 0, 0, \ldots, 0)$) is transformed into $\sigma_i^2 v_i$, so it's an eigenvector whose associated eigenvalue is proportional to the variance of the ith component.

Dimensionality Reduction and Component Analysis

Therefore, in order to find out which elements can be discarded, we can sort the eigenvalues so that the following is true:

$$\lambda_1 \leqslant \lambda_2 \leqslant \ldots \leqslant \lambda_n$$

The corresponding eigenvectors ($v_1, v_2, \ldots, v_n$) determine, respectively, the component corresponding to the largest variance, and so on, until the last one. Formally, we define such eigenvectors as **principal components**; therefore, the first principal component is the direction associated with the largest variance, the second principal component is orthogonal to the first one, and it's associated with the second largest variance, and so forth. This concept is shown in the following screenshot, in the case of a bidimensional dataset:

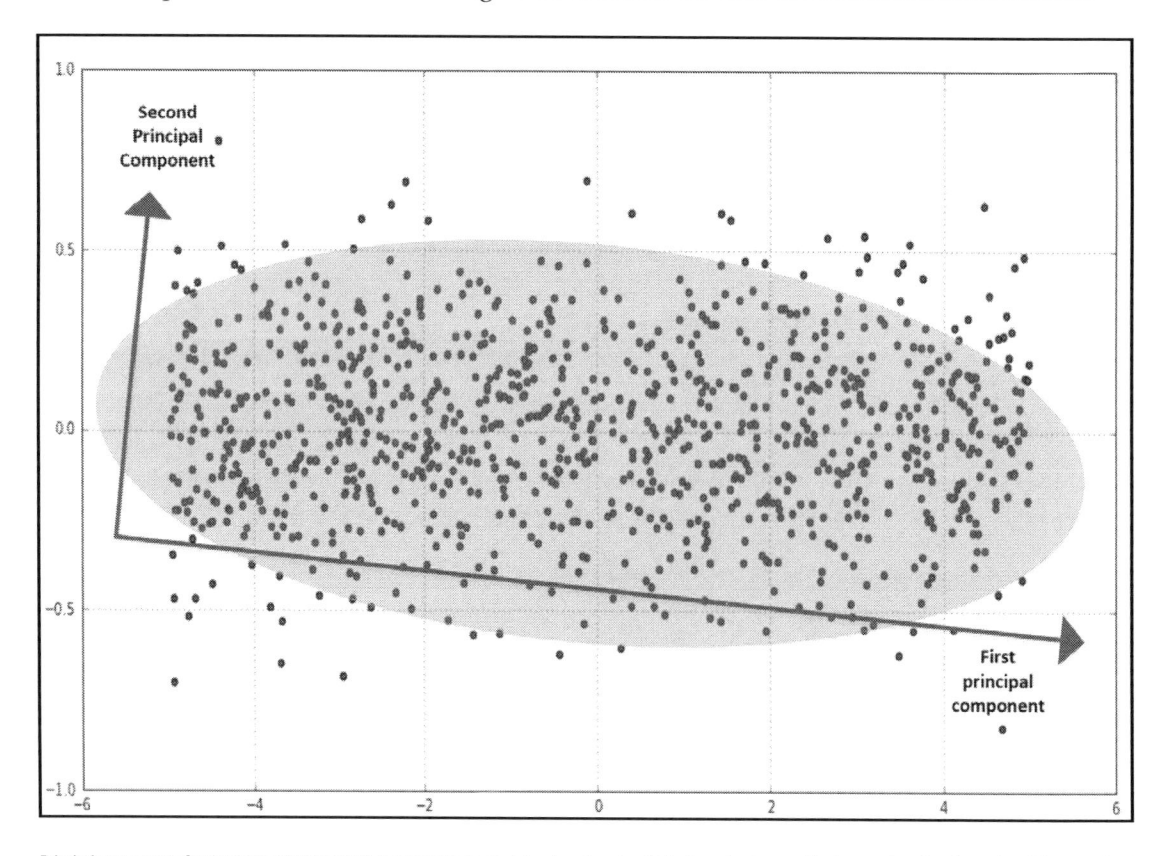

Principal components of a bidimensional dataset; the first principal component lies along the axis with the largest variance, while the second one is orthogonal, and it's proportional to the residual variance

At this point, the problem is almost solved; in fact, if we only select the first k principal components ($v_i \in \Re^{n \times 1}$), we can build a transformation matrix, $A_k \in \Re^{n \times k}$, so as to have the eigenvectors associated to the first k eigenvalues as rows:

$$A_k = \begin{pmatrix} \bar{v}_1^{(1)} & \cdots & \bar{v}_k^{(1)} \\ \vdots & \ddots & \vdots \\ \bar{v}_n^{(1)} & \cdots & \bar{v}_k^{(1)} \end{pmatrix}$$

Hence, we can transform the entire dataset by using the following matrix multiplication:

$$Z = XA_k \text{ where } Z \in \mathbb{R}^{m \times k}$$

The new dataset, Z, has a dimensionality equal to $k < (or <<) n$, and it contains an amount of the original variance proportional to the number of components. For example, considering the example shown in the previous screenshot, if we select a single component, all of the vectors are transformed into points along the first principal component. Of course, there's some loss of information, which must be considered case by case; in the following sections, we are going to discuss how to evaluate such loss and make a reasonable decision. Now, we will briefly show how the principal components can be extracted in an efficient way.

PCA with Singular Value Decomposition

Even though we are going to employ complete PCA implementations, it will be helpful to understand how such a process can be carried out efficiently. Of course, the most obvious way to proceed is based on the calculation of the sample covariance matrix, its eigendecomposition (which will output the eigenvalues and the corresponding eigenvectors), and then finally, it's possible to build the transformation matrix. This method is straightforward, but unfortunately, it's also inefficient. The main reason is that we need to compute the sample covariance matrix, which can be a very long task for large datasets.

A much more efficient way is provided by **Singular Value Decomposition (SVD)**, which is a linear algebra procedure with some important features: it can operate directly on the dataset, it can be stopped when the desired number of components has been extracted, and there are incremental versions that can work with small batches, overcoming the problem of memory shortages. In particular, considering the dataset, $X \in \Re^{m \times n}$, the SVD can be expressed as follows:

$$X = U\Lambda V^T \text{ where } U \in \mathbb{R}^{m \times m}, \Lambda = diag(n \times n), V \in \mathbb{R}^{n \times n}$$

U is a unitary matrix (that is, $UU^T = U^TU = I$, so $U^T = U^{-1}$) containing the left-hand singular vectors as rows (the eigenvectors of XX^T); V (unitary, too) contains the right-hand singular vectors as rows (corresponding to the eigenvectors of X^TX), while Λ is a diagonal matrix containing the singular values of $m\Sigma_s$ (which are the square roots of the eigenvalues of both XX^T and X^TX). The eigenvalues are sorted by descending order, and the eigenvectors are rearranged in order to match the corresponding positions. As the $1/m$ factor is a multiplicative constant, it doesn't affect the relative magnitude of the eigenvalues; therefore, the sorting order remains unchanged. Hence, we can work directly with V or U and select the first top k eigenvalues from Λ. In particular, we can observe the following result (as the transformation matrix, A, is equal to V):

$$Z = XA = U\Lambda V^T A = U\Lambda V^T V = U\Lambda$$

Therefore, by using the truncated version of U_k (containing only the top k eigenvectors) and Λ_k (containing only the top k eigenvalues), we can directly obtain the lower-dimensional transformed dataset (with k components), as follows:

$$Z_k = U_k \Lambda_k$$

This method is fast, effective, and can easily scale when the dataset is too large to fit into the memory. Even though we are not working with such scenarios in this book, it's helpful to mention the scikit-learn `TruncatedSVD` class (which performs SVD limited to k top eigenvalues) and `IncrementalPCA` class (which performs PCA on small batches). For our purposes, we will employ the standard `PCA` class and some important variants, which require the whole dataset to fit into the memory.

Whitening

An important application of the SVD is the **whitening** procedure, which forces the dataset, X, with a null mean (that is, $E[X] = 0$ or zero-centered), to have an identity covariance matrix, C, (which is real and symmetric). This method is extremely helpful, to improve the performance of many supervised algorithms, which can benefit from a uniform single variance shared by all components.

Applying the decomposition to C, we obtain the following:

$$C = E[X^T X] = V\Lambda V^T = I$$

The columns of the matrix V are the eigenvectors of C, while Λ is a diagonal matrix containing the eigenvalues (remember that the SVD outputs singular values, which are the square roots of the eigenvectors). Hence, we need to find a linear transformation, $z = Ax$, so that $E[Z^T Z] = I$. This is straightforward when using the previous decomposition:

$$C_W = E[Z^T Z] = E[AX^T X A] = AE[X^T X]A^T = AV\Lambda V^T A^T = I$$

From the previous equation, we can derive the expression for the transformation matrix, A:

$$AA^T = V\Lambda^{-1}V^T = I \Rightarrow A = V\Lambda^{-\frac{1}{2}}$$

Now, we'll show the effects of whitening with a small test dataset, as follows:

```
import numpy as np

from sklearn.datasets import make_blobs

X, _ = make_blobs(n_samples=300, centers=1, cluster_std=2.5,
random_state=1000)

print(np.cov(X.T))
```

The output of the previous block, showing the covariance matrix of the dataset, is as follows:

```
[[6.37258226 0.40799363]
 [0.40799363 6.32083501]]
```

The `whiten()` function, used to perform whitening on a generic dataset (zero-centering is part of the process), is shown in the following snippet (the `correct` parameter forces scale correction after whitening):

```
import numpy as np

def zero_center(X):
    return X - np.mean(X, axis=0)

def whiten(X, correct=True):
    Xc = zero_center(X)
    _, L, V = np.linalg.svd(Xc)
    W = np.dot(V.T, np.diag(1.0 / L))
    return np.dot(Xc, W) * np.sqrt(X.shape[0]) if correct else 1.0
```

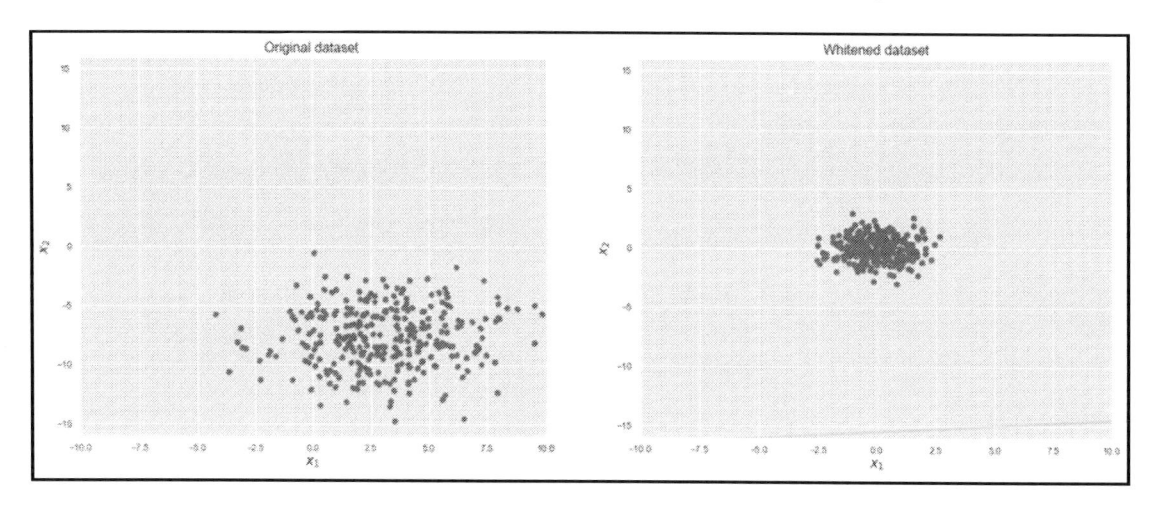

Dimensionality Reduction and Component Analysis

The result of whitening applied to the X array is shown in the following screenshot:

Original dataset (left); whitened dataset (right)

We can now check the new covariance matrix, as follows:

```
import numpy as np

Xw = whiten(X)
print(np.cov(Xw.T))
```

The output is as follows:

```
[[1.00334448e+00 1.78229783e-17]
 [1.78229783e-17 1.00334448e+00]]
```

As is possible to see, the matrix is now an identity (with a minimum error), and the dataset also has a null mean.

PCA with the MNIST dataset

Now, let's apply the PCA, in order to reduce the dimensionality of the MNIST dataset. We are going to use the compressed version (1,797, 8 × 8 images) provided by scikit-learn, but none of our considerations will be affected by this choice. Let's start by loading and normalizing the dataset:

```
from sklearn.datasets import load_digits

digits = load_digits()
X = digits['data'] / np.max(digits['data'])
```

From the theoretical discussion, we know that the magnitude of the eigenvalues of the covariance matrix is proportional to the relative importance (that is, the explained variance, and therefore the informative content) of the corresponding principal component. Therefore, if they are sorted in descending order, it's possible to compute the following differences:

$$\lambda_2 - \lambda_1, \lambda_3 - \lambda_2, \ldots, \lambda_n - \lambda_{n-1}$$

As the importance tends to decrease when the number of components $k \rightarrow n$, we can select the optimal k by picking the first largest difference, which indicates a substantial drop in the amount of explained variance by all of the following components. In order to better understand this mechanism, let's compute the eigenvalues and their differences (as the covariance matrix, C, is positive semi-definite, we are sure that $\lambda_i \geq 0 \ \forall \ i \in (1, n)$):

```
import numpy as np

C = np.cov(X.T)
l, v = np.linalg.eig(C)
l = np.sort(l)[::-1]
d = l[:l.shape[0]-1] - l[1:]
```

Dimensionality Reduction and Component Analysis

The differences for the flattened images (64-dimensional arrays) are shown in the following screenshot:

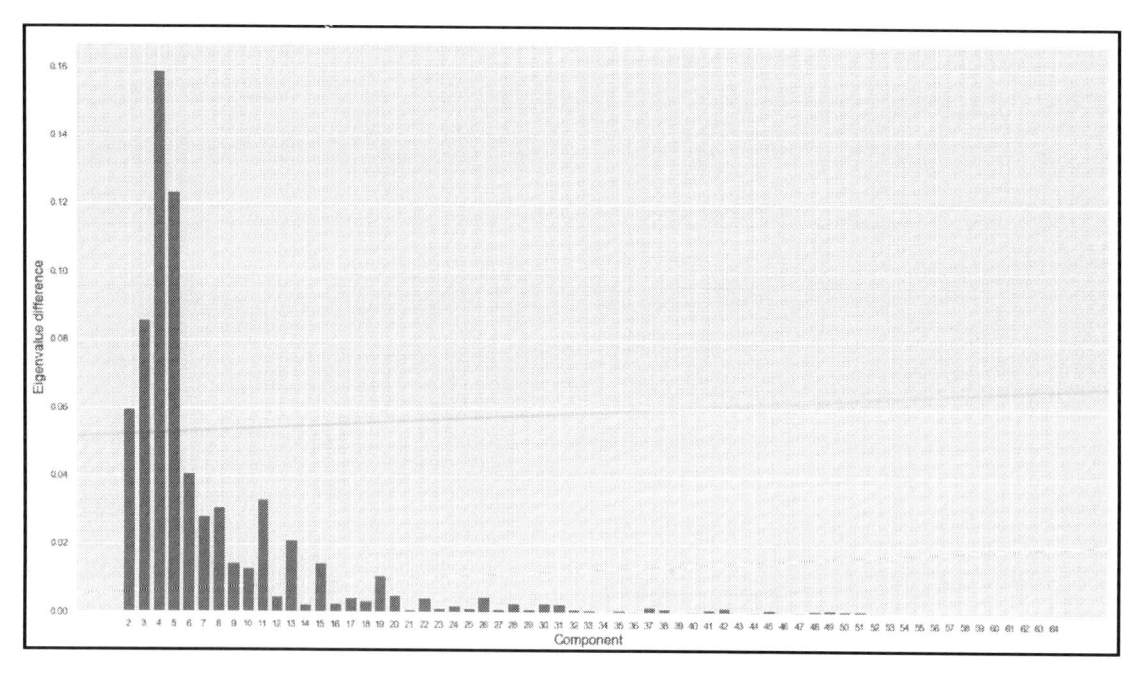

Eigenvalue differences for each principal component

As is possible to see, the differences for the first principal components are very large, and a maximum is reached in correspondence with the fourth principal component ($\lambda_4 - \lambda_3$); however, the next difference is still very high, while there's an abrupt drop corresponding to λ_6. At this point, the trend is almost stable (apart from some residual oscillations) until λ_{11}, and then it begins to decrease very rapidly, tending toward zero. As we still want to have square images, we are going to choose $k = 16$ (which is equivalent to dividing each side by four). In another task, you could choose, for example, $k = 15$, or even $k = 8$; however, in order to have a better understanding of the error induced by the dimensionality reduction, it will be helpful to analyze the explained variance, too. Hence, let's start by performing PCA:

```
from sklearn.decomposition import PCA

pca = PCA(n_components=16, random_state=1000)
digits_pca = pca.fit_transform(X)
```

The `digits_pca` array is obtained after fitting the model and projecting all of the samples onto the subspace corresponding to the first 16 principal components. If we want to compare the original images with their reconstructions, we need to invoke the `inverse_transform()` method, which performs the projection onto the original space. So, if the PCA is, in this case, a transformation, $f(x): \Re^{64} \to \Re^{16}$, the inverse transform is $g(z): \Re^{16} \to \Re^{64}$. The comparison between the first 10 digits and their reconstruction is shown in the following screenshot:

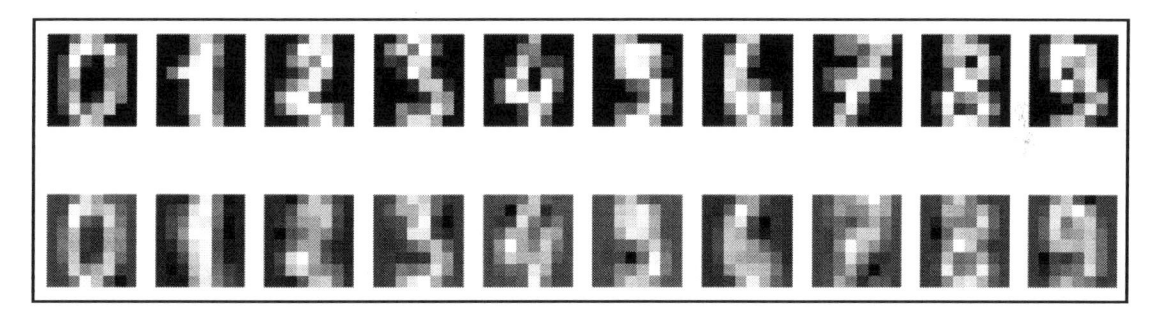

Original samples (top row); reconstructions (bottom row)

The reconstructions are clearly lossy, but the digits are still distinguishable. Now, let's check the total explained variance by summing all of the values of the `explained_variance_ratio_` array, which contains the relative amount of explained variance for every component (so that the sum for any $k < n$ components is always less than 1):

```
print(np.sum(pca.explained_variance_ratio_))
```

The output of the previous snippet is as follows:

```
0.8493974642542452
```

Hence, with dimensionality reduction to 16 components, we are explaining about 85% of the original variance, which is a reasonable value, considering that we are discarding 48 components for each sample.

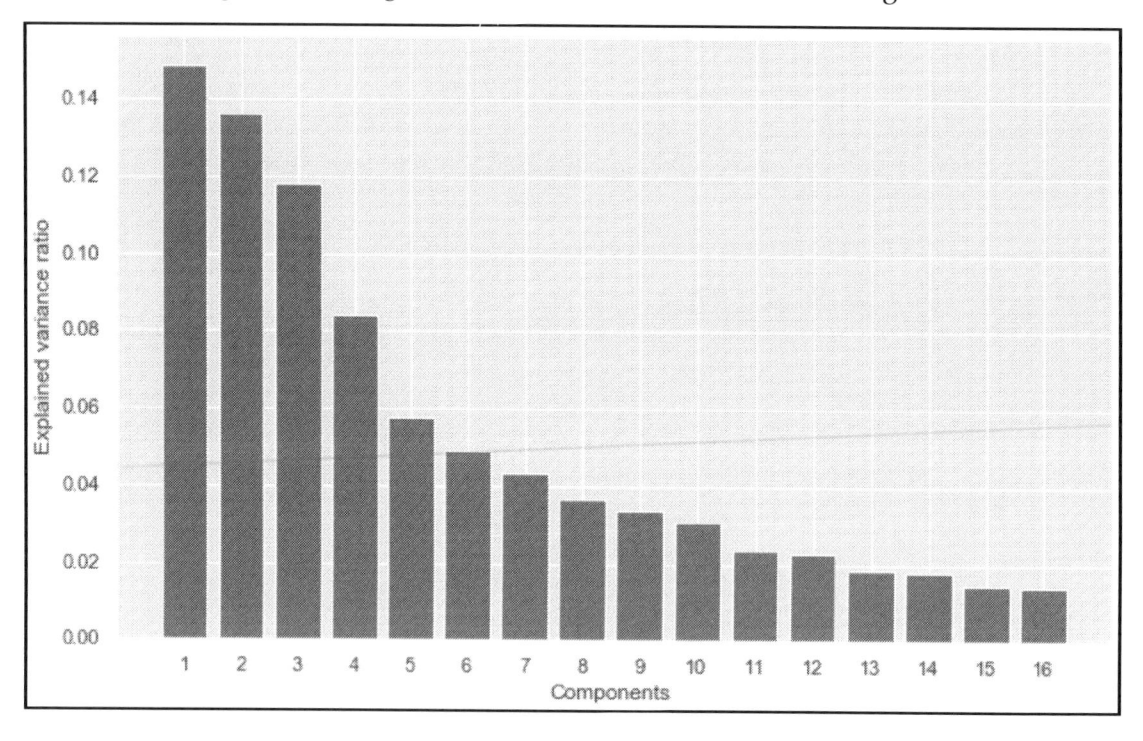

Dimensionality Reduction and Component Analysis

The plot showing all of the single contributions is shown in the following screenshot:

Explained variance ratio corresponding to each principal component

As expected, the contribution tends to decrease, because the first principal components are, in this case, responsible; for example, for the color a line (such as black or white), while the remaining ones contribute to the shades of gray. Such behavior is very common, and is observable in almost every case. Through this diagram, it's also easy to find the extra loss, for a further reduction. For example, we can immediately find out that a drastic limitation to 3 components will explain about 40% of the original variance; so, the remaining 45% is split into the remaining 13 components. I invite you to repeat this example, trying to find the minimum number of components needed by a human being to distinguish all of the digits.

Kernel PCA

Sometimes, datasets are not linearly separable, and standard PCA is not able to extract the correct principal components. The process is not dissimilar to the one discussed in Chapter 3, *Advanced Clustering*, when we faced the problem of non-convex clusters. In that case, some algorithms were not able to perform successful separation because of the geometry. In this case, the goal is to distinguish between different classes (in a pure, unsupervised scenario, we think about specific groupings) according to the structure of the principal components. Therefore, we want to work with the transformed dataset, Z, and detect the presence of distinguishable thresholds. For example, let's consider the following screenshot:

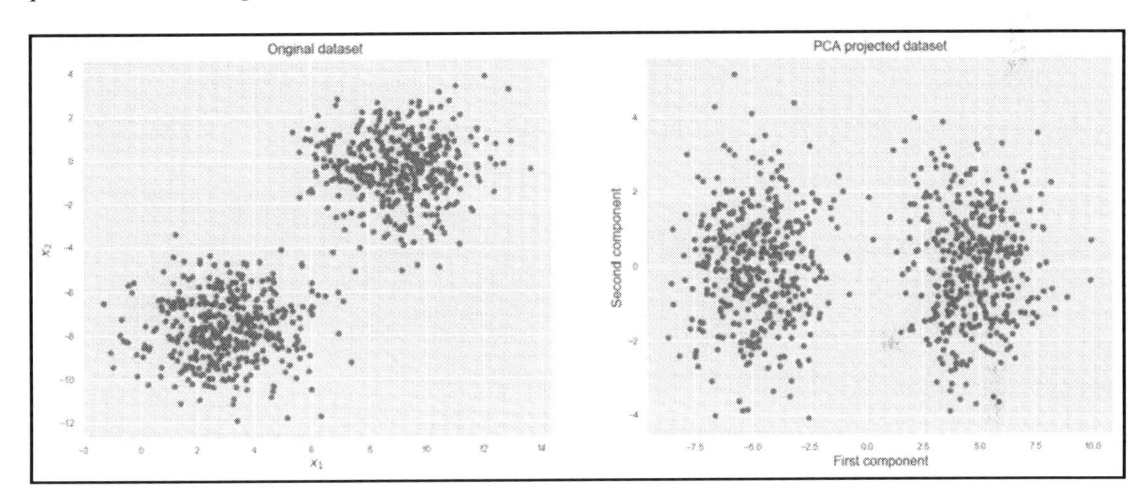

Original dataset (left); PCA projected version (right)

Dimensionality Reduction and Component Analysis

As the original dataset is linearly separable, after PCA projection, we can immediately find the threshold that allows detecting the first component (which is the only one really needed), in order to distinguish between the two blobs. However, if the dataset is not linearly separable, we get an unacceptable result, as shown in the following screenshot:

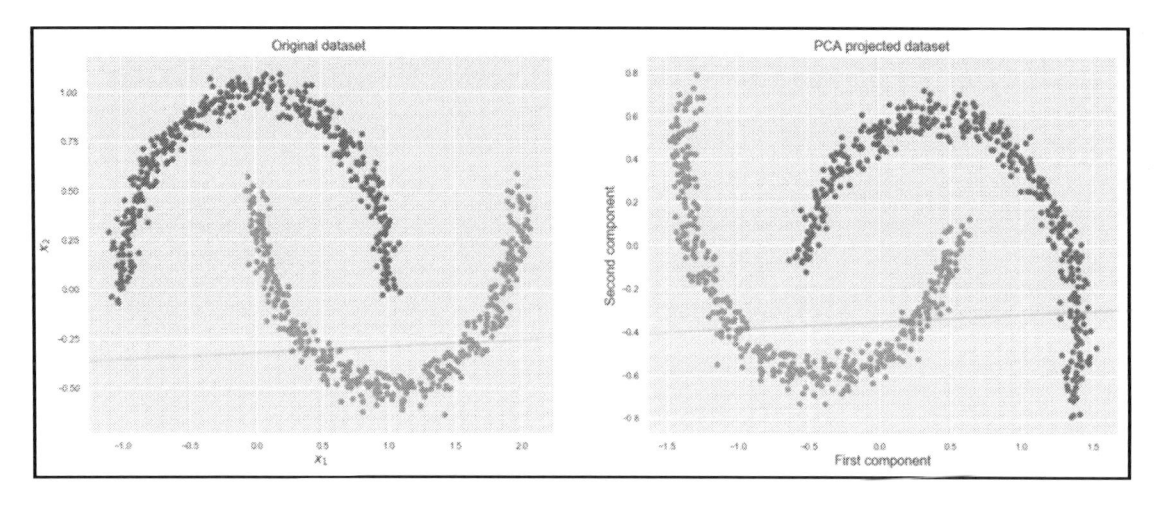

Original dataset (left); PCA projected version (right)

When the geometry is more complex, finding distinguishable thresholds can be impossible. However, we know that the projection of data onto a higher-dimensional space can make them linearly separable. In particular, if $x \in \Re^n$, we could choose an appropriate function, $f(x)$, so that $y = f(x) \in \Re^p$, with $p \gg n$. Unfortunately, applying this transformation to the entire dataset can be very expensive; in fact, given a transformation matrix, A, (with n components), a single principal component, $a^{(t)}$, after the projection, can be written as follows (remember that they are the eigenvectors of the covariance matrix):

$$\bar{v}^{(t)} = \sum_i (m\bar{x}_i^T \cdot \bar{x}_i)\bar{x}_i = \sum_i \beta_{it}\bar{x}_i \Rightarrow \bar{a}^{(t)} = \sum_i \alpha_{it} f(\bar{x}_i)$$

Therefore, the transformation of a single vector becomes the following:

$$\bar{z}_j = \bar{v}^{(t)T}\bar{x}_i \Rightarrow \bar{w}_j = \left(\sum_i \alpha_{it} f(\bar{x}_i)\right)^T f(\bar{x}_j)$$

As is possible to see, the transformation requires the computation of the dot product, $f(x_i)^T f(x_j)$. In these cases, we can employ the so-called **kernel trick**, which states that there are specific functions, $K(\bullet, \bullet)$, called kernels, with an interesting property, as follows:

$$K(\bar{x}_i, \bar{x}_j) = f(\bar{x}_i)^T f(\bar{x}_j)$$

In other words, we can compute the projection onto the principal components in a higher-dimensional space by simply computing the kernel for every couple of points, instead of performing a dot product, which requires n multiplications after the computation of $f(\bullet)$.

Some common kernels are as follows:

- The **Radial Basis Function (RBF)**, or Gaussian, kernel:

$$K(\bar{x}_i, \bar{x}_j) = e^{-\frac{\|\bar{x}_i - \bar{x}_j\|^2}{\sigma^2}} \quad or \quad e^{-\gamma \|\bar{x}_i - \bar{x}_j\|^2}$$

- The polynomial kernel, with a degree of p: $K(\bar{x}_i, \bar{x}_j) = (a + b\bar{x}_i^T \cdot \bar{x}_j)^p$

- The sigmoid kernel:

$$K(\bar{x}_i, \bar{x}_j) = \frac{e^{2(a+b\bar{x}_i^T \cdot \bar{x}_j)} - 1}{e^{2(a+b\bar{x}_i^T \cdot \bar{x}_j)} + 1}$$

The procedure is still rather expensive for very large datasets (but it's possible to precompute and store the kernel values, in order to avoid the extra time), but it's much more efficient than a standard projection. Moreover, it has the advantage of allowing for the extraction of the principal components in a space where linear discrimination is possible. Now, let's apply an RBF kernel PCA to the half-moon dataset that was shown in the previous screenshot. The gamma parameter is equal to $1/\sigma^2$. In this particular case, the main problem is the presence of a double overlap. Considering that the original standard deviation is about 1.0 (that is, also $\sigma^2 = 1$), we need at least three standard deviations in order to distinguish between them properly; therefore, we are going to set $\gamma = 10$:

```
from sklearn.datasets import make_moons
from sklearn.decomposition import KernelPCA

X, Y = make_moons(n_samples=800, noise=0.05, random_state=1000)

kpca = KernelPCA(n_components=2, kernel='rbf', gamma=10.0,
random_state=1000)
X_pca = kpca.fit_transform(X)
```

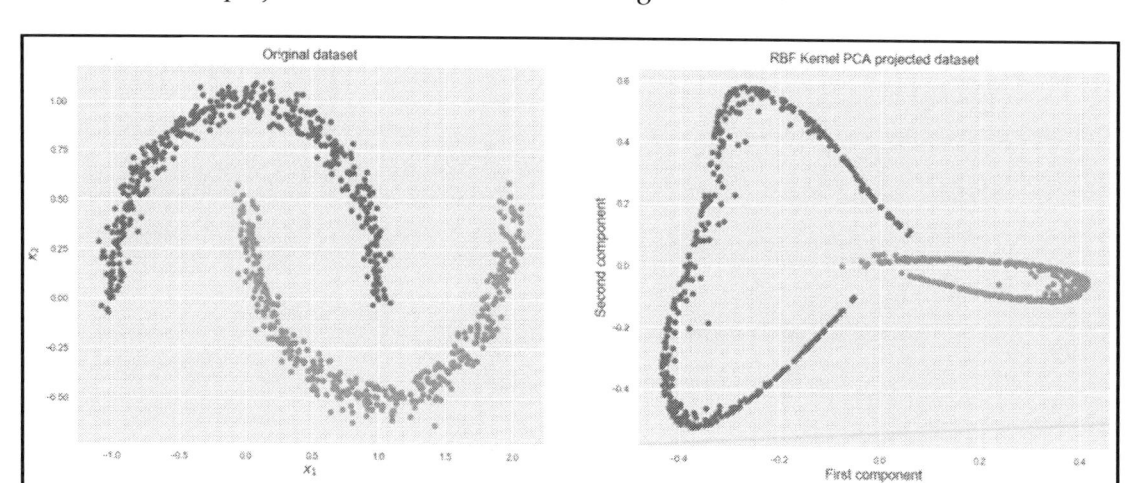

The result of the projection is shown in the following screenshot:

Original dataset (left); kernel PCA projected version (right)

As is possible to see, even in this case, the first component is enough to make a decision (with minimum tolerance, due to the noise), and setting a threshold at zero allows separation of the dataset. I invite the reader to test the effects of the other kernels and apply them, in order to distinguish between the MNIST subsets containing all zeros and ones.

Adding more robustness to heteroscedastic noise with factor analysis

One of the main problems with standard PCA is the intrinsic weakness of such a model in terms of heteroscedastic noise. If you are not familiar with this terminology, it will be helpful to introduce two definitions. A multivariate decorrelated noise term is characterized by a diagonal covariance matrix, C, which can have two different configurations, as follows:

- $C = diag(\sigma^2, \sigma^2, ..., \sigma^2)$: In this case, the noise is defined as **homoscedastic** (all of the components have the same variance).
- $C = diag(\sigma_1^2, \sigma_2^2, ..., \sigma_n^2)$, with $\sigma_1^2 \neq \sigma_2^2 \neq ... \neq \sigma_n^2$: In this case, the noise is defined as **heteroscedastic** (every component has its own variance).

It's possible to prove that, when the noise is homoscedastic, PCA can easily manage it, because the explained variances of single components are affected by the noise term in the same way (that is, this is equivalent to the absence of noise). Conversely, when the noise is heteroscedastic, the performance of PCA drops, and the result could be absolutely unacceptable. For this reason, Rubin and Thayer (in *EM algorithms for ML factor analysis, Rubin D. and Thayer D., Psychometrika, 47, 1982*) proposed an alternative dimensionality reduction method, called **factor analysis**, which can solve this kind of problem.

Let's suppose that we have a zero-centered dataset, X, containing m samples $x_i \in \mathfrak{R}^n$. Our goal is to find a set of latent variables, $z_i \in \mathfrak{R}^p$ (with $p < n$), and a matrix, A (called a factor-loading matrix), so that each sample can be rewritten, as follows:

$$\bar{x}_i = A\bar{z}_i + \bar{n} \text{ where } \bar{z}_i \sim N(0, I) \text{ and } \bar{n} \sim N(0, C_n) \text{ with } C_n = diag(\sigma_1^2, \sigma_2^2, \ldots, \sigma_n^2)$$

Hence, we are now assuming that a sample, x_i is a combination of a set of Gaussian latent variables, plus an additional heteroscedastic noise term. As latent variables have lower dimensionality, the problem is very similar to standard PCA, with the main difference that now, we are taking into account the heteroscedastic noise (of course, the term n can also be null, or homoscedastic). Therefore, when the components (that is, the latent variables) are determined, the impact of the different noise variances is included in the model, with the final effect of partial filtering (denoising). In the aforementioned paper, the authors proposed an optimization algorithm, which is not very formally complex, but which requires many mathematical manipulations (for this reason, we are omitting any proof). This method is based on the **Expectation Maximization** (**EM**) algorithm, which facilitates finding the parameter set that maximizes the log-likelihood. In this book, instead of discussing all of the mathematical details (which can be found in the original paper), let's check the properties of this method and compare the results with standard PCA.

Let's start by loading the Olivetti faces dataset, zero-centering it, and creating a heteroscedastic noisy version, as follows:

```
import numpy as np

from sklearn.datasets import fetch_olivetti_faces

faces = fetch_olivetti_faces(shuffle=True, random_state=1000)
X = faces['data']
Xz = X - np.mean(X, axis=0)

C = np.diag(np.random.uniform(0.0, 0.1, size=Xz.shape[1]))
Xnz = Xz + np.random.multivariate_normal(np.zeros(shape=Xz.shape[1]), C,
size=Xz.shape[0])
```

Dimensionality Reduction and Component Analysis

A few original and noisy images are shown in the following screenshot:

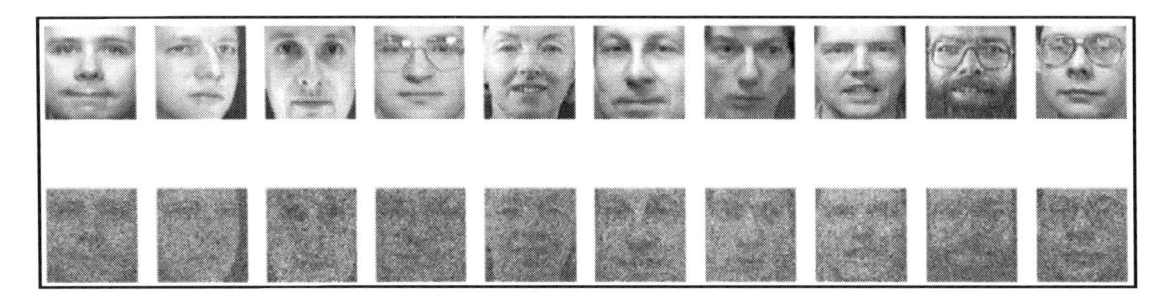

Original images (upper line); noisy versions (lower line)

Now, let's evaluate the average log-likelihood (through the `score()` method, available in both `PCA` and `FactorAnalysis` classes) for the following:

- PCA, with the original dataset and `128` components
- PCA, with the noisy dataset and `128` components
- Factor analysis, with the noisy dataset and `128` components (latent variables)

In the following snippet, all 3 models are instantiated and trained:

```
from sklearn.decomposition import PCA, FactorAnalysis

pca = PCA(n_components=128, random_state=1000)
pca.fit(Xz)
print('PCA log-likelihood(Xz): {}'.format(pca.score(Xz)))

pcan = PCA(n_components=128, random_state=1000)
pcan.fit(Xnz)
print('PCA log-likelihood(Xnz): {}'.format(pcan.score(Xnz)))

fa = FactorAnalysis(n_components=128, random_state=1000)
fa.fit(Xnz)
print('Factor Analysis log-likelihood(Xnz): 
{}'.format(fa.score(Xnz)))
```

The output of the previous snippet is as follows:

```
PCA log-likelihood(Xz): 4657.3828125
PCA log-likelihood(Xnz): -2426.302304948351
Factor Analysis log-likelihood(Xnz): 1459.2912218162423
```

These results show the effectiveness of factor analysis in the presence of heteroscedastic noise. The maximum average log-likelihood achieved by the PCA is about 4657, which drops to -2426 in the presence of noise. Conversely, factor analysis achieves an average log-likelihood of about 1,460, which is much larger than the one obtained using PCA (even if the effect of the noise has not been complete filtered out). Therefore, whenever the dataset contains (or the data scientist suspects that it contains) heteroscedastic noise (for example, the samples are obtained as a superimposition of sources captured by different instruments), I strongly suggest considering factor analysis as the primary dimensionality reduction method. Of course, if other conditions (for example, non-linearity, sparseness, and so on) are requested, the other methods that were discussed in the chapter could be evaluated before making a final decision.

Sparse PCA and dictionary learning

Standard PCA is generally a dense decomposition; this is to say that the vectors, once transformed, are linear combinations of all of the components with not-null coefficients:

$$\bar{z}_i = V^T \bar{x}_i = (\bar{v}_{11}\bar{x}_{i1} + \bar{v}_{21}\bar{x}_{i1} + \ldots + \bar{v}_{n1}\bar{x}_{in}) + \ldots = \alpha_1 \bar{x}_i 1 + \ldots + \alpha_n \bar{x}_i n$$

In the previous expression, the coefficients, α_i, are almost always different from zero, so all of the components are involved in the rebuilding process. For dimensionality reduction purposes, this is not an issue, because we are more interested in the variance explained by each component, in order to limit them. However, there are some tasks for which it's helpful to analyze a larger set of **building atoms**, with the assumption that each vector can be expressed as a sparse combination of them. The most classic example is a text corpus, where the dictionary contains many more terms than the one involved in every single document. These kinds of models are often called **dictionary learning** algorithms, because the set of atoms defines a sort of dictionary, containing all of the words that can be employed to create new samples. When the number of the atoms, *k*, is larger than the dimensionality of the samples, *n*, the dictionary is called **over-complete**, and the representations are often sparse. Conversely, when *k* < *n*, the dictionary is called **under-complete,** and the vectors need to be denser.

Such learning problems can easily be solved through the minimization of a function, by imposing a penalty on the L_1 norm of the solution. The reason that this constraint induces sparsity is beyond the scope of this book, but those that are interested can find a longer discussion in *Mastering Machine Learning Algorithms, Bonaccorso G., Packt Publications*, 2018.

The problem of dictionary learning (as well as sparse PCA) can be formally expressed as follows:

$$\begin{cases} argmin_{U,V} \|X - UV\|^2 + \alpha \|V\|_1 \\ \|U_k\| = 1 \end{cases}$$

This is a particular case of an algorithm, where the components, U_k, are forced to have unit lengths (unless there is the `normalize_components=False` parameter), and the coefficients, V, are penalized, in order to increase their sparsity (which is proportional to the coefficient, α).

Let's consider the MNIST dataset, performing sparse PCA with 30 components (which yields an under-complete dictionary) and a medium-high sparsity level (for example, α = 2.0). The array, X, is supposed to contain normalized samples, and is shown in the following PCA example:

```
from sklearn.decomposition import SparsePCA

spca = SparsePCA(n_components=30, alpha=2.0, normalize_components=True,
random_state=1000)
spca.fit(X)
```

At the end of the training process, the `components_` array contains the atoms, which are shown in the following screenshot:

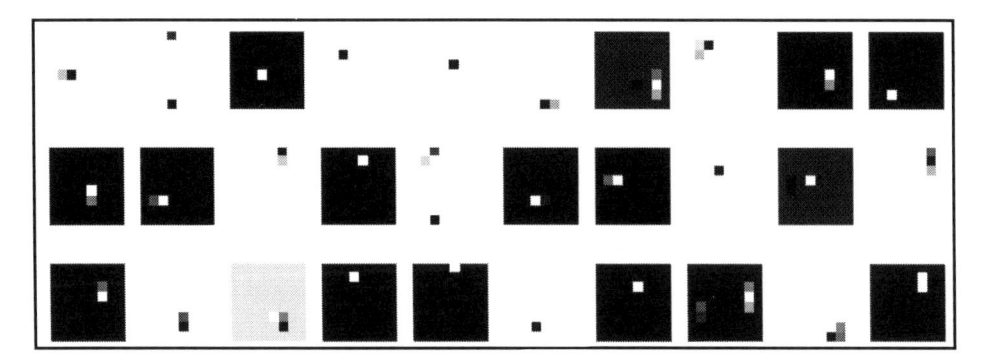

Components extracted by the sparse PCA algorithm

It's not difficult to understand that every digit can be composed using these atoms; however, the amount of sparsity cannot be extremely great, considering the number of atoms. Let's consider, for example, the transformation of the digit X[0]:

```
y = spca.transform(X[0].reshape(1, -1)).squeeze()
```

The absolute values of the coefficients are shown in the following screenshot:

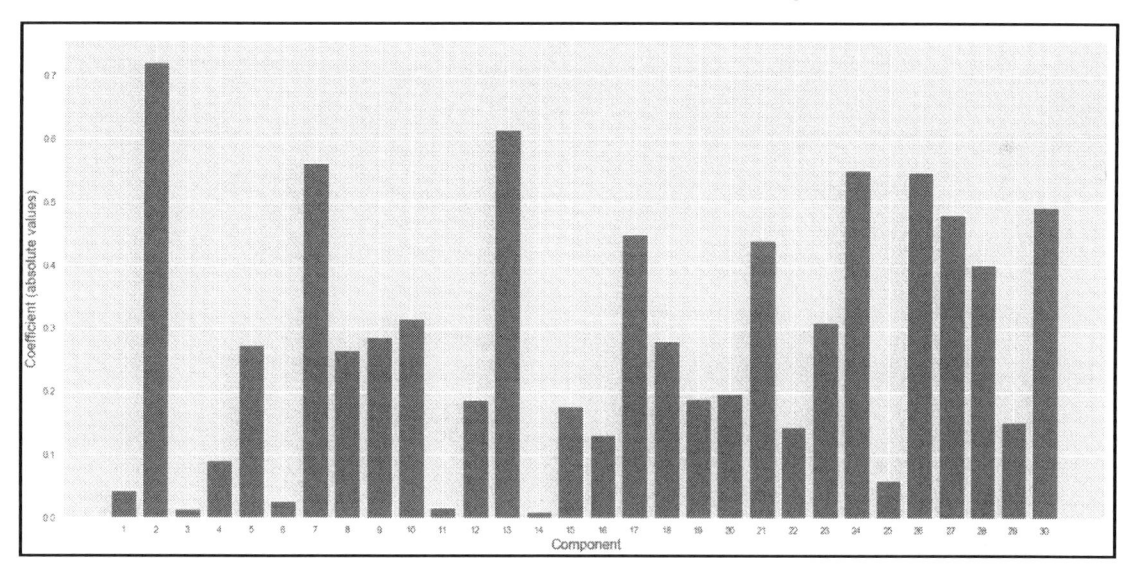

Absolute coefficients for the sparse transformation of the digit X[0]

There are clearly some dominant components (for example, **2**, **7**, **13**, **17**, **21**, **24**, **26**, **27**, and **30**), some secondary ones (for example, **5**, **8**, and so on) and some null or negligible ones (for example, **1**, **3**, **6**, and so on). If the sparsity level is increased with the same code length (30 components), the coefficients corresponding to the null components will drop to zero, while if the code length is also increased (for example, *k = 100*), the dictionary will become over-complete, and the number of null coefficients will increase, too.

Non-Negative Matrix Factorization

When the dataset, X, is non-negative, it is possible to apply a factorization technique, which has been proven (for example, in *Learning the parts of objects by non-negative matrix factorization, Lee D. D., and Seung, S. H., Nature, 401, 10/1999*) to be more reliable when the goal of the task is to extract atoms that correspond to the structural parts of the samples. For example, in the case of images, they are supposed to be geometrical elements or even more complex parts. The main condition imposed by **Non-Negative Matrix Factorization (NNMF)** is that all of the matrices involved must be non-negative and $X = UV$. Hence, once a norm, N, has been defined (for example, Frobenius), the simple objective becomes the following:

$$min_{U,V} \|X - UV\|_N$$

As this is not generally acceptable when sparsity is also needed (and, moreover, to allow for greater flexibility in changing the solution to meet specific requirements), the problem is often expressed (such as in scikit-learn) by adding penalties on both Frobenius (a matrix extension of L_2) and L_1 norms (for example, in ElasticNet):

$$min_{U,V} \left[\|X - UV\|_N + \alpha\beta(\|U\|_1 + \|V\|_1) + \frac{1}{2}\alpha(1-\beta)\left(\|U\|^2_{Frob} + \|V\|^2_{Frob}\right) \right]$$

Double regularization allows you to obtain both sparsity and a better match between the components and the parts of the samples, by avoiding an effect similar to the overfitting of supervised models (as the solution is sub-optimal, it also more flexible in adapting to new samples drawn from the same data-generating process; this increases the likelihood generally achievable).

Now, let's consider the MNIST dataset, and let's decompose it into 50 atoms, initially setting $\alpha = 2.0$ and $\beta = 0.1$ (called `l1_ratio` in scikit-learn). This configuration will force medium sparsity and a strong L2/Frobenius regularization. The process is straightforward and analogous to sparse PCA:

```
from sklearn.decomposition import NMF

nmf = NMF(n_components=50, alpha=2.0, l1_ratio=0.1, random_state=1000)
nmf.fit(X)
```

Chapter 7

At the end of the training process, the components (atoms) are as shown in the following screenshot:

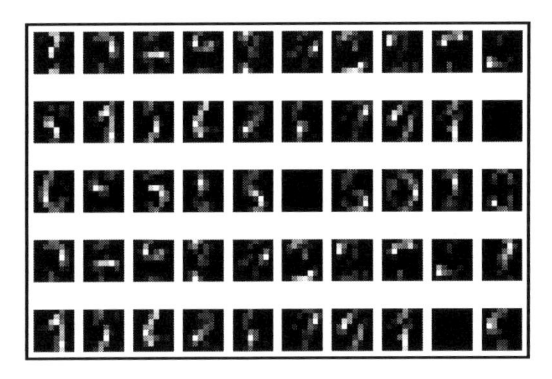

Atoms extracted by the NNMF algorithm

Contrary to what we observed for standard dictionary learning, the atoms are now much more structured, and they reproduce specific parts of the digits (for example, vertical or horizontal strokes, circles, dots, and so on); therefore, we can expect more sparse representations, because fewer components are enough to build a digit. Considering the example shown in the previous section (the digit X[0]), the absolute contributions of all of the components are the ones reported in the following diagram:

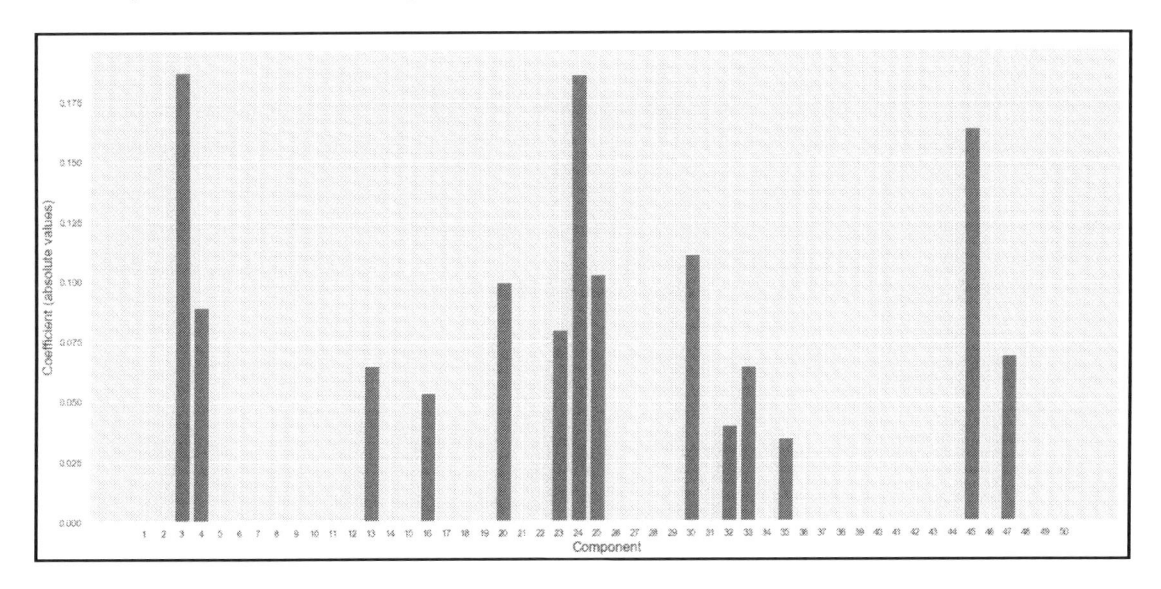

Absolute coefficients for the NNMF of the digit X[0]

Three components are dominant (**3, 24,** and **45**); hence, we can try to express the sample as a combination of them. The coefficients are, respectively, 0.19, 0.18, and 0.16. The result is shown in the following screenshot (the digit X[0] is the representation of zero):

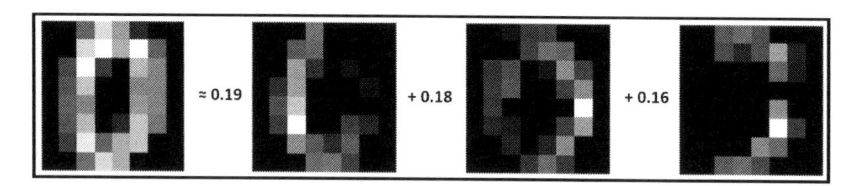

Deconstruction of the digit X[0], based on three main components

It's interesting to note how the algorithm has selected the atoms. Even if this process is strongly influenced by the *α* and *β* parameters, and by the norm, we can observe that, for example, the third atom (the first in the screenshot) can be shared by many zeros, threes, and eights; the last atom is helpful for both zeros and nines. An over-complete dictionary with a weaker L_1 penalty may be helpful whenever the granularity of the atoms is too coarse. Of course, each problem requires specific solutions; hence, I strongly suggest checking the structure of the atoms with a domain expert. As an exercise, I invite you to apply the NNMF to another dataset of small images (for example, Olivetti, Cifar-10, or STL-10), and try to find the right parameters necessary to isolate a fixed number of structural parts (for example, for faces, they can be eyes, noses, and mouths).

Independent Component Analysis

When working with standard PCA (or other techniques, such as factor analysis), the components are uncorrelated, but it's not guaranteed that they are statistically independent. In other words, let's suppose that we have a dataset, *X*, drawn from a joint probability distribution, *p(X)*; if there are *n* components, we cannot always be sure that the following equality holds:

$$p(x_1, x_2, \ldots, x_n) = p(x_1)p(x_2)\ldots p(x_n)$$

However, there are many important tasks, based on a common model called the **cocktail party**. In such scenarios, we can suppose (or we know) that many different and independent sources (for example, voices and music) overlap and generate a single signal. At this point, our goal is to try to separate the sources by applying a linear transformation to each sample. Let's consider a whitened dataset, X (so all of the components have the same informative content), which we can assume to be sampled from a Gaussian distribution N(0, I) (this is not a restrictive condition, because the overlap of many different sources easily converges to a normal distribution). Therefore, the goal can be expressed as follows:

$$\bar{x}_i = A\bar{z}_i \ \forall\ \bar{x}_i \in X \ and \ p(\bar{z};\theta) = \alpha \sum_k e^{f_k(\bar{z})}$$

In other words, we are expressing each sample as a product of a number of independent factors, with a prior distribution based on an exponential function. The only condition that must be absolutely enforced is the non-Gaussianity (otherwise, the components become indistinguishable); hence, the functions, $f_k(z)$, cannot be quadratic polynomials. In practice, we would also like to include moderate sparseness, so we expect peaked and heavy-tailed distributions (that is, the probability is high only in a very short range, and then abruptly drops to almost zero). Such a condition can be verified by checking the normalized fourth moment, called **kurtosis**:

$$Kurtosis(X) = E\left[\left(\frac{x - \mu_x}{\sigma_x}\right)^4\right]$$

For a Gaussian distribution, the kurtosis is 3. As this is often a reference value, all of the distributions with *Kurtosis(X) > 3* are called super-Gaussian or **leptokurtic**, while the ones with *Kurtosis(X) < 3* are called sub-Gaussian or **platykurtic**. An example of the former class of distribution is the Laplace one, which is shown in the following screenshot:

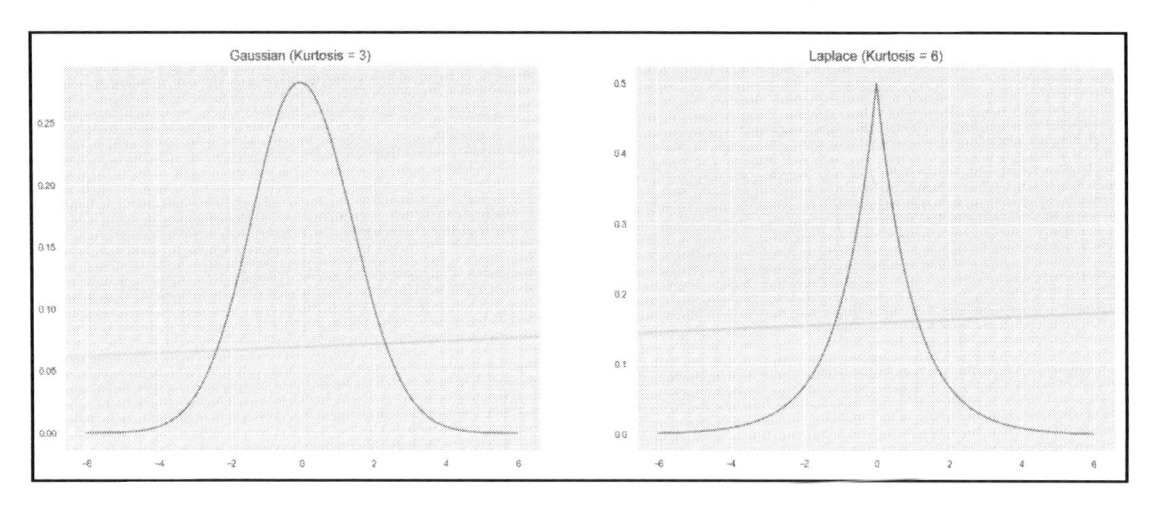

Probability density functions of Gaussian distribution (left) and Laplace distribution (right)

Unfortunately, the use of kurtosis is discouraged by its lack of robustness, with respect to outliers (that is, as it involves the fourth power, even a small value can be amplified and can alter the final result; for example, a noisy Gaussian with outliers on the tails can appear super-Gaussian). For this reason, the authors Hyvarinen and Oja (in *Independent Component Analysis: Algorithms and Applications, Hyvarinen A. and Oja, E., Neural Networks* 13, 2000) proposed an algorithm called **fast Independent Component Analysis (FastICA)**, based on the concept of **negentropy**. We are not going to describe the whole model in this book; however, it would be helpful to understand the basic ideas. It is possible to prove that, between all distributions with the same variance, the Gaussian has the largest entropy. Hence, if the dataset, *X* (zero-centered), has been drawn from a distribution with covariance, Σ, it is possible to define the negentropy of *X* as the difference between the entropy of a Gaussian $N(0, ;\Sigma)$ and the entropy of *X*:

$$H_N(X) = H(N(0, \Sigma)) - H(X)$$

Therefore, our goal is to reduce $H_N(X)$ (which is always greater than or equal to zero) by reducing $H(X)$. The FastICA algorithm is based on an approximation of $H_N(X)$ through a combination of specific functions. The most common, called **logcosh** (which is also the default in scikit-learn), is as follows:

$$f(x) = \frac{1}{a} \log(\cosh(ax))$$

With this trick, the negentropy can be optimized more easily, and the final decomposition is certain to contain independent components. Now, let's apply the FastICA algorithm to the MNIST dataset (in order to force better precision, we are setting `max_iter=10000` and `tol=1e-5`):

```
from sklearn.decomposition import FastICA

ica = FastICA(n_components=50, max_iter=10000, tol=1e-5, random_state=1000)
ica.fit(X)
```

The 50 independent components (always available through the `components_` instance variable) found by the algorithm are shown in the following screenshot:

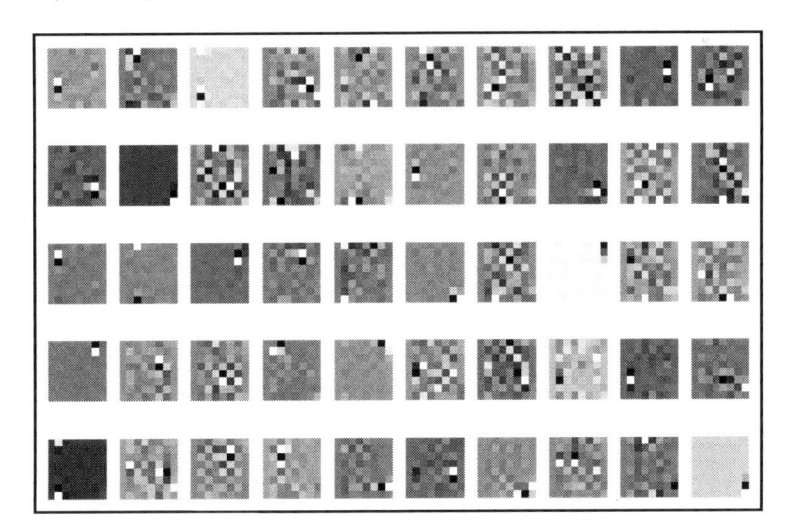

Independent components extracted by FastICA

In this case, the components are immediately recognizable as parts of the digits (I invite the reader to repeat the example by reducing and increasing the number of components up to 64, which is the maximum number, considering the dimensionality of the dataset). The components tend to reach the mean positions of the corresponding distributions; hence, with a smaller number, it's possible to distinguish more structured patterns (which can be considered different overlapping signals), while a larger number of components leads to more feature-centered elements. However, contrary to NNMF, FastICA doesn't guarantee extracting actual parts of the samples, but rather, more complete regions. In other words, while NNMF can easily detect, for example, some single strokes, FastICA tends to consider the samples as a sum of different signals, which, in the case of images, often involves the entire dimensionality of the samples, unless the number of components is drastically increased. To better understand this concept, let's consider the Olivetti faces dataset, which contains 400 64 × 64 grayscale portraits:

```
from sklearn.datasets import fetch_olivetti_faces

faces = fetch_olivetti_faces(shuffle=True, random_state=1000)
```

The first 10 faces are shown in the following screenshot:

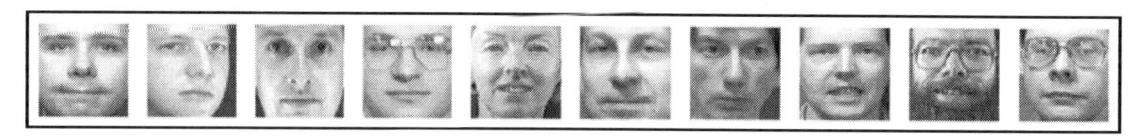

Sample faces extracted from the Olivetti faces dataset

Now, let's extract 100 independent components:

```
ica = FastICA(n_components=100, max_iter=10000, tol=1e-5, random_state=1000)
ica.fit(faces['data'])
```

The first 50 components are plotted in the following screenshot:

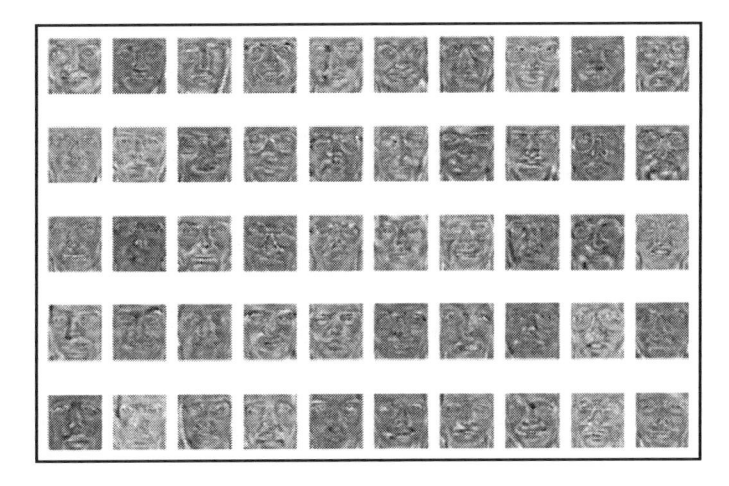

50 (out of 100) independent components extracted by FastICA

As you can see, each component is similar to a **meta-face** (sometimes called an eigenface), with some specific, dominant features together with secondary contributions, due to all of the remaining ones (even if they are not immediately recognizable in a precise sample set). The effect becomes even more evident when the number of components is increased to 350, as follows:

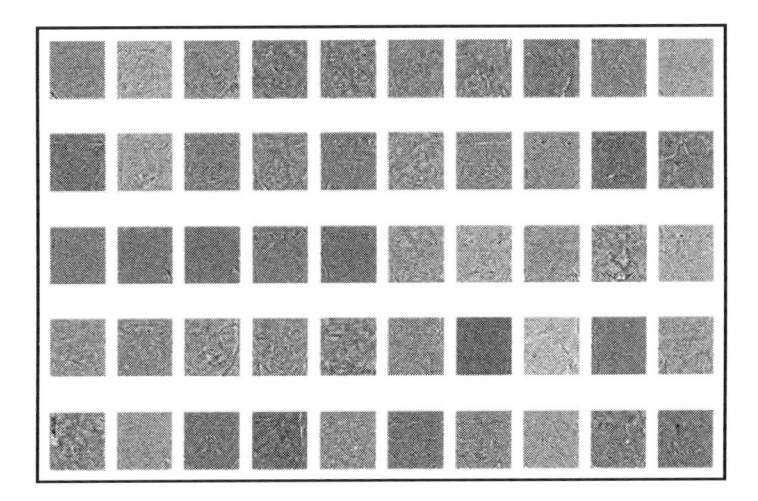

50 (out of 350) independent components extracted by FastICA

In this case, the secondary features are less dominant, because there are more overlapping distributions, and each of them is centered on a more atomic eigenface. Of course, the optimal number of components cannot be defined without complete domain knowledge. For example, in the case of the Olivetti faces dataset, it could be helpful to identify either particular subelements (for example, the position of glasses) or more complete facial expressions. In the former case, a larger number of components yields more focused solutions (even if they are globally less distinguishable), while in the latter, a smaller number (such as in the previous example) produces more complete outcomes, where it's possible to evaluate different influencing factors. In terms of signals, the number of components should be equal to the number of expected overlapping factors (assuming their independence). For example, an audio signal can contain a recording of a person talking in an airport, with a background voice announcing a flight. In this case, the scenario can be made up of three components: two voices and noise. As the noise will be partially split into the dominant components, the final number will be equal to two.

Topic modeling with Latent Dirichlet Allocation

We will now consider another kind of decomposition that is extremely helpful when working with text documents (that is, NLP). The theoretical part is not very easy, because it requires deep knowledge of probability theory and statistical learning (it can be found in the original paper *Latent Dirichlet Allocation, Journal of Machine Learning Research, Blei D., Ng A., and Jordan M., 3, (2003) 993-1022*); therefore, we are only going to discuss the main elements, without any mathematical references (a more compact description is also present in *Machine Learning Algorithms Second Edition, Bonaccorso, G., Packt Publications, 2018*). Let's consider a set of text documents, d_j (called a **corpus**), whose atoms (or components) are the words, w_i:

$$d_j = \{w_{j1}, w_{j2}, \ldots, w_{jm}\} \text{ and } Corpus = \{d_1, d_2, \ldots, d_p\}$$

After collecting all of the words, we can build a dictionary:

$$Dictionary = \{w_1, w_2, \ldots, w_n\}$$

We can also state the following inequality ($N(\bullet)$ counts the number of elements of a set):

$$N(d_j) \ll N(Dictionary) \ \forall j \in Corpus$$

This means that the distribution of the words between the documents is sparse, because only a few words are used in a single document, and the choice for the former is the symmetric Dirichlet distribution (the model is named after it), which is extremely sparse (moreover, it's the conjugate prior for categorical distribution, which is a one-trial multinomial one, so is quite easy to incorporate into the model). The probability density function (as the distribution is symmetric, the parameter $\alpha_i = \alpha \ \forall \ i$) is as follows:

$$p(\bar{x}, \bar{\alpha}) = \frac{\Gamma(\sum_k \alpha_k)}{\prod_k \Gamma(\alpha_k)} \prod_k x_k^{\alpha_k - 1} = \frac{\Gamma(\alpha k)}{\Gamma(\alpha)^k} \prod_k x_k^{\alpha - 1} \quad (for\ the\ symmetry)$$

Now, let's consider a semantic grouping of the documents into topics, t_k, and suppose that every topic is characterized by a small number of peculiar words:

$$t_k = \{w_{k1}, w_{k2}, \ldots, w_{kt}\} \ and \ Topics = \{t_1, t_2, \ldots, t_k\}$$

This means that the distribution of words between topics is also sparse. Therefore, we have full joint probability (words, topics), and we want to determine the conditional probabilities $p(w_i | t_k)$ and $p(t_k | w_i)$. In other words, given a document, which is a collection of terms (each of them has a marginal probability $p(w_i)$), we want to compute the probability that such a document belongs to a specific topic. As a document is softly assigned to all of the topics (that is, it can belong to more than one topic, to different degrees), we need to consider a sparse topic-document distribution from which the topic-mixtures (θ_i) are drawn:

$$\theta_i \sim Dir(\alpha)$$

In an analogous way, we need to consider the topic-word distribution (as a word can be shared by more topics, to different degrees) from which we can draw topic-word-mixture samples, β_j:

$$\beta_j \sim Dir(\gamma)$$

Latent Dirichlet Allocation (LDA) is a generative model (the training goal, in a simplistic way, consists of finding the optimal parameters α and γ) that is able to extract a fixed number of topics from a corpus and characterize them with a set of words. Given a sample document, it is able to assign it to a topic by providing the topic-mixture probability vector ($\theta_i = (p(t_1), p(t_2), \ldots, p(t_k))$); it can also work with unseen documents (using the same dictionary).

Dimensionality Reduction and Component Analysis

Now, let's apply the LDA to a subset of the 20 newsgroups dataset, which contains thousands of messages publicly released for NLP research. In particular, we want to model the rec.autos and comp.sys.mac.hardware subgroups. We can use the built-in scikit-learn fetch_20newsgroups() function, asking to strip all of the unnecessary headers, footers, and quotes (other posts attached to an answer):

```
from sklearn.datasets import fetch_20newsgroups

news = fetch_20newsgroups(subset='all', categories=('rec.autos',
'comp.sys.mac.hardware'), remove=('headers', 'footers', 'quotes'),
random_state=1000)

corpus = news['data']
labels = news['target']
```

At this point, we need to vectorize the corpus. In other words, we need to transform each document into a sparse vector containing the frequency (count) of each word in the vocabulary:

$$d_j = \{w_1, w_2, \ldots, w_p\} \quad \Rightarrow \quad f(d_j) = \{n(w_1), n(w_2), \ldots, n(w_N)\}$$

We are going to perform this step using the CountVectorizer class, asking to strip the accents and remove the stop words (for example, in English, and, the, and so on) that have a very high relative frequency, but are not representative. Moreover, we are forcing the tokenizer to exclude all of the tokens that are not pure text (by setting token_pattern='[a-z]+'). In other contexts, this pattern could be different, but in this case, we don't want to rely on numbers and symbols:

```
from sklearn.feature_extraction.text import CountVectorizer

cv = CountVectorizer(strip_accents='unicode', stop_words='english',
analyzer='word', token_pattern='[a-z]+')
Xc = cv.fit_transform(corpus)

print(len(cv.vocabulary_))
```

The output of the previous snippet is as follows:

```
14182
```

Hence, each document is a 14,182-dimensional sparse vector (it's obvious that the majority of values are null). We can now perform LDA by imposing n_components=2, because we expect to extract two topics:

```
from sklearn.decomposition import LatentDirichletAllocation

lda = LatentDirichletAllocation(n_components=2, learning_method='online',
max_iter=100, random_state=1000)
Xl = lda.fit_transform(Xc)
```

After the training process, the components_ instance variable contains the relative frequency (in terms of counts) of each couple (word and topic). Hence, in our case, its shape is (2, 14, 182), and the components_[i, j] element, with $i \in (0, 1)$ and $j \in (0, 14, 181)$, can be interpreted as the importance of the word, j, in order to define the topic, i. Therefore, we would be interested in checking, for example, the top 10 words for both topics:

```
import numpy as np

Mwts_lda = np.argsort(lda.components_, axis=1)[::-1]

for t in range(2):
    print('\nTopic ' + str(t))
    for i in range(10):
        print(cv.get_feature_names()[Mwts_lda[t, i]])
```

The output is as follows:

```
Topic 0
compresion
progress
deliberate
dependency
preemptive
wv
nmsu
bpp
coexist
logically

Topic 1
argues
compromising
overtorque
moly
forbid
cautioned
sauber
```

Dimensionality Reduction and Component Analysis

```
explosion
eventual
agressive
```

It's easy (considering some very peculiar terms) to understand that `Topic 0` has been assigned to `comp.sys.mac.hardware`, and the other one to `rec.autos` (unfortunately, this process cannot be based on autodetection, because the semantic must be interpreted by a human being). In order to evaluate the model, let's consider two sample messages, as follows:

```
print(corpus[100])
print(corpus[200])
```

The output, limited to a few lines, is as follows:

```
I'm trying to find some information on accelerator boards for the SE. Has
anyone used any in the past, especially those from Extreme Systems, Novy or
MacProducts? I'm looking for a board that will support extended video,
especially Radius's two-page monitor. Has anyone used Connectix Virtual in
conjunction with their board? Any software snafus? Are there any stats
anywhere on the speed difference between a board with an FPU and one
without? Please send mail directly to me. Thanks.

...

The new Cruisers DO NOT have independent suspension in the front.  They
still
run a straight axle, but with coils.  The 4Runner is the one with
independent
front.  The Cruisers have incredible wheel travel with this system.

The 91-up Cruiser does have full time 4WD, but the center diff locks in
low range.  My brother has a 91 and is an incredibly sturdy vehicle which
has done all the 4+ trails in Moab without a tow.  The 93 and later is even
better with the bigger engine and locking diffs.
```

Therefore, the first post is clearly related to graphics, while the second one is a political message. Let's compute the topic-mixtures for both of them, as follows:

```
print(Xl[100])
print(Xl[200])
```

The output is as follows:

```
[0.98512538 0.01487462]
[0.01528335 0.98471665]
```

So, the first message has about 98% probability belonging to `Topic 0`, while the second one is almost hardly assigned to `Topic 1`. This confirms that the decomposition has worked properly. In order to get a better insight into the overall distribution, it will be helpful to visualize the mixtures for the messages belonging to each category, as shown in the following screenshot:

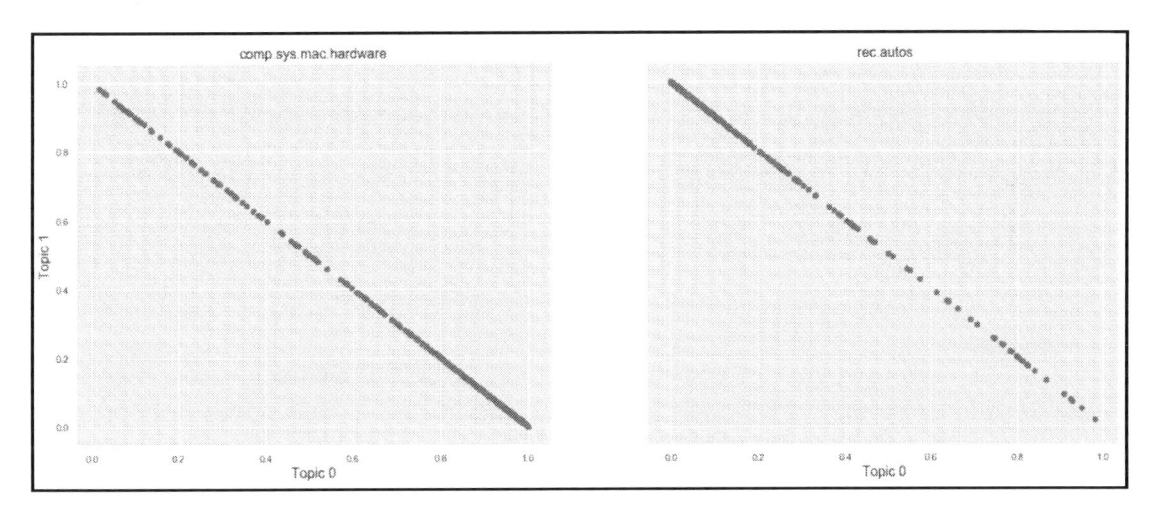

Topic-mixtures for comp.sys.mac.hardware (left) and rec.autos (right)

As you can see, the topics are almost orthogonal. The majority of the messages belonging to `rec.autos` have $p(t_0) < 0.5$ and $p(t_1) > 0.5$, while there's a slight overlap for `comp.sys.mac.hardware`, where the group of messages that do not have $p(t_0) > 0.5$ and $p(t_1) < 0.5$ is a little bit larger. This is probably due to the presence of words that can qualify both topics with the same importance (for example, the terms *discussion* or *debate* could be equally present in both newsgroups). As an exercise, I invite you to employ more subsets and try to prove the orthogonality of the topics and detect the words that could lead to incorrect assignments.

Summary

In this chapter, we presented different techniques that can be employed for both dimensionality reduction and dictionary learning. PCA is a very well-known method that involves finding the most import components of the dataset associated with the directions where the variance is larger. This method has the double effect of diagonalizing the covariance matrix and providing an immediate measure of the importance of each feature, so as to simplify the selection and maximize the residual explained variance (the amount of variance that it is possible to explain with a smaller number of components). As PCA is intrinsically a linear method, it cannot often be employed with non-linear datasets. For this reason, a kernel-based variant has been developed. In our example, you saw how an RBF kernel is able to project a non-linearly separable dataset onto a subspace, where PCA can determine a discriminant component.

Sparse PCA and dictionary learning are widely used techniques that are employed when it's necessary to extract building atoms that can be mixed (in a linear combination), in order to produce samples. In many cases, the goal is to find a so-called over-complete dictionary, which is equivalent to saying that we expect many more atoms than the ones actually employed to build each sample (that's why the representation is sparse). While PCA can extract uncorrelated components, it seldom fails to find statistically independent ones. For this reason, we introduced the concept of ICA, which is a technique that was developed in order to extract overlapped sources from samples that can be thought of as the sum of independent causes (for example, voices or visual elements). Another method with peculiar features is the NNMF, which can produce both a sparse representation and a set of components resembling specific parts of the samples (for example, for a face, they can represent eyes, noses, and so on). The last section covered the concept of LDA, which is a topic modeling technique that can be employed to find topic-mixtures, given a corpus of documents (that is, the probability that a document belongs to each specific topic).

In the next chapter, we will introduce some neural models based on the unsupervised paradigm. In particular, deep belief networks, autoencoders, and models that can extract the principal component of a dataset without the eigendecomposition (nor SVD) of the covariance matrix, will be discussed.

Questions

1. A dataset, X, has a covariance matrix $C=diag(2, 1)$. What do you expect from PCA?
2. Considering the previous question, if X is zero-centered and the ball, $B_{0.5}(0, 0)$, is empty, can we suppose that a threshold of $x = 0$ (the first principal component) allows for horizontal discrimination?
3. The components extracted by PCA are statistically independent. Is this correct?
4. A distribution with $Kurt(X) = 5$ is suitable for ICA. Is this correct?
5. What is the NNMF of a dataset, X, containing the samples (1, 2) and (0, -3)?
6. A corpus of 10 documents is associated with a dictionary with 10 terms. We know that the fixed length of each document is 30 words. Is the dictionary over-complete?
7. Kernel PCA is employed with a quadratic kernel. If the original dimensionality is 2, what is the dimensionality of the new space where the PCA is performed?

Further reading

- *Online Dictionary Learning for Sparse Coding*, J. Mairal, F. Bach, J. Ponce, and G. Sapiro, 2009
- *Learning the parts of objects by non-negative matrix factorization*, Lee D. D., Seung S. H., Nature, 401, 10/1999
- *EM algorithms for ML factor analysis*, Rubin D., and Thayer D., Psychometrika, 47, 1982
- *Independent Component Analysis: Algorithms and Applications*, Hyvarinen A. and Oja E., Neural Networks 13, 2000
- *Mathematical Foundations of Information Theory*, Khinchin A. I., Dover Publications
- *Latent Dirichlet Allocation, Journal of Machine Learning Research*, Blei D., Ng A., and Jordan M., 3, (2003) 993-1022
- *Machine Learning Algorithms Second Edition*, Bonaccorso G., Packt Publishing, 2018
- *Mastering Machine Learning Algorithms*, Bonaccorso G., Packt Publishing, 2018

8
Unsupervised Neural Network Models

In this chapter, we will discuss some neural models that can be employed for unsupervised tasks. The choice of neural networks (often deep ones) allows you to address the complexity of high-dimensional datasets with particular features that need sophisticated processing units (for example, images).

In particular, we will cover the following:

- Autoencoders
- Denoising autoencoders
- Sparse autoencoders
- Variational autoencoders
- PCA neural networks:
- Sanger's network
- Rubner-Tavan's network
- Unsupervised **Deep Belief Networks (DBN)**

Technical requirements

The code presented in this chapter requires the following:

- Python 3.5+ (The `Anaconda distribution` is highly recommended)
- The following libraries:
    - SciPy 0.19+
    - NumPy 1.10+
    - scikit-learn 0.20+
    - pandas 0.22+
    - Matplotlib 2.0+
    - seaborn 0.9+
    - TensorFlow 1.5+
    - deep-belief-network (https://github.com/albertbup/deep-belief-network)

The examples are available in the GitHub repository, at https://github.com/PacktPublishing/HandsOn-Unsupervised-Learning-with-Python/Chapter08.

Autoencoders

In `Chapter 7`, *Dimensionality Reduction And Component Analysis*, we discussed some common methods that can be employed to reduce the dimensionality of a dataset, given its peculiar statistical properties (for example, the covariance matrix). However, when complexity increases, even **kernel principal component analysis (kernel PCA)** might be unable to find a suitable lower-dimensional representation. In other words, the loss of information can overcome a threshold that guarantees the possibility of rebuilding the samples effectively. **Autoencoders** are models that exploit the extreme non-linearity of neural networks, in order to find low-dimensional representations of a given dataset. In particular, let's assume that X is a set of samples drawn from a data-generating process, $p_{data}(x)$. For simplicity, we will consider $x_i \in \Re^n$, but there are no restrictions on the structure of the support (for example, for RGB images, $x_i \in \Re^{n \times m \times 3}$). An autoencoder is formally split into two components: there is an encoder, which transforms a high-dimensional input into shorter code, and a decoder, which performs an inverse operation (as shown in the following diagram):

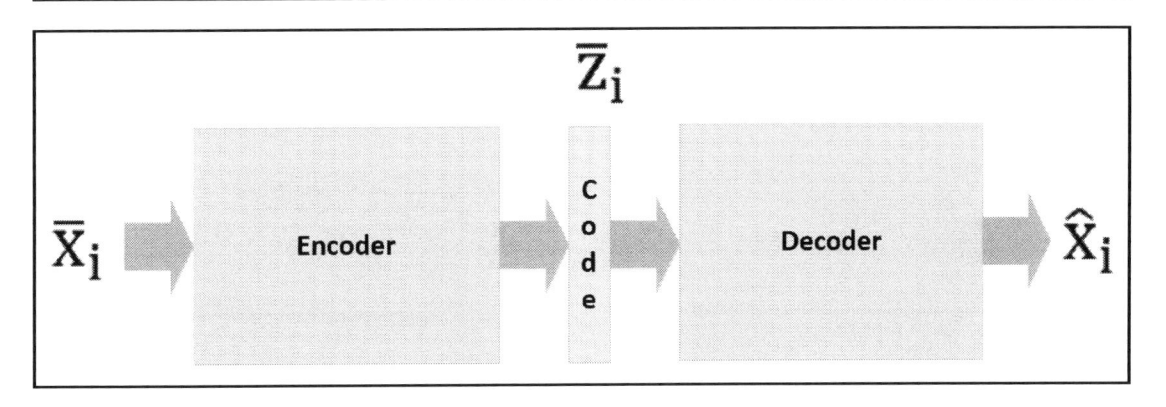

Structural schema of a generic autoencoder

If the code is a p-dimensional vector, the encoder can be defined as a parameterized function, $e(\bullet)$:

$$\bar{z}_i = e(\bar{x}_i, \bar{\theta}_e) \text{ where } \bar{x}_i \in \mathbb{R}^n \text{ and } \bar{z}_i \in \mathbb{R}^p$$

In an analogous way, the decoder is another parameterized function, $d(\bullet)$:

$$\hat{x}_i = d(\bar{z}_i, \bar{\theta}_d) \text{ where } \hat{x}_i \in \mathbb{R}^n \text{ and } \bar{z}_i \in \mathbb{R}^p$$

Therefore, a full autoencoder is a composite function that, given an input sample, x_i, provides an optimal reconstruction as output:

$$\hat{x}_i = d(e(\bar{x}_i, \bar{\theta}_e), \bar{\theta}_d) = g(\bar{x}_i, \bar{\theta})$$

As they are generally implemented through neural networks, an autoencoder is trained using the back-propagation algorithm, very often based on the mean square error cost function:

$$C(X, \hat{X}, \bar{\theta}) = \frac{1}{m} \sum_i \left(\bar{x}_i - g(\bar{x}_i, \bar{\theta})\right)$$

Alternatively, considering the data-generating process, we can re-express the goal considering a parameterized conditional distribution, $q(\bullet)$:

$$q(\hat{x}_i | \bar{x}_i) = p(e(\bar{x}_i, \bar{\theta}_e), \bar{\theta}_d | \bar{x}_i)$$

Hence, the cost function can now become, for example, the Kullback-Leibler divergence between $p_{data}(\cdot)$ and $q(\cdot)$:

$$D_{KL}(p_{data}||q) = \sum_i p_{data}(\bar{x}_i) \log \frac{p_{data}(\bar{x}_i)}{q(\hat{x}_i|\bar{x}_i)} = -H(p_{data}) + H(p_{data}, q) = H(p_{data}, q) + k$$

As the entropy of p_{data} is a constant, it can be excluded by the optimization process; therefore, the minimization of the divergence is equivalent to minimizing the cross-entropy between p_{data} and q. The Kullback-Leibler cost function is equivalent to the mean square error, if p_{data} and q are assumed to be Gaussian, so both approaches are interchangeable. In some cases, when the data is normalized in the range (0, 1), it's possible to employ a Bernoulli distribution for either p_{data} and q. Formally, this is not completely correct, as a Bernoulli distribution is binary and $x_i \in \{0, 1\}^d$; however, the employment of sigmoid output units also guarantees successful optimization for continuous samples, $x_i \in (0, 1)^d$. In this case, the cost function becomes the following:

$$H(p_{data}, q) = -\sum_i \hat{x}_i \log(\hat{x}_i) + (1 - \hat{x}_i)\log(1 - \hat{x}_i)$$

Example of a deep convolutional autoencoder

Let's implement a deep convolutional autoencoder based on TensorFlow and the Olivetti faces dataset (which is relatively small, but offers a good level of expressivity). Let's start by loading the images and preparing the training set:

```
from sklearn.datasets import fetch_olivetti_faces

faces = fetch_olivetti_faces(shuffle=True, random_state=1000)
X_train = faces['images']
```

The samples are 400, 64 × 64 grayscale images that we are going to resize to 32 × 32, in order to speed up computation and avoid memory issues (this operation will cause a slight loss of visual precision, and you can remove it if you have enough computational resources). We can now define the main constants (the number of epochs (`nb_epochs`), `batch_size`, and `code_length`) and the `graph`:

```
import tensorflow as tf

nb_epochs = 600
batch_size = 50
```

```
code_length = 256
width = 32
height = 32

graph = tf.Graph()
```

Hence, we are going to train the model for 600 epochs, with 50 samples per batch. As each image is *64 × 64 = 4,096*, the compression ratio is *4,096/256 = 16* times. Of course, this choice is not a rule, and I invite you to always check for different configurations, in order to maximize both the convergence speed and the final accuracy. In our case, we are modeling the encoder with the following layers:

- 2D convolution with 16 (3 × 3) filters, (2 × 2) strides, ReLU activation, and the same padding
- 2D convolution with 32 (3 × 3) filters, (1 × 1) strides, ReLU activation, and the same padding
- 2D convolution with 64 (3 × 3) filters, (1 × 1) strides, ReLU activation, and the same padding
- 2D convolution with 128 (3 × 3) filters, (1 × 1) strides, ReLU activation, and the same padding

The decoder exploits a sequence of transpose convolutions (also called **deconvolutions**):

- 2D transpose convolution with 128 (3 × 3) filters, (2 × 2) strides, ReLU activation, and the same padding
- 2D transpose convolution with 64 (3 × 3) filters, (1 × 1) strides, ReLU activation, and the same padding
- 2D transpose convolution with 32 (3 × 3) filters, (1 × 1) strides, ReLU activation, and the same padding
- 2D transpose convolution with 1 (3 × 3) filter, (1 × 1) strides, Sigmoid activation, and the same padding

The loss function is based on the L_2 norm of the difference between the reconstructions and the original images. The optimizer is Adam, with a learning rate of *η=0.001*. The encoder part of the TensorFlow DAG is as follows:

```
import tensorflow as tf

with graph.as_default():
    input_images_xl = tf.placeholder(tf.float32,
                                    shape=(None, X_train.shape[1],
X_train.shape[2], 1))
    input_images = tf.image.resize_images(input_images_xl, (width, height),
```

```
                method=tf.image.ResizeMethod.BICUBIC)

    # Encoder
    conv_0 = tf.layers.conv2d(inputs=input_images,
                              filters=16,
                              kernel_size=(3, 3),
                              strides=(2, 2),
                              activation=tf.nn.relu,
                              padding='same')

    conv_1 = tf.layers.conv2d(inputs=conv_0,
                              filters=32,
                              kernel_size=(3, 3),
                              activation=tf.nn.relu,
                              padding='same')

    conv_2 = tf.layers.conv2d(inputs=conv_1,
                              filters=64,
                              kernel_size=(3, 3),
                              activation=tf.nn.relu,
                              padding='same')
    conv_3 = tf.layers.conv2d(inputs=conv_2,
                              filters=128,
                              kernel_size=(3, 3),
                              activation=tf.nn.relu,
                              padding='same')
```

The code part of the DAG is as follows:

```
import tensorflow as tf

with graph.as_default():
    # Code layer
    code_input = tf.layers.flatten(inputs=conv_3)

    code_layer = tf.layers.dense(inputs=code_input,
                                 units=code_length,
                                 activation=tf.nn.sigmoid)
    code_mean = tf.reduce_mean(code_layer, axis=1)
```

The decoder part of the DAG is as follows:

```
import tensorflow as tf

with graph.as_default():
    # Decoder
    decoder_input = tf.reshape(code_layer, (-1, int(width / 2), int(height / 2), 1))
```

```
        convt_0 = tf.layers.conv2d_transpose(inputs=decoder_input,
                                              filters=128,
                                              kernel_size=(3, 3),
                                              strides=(2, 2),
                                              activation=tf.nn.relu,
                                              padding='same')

        convt_1 = tf.layers.conv2d_transpose(inputs=convt_0,
                                              filters=64,
                                              kernel_size=(3, 3),
                                              activation=tf.nn.relu,
                                              padding='same')

        convt_2 = tf.layers.conv2d_transpose(inputs=convt_1,
                                              filters=32,
                                              kernel_size=(3, 3),
                                              activation=tf.nn.relu,
                                              padding='same')

        convt_3 = tf.layers.conv2d_transpose(inputs=convt_2,
                                              filters=1,
                                              kernel_size=(3, 3),
                                              activation=tf.sigmoid,
                                              padding='same')
        output_images = tf.image.resize_images(convt_3, (X_train.shape[1],
X_train.shape[2]),
method=tf.image.ResizeMethod.BICUBIC)
```

The `loss` function and the Adam optimizer are defined in the following snippet:

```
import tensorflow as tf

with graph.as_default():
    # Loss
    loss = tf.nn.l2_loss(convt_3 - input_images)

    # Training step
    training_step = tf.train.AdamOptimizer(0.001).minimize(loss)
```

Once the full DAG has been defined, we can initialize the session and all of the variables:

```
import tensorflow as tf

session = tf.InteractiveSession(graph=graph)
tf.global_variables_initializer().run()
```

Unsupervised Neural Network Models

Once TensorFlow has been initialized, the training process can be started, as follows:

```
import numpy as np

for e in range(nb_epochs):
    np.random.shuffle(X_train)

    total_loss = 0.0
    code_means = []

    for i in range(0, X_train.shape[0] - batch_size, batch_size):
        X = np.expand_dims(X_train[i:i + batch_size, :, :],
axis=3).astype(np.float32)

        _, n_loss, c_mean = session.run([training_step, loss, code_mean],
                                        feed_dict={
                                            input_images_xl: X
                                        })
        total_loss += n_loss
        code_means.append(c_mean)

    print('Epoch {}) Average loss per sample: {} (Code mean: {})'.
          format(e + 1, total_loss / float(X_train.shape[0]),
np.mean(code_means)))
```

The output of the previous snippet is as follows:

```
Epoch 1) Average loss per sample: 11.933397521972656 (Code mean:
0.5420681238174438)
Epoch 2) Average loss per sample: 10.294102325439454 (Code mean:
0.4132006764411926)
Epoch 3) Average loss per sample: 9.917563934326171 (Code mean:
0.38105469942092896)
...
Epoch 600) Average loss per sample: 0.4635812330245972 (Code mean:
0.42368677258491516)
```

At the end of the training process, the average loss per sample is about 0.46 (considering 32 × 32 images), and the mean of the codes is 0.42. This value indicates that the encoding is rather dense, because the single values are expected to be uniformly distributed in the range (0, 1); therefore, the average is 0.5. In this case, we are not interested in this datum, but we are going to compare the result when looking for sparsity, too.

The output of the autoencoder for some sample images is shown in the following diagram:

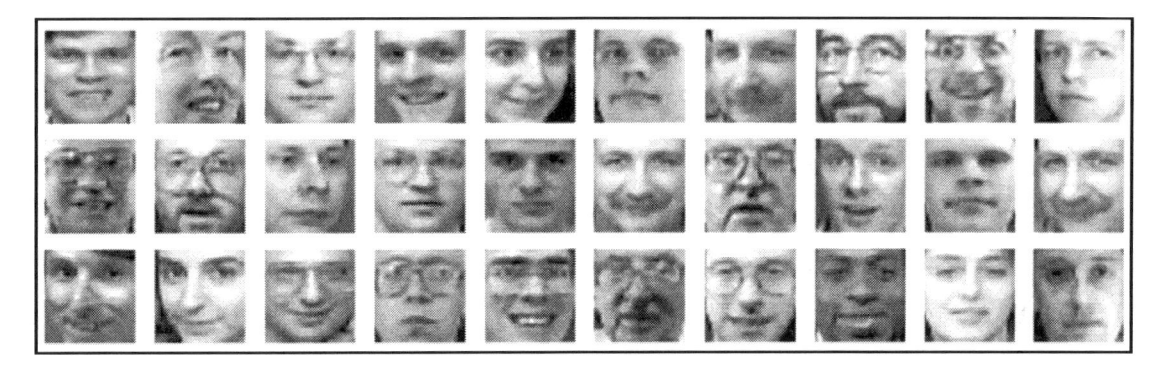

Sample output of the deep convolutional autoencoder

The quality of the reconstruction is partially affected by the upsizing to 64 × 64; however, better results can be obtained by reducing the compression ratio and increasing the code length.

Denoising autoencoders

A very helpful application of autoencoders is not strictly related to their ability to find lower-dimensional representations, but relies on the transformation process from input to output. In particular, let's assume a zero-centered dataset, X, and a noisy version whose samples have the following structure:

$$\bar{x}_i^n = \bar{x}_i + \bar{n}(i) \ \ where \ \ \bar{n}(i) \sim N(0, \Sigma)$$

In this case, the goal of the autoencoder is to remove the noisy term and recover the original sample, x_i. From a mathematical viewpoint, there are no particular differences between standard and **denoising autoencoders**; however, it's important to consider the capacity needs for such models. As they have to recover original samples, given a corrupted input (whose features occupy a much larger sample space), the amount and dimension of layers might be larger than for a standard autoencoder. Of course, considering the complexity, it's impossible to have clear insight without a few tests; therefore, I strongly suggest starting with smaller models and increasing the capacity until the optimal cost function reaches a suitable value. For the addition of noise, there are a few possible strategies:

- Corrupting the samples contained in each batch (throughout the epochs).
- Using a noise layer as input 1 for the encoder.

Unsupervised Neural Network Models

- Using a dropout layer as input 1 for the encoder (for example, with salt-and-pepper noise). In this case, the probability of dropout can be fixed, or it can be randomly sampled in a predefined interval (for example, (0.1, 0.5)).

If the noise is assumed to be Gaussian (which is the most common choice), it's possible to generate both homoscedastic and heteroscedastic noise. In the first case, the variance is kept constant for all components (that is, $n(i) \sim N(0, \sigma^2 I)$), while in the latter, every component has its own variance. Depending on the nature of the problem, another solution might be more appropriate; however, when there are no restrictions, it's always preferable to employ heteroscedastic noise, in order to increase the overall robustness of the system.

Adding noise to the deep convolutional autoencoder

In this example, we are going to modify the previously developed deep convolutional autoencoder, in order to manage noisy input samples. The DAG is almost equivalent, with the difference that, now, we need to feed both noisy and original images:

```
import tensorflow as tf

with graph.as_default():
    input_images_xl = tf.placeholder(tf.float32,
                                     shape=(None, X_train.shape[1], X_train.shape[2], 1))
    input_noisy_images_xl = tf.placeholder(tf.float32,
                                           shape=(None, X_train.shape[1], X_train.shape[2], 1))
    input_images = tf.image.resize_images(input_images_xl, (width, height),
method=tf.image.ResizeMethod.BICUBIC)
    input_noisy_images = tf.image.resize_images(input_noisy_images_xl, (width, height),
method=tf.image.ResizeMethod.BICUBIC)

    # Encoder
    conv_0 = tf.layers.conv2d(inputs=input_noisy_images,
                              filters=16,
                              kernel_size=(3, 3),
                              strides=(2, 2),
                              activation=tf.nn.relu,
                              padding='same')
    ...
```

The `loss` function, of course, is computed by considering the original images:

```
...

# Loss
loss = tf.nn.l2_loss(convt_3 - input_images)

# Training step
training_step = tf.train.AdamOptimizer(0.001).minimize(loss)
```

After the standard initialization of the variables, we can start the training process, considering an additive noise, $n_i \sim N(0, 0.45)$ (that is, $\sigma \approx 0.2$):

```
import numpy as np

for e in range(nb_epochs):
    np.random.shuffle(X_train)

    total_loss = 0.0
    code_means = []

    for i in range(0, X_train.shape[0] - batch_size, batch_size):
        X = np.expand_dims(X_train[i:i + batch_size, :, :],
axis=3).astype(np.float32)
        Xn = np.clip(X + np.random.normal(0.0, 0.2, size=(batch_size,
X_train.shape[1], X_train.shape[2], 1)), 0.0, 1.0)

        _, n_loss, c_mean = session.run([training_step, loss, code_mean],
                                        feed_dict={
                                            input_images_xl: X,
                                            input_noisy_images_xl: Xn
                                        })
        total_loss += n_loss
        code_means.append(c_mean)

    print('Epoch {}) Average loss per sample: {} (Code mean: {})'.
          format(e + 1, total_loss / float(X_train.shape[0]),
np.mean(code_means)))
```

Once the model has been trained, it's possible to test it with a few noisy samples. The results are shown in the following screenshot:

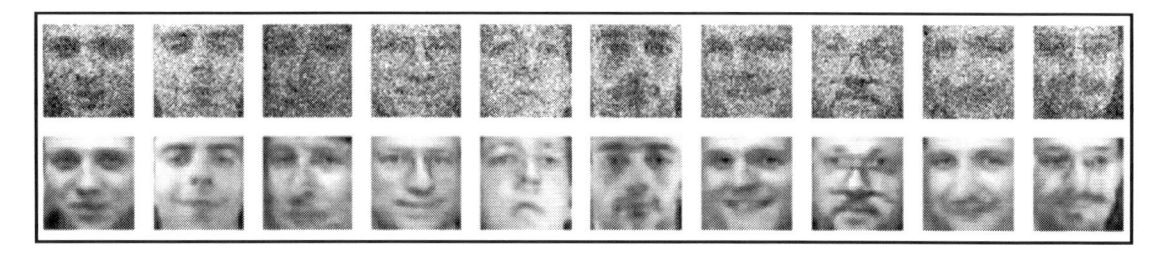

Noisy samples (upper row); denoised images (lower row)

As you can see, the autoencoder has successfully learned how to denoise the input images, even when they are quite corrupt. I invite you to test the model with other datasets, looking for the maximum noise variance that allows for a reasonably good reconstruction.

Sparse autoencoders

The code generated by a standard autoencoder is generally dense; however, as discussed in Chapter 7, *Dimensionality Reduction and Component Analysis*, sometimes, it's preferable to work with over-complete dictionaries and sparse encodings. The main strategy to accomplish this goal is to simply add an L_1 penalty (on the code layer) to the cost function:

$$C_s(X, \hat{X}, \bar{\theta}) = C(X, \hat{X}, \bar{\theta}) + \alpha \sum_i \|\bar{z}_i\|_1$$

The α constant determines the amount of sparseness that will be reached. Of course, as the optimum of C_s doesn't correspond to the original one, in order to achieve the same accuracy, more epochs and a longer code layer are often needed. Another method, proposed by Andrew Ng (in *Sparse Autoencoder*, CS294A, Stanford University) is based on a slightly different approach. The code layer is considered a set of independent Bernoulli random variables; therefore, given another set of Bernoulli variables with a small mean (for example, $p_r \sim B(0.05)$), it's possible to try to find the optimal code that also minimizes the Kullback-Leibler divergence between z_i and such a reference distribution:

$$Ls_i = \sum_j D_{KL}(\bar{z}_i^j \| p_r) = \sum_j p_r \log \frac{p_r}{\bar{z}_i^j} + (1 - p_r) \log \frac{1 - p_r}{1 - \bar{z}_i^j}$$

Therefore, the new cost function becomes the following:

$$C_s(X, \hat{X}, \bar{\theta}) = C(X, \hat{X}, \bar{\theta}) + \alpha \sum_i Ls_i$$

The final effect is not very different from the one achieved using the L_1 penalty. In fact, in both cases, the model is forced to learn a sub-optimal representation, also trying to minimize an objective that, if considered alone, would lead the output code to always become null. Hence, the full cost function will reach a minimum that guarantees both the reconstruction ability and the sparseness (which must always be balanced with the code length). So, in general, the longer the code, the larger the sparseness that it is possible to achieve.

Adding a sparseness constraint to the deep convolutional autoencoder

In this example, we want to increase the sparsity of the code by using an L_1 penalty. The DAG and the training process are exactly the same as the main example, and the only difference is the `loss` function, which now becomes the following:

```
...
sparsity_constraint = 0.01 * tf.reduce_sum(tf.norm(code_layer, ord=1, axis=1))
loss = tf.nn.l2_loss(convt_3 - input_images) + sparsity_constraint
...
```

We have added a sparsity constraint with $\alpha = 0.01$; therefore, we can retrain the model by checking the average code length. The output of the process is as follows:

```
Epoch 1) Average loss per sample: 12.785746307373048 (Code mean: 0.30300647020339966)
Epoch 2) Average loss per sample: 10.576686706542969 (Code mean: 0.16661183536052704)
Epoch 3) Average loss per sample: 10.204148864746093 (Code mean: 0.15442773699760437)
...
Epoch 600) Average loss per sample: 0.8058895015716553 (Code mean: 0.028538944199681282)
```

As you can see, the code has now become extremely sparse, with a final mean equal to about 0.03. This piece of information indicates that the majority of the code values are close to zero, and only a few of them can be considered when decoding the image. As an exercise, I invite you to analyze the code for a set of selected images, trying to understand the semantics of their values according to their activation/inactivation.

Variational autoencoders

Let's consider a dataset, X, drawn from a data generating process, p_{data}. A variational autoencoder is a generative model (based on the main concepts of a standard autoencoder), which was proposed by Kingma and Welling (in *Auto-Encoding Variational Bayes, Kingma D. P. and Welling M., arXiv:1312.6114 [stat.ML]*), aimed at reproducing the data-generating process. In order to achieve this goal, we need to start from a generic model based on a set of latent variables, z, and a set of learnable parameters, θ. Given a sample, $x_i \in X$, the probability of the model is p(x, z; θ). Hence, the goal of the training process is to find the optimal parameters that maximize the likelihood, p(x; θ), which can be obtained by marginalizing the full joint probability:

$$p(\bar{x};\bar{\theta}) = \int p(\bar{x},\bar{z};\bar{\theta})dz = \int p(\bar{x}|\bar{z};\bar{\theta})p(\bar{z};\bar{\theta})dz$$

The previous expression is straightforward, but unfortunately, it's seldom tractable in a closed form. The main reason is that we have no valid pieces of information about the prior, p(z; θ). Moreover, even assuming, for example, that $z \sim N(0, \Sigma)$ (for example, N(0, I)), the probability of finding valid samples is extremely sparse. In other words, given a value, z, it is very unlikely that we will generate a sample that actually belongs to p_{data}, too. In order to solve this problem, the authors proposed a variational approach, which we are going to briefly look at (a full explanation is present in the aforementioned paper). Assuming the structure of a standard autoencoder, we can introduce a proxy parameterized distribution by modeling the encoder as $q(z|x; \theta_q)$. At this point, we can compute the Kullback-Leibler divergence between q(•) and the actual conditional probability, p(z|x; θ):

$$D_{KL}(q\|p) = \sum_z q(\bar{z}|\bar{x};\bar{\theta}_q) \log\frac{q(\bar{z}|\bar{x};\bar{\theta}_q)}{p(\bar{z}|\bar{x};\bar{\theta})} = E_z[\log q(\bar{z}|\bar{x};\bar{\theta}_q)] - E_z[\log p(\bar{z}|\bar{x};\bar{\theta})] =$$
$$= E_z[\log q(\bar{z}|\bar{x};\bar{\theta}_q)] - E_z[\log p(\bar{x}|\bar{z};\bar{\theta}) - \log p(\bar{z};\bar{\theta}) + \log p(\bar{x};\bar{\theta})]$$

As the expected value operators work on z, the last term can be extracted and moved to the left-hand side of the expression, becoming the following:

$$log\ p(\bar{x}; \bar{\theta}) - D_{KL}(q||p) = E_z[log\ q(\bar{z}|\bar{x}; \bar{\theta}_q) - log\ p(\bar{x}|\bar{z}; \bar{\theta}) - log\ p(\bar{z}; \bar{\theta})] =$$
$$= E_z[log\ p(\bar{x}|\bar{z}; \bar{\theta})] - D_{KL}(q||p(\bar{z}; \bar{\theta}))$$

After another simple manipulation, the previous equation becomes the following:

$$log\ p(\bar{x}; \bar{\theta}) = E_z[log\ p(\bar{x}|\bar{z}; \bar{\theta})] - D_{KL}(q||p(\bar{z}; \bar{\theta})) + D_{KL}(q||p) =$$
$$= ELBO_{\bar{\theta}} + D_{KL}(q||p)$$

The left-hand side is the log-likelihood of the samples under the model, while the right-hand side is the sum of a non-negative term (the KL-divergence) and another term called the **Evidence Lower Bound (ELBO)**:

$$ELBO_{\bar{\theta}} = -D_{KL}(q||p(\bar{z}; \bar{\theta})) + E_z[log\ p(\bar{x}|\bar{z}; \bar{\theta})]$$

As we will discuss, working with the ELBO is easier than dealing with the remaining part of the formula, and, as KL-divergence cannot introduce a negative contribution, if we maximize the ELBO, we also maximize the log-likelihood.

We previously defined $p(z; \theta) = N(0, I)$; therefore, we can model $q(z|x; \theta)$ as a multivariate Gaussian, where the two parameter sets (the mean vector and covariance matrix) are represented by a split probabilistic encoder. In particular, given a sample, x, the encoder now has to output both a mean vector, $\mu(z|x; \theta_q)$, and a covariance matrix, $\Sigma(z|x; \theta_q)$. For simplicity, we can assume the matrix to be diagonal, so the two components have exactly the same structure. The resulting distribution is $q(z|x; \theta_q) = N(\mu(z|x; \theta_q), \Sigma(z|x; \theta_q))$; therefore, the first term of the ELBO is the negative KL-divergence between two Gaussian distributions:

$$D_{KL}(N(\mu(\bar{z}|\bar{x}; \bar{\theta}_q), \Sigma(\bar{z}|\bar{x}; \bar{\theta}_q))||N(0, I) = \frac{1}{2}\left(tr(\Sigma(\bar{z}|\bar{x}; \bar{\theta}_q) + \mu(\bar{z}|\bar{x}; \bar{\theta}_q)^T \mu(\bar{z}|\bar{x}; \bar{\theta}_q) - log|\Sigma(\bar{z}|\bar{x}; \bar{\theta}_q)| - p\right)$$

In the previous formula, p is the code length, so it is the dimension of both the mean and the diagonal covariance vectors. The expression on the right-hand side is very easy to compute, because Σ is diagonal (that is, the trace is the sum of the elements, and the determinant is the product). However, the maximization of this formula, although correct, is not a differentiable operation when the **Stochastic Gradient Descent (SGD)** algorithm is employed. In order to overcome this problem, the authors suggested reparametrizing the distribution.

When a batch is presented, a normal distribution is sampled, obtaining $\alpha \sim N(0, I)$. Using this value, it's possible to build the required sample by using the output of the probabilistic encoder: $\mu(z|x; \theta_q) + \alpha \cdot \Sigma(z|x; \theta_q)^2$. This expression is differentiable, as α is constant during each batch (of course, as $\mu(z|x; \theta_q)$ and $\Sigma(z|x; \theta_q)$ are parameterized with neural networks, they are differentiable).

The second term on the right-hand side of the ELBO is the expected value of $log\ p(x|z; \theta)$. It's easy to see that such an expression corresponds to the cross-entropy between the original distribution and the reconstruction:

$$E_z[log\ p(\bar{x}|\bar{z}; \bar{\theta})] = \sum_z p(\bar{z}|\bar{x}; \bar{\theta}) log\ p(\bar{x}|\bar{z}; \bar{\theta}) = -H(p(\bar{z}|\bar{x}; \bar{\theta}), p(\bar{x}|\bar{z}; \bar{\theta}))$$

This is the cost function of a standard autoencoder, which we are going to minimize with the assumption of working with Bernoulli distributions. So, the formula becomes the following:

$$H = -\sum_i p(\bar{x}|\bar{z}; \bar{\theta}) log(p(\bar{x}|\bar{z}; \bar{\theta})) + (1 - p(\bar{x}|\bar{z}; \bar{\theta})) log(1 - p(\bar{x}|\bar{z}; \bar{\theta}))$$

Example of a deep convolutional variational autoencoder

In this example, we want to build and train a deep convolutional variational autoencoder based on the Olivetti faces dataset. The structure is very similar to the one employed in our first example. The encoder has the following layers:

- 2D convolution with 16 (3 × 3) filters, (2 × 2) strides, ReLU activation, and the same padding
- 2D convolution with 32 (3 × 3) filters, (1 × 1) strides, ReLU activation, and the same padding
- 2D convolution with 64 (3 × 3) filters, (1 × 1) strides, ReLU activation, and the same padding
- 2D convolution with 128 (3 × 3) filters, (1 × 1) strides, ReLU activation, and the same padding

The decoder has the following transpose convolutions:

- 2D transpose convolution with 128 (3 × 3) filters, (2 × 2) strides, ReLU activation, and the same padding
- 2D transpose convolution with 128 (3 × 3) filters, (2 × 2) strides, ReLU activation, and the same padding
- 2D transpose convolution with 32 (3 × 3) filters, (1 × 1) strides, ReLU activation, and the same padding
- 2D transpose convolution with 1 (3 × 3) filter, (1 × 1) strides, Sigmoid activation, and the same padding

The generation of noise is completely managed by TensorFlow, and it's based on the trick explained in the theoretical section. The first part of the DAG, containing the graph definition and the encoder, is shown in the following snippet:

```
import tensorflow as tf

nb_epochs = 800
batch_size = 100
code_length = 512
width = 32
height = 32

graph = tf.Graph()

with graph.as_default():
    input_images_xl = tf.placeholder(tf.float32,
                                     shape=(batch_size, X_train.shape[1], X_train.shape[2], 1))
    input_images = tf.image.resize_images(input_images_xl, (width, height),
                                          method=tf.image.ResizeMethod.BICUBIC)

    # Encoder
    conv_0 = tf.layers.conv2d(inputs=input_images,
                              filters=16,
                              kernel_size=(3, 3),
                              strides=(2, 2),
                              activation=tf.nn.relu,
                              padding='same')

    conv_1 = tf.layers.conv2d(inputs=conv_0,
                              filters=32,
                              kernel_size=(3, 3),
                              activation=tf.nn.relu,
                              padding='same')
    conv_2 = tf.layers.conv2d(inputs=conv_1,
```

```
                            filters=64,
                            kernel_size=(3, 3),
                            activation=tf.nn.relu,
                            padding='same')

    conv_3 = tf.layers.conv2d(inputs=conv_2,
                              filters=128,
                              kernel_size=(3, 3),
                              activation=tf.nn.relu,
                              padding='same')
```

The part of the DAG where the code layers are defined is as follows:

```
import tensorflow as tf

with graph.as_default():
    # Code layer
    code_input = tf.layers.flatten(inputs=conv_3)

    code_mean = tf.layers.dense(inputs=code_input,
                                units=width * height)

    code_log_variance = tf.layers.dense(inputs=code_input,
                                        units=width * height)

    code_std = tf.sqrt(tf.exp(code_log_variance))
```

The decoder part of the DAG is as follows:

```
import tensorflow as tf

with graph.as_default():
    # Decoder
    decoder_input = tf.reshape(sampled_code, (-1, int(width / 4),
int(height / 4), 16))

    convt_0 = tf.layers.conv2d_transpose(inputs=decoder_input,
                                         filters=128,
                                         kernel_size=(3, 3),
                                         strides=(2, 2),
                                         activation=tf.nn.relu,
                                         padding='same')

    convt_1 = tf.layers.conv2d_transpose(inputs=convt_0,
                                         filters=128,
                                         kernel_size=(3, 3),
                                         strides=(2, 2),
                                         activation=tf.nn.relu,
```

```
                                           padding='same')
    convt_2 = tf.layers.conv2d_transpose(inputs=convt_1,
                                           filters=32,
                                           kernel_size=(3, 3),
                                           activation=tf.nn.relu,
                                           padding='same')

    convt_3 = tf.layers.conv2d_transpose(inputs=convt_2,
                                           filters=1,
                                           kernel_size=(3, 3),
                                           padding='same')

    convt_output = tf.nn.sigmoid(convt_3)
    output_images = tf.image.resize_images(convt_output, (X_train.shape[1],
X_train.shape[2]),
method=tf.image.ResizeMethod.BICUBIC)
```

The last part of the DAG contains the loss function and the Adam optimizer, as follows:

```
import tensorflow as tf

with graph.as_default():
    # Loss
    reconstruction =
tf.nn.sigmoid_cross_entropy_with_logits(logits=convt_3,
labels=input_images)
    kl_divergence = 0.5 * tf.reduce_sum(
            tf.square(code_mean) + tf.square(code_std) - tf.log(1e-8 +
tf.square(code_std)) - 1, axis=1)

    loss = tf.reduce_sum(tf.reduce_sum(reconstruction) + kl_divergence)

    # Training step
    training_step = tf.train.AdamOptimizer(0.001).minimize(loss)
```

The loss function is made up of two components:

1. The reconstruction loss, based on the cross-entropy
2. The Kullback-Leibler divergence between the code distribution and the reference normal distribution

At this point, as usual, we can initialize the session and all of the variables and begin the training procedure for 800 epochs and 100 samples per batch:

```
import tensorflow as tf
import numpy as np

session = tf.InteractiveSession(graph=graph)
```

Unsupervised Neural Network Models

```
tf.global_variables_initializer().run()

for e in range(nb_epochs):
    np.random.shuffle(X_train)
    
    total_loss = 0.0
    
    for i in range(0, X_train.shape[0] - batch_size, batch_size):
        X = np.zeros((batch_size, 64, 64, 1), dtype=np.float32)
        X[:, :, :, 0] = X_train[i:i + batch_size, :, :]
        
        _, n_loss = session.run([training_step, loss],
                                feed_dict={
                                    input_images_xl: X
                                })
        total_loss += n_loss
    
    print('Epoch {}) Average loss per sample: {}'.format(e + 1, total_loss 
/ float(batch_size)))
```

At the end of the training process, we can test the reconstruction of a few samples. The result is shown in the following screenshot:

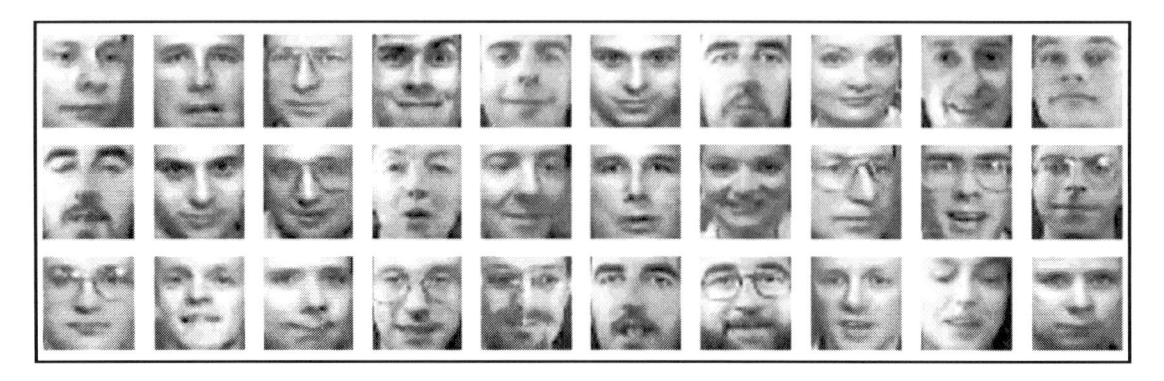

Sample reconstructions produced by the variational autoencoder

As an exercise, I invite the reader to modify the DAG, in order to accept generic input codes and evaluate the generative properties of the model. Alternatively, it's possible to obtain the code for a training sample and apply some noise, in order to observe the effect on the output reconstruction.

Hebbian-based principal component analysis

In this section, we are going to analyze two neural models (Sanger's and Rubner-Tavan's networks) that can perform **principal component analysis (PCA)** without the need of either eigendecomposing the covariance matrix or performing truncated SVD. They are both based on the concept of **Hebbian learning** (for further details, please refer to Dayan, P. and Abbott, L. F., *Theoretical Neuroscience, The MIT Press,* 2005 or Bonaccorso, G., *Mastering Machine Learning Algorithms,* Packt, 2018), which is one of the first mathematical theories about the dynamics of very simple neurons. Nevertheless, such concepts have very interesting implications, in particular in the field of component analysis. In order to better understand the dynamics of networks, it will be helpful to provide a quick overview of the basic model of a neuron. Let's consider an input, $x \in \Re^n$, and a weight vector, $w \in \Re^n$. A neuron performs the dot product (without bias), in order to produce the scalar output, y:

$$y = \bar{w}^T \bar{x}$$

Now, if we imagine two neurons, the first one is called the pre-synaptic unit and the other the post-synaptic one. **Hebb's rule** states that the synaptic strength must increase when both pre- and post-synaptic units output values with the same sign (in particular, both positive), while it must be weakened when the signs are different. The mathematical expression of such a concept is as follows:

$$\Delta \bar{w} = \eta y \bar{x} = \eta (\bar{w}^T \bar{x}) \bar{x}$$

The constant, η, is the learning rate. A full analysis is beyond the scope of this book, but it's possible to prove that a Hebbian neuron (with some very simple modifications, needed to control the growth of w) modifies the synaptic weights so that, after a sufficiently large number of iterations, it aligns along the first principal component of a dataset, X. Starting from this result (which we will not prove), we can introduce Sanger's network.

Sanger's network

The Sanger's network model was proposed by Sanger (in Sanger, T. D., *Optimal Unsupervised Learning in a Single-Layer Linear Feedforward Neural Network, Neural Networks*, 2, 1989), in order to extract the first *k* principal components of a dataset, *X*, in descending order, with an online procedure (conversely, a standard PCA is a batch process that requires the entire dataset). Even if there's an incremental algorithm based on a particular version of SVD, the main advantage of these neural models is their intrinsic ability to work with single samples without any loss of performance. Before showing the structure of the network, it's necessary to introduce a modification to Hebb's rule, called **Oja's rule**:

$$\Delta \bar{w} = \eta y \bar{x} - \alpha y^2 \bar{w}$$

This rule was introduced in order to solve the problem of the infinite growth of standard Hebbian neurons. In fact, it's easy to understand that if the dot product, $w^T x$, is positive, Δw will update the weights by increasing the magnitude of *w* more and more. Hence, after a large number of iterations, the model can encounter an overflow. Oja's rule overcomes this problem by introducing an auto-limitation that forces the weight magnitude to saturate without affecting the ability of the neuron to find the orientation of the first principal component. In fact, denoting the weight vector after the kth iteration with w_k, it's possible to prove the following:

$$\lim_{k \to \infty} |w_k| = \frac{1}{\sqrt{\alpha}}$$

Sanger's network is based on a modified version of Oja's rule, defined as **Generalized Hebbian Learning** (GHL). Let's suppose that we have a dataset, *X*, containing *m* vectors, $x_i \in \Re^n$. The structure of the network is shown in the following diagram:

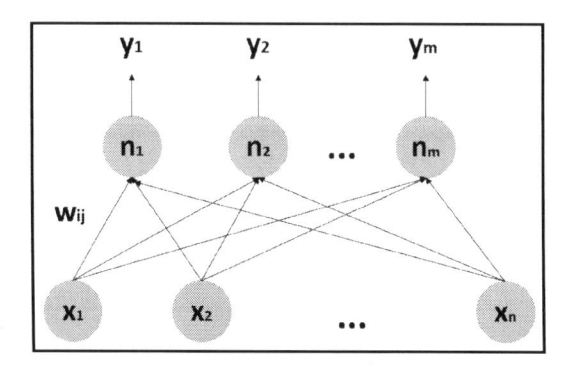

Structure of a generic Sanger's network

The weights are organized into a matrix, W = {w_{ij}} (w_{ij} is the weight connecting the pre-synaptic unit, i, with the post-synaptic unit, j); therefore, the activation of the output can be computed by using the following formula:

$$\bar{y} = W\bar{x}$$

However, in this kind of network, we are more interested in the final weights, because they must be equal to the first n principal components. Unfortunately, if we apply Oja's rule without any modification, all of the neurons will find the same component (the first one); hence, a different strategy must be employed. From the theory, we know that the principal components must be orthogonal; therefore, if w_1 is the vector with the orientation of the first components, we can force w_2 to become orthogonal to w_1, and so on. This method is based on the **Gram-Schmidt orthonormalization procedure**. Let's consider two vectors—w_1 which has already converged, and w_{20}, which, without any intervention, will also converge to w_1. We can find the orthogonal component of w_{20} by considering the projection of this vector onto w_1:

$$P_{\bar{w}_1}(\bar{w}_{20}) = (\bar{w}_1^T \bar{w}_{20}) \frac{\bar{w}_1}{\|\bar{w}_1\|}$$

At this point, the orthogonal component, w_2, is equal to the following:

$$\bar{w}_2 = \bar{w}_{20} - P_{\bar{w}_1}(\bar{w}_{20})$$

The third component must be orthogonal to w_1 and w_2, so the process must be repeated for all n units, until the final convergence. Moreover, we are now working with already converged components, but rather with a dynamic system that is updated in parallel; therefore, it's necessary to incorporate this procedure into a learning rule, as follows:

$$\Delta w_{ij} = \eta \left(y_i \bar{x}_j - y_i \sum_{k=1}^{i} w_{kj} y_k \right)$$

The previous update refers to a single weight, w_{ij}, given an input, x. As is easy to understand, the first part is the standard Hebb's rule, while the remaining part is the orthogonalizing term, which is extended to all of the units preceding y_i.

In a matrix form, the update becomes the following:

$$\Delta W = \eta \left(\bar{y}\bar{x}^T - Tril(\bar{y}\bar{y}^T)W \right) \quad where \quad \bar{y}\bar{y}^T = W\bar{x}\bar{x}^T W^T$$

The *Tril(•)* function computes the lower-triangular part of a square matrix. The convergence proof is non-trivial, but it's possible to see how this model converges to the first n principal components in descending order, under the mild condition that η decreases monotonically:

$$\lim_{t \to \infty} \eta_t = 0$$

Such a constraint is not difficult to implement; however, in general, the algorithm can also reach the convergence when $\eta < 1$ and is kept constant during the iterations.

An example of Sanger's network

Let's consider a sample bidimensional zero-centered dataset, obtained with the scikit-learn `make_blobs()` utility function:

```
import numpy as np

def zero_center(Xd):
    return Xd - np.mean(Xd, axis=0)

X, _ = make_blobs(n_samples=500, centers=3, cluster_std=[5.0, 1.0, 2.5],
random_state=1000)
Xs = zero_center(X)

Q = np.cov(Xs.T)
eigu, eigv = np.linalg.eig(Q)

print('Covariance matrix: {}'.format(Q))
print('Eigenvalues: {}'.format(eigu))
print('Eigenvectors: {}'.format(eigv.T))
```

The output of the previous snippet is as follows:

```
Covariance matrix: [[18.14296606  8.15571356]
 [ 8.15571356 22.87011239]]
Eigenvalues: [12.01524122 28.99783723]
Eigenvectors: [[-0.79948496  0.60068611]
 [-0.60068611 -0.79948496]]
```

The eigenvalues are about 12 and 29, respectively, indicating that the first principal component (which corresponds to the first row of the transposed eigenvector matrix, so (-0.799, 0.6)) is much shorter than the second one. Of course, in this case, we have already computed the principal components by eigendecomposing the covariance matrix, but that has only been done for didactic purposes. The Sanger's network will extract the components in descending order; therefore, we expect to find the second column as the first column, and the first column as the second column of the weight matrix. Let's start by initializing the weights and the training constants:

```
import numpy as np

n_components = 2
learning_rate = 0.01
nb_iterations = 5000
t = 0.0

W_sanger = np.random.normal(scale=0.5, size=(n_components, Xs.shape[1]))
W_sanger /= np.linalg.norm(W_sanger, axis=1).reshape((n_components, 1))
```

> **TIP**: In order to reproduce the example, it's necessary to set the random seed equal to 1,000; that is, `np.random.seed(1000)`.

In this case, we are performing a fixed number of iterations (5,000); however, I invite you to modify the example, in order to employ a tolerance and a stop criterion based on the norm (for example, Frobenius) of the difference between the weights computed at two subsequent time steps (this method can speed up the training by avoiding useless iterations).

The initial configuration is shown in the following diagram:

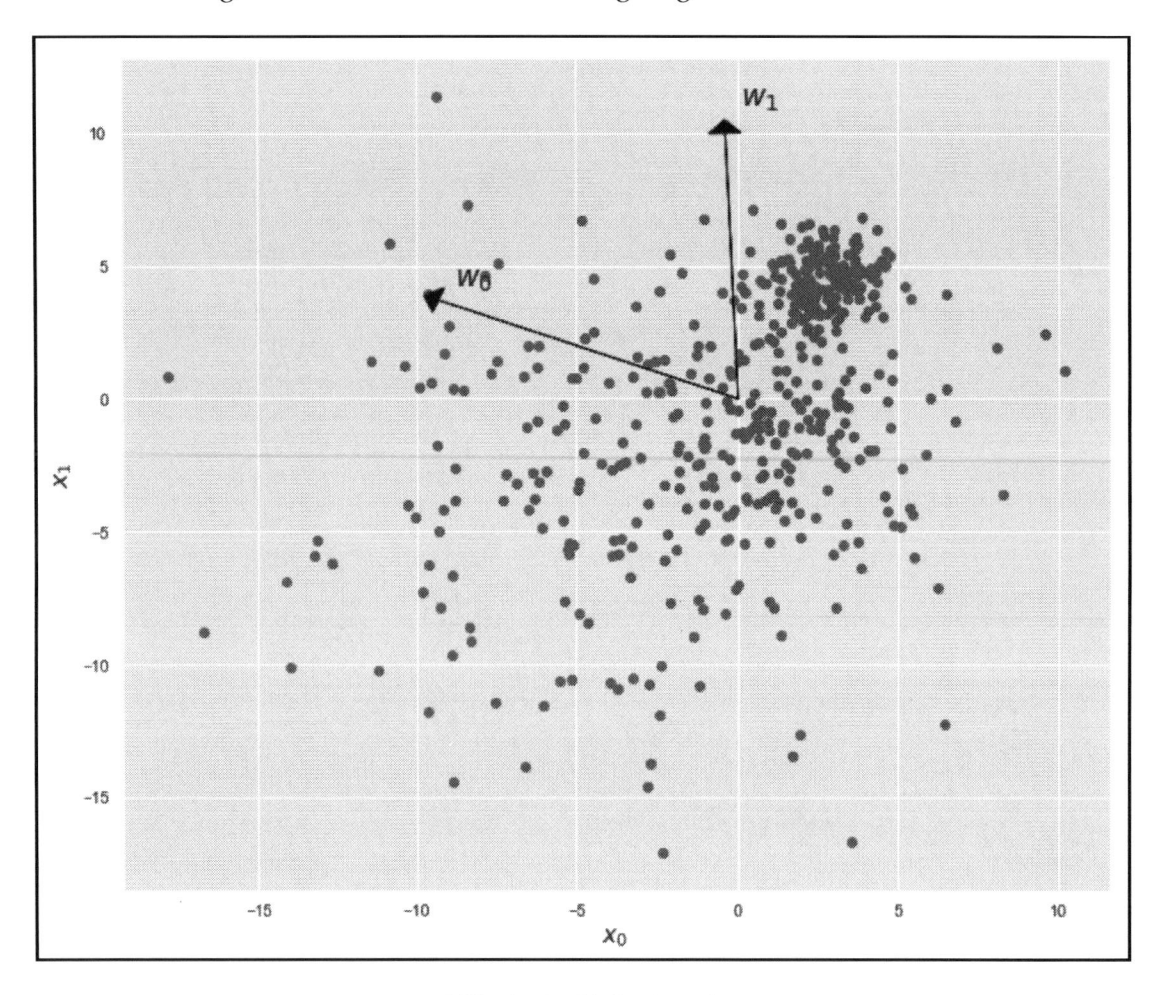

Initial configuration of the Sanger's network

At this point, we can start the training cycle, as follows:

```
import numpy as np

for i in range(nb_iterations):
    dw = np.zeros((n_components, Xs.shape[1]))
    t += 1.0

    for j in range(Xs.shape[0]):
        Ysj = np.dot(W_sanger, Xs[j]).reshape((n_components, 1))
        QYd = np.tril(np.dot(Ysj, Ysj.T))
        dw += np.dot(Ysj, Xs[j].reshape((1, X.shape[1]))) - np.dot(QYd, W_sanger)

    W_sanger += (learning_rate / t) * dw
    W_sanger /= np.linalg.norm(W_sanger, axis=1).reshape((n_components, 1))

print('Final weights: {}'.format(W_sanger))
print('Final covariance matrix: {}'.format(np.cov(np.dot(Xs, W_sanger.T).T)))
```

The output of the previous snippet is as follows:

```
Final weights: [[-0.60068611 -0.79948496]
 [-0.79948496  0.60068611]]
Final covariance matrix: [[ 2.89978372e+01 -2.31873305e-13]
 [-2.31873305e-13 1.20152412e+01]]
```

Unsupervised Neural Network Models

As you can see, the final covariance matrix is decorrelated, as expected, and the weights have converged to the eigenvectors of C. The final configuration of the weights (the principal components) is shown in the following diagram:

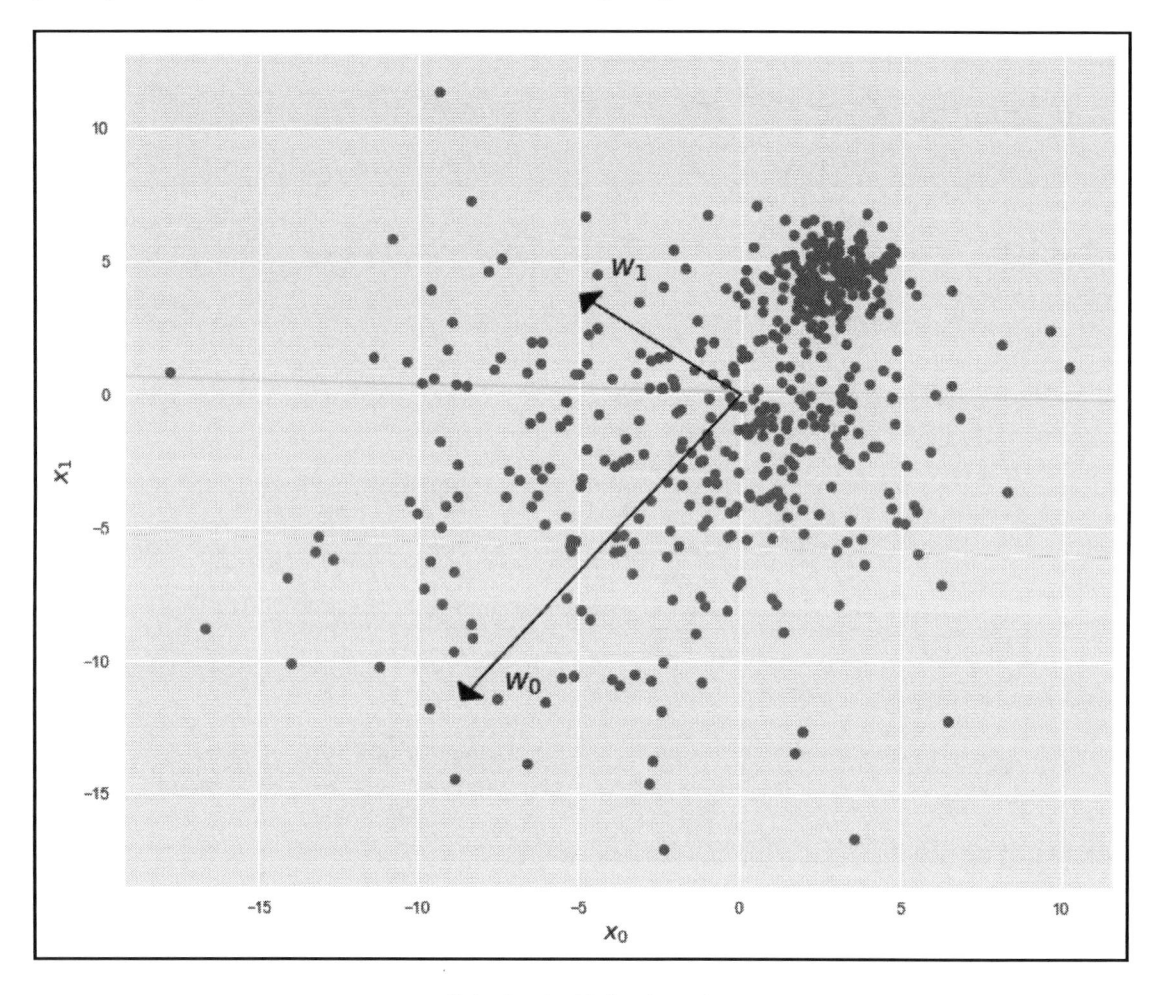

Final configuration of the Sanger's network

The first principal component corresponds to the weight, w_0, and it's the largest, while w_1 is the second component. I invite you to test the network with higher-dimensional datasets and compare the performance with the standard algorithms, based on the SVD or eigendecomposition of the covariance matrix.

Rubner-Tavan's network

Another neural network that can perform PCA was proposed by Rubner and Tavan (in Rubner, J. and Tavan, P., *A Self-Organizing Network for Principal-Components Analysis*, *Europhysics Letters*, 10(7), 1989). Their approach, however, is based on the decorrelation of the covariance matrix, which is the final result of PCA (that is, it is like operating with a bottom-up strategy, while the standard procedure is top-down). Let's consider a zero-centered dataset, X, and a network whose output is $y \in \Re^m$ vectors. Therefore, the covariance matrix of the output distribution is as follows:

$$C = \frac{1}{n_{samples}} \begin{pmatrix} \sum_i y_{i1} y_{i1} & \cdots & \sum_i y_{i1} y_{im} \\ \vdots & \ddots & \vdots \\ \sum_i y_{im} y_{i1} & \cdots & \sum_i y_{im} y_{im} \end{pmatrix}$$

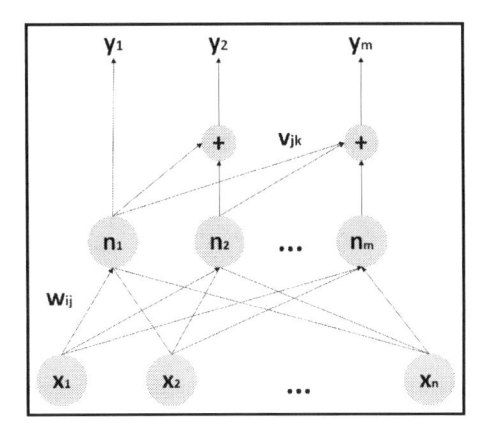

Structure of a generic Rubner-Tavan's network

As you can see, the main difference from a Sanger's network is the presence of summing nodes before each output unit (except for the first one). This approach is called **hierarchical lateral connection**, because every node, y_i ($i > 0$), is made up of a direct component, n_i, summed to all previous weighted output. Hence, assuming the notation, $v^{(i)}$, to indicate the ith component of the vector, i, the output of the network is as follows:

$$\bar{y}^{(i)} = \sum_{j=1}^{m} w_{ij} \bar{x}^{(j)} + \sum_{k=1}^{i-1} v_{jk} \bar{y}^{(k)}$$

It has been proven that this model, with a particular weight update rule (which we are going to discuss), converges to a single, stable, fixed point, and the output is forced to become mutually decorrelated. Looking at the structure of the model, the operating sequence is as follows:

- The first output is kept unchanged
- The second output is forced to become decorrelated with the first one
- The third output is forced to become decorrelated with both the first and the second ones, and so on
- The last output is forced to become decorrelated with all previous ones

After a number of iterations, every production, $y_i y_j$, with $i \neq j$, becomes null, and C becomes a diagonal covariance matrix. Moreover, in the aforementioned paper, the authors proved that the eigenvalues (which correspond to the variances) are sorted in descending order; therefore, it's possible to select the top p components by taking the sub-matrix containing the first p rows and columns.

A Rubner-Tavan network is updated by using two different rules, one for each weight layer. The internal weights, w_{ij}, are updated by using Oja's rule:

$$\Delta w_{ij} = \eta \bar{y}^{(i)} \left(\bar{x}^{(j)} - w_{ij} \bar{y}^{(i)} \right)$$

This rule guarantees the extraction of the principal components without the infinite growth of w_{ij}. Instead, the external weights, v_{jk}, are updated by using an **anti-Hebbian rule**:

$$\Delta v_{jk} = -\eta \bar{y}^{(j)} \left(\bar{y}^{(k)} + v_{jk} \bar{y}^{(j)} \right) \quad \forall i \neq k$$

The first term of the previous formula, $-\eta y^{(j)} y^{(k)}$, is responsible for the decorrelation, while the second one, analogous to Oja's rule, acts as a self-limiting regularizer that prevents the weights from overflowing. In particular, the $-\eta y^{(i)} y^{(k)}$ term can be interpreted as a feedback signal for the update rule, Δw_{ij}, which is influenced by the actual output corrected by the Δv_{jk} term. Considering the behavior of the Sanger's network, it's not easy to understand that, once the output is decorrelated, the internal weights w_{ij} become orthogonal, representing the first principal components of X.

In matrix form, the weights, w_{ij}, can immediately be arranged into $W = \{w_{ij}\}$, so that at the end of the training process, every column is an eigenvector of C (in descending order). Instead, for the external weights, v_{jk}, we need to use the $Tril(\bullet)$ operator again:

$$V = Tril_{V(i,j)=0 \ if \ i=j} \begin{pmatrix} \bar{v}_1 \\ \vdots \\ \bar{v}_m \end{pmatrix} = \begin{pmatrix} 0 & 0 & \cdots & 0 \\ \bar{v}_{21} & 0 & \cdots & 0 \\ \vdots & \vdots & \ddots & \vdots \\ \bar{v}_{m1} & \bar{v}_{m2} & \cdots & 0 \end{pmatrix}$$

Therefore, the output at the iteration t+1 becomes the following:

$$\bar{y}^{(t+1)} = W^T \bar{x} + V \bar{y}^{(t)}$$

It's interesting to note that such a network has a recurrent output; therefore, once an input is applied, a few iterations are necessary to allow y to stabilize (ideally, the update must continue until $||y^{(t+1)} - y^{(t)}|| \to 0$).

An example of a Rubner-Tavan's network

In this example, we will use the dataset defined in the example of a Sanger's network, in order to perform principal component extraction using the Rubner-Tavan's network. For our convenience, let's recompute the eigendecomposition:

```
import numpy as np

Q = np.cov(Xs.T)
eigu, eigv = np.linalg.eig(Q)

print('Eigenvalues: {}'.format(eigu))
print('Eigenvectors: {}'.format(eigv.T))
```

The output of the previous snippet is as follows:

```
Eigenvalues: [12.01524122 28.99783723]
Eigenvectors: [[-0.79948496  0.60068611]
 [-0.60068611 -0.79948496]]
```

We can now initialize the hyperparameters, as follows:

```
n_components = 2
learning_rate = 0.0001
max_iterations = 1000
stabilization_cycles = 5
```

Unsupervised Neural Network Models

```
threshold = 0.00001

W = np.random.normal(0.0, 0.5, size=(Xs.shape[1], n_components))
V = np.tril(np.random.normal(0.0, 0.01, size=(n_components, n_components)))
np.fill_diagonal(V, 0.0)

prev_W = np.zeros((Xs.shape[1], n_components))
t = 0
```

Hence, we have chosen to employ a stopping threshold equal to 0.00001 (the comparison is based on the Frobenius norm of two consecutive computations of the weight matrix) and a maximum of 1,000 iterations. We also set five stabilization cycles and a fixed learning rate, $\eta=0.0001$. We can start the learning process, as follows:

```
import numpy as np

while np.linalg.norm(W - prev_W, ord='fro') > threshold and t < max_iterations:
    prev_W = W.copy()
    t += 1

    for i in range(Xs.shape[0]):
        y_p = np.zeros((n_components, 1))
        xi = np.expand_dims(Xs[i], 1)
        y = None

        for _ in range(stabilization_cycles):
            y = np.dot(W.T, xi) + np.dot(V, y_p)
            y_p = y.copy()

        dW = np.zeros((Xs.shape[1], n_components))
        dV = np.zeros((n_components, n_components))

        for t in range(n_components):
            y2 = np.power(y[t], 2)
            dW[:, t] = np.squeeze((y[t] * xi) + (y2 * np.expand_dims(W[:, t], 1)))
            dV[t, :] = -np.squeeze((y[t] * y) + (y2 * np.expand_dims(V[t, :], 1)))

        W += (learning_rate * dW)
        V += (learning_rate * dV)

        V = np.tril(V)
        np.fill_diagonal(V, 0.0)

        W /= np.linalg.norm(W, axis=0).reshape((1, n_components))
```

```
print('Final weights: {}'.format(W))
```

The output of the previous block is as follows:

```
Final weights: [[-0.60814345 -0.80365858]
 [-0.79382715  0.59509065]]
```

As expected, the weights converged to the eigenvectors of the covariance matrix. Let's also compute the final covariance matrix, in order to check its values:

```
import numpy as np

Y_comp = np.zeros((Xs.shape[0], n_components))

for i in range(Xs.shape[0]):
    y_p = np.zeros((n_components, 1))
    xi = np.expand_dims(Xs[i], 1)

    for _ in range(stabilization_cycles):
        Y_comp[i] = np.squeeze(np.dot(W.T, xi) + np.dot(V.T, y_p))
        y_p = y.copy()

print('Final covariance matrix: {}'.format(np.cov(Y_comp.T)))
```

The output is as follows:

```
Final covariance matrix: [[28.9963492  0.31487817]
 [ 0.31487817 12.01606874]]
```

Again, the final covariance matrix is decorrelated (up to a negligible error). Rubner-Tavan's networks are generally faster than Sanger's networks, because of the anti-Hebbian feedback that speeds up the convergence; therefore, they should be the first choice when such models are employed. However, it's very important to tune the learning rate, in order to avoid oscillations. I suggest starting with a small value and slightly incrementing it until the number of iterations reaches its minimum. Alternatively, it's possible to start with a higher learning rate that allows for faster initial corrections, and to progressively reduce it by using linear (as with the Sanger's network) or exponential decay.

Unsupervised deep belief networks

In this section, we will discuss a very famous generative model that, in an unsupervised scenario, can be employed in order to perform the dimensionality reduction of input dataset X, drawn from a predefined data-generating process. As this book has no particular prerequisites and the mathematical complexity is quite high, we are going to briefly introduce the concepts, without proofs, nor a deep analysis of the structures of the algorithms. Before discussing **deep belief networks** (**DBN**), it's necessary to introduce another model, the **Restricted Boltzmann Machine** (**RBM**), which can be considered a building block for a DBN.

Restricted Boltzmann Machines

This network, also known as **Harmonium**, was proposed in *Information Processing in Dynamical Systems: Foundations of Harmony Theory, Parallel Distributed Processing, Vol 1, The MIT Press*, 1986) as a probabilistic generative model. In other words, the goal of an RBM is learning an unknown distribution (that is, a data-generating process), in order to generate all possible samples. The generic structure is shown in the following diagram:

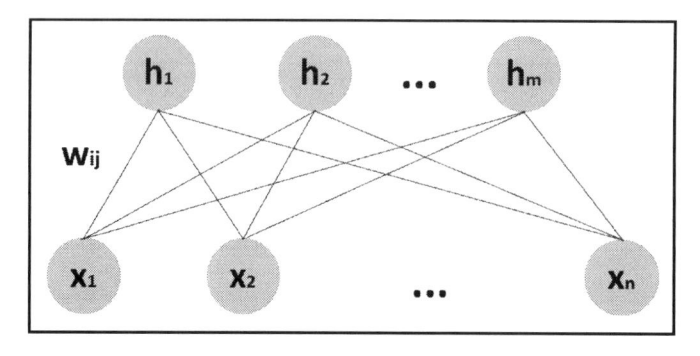

Structure of a generic Restricted Boltzmann Machine

The neurons, x_i, are observable (that is, they represent the vectors that are generated by the process that the RBM has to learn), while h_j are latent (that is, they are hidden and contribute to the values assumed by x_i). Without any further details, we need to say that this model has the structure of a **Markov random field** (**MRF**), thanks to the fact that there are no connections between neurons of the same layer (that is, the graph describing the network is bipartite). An important property of MRFs is the possibility to model the full joint probability, $p(x, h; \theta)$, with a Gibbs distribution:

$$p(\bar{x}, \bar{h}; \bar{\theta}) = \frac{1}{Z} e^{-E(\bar{x}, \bar{h}, \bar{\theta})}$$

The exponent, $E(x, h, \theta)$, plays the role of the energy of a physical system, and, in our case, it is equal to the following:

$$E(\bar{x}, \bar{h}) = -\sum_i \sum_j w_{ij} \bar{x}_i \bar{h}_j - \sum_i b_i \bar{x}_i - \sum_j c_j \bar{h}_j \text{ and } \bar{\theta} = \{\bar{w}, \bar{b}, \bar{c}\}$$

The main assumption for this formula is that all of the neurons are Bernoulli distributed (that is, $x_i, h_j \sim B(0, 1)$) and the terms b_i and c_j are biases for the observable and latent units. Given a data-generating process, p_{data}, an RBM must be optimized so that the likelihood, $p(x; \theta)$, is maximized. Skipping all of the intermediate steps (which can be found in the aforementioned paper), it's possible to prove the following:

$$\begin{cases} p(\bar{x}_i = 1|\bar{h}) = \sigma\left(\sum_j w_{ij} \bar{h}_j + \bar{b}_i\right) \\ p(\bar{h}_j = 1|\bar{x}) = \sigma\left(\sum_i w_{ij} \bar{x}_j + \bar{c}_j\right) \end{cases}$$

In the previous formulas, $\sigma(\bullet)$ is the sigmoid function. Given these two expressions, it's possible to derive (the manipulations are omitted) the gradient of the log-likelihood with respect to all learnable variables:

$$\begin{cases} \nabla_{w_{ij}} L(\bar{\theta}; \bar{x}) = p(\bar{h}_j = 1|\bar{x}) \bar{x}_i - \sum_{\bar{x}} p(\bar{x}; \bar{\theta}) p(\bar{h}_j = 1|\bar{x}) \bar{x}_i \\ \nabla_{\bar{b}_i} L(\bar{\theta}; \bar{x}) = \bar{x}_i - \sum_{\bar{x}} p(\bar{x}; \bar{\theta}) \bar{x}_i \\ \nabla_{\bar{c}_j} L(\bar{\theta}; \bar{x}) = p(\bar{h}_j = 1|\bar{x}) - \sum_{\bar{x}} p(\bar{x}; \bar{\theta}) p(\bar{h}_j = 1|\bar{x}) \end{cases}$$

It's straightforward to understand that the first term of all of the gradients is extremely easy to compute, while all of the second terms require a sum over all of the possible observable values. This is clearly an intractable problem that cannot be solved in a closed form. For this reason, Hinton (in Hinton, G., *A Practical Guide to Training Restricted Boltzmann Machines*, Dept. Computer Science, University of Toronto, 2010) proposed an algorithm called **Contrastive Divergence**, which can be employed to find an approximate solution. The explanation of this method requires knowledge of Markov chains (which is not a prerequisite); however, we can summarize the strategy by saying that it computes an approximation of the gradient through a finite (and small) number of sampling steps (in general, a single step is enough to obtain good results). This method allows the very efficient training of an RBM and makes deep belief networks easy to use and extremely effective.

Deep belief networks

A DBN is a stacked model based on RBMs. The generic structure is shown in the following diagram:

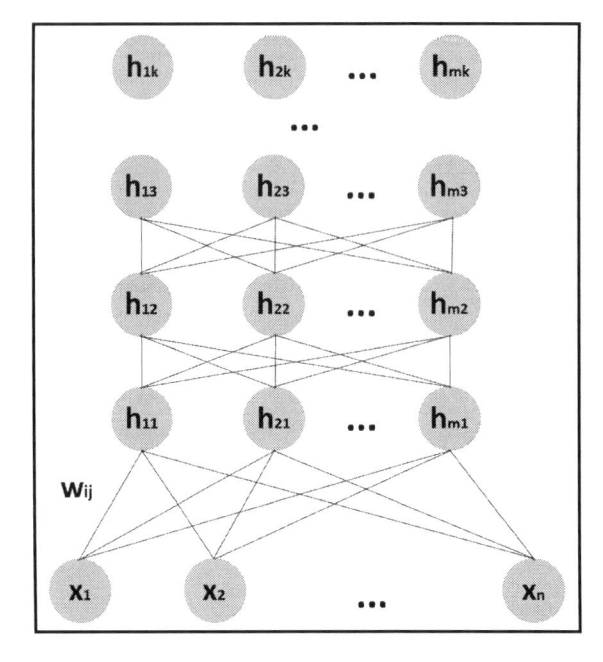

Structure of a generic DBN

The first layer contains visible units, while all of the remaining ones are latent. In an unsupervised scenario, the goal is to learn an unknown distribution, finding out the internal representation of the samples. In fact, when the number of latent units is smaller than the input ones, the model learns how to encode the distribution by using lower-dimensional subspace. Hinton and Osindero (in Hinton, G. E., and Osindero, S., *A Fast Learning Algorithm for Deep Belief Nets, Teh Y. W., Neural Computation*, 18/7, 2005) proposed a step-wise greedy training procedure (which is the one normally implemented). Each couple of layers is considered an RBM and is trained by using the Contrastive Divergence algorithm. Once an RBM has been trained, the hidden layer becomes the observable layer of the subsequent RBM, and the process is continued until the last one. Therefore, a DBN develops a sequence of internal representations (that's why it's defined as a deep network), where every level is trained on lower-level features. The process is not dissimilar to a variational autoencoder; however, in this case, the structure of the model is more rigid (for example, it's not possible to employ convolutional units). Moreover, the output is not a reconstruction of the input, but rather an internal representation. Therefore, considering the formulas discussed in the previous section, if it's necessary to invert the process (that is, given an internal representation, obtaining an input), it's necessary to sample from the topmost layer, applying the following formula:

$$p(\bar{x}_i = 1|\bar{h}) = \sigma \left(\sum_j w_{ij} \bar{h}_j + \bar{b}_i \right)$$

Of course, the process must be repeated backward, until the actual input layer has been reached. DBNs are very powerful (with, for example, several scientific applications in the field of astrophysics), even if their structure is not flexible like other, more recent models; however, the complexity is generally higher, and therefore, I always suggest starting with smaller models, increasing the number of layers and/or neurons only if the final accuracy is not adequate for the specific purpose.

Example of an unsupervised DBN

In this example, we want to employ a DBN in order to find a low-dimensional representation of the MNIST dataset. As the complexity of these models can easily grow, we are going to limit the process to 500 random samples. The implementation is based on the deep-belief-network package (https://github.com/albertbup/deep-belief-network), which supports both NumPy and TensorFlow. In the former case, the classes (whose names remain unchanged) must be imported from the `dbn` package, while in the latter, the package is `dbn.tensorflow`. In this example, we are going to use the NumPy version, which has fewer requirements, but the reader is invited to check the TensorFlow version, too.

Unsupervised Neural Network Models

Let's start by loading and normalizing the dataset, as follows:

```
import numpy as np

from sklearn.datasets import load_digits
from sklearn.utils import shuffle

nb_samples = 500

digits = load_digits()

X_train = digits['data'] / np.max(digits['data'])
Y_train = digits['target']

X_train, Y_train = shuffle(X_train, Y_train, random_state=1000)
X_train = X_train[0:nb_samples]
Y_train = Y_train[0:nb_samples]
```

We can now instantiate the `UnsupervisedDBN` class, with the following structure:

1. 64 input neurons (implicitly detected from the dataset)
2. 32 sigmoid neurons
3. 32 sigmoid neurons
4. 16 sigmoid neurons

Hence, the last representation is made up of 16 values (one quarter of the original dimensionality). We are setting a learning rate of $\eta=0.025$ and 16 samples per batch (of course, you are invited to check out other configurations, in order to minimize the reconstruction error). The following snippet initializes and trains the model:

```
from dbn import UnsupervisedDBN

unsupervised_dbn = UnsupervisedDBN(hidden_layers_structure=[32, 32, 16],
                                    learning_rate_rbm=0.025,
                                    n_epochs_rbm=500,
                                    batch_size=16,
                                    activation_function='sigmoid')

X_dbn = unsupervised_dbn.fit_transform(X_train)
```

At the end of the training process, we can analyze the distribution, after projecting it onto a bidimensional space. As usual, we are going to employ the t-SNE algorithm, which guarantees finding the most similar low-dimensional distribution:

```
from sklearn.manifold import TSNE

tsne = TSNE(n_components=2, perplexity=10, random_state=1000)
X_tsne = tsne.fit_transform(X_dbn)
```

The plot of the projected samples is shown in the following diagram:

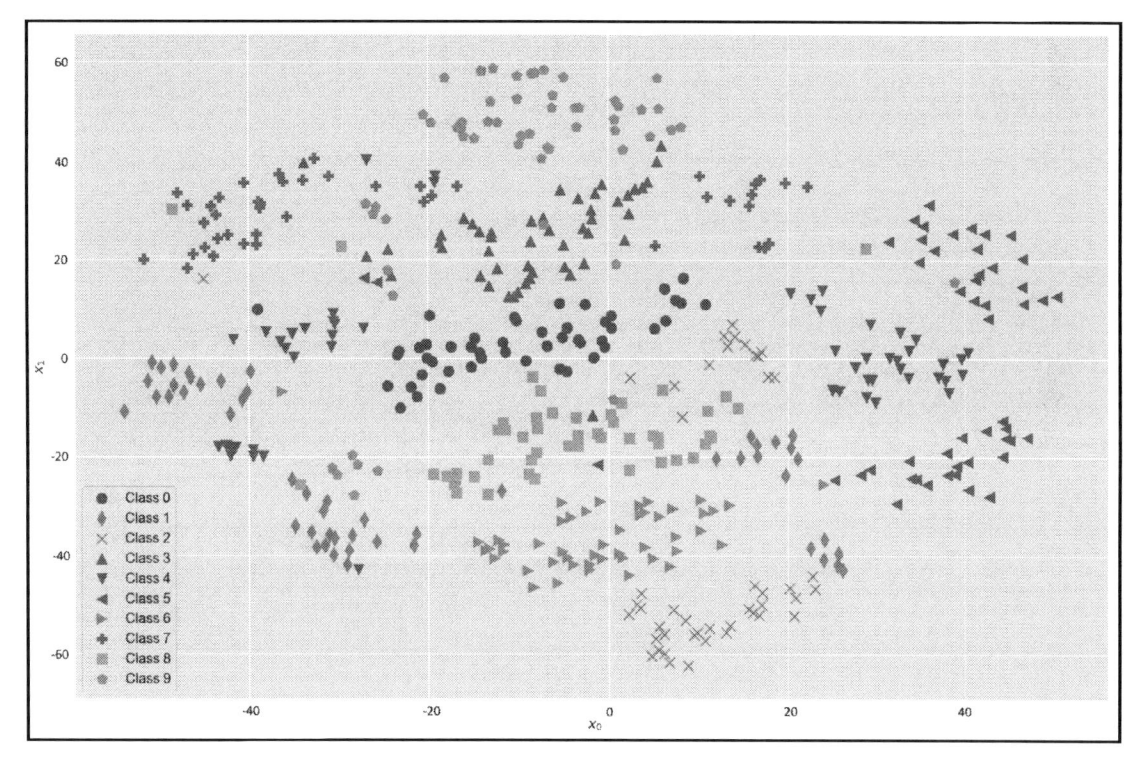

t-SNE plot of the unsupervised DBN output representations

As you can see, most of the blocks are quite cohesive, indicating that the peculiar properties of a digit have been successfully represented in the lower-dimensional space. In some cases, the same digit group is split into more clusters, but in general, the amount of noisy (isolated) points is extremely low. For example, the group containing the digit 2 is indicated with the symbol x. The majority of the samples are in the range $0 < x_0 < 30$, $x_1 < -40$; however, a subgroup is also located in the range $-10 < x_1 < 10$. If we check the neighbors of this small cluster, they are made up of samples representing the digit 8 (represented by a square). It's easy to understand that some malformed twos are very similar to malformed eights, and this justifies the split of the original cluster. From a statistical viewpoint, the explained variance can have a different impact. In some cases, a few components are enough to determine the peculiar features of a class, but this cannot generally be true. When samples belonging to different classes show similarities, a distinction can only be made thanks to the variance of the secondary components. This consideration is very important when working with datasets containing almost (or even partially) overlapping samples. The main task of the data scientist, when performing dimensionality reduction, is not to check the overall explained variance, but rather, to understand whether there are regions that are negatively affected by the dimensionality reduction. In such situations, it's possible to either define multiple detection rules (for example, when a sample, $x_i \in R_1$ or $x_i \in R_4 \to x_i$, has the y_k label) or to try to avoid models that create this segmentation (in this case, you are invited to test more complex DBNs and higher-dimensional output representations).

Summary

In this chapter, we discussed some quite common neural models that are employed for solving unsupervised tasks. Autoencoders allow you to find the low-dimensional representation of a dataset without specific limits to its complexity. In particular, the use of deep convolutional networks helps to detect and learn both high-level and low-level geometrical features that can lead to a very accurate reconstruction when the internal code is much shorter than the original dimensionality too. We also discussed how to add sparsity to an autoencoder, and how to use these models to denoise samples. A slightly different variant of a standard autoencoder is a variational autoencoder, which is a generative model that can improve the ability to learn the data-generating process from which a dataset is supposed to be drawn.

Sanger's and Rubner-Tavan's networks are neural models that are able to extract the first k principal components of a dataset without any statistical preprocessing. They also have the advantage of working naturally in an online fashion (while standard PCA often requires the whole dataset, even if there is an incremental variant whose performances are slightly worse than the offline algorithm), and of extracting components in descending order. The last models that we discussed were DBNs in an unsupervised context. We described the generative properties of their building blocks, RBM, and then we analyzed how such models can learn internal (normally lower-dimensional) representations of a data-generating process.

In the next chapter, we will discuss other neural models—**Generative Adversarial Networks** (**GANs**) and **Self-Organizing Maps** (**SOMs**). The former can learn an input distribution and generate new samples drawn from it, while the latter is based on the functioning of some specific areas of the brain, and train their units in order to be receptive to specific input patterns.

Questions

1. In an autoencoder, both the encoder and decoder must be structurally symmetric. Is this correct?
2. Given a dataset, X, and its transformation, Y, based on the code yielded by an autoencoder, all of the information contained in X can be found in Y. Is this correct?
3. A code, $z_i \in (0, 1)^{128}$ has $sum(z_i) = 36$. Is it sparse?
4. If $std(z_i) = 0.03$, is the code sparse?
5. A Sanger's network requires covariance matrix columns as input vectors. Is this correct?
6. How can we determine the importance of each component extracted by a Rubner-Tavan network?
7. Given a random vector, $h_i \in \Re^m$ (m is the output dimensionality of a DBN), is it possible to determine the most likely corresponding input sample?

Further reading

- *Stacked Denoising Autoencoders: Learning Useful Representations in a Deep Network with a Local Denoising Criterion, Vincent, P., Larochelle, H., Lajoie, I., Bengio, Y., and Manzagol, P., Journal of Machine Learning Research 11*, 2010
- *Sparse Autoencoder, CS294A, Ng, A., Stanford University*
- *Auto-Encoding Variational Bayes, Kingma. D. P. and Welling, M., arXiv:1312.6114 [stat.ML]*
- *Theoretical Neuroscience, Dayan, P. and Abbott, L. F., The MIT Press, 2005*

- *Optimal Unsupervised Learning in a Single-Layer Linear Feedforward Neural Network, Neural Networks, Sanger, T. D., 2, 1989*
- *A Self-Organizing Network for Principal-Components Analysis, Europhysics Letters, Rubner, J. and Tavan, P., 10(7), 1989*
- *Information Processing in Dynamical Systems: Foundations of Harmony Theory, Parallel Distributed Processing, Smolensky, Paul, Vol 1, The MIT Press, 1986*
- *A Practical Guide to Training Restricted Boltzmann Machines,* Hinton, G., Dept. Computer Science, University of Toronto, 2010
- *A Fast Learning Algorithm for Deep Belief Nets,* Hinton G. E., Osindero S., and Teh Y. W., *Neural Computation, 18/7, 2005*
- *Machine Learning Algorithms, Second Edition,* Bonaccorso, G., Packt, 2018
- *Mastering Machine Learning Algorithms,* Bonaccorso, G., Packt, 2018

9
Generative Adversarial Networks and SOMs

In this chapter, we will finish our journey through the world of unsupervised learning, discussing some very popular neural models that can be employed to perform a data generating process and new samples that can be drawn from it. Moreover, we will analyze the functionality of self-organizing maps, which can adapt their structures so that specific units become responsive to distinct input patterns.

In particular, we will discuss the following topics:

- **Generative adversarial networks (GANs)**
- **Deep convolutional GANs (DCGANs)**
- **Wasserstein GANs (WGANs)**
- **Self-organizing maps (SOMs)**

Technical requirements

The code that will be presented in this chapter will require the following:

- Python 3.5+ (the Anaconda distribution (https://www.anaconda.com/distribution/) is highly recommended)
- Libraries, as follows:
    - SciPy 0.19+
    - NumPy 1.10+
    - scikit-learn 0.20+
    - pandas 0.22+
    - Matplotlib 2.0+

- seaborn 0.9+
- TensorFlow 1.5+
- Keras 2+ (only for the dataset utility functions)

The examples are available in the GitHub repository, at https://github.com/PacktPublishing/HandsOn-Unsupervised-Learning-with-Python/Chapter09.

Generative adversarial networks

These generative models were proposed by Goodfellow and other researchers (in *Generative Adversarial Networks, Goodfellow I. J., Pouget-Abadie J., Mirza M., Xu B., Warde-Farley D., Ozair S., Courville A., and Bengio Y., arXiv:1406.2661 [stat.ML]*) in order to exploit the power of **adversarial training**, along with the flexibility of deep neural networks. Without the need for too many technical details, we can introduce the concept of adversarial training as a technique based on game theory, whose goal it is to optimize two agents that play against one another. When one agent tries to cheat its opponent, the other agent has to learn how to distinguish between correct and fake input. In particular, a GAN is a model that's split into two well-defined components:

- A **generator**
- A **discriminator** (also known as a **critic**)

Let's start by supposing that we have a data generating process, p_{data}, and a dataset, X, of m samples drawn from it:

$$X = \{\bar{x}_1, \bar{x}_2, \ldots, \bar{x}_m\} \quad where \quad \bar{x}_i \in \mathbb{R}^n$$

For simplicity, the dataset is assumed to have a single dimension; however, this is not a constraint, nor a limitation. The generator is a parameterized function (normally using a neural network) that is fed with a noisy sample and provides an n-dimensional vector as output:

$$\hat{x}_i = g(\bar{z}_i; \bar{\theta}_g) \quad where \quad \hat{x}_i \in \mathbb{R}^n \ and \ \bar{z}_i \sim U(-1, 1)$$

In other words, the generator is a transformation of a uniform distribution into another distribution, $p_g(x)$, over the samples $x \in \Re^n$. The main goal of a GAN is as follows:

$$p_g(\bar{x}) \rightarrow p_{data}(\bar{x})$$

However, contrary to autoencoders, in which such an objective is achieved through a direct training of the whole model, in a GAN the goal is pursued through a game played between the generator and discriminator, which is another parameterized function that takes a sample, $x_i \in \Re^n$, and returns a probability:

$$p_i = d\left(\bar{x}_i; \bar{\theta}_d\right) \text{ where } \bar{x}_i \in \mathbb{R}^n \text{ and } p_i \in (0,1)$$

The role of the discriminator is to distinguish between samples drawn from p_{data} (which returns large probabilities) and samples generated by $g(z; \theta_g)$ (which returns low probabilities). However, as the generator's goal is to become more and more able to reproduce p_{data}, its role is to learn how to cheat the discriminator with samples that are drawn from an almost perfect reproduction of the data generating process. Therefore, considering the discriminator, the goal is to maximize the following conditions:

$$\begin{cases} \log\left(d(\bar{x}; \bar{\theta}_d)\right) & if \ \bar{x}_i \sim p_{data} \\ \log\left(1 - d(g(\bar{z}; \bar{\theta}_g); \bar{\theta}_d)\right) & otherwise \end{cases}$$

However, this is a **minimax game**, which means that the two opponents, A and B, must try to minimize (A) and maximize (B), the same objective. In this case, the goal of the generator is to minimize the second term of the previous double cost function:

$$\log\left(1 - d(g(\bar{z}; \bar{\theta}_g); \bar{\theta}_d)\right)$$

In fact, when both agents succeed in optimizing the objective, the discriminator will be able to distinguish between samples drawn from p_{data} and outliers, and the generator will be able to output synthetic samples belonging to p_{data}. It must be clear, however, that the problem can be expressed by using a single objective, and the goal of the training process is to find out the optimal parameter set, $\theta = \{\theta_d, \theta_g\}$, so that the discriminator maximizes it while the generator minimizes it. Both agents must be optimized at the same time, but in practice, the process is alternated (for example, generator, discriminator, generator, and so on). In a more compact form, the objective can be expressed as follows:

$$V(g,d) = E_{\bar{x} \sim p_{data}}\left[\log\left(d(\bar{x}; \bar{\theta}_d)\right)\right] + E_{\bar{z} \sim p_{noise}}\left[\log\left(1 - d(g(\bar{z}; \bar{\theta}_g); \bar{\theta}_d)\right)\right] = V_{data}(d) + V_{noise}(g,d)$$

Hence, the optimum is reached by solving the following problem:

$$\bar{\theta}_{opt} = argmax_{\bar{\theta}_d} \, argmin_{\bar{\theta}_g} V(g,d)$$

According to the game theory, this is a non-cooperative game that admits a **Nash equilibrium** point. When such a condition is met, if we assume that both players are aware of the opponents' strategies, they have no reason to change their own strategy anymore. In the context of a GAN, this condition implies that once the equilibrium is reached (even just theoretically), the generator can continue to output samples, being sure that they won't be misclassified by the discriminator. At the same time, the discriminator has no reason to change its strategy, because it can perfectly distinguish between p_{data} and any other distributions. From a dynamic viewpoint, the training speed of both components is asymmetrical. While the generator usually needs more iterations, the discriminator can converge very quickly. However, such a premature convergence can be very dangerous for the overall performance. In fact, the generator also reaches its optimum thanks to the feedback provided by the discriminator. Unfortunately, when the gradient is very small, this contribution becomes negligible, with the obvious consequence that the generator misses the chance to improve its ability to output better samples (for example, when the samples are images, their quality can remain very low, even with complex architectures). Such a condition is not dependent on the intrinsic lack of capacity of the generator, but rather, on the limited number of corrections that it starts to apply once the discriminator has converged (or is very close to doing so). In practice, as there are no specific rules, the only valid suggestion is to check both of the loss functions during the training process. If the discriminator loss decreases too quickly, while the generator loss remains large, it's often preferable to interleave more generator training steps with a single discriminator step.

Analyzing a GAN

Let's suppose that we have a GAN that has been properly trained by using a dataset X, drawn from $p_{data}(x)$. Goodfellow, et al., proved that, given the generator distribution $p_g(x)$, the optimal discriminator is as follows:

$$d_{opt}(\bar{x}) = \frac{p_{data}(\bar{x})}{p_{data}(\bar{x}) + p_g(\bar{x})}$$

The global objective can be rewritten by using the optimal discriminator:

$$V(d_{opt}) = E_{\bar{x} \sim p_{data}}\left[log\left(d_{opt}(\bar{x}; \bar{\theta}_d)\right)\right] + E_{\bar{x} \sim p_g}\left[log\left(1 - d_{opt}(\bar{x}; \bar{\theta}_d)\right)\right]$$

We can now expand the previous expression:

$$V(d_{opt}) = E_{\bar{x} \sim p_{data}} \left[log \left(\frac{p_{data}(\bar{x})}{p_{data}(\bar{x}) + p_g(\bar{x})} \right) \right] + E_{\bar{x} \sim p_g} \left[log \left(\frac{p_g(\bar{x})}{p_{data}(\bar{x}) + p_g(\bar{x})} \right) \right]$$

Now, let's consider the Kullback-Leibler divergence between two distributions, *a* and *b*:

$$D_{KL})(a||b) = \sum_x a(x) \, log \frac{a(x)}{b(x)} = E_x \left[log \frac{a(x)}{b(x)} \right]$$

Considering the previous expression, after a few simple manipulations, it's easy to prove the following equality:

$$\frac{1}{2} V(d_{opt}) + log(2) = \frac{1}{2} D_{KL} \left(p_{data} || \frac{p_{data} + p_g}{2} \right) + \frac{1}{2} D_{KL} \left(p_g || \frac{p_{data} + p_g}{2} \right) = D_{JS}(p_{data}||p_g)$$

Hence, the objective can be expressed as a function of the **Jensen-Shannon divergence** between the data generating process and the generator distribution. The main differences with the Kullback-Leibler divergence are that $0 \leq D_{JS}(p_{data}||p_g) \leq log(2)$, and it's symmetric. This reformulation is not surprising, because the true goal of GAN is to be a generative model that can successfully reproduce p_{data}, as shown in the following diagram:

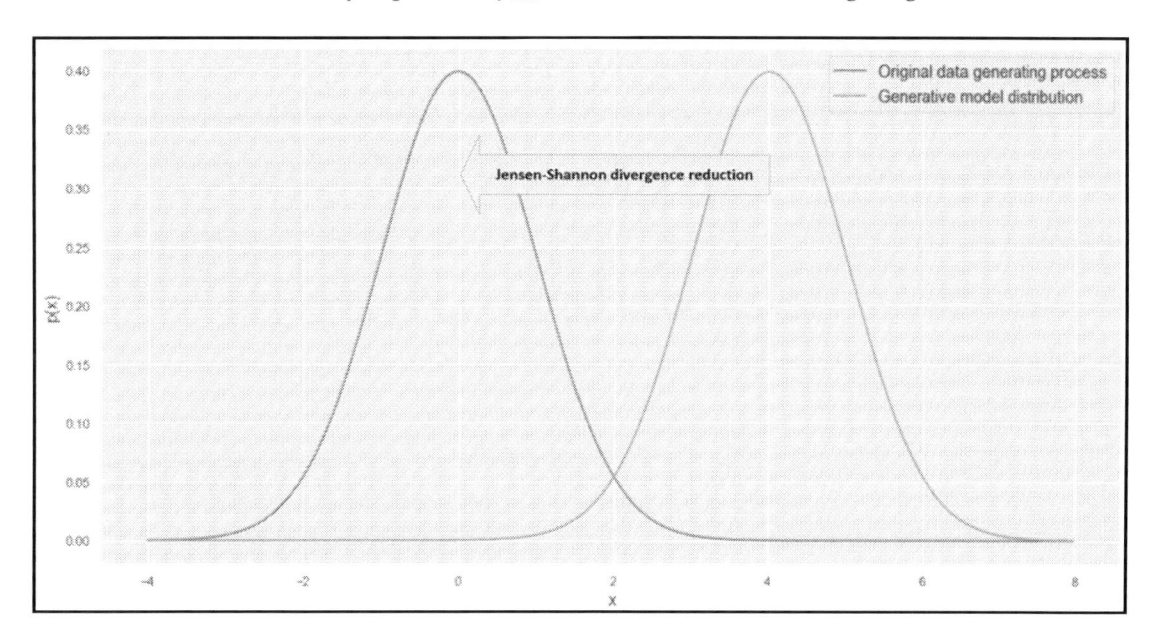

The goal of a GAN is to move the generative model distribution in the direction of p_{data}, trying to maximize the overlap

The initial distribution is generally completely different from the target one; therefore, a GAN must both reshape and shift it towards p_{data}. When the overlap is complete, the Jensen-Shannon divergence reaches its minimum, and the optimization is complete. However, as we are going to discuss in the next sections, this process, because of the property of the Jensen-Shannon divergence, doesn't always run so smoothly, and the GAN can reach suboptimal minima very far from the desired final configuration.

Mode collapse

Given a probability distribution, the value that occurs most often (in the discrete case), or the one that corresponds to a maximum of the probability density function (in a continuous scenario), is called the **mode**. If we consider the latter case, a distribution whose PDF has a single maximum is called **unimodal**. When there are two local maxima, it's called **bimodal,** and so on (in general, when there are many modes, the distribution is simply called **multimodal**). Two examples are shown in the following screenshot:

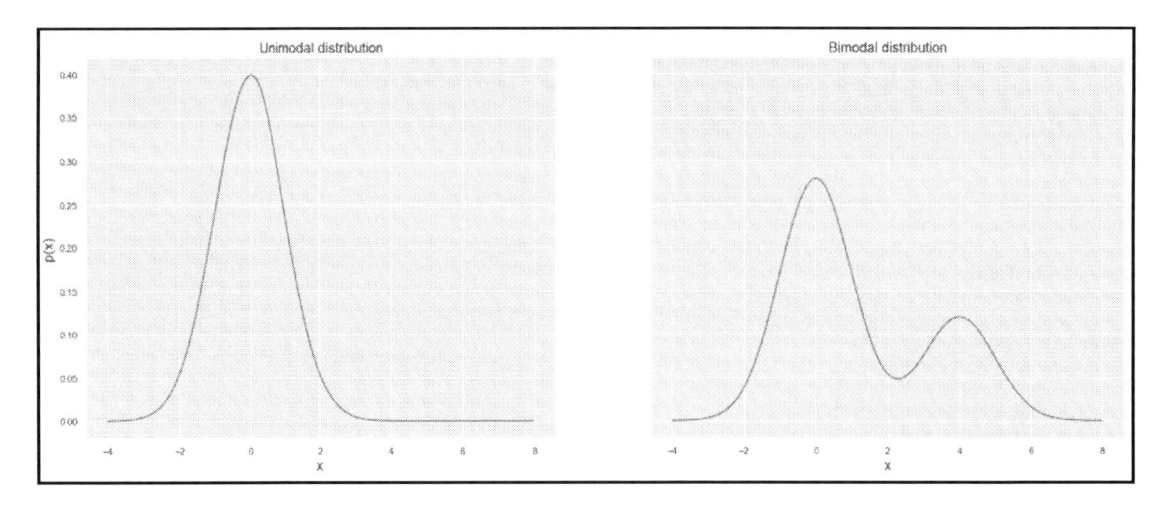

Examples of unimodal (left) and bimodal (right) distributions

When working with complex datasets, we cannot easily estimate the number of modes; however, it's reasonable to suppose that the data generating process is a multimodal one. Sometimes, when the samples are based on a common structure, there can be a dominant mode and several secondary ones; but in general, the probability of having a single mode is very low if the samples are structurally different (of course, a single mode is possible if there are slight modifications of the same basic element, but this is not a valid case to take into account).

Now, let's imagine that we are working with a multimodal distribution of face pictures (such as those in the example that we are going to discuss in the next section). What's the content of a mode? It's hard to answer this question precisely, but it's very easy to understand that the face corresponding to a maximum of the data generating process should contain the elements that are most common in the dataset (for example, if 80% of the people have a beard, we can reasonably suppose that the mode will contain it).

One of the most famous and tough problems that we face when working with GANs is called **mode collapse**, and it involves a suboptimal final configuration, wherein the generator freezes around a mode and keeps providing the same kinds of sample as output. The reason for such a situation is extremely complex to analyze (indeed, there are only theories), but we can understand why it happens if we rethink the minimax game. As we are going to train two different components, even if the Nash equilibrium is guaranteed, it can happen that after a few iterations, the discriminator becomes very selective with respect to the most common patterns. Of course, as the generator is trained in order to deceive the discriminator, the easiest way to achieve this goal is by simply avoiding all samples far from the mode. This behavior increases the selectivity of the discriminator and creates a feedback process that makes the GAN collapse into a state where only a small region of the data generating process is present.

In terms of gradients, the pieces of information provided by the discriminator for the optimization of the generator soon become very scarce, because the most common samples won't need any adjustment. On the other hand, as the generator starts to avoid all those samples whose $p(x)$ is not close to the maximum, they don't expose the discriminator to new, potentially valid samples, so the gradient will remain very small, until it vanishes to zero. Unfortunately, there are no global strategies that can be employed to avoid this problem, but in this chapter, we will discuss one of the methods proposed in order to mitigate the risk of mode collapse (WGANs). In particular, we are going to focus our attention on the limitations of the Jensen-Shannon divergence, which, in some cases, can lead the GAN to a suboptimal configuration for the absence of large gradients. In this introduction, it's important that readers not familiar with these models become aware of the risks and are able to recognize the mode collapse when it happens.

At this point, we can move on to the practical side of things and model a real GAN, using TensorFlow.

Example of a deep convolutional GAN

We can now implement a DCGAN, based on the model proposed in *Unsupervised Representation Learning with Deep Convolutional Generative Adversarial Networks, Radford A., Metz L., and Chintala S., arXiv:1511.06434 [cs.LG]*, and the Olivetti faces dataset, which is small enough to allow for a quick training phase.

Let's start by loading the dataset and normalizing the values in the range (*-1, 1*), as follows:

```
from sklearn.datasets import fetch_olivetti_faces

faces = fetch_olivetti_faces(shuffle=True, random_state=1000)

X_train = faces['images']
X_train = (2.0 * X_train) - 1.0

width = X_train.shape[1]
height = X_train.shape[2]
```

A few sample faces are shown in the following screenshot:

Sample faces drawn from the Olivetti faces dataset

Even if the structure of all of the faces resembles the same patterns, there are subtle differences in the shapes of the eyes (with and without glasses), nose, and mouth. Moreover, some people have a beard, and the expressions are quite different (smiling, serious, staring at something far from the camera, and so on). Therefore, we need to expect a multimodal distribution, probably with a main mode corresponding to the average facial structure and several other modes corresponding to subsets with specific, common features.

At this point, we can define the main constants, as follows:

```
nb_samples = 400
code_length = 512
nb_epochs = 500
batch_size = 50
nb_iterations = int(nb_samples / batch_size)
```

There are 400 64 × 64 grayscale samples (corresponding to 4,096 components per sample). In this example, we have chosen to employ a noise code vector with 512 components and train the model for 500 epochs, with 50 sample batches. Such values are not based on golden rules, because (particularly for GANs) it's almost impossible to know which setting will yield the optimal results. Hence, as usual, I strongly suggest checking different hyperparameter sets before making a decision.

When the training process is not too long, it's possible to check the average losses for both the generator and discriminator with a set of uniformly sampled hyperparameters (for example, *batch size* ∈ *{20, 50, 100, 200}*). If, for example, an optimal value seems to exist in the range *(50, 100)*, a good strategy is to extract some random values and retrain the model. Such a process can be repeated until the differences between sampled values are negligible. Of course, considering the complexity of these models, a thorough search can only be carried out with dedicated hardware (that is, multiple GPUs or TPUs); therefore, another suggestion is to start with tested configurations (even if the context is different) and apply small modifications, in order to optimize them for the specific task. In this example, we are setting many values according to the original paper, but I invite the reader to rerun the code after custom changes and observe the differences.

We can now define the DAG for the generator, which is based on the following structure:

- 2D convolution with 1,024 (4 × 4) filters with (1, 1) strides, valid padding, and linear output
- Batch normalization and leaky ReLU activation (which is more performant when the input values are negative; in fact, a standard ReLU has a null gradient when $x < 0$, while a leaky ReLU has a constant, small gradient that allows for slight modifications)
- 2D convolution with 512 (4 × 4) filters with (2, 2) strides, the same padding, and linear output
- Batch normalization and leaky ReLU activation
- 2D convolution with 256 (4 × 4) filters with (2, 2) strides, the same padding, and linear output
- Batch normalization and leaky ReLU activation
- 2D convolution with 128 (4 × 4) filters with (2, 2) strides, the same padding, and linear output
- Batch normalization and leaky ReLU activation
- 2D convolution with 1 (4 × 4) filter with (2, 2) strides, the same padding, and hyperbolic tangent output

The code for the generator is shown in the following snippet:

```python
import tensorflow as tf

def generator(z, is_training=True):
    with tf.variable_scope('generator'):
        conv_0 = tf.layers.conv2d_transpose(inputs=z,
                                            filters=1024,
                                            kernel_size=(4, 4),
                                            padding='valid')

        b_conv_0 = tf.layers.batch_normalization(inputs=conv_0, training=is_training)

        conv_1 = tf.layers.conv2d_transpose(inputs=tf.nn.leaky_relu(b_conv_0),
                                            filters=512,
                                            kernel_size=(4, 4),
                                            strides=(2, 2),
                                            padding='same')

        b_conv_1 = tf.layers.batch_normalization(inputs=conv_1, training=is_training)

        conv_2 = tf.layers.conv2d_transpose(inputs=tf.nn.leaky_relu(b_conv_1),
                                            filters=256,
                                            kernel_size=(4, 4),
                                            strides=(2, 2),
                                            padding='same')

        b_conv_2 = tf.layers.batch_normalization(inputs=conv_2, training=is_training)

        conv_3 = tf.layers.conv2d_transpose(inputs=tf.nn.leaky_relu(b_conv_2),
                                            filters=128,
                                            kernel_size=(4, 4),
                                            strides=(2, 2),
                                            padding='same')

        b_conv_3 = tf.layers.batch_normalization(inputs=conv_3, training=is_training)

        conv_4 = tf.layers.conv2d_transpose(inputs=tf.nn.leaky_relu(b_conv_3),
                                            filters=1,
                                            kernel_size=(4, 4),
```

```
                                      strides=(2, 2),
                                      padding='same')

        return tf.nn.tanh(conv_4)
```

The code is straightforward, but it's helpful to clarify the need for a variable scope context (defined through the command `tf.variable_scope('generator')`). As we need to train the model with an alternate fashion, when the generator is being optimized, only its variables must be updated. Therefore, we have defined all of the layers inside a named scope that allows forcing the optimizer to only work a subset of all trainable variables.

The DAG for the discriminator is based on the following symmetrical structure:

- 2D convolution with 128 (4 × 4) filters with (2, 2) strides, the same padding, and leaky ReLU output
- 2D convolution with 256 (4 × 4) filters with (2, 2) strides, the same padding, and linear output
- Batch normalization and leaky ReLU activation
- 2D convolution with 512 (4 × 4) filters with (2, 2) strides, the same padding, and linear output
- Batch normalization and leaky ReLU activation
- 2D convolution with 1,024 (4 × 4) filters with (2, 2) strides, the same padding, and linear output
- Batch normalization and leaky ReLU activation
- 2D convolution with 1 (4 × 4) filters with (2, 2) strides, valid padding, and linear output (the output is expected to be a sigmoid, which can represent a probability, but we are going to perform this transformation directly inside of the loss function)

The code for the discriminator is as follows:

```
import tensorflow as tf

def discriminator(x, is_training=True, reuse_variables=True):
    with tf.variable_scope('discriminator', reuse=reuse_variables):
        conv_0 = tf.layers.conv2d(inputs=x,
                                  filters=128,
                                  kernel_size=(4, 4),
                                  strides=(2, 2),
                                  padding='same')

        conv_1 = tf.layers.conv2d(inputs=tf.nn.leaky_relu(conv_0),
                                  filters=256,
```

```
                              kernel_size=(4, 4),
                              strides=(2, 2),
                              padding='same')

        b_conv_1 = tf.layers.batch_normalization(inputs=conv_1,
training=is_training)

        conv_2 = tf.layers.conv2d(inputs=tf.nn.leaky_relu(b_conv_1),
                              filters=512,
                              kernel_size=(4, 4),
                              strides=(2, 2),
                              padding='same')

        b_conv_2 = tf.layers.batch_normalization(inputs=conv_2,
training=is_training)

        conv_3 = tf.layers.conv2d(inputs=tf.nn.leaky_relu(b_conv_2),
                              filters=1024,
                              kernel_size=(4, 4),
                              strides=(2, 2),
                              padding='same')

        b_conv_3 = tf.layers.batch_normalization(inputs=conv_3,
training=is_training)

        conv_4 = tf.layers.conv2d(inputs=tf.nn.leaky_relu(b_conv_3),
                              filters=1,
                              kernel_size=(4, 4),
                              padding='valid')

        return conv_4
```

Also, in this case, we need to declare a dedicated variable scope. However, as the discriminator is employed in two different contexts (that is, the evaluation of true samples and that of generated ones), we need to ask for the variable reused in the second declaration. If such a flag is not set, every call to the function will produce new variable sets, corresponding to different discriminators.

Once the two main components have been declared, we can initialize the graph and set up the whole DAG for the GAN, as follows:

```
import tensorflow as tf

graph = tf.Graph()

with graph.as_default():
    input_x = tf.placeholder(tf.float32, shape=(None, width, height, 1))
```

```
    input_z = tf.placeholder(tf.float32, shape=(None, code_length))
    is_training = tf.placeholder(tf.bool)

    gen = generator(z=tf.reshape(input_z, (-1, 1, 1, code_length)),
is_training=is_training)

    discr_1_l = discriminator(x=input_x, is_training=is_training,
reuse_variables=False)
    discr_2_l = discriminator(x=gen, is_training=is_training,
reuse_variables=True)

    loss_d_1 = tf.reduce_mean(
tf.nn.sigmoid_cross_entropy_with_logits(labels=tf.ones_like(discr_1_l),
logits=discr_1_l))
    loss_d_2 = tf.reduce_mean(
tf.nn.sigmoid_cross_entropy_with_logits(labels=tf.zeros_like(discr_2_l),
logits=discr_2_l))
    loss_d = loss_d_1 + loss_d_2

    loss_g = tf.reduce_mean(
tf.nn.sigmoid_cross_entropy_with_logits(labels=tf.ones_like(discr_2_l),
logits=discr_2_l))

    variables_g = [variable for variable in tf.trainable_variables() if
variable.name.startswith('generator')]
    variables_d = [variable for variable in tf.trainable_variables() if
variable.name.startswith('discriminator')]

    with
tf.control_dependencies(tf.get_collection(tf.GraphKeys.UPDATE_OPS)):
        training_step_d = tf.train.AdamOptimizer(0.0001,
beta1=0.5).minimize(loss=loss_d, var_list=variables_d)
        training_step_g = tf.train.AdamOptimizer(0.0005,
beta1=0.5).minimize(loss=loss_g, var_list=variables_g)
```

The first block contains the declaration of the placeholders. For the sake of clarity, while the purpose of `input_x` and `input_z` is quite easy to understand, `is_training` can be less obvious. The goal of this Boolean flag is to allow for disabling the batch normalization during the production phase (it must only be active during the training one). The next steps consist of declaring the generator and two discriminators (they are formally the same, as the variables are shared, but one is fed with true samples, and the other must evaluate the output of the generator). Then, it's time to define the loss functions, which are based on a trick that speeds up the computation and increases the numerical stability.

The function `tf.nn.sigmoid_cross_entropy_with_logits()` accepts a *logit* (that's why we haven't directly applied the sigmoid transformation to the discriminator output), and allows us to perform the following vectorial computation:

$$L = -x_{label} \log(\sigma(x_{logit})) - (1 - x_{label}) \log(1 - \sigma(x_{logit}))$$

Therefore, as `loss_d_1` is the loss function for the true samples, we use the operator `tf.ones_like()` to set all of the labels equal to 1; therefore, the second term of the sigmoid cross-entropy becomes null, and the result is as follows:

$$L_{d1} = \frac{1}{batch\ size} \sum_i \log(\sigma(x_i))$$

Conversely, `loss_d_2` requires exactly the second term of the sigmoid cross-entropy; therefore, we set all of the labels equal to zero, in order to obtain the loss function:

$$L_{d2} = \frac{1}{batch\ size} \sum_i \log(1 - \sigma(x_i))$$

The same concept is applied to the generator loss function. The next steps are required to define two Adam optimizers. As we explained before, we need to isolate the variables, in order to perform an interlaced training; hence, the `minimize()` functions are now fed with both the losses and the variable sets that must be updated. The context declaration `tf.control_dependencies(tf.get_collection(tf.GraphKeys.UPDATE_OPS))` is suggested in the official TensorFlow documentation, whenever a batch normalization is employed and its goal is to allow the execution of the training steps only after the computation of means and variances (for further details about this technique, please check the original paper: *Batch Normalization: Accelerating Deep Network Training by Reducing Internal Covariate Shift*, Ioffe S. and Szegedy C., arXiv:1502.03167 [cs.LG]).

At this point, we can create a session and initialize all of the variables, as follows:

```
import tensorflow as tf

session = tf.InteractiveSession(graph=graph)
tf.global_variables_initializer().run()
```

Once everything is ready, the training process can be started. The following snippet shows code that performs an alternate training of the discriminator and generator:

```
import numpy as np

samples_range = np.arange(nb_samples)

for e in range(nb_epochs):
    d_losses = []
    g_losses = []

    for i in range(nb_iterations):
        Xi = np.random.choice(samples_range, size=batch_size)
        X = np.expand_dims(X_train[Xi], axis=3)
        Z = np.random.uniform(-1.0, 1.0, size=(batch_size, code_length)).astype(np.float32)

        _, d_loss = session.run([training_step_d, loss_d],
                                feed_dict={
                                    input_x: X,
                                    input_z: Z,
                                    is_training: True
                                })
        d_losses.append(d_loss)

        Z = np.random.uniform(-1.0, 1.0, size=(batch_size, code_length)).astype(np.float32)

        _, g_loss = session.run([training_step_g, loss_g],
                                feed_dict={
                                    input_x: X,
                                    input_z: Z,
                                    is_training: True
                                })
        g_losses.append(g_loss)

    print('Epoch {}) Avg. discriminator loss: {} - Avg. generator loss: {}'.format(e + 1, np.mean(d_losses), np.mean(g_losses)))
```

In both steps, we feed the network with a batch of true images (which won't be used during the generator optimization) and uniformly sampled code, Z, where each component is $z_i \sim U(-1, 1)$. In order to mitigate the risk of mode collapse, we are going to shuffle the set at the beginning of each iteration. This is not a robust method, but it at least guarantees avoiding the intercorrelations that could lead the GAN to a suboptimal configuration.

At the end of the training process, we can generate a few sample faces, as follows:

```
import numpy as np

Z = np.random.uniform(-1.0, 1.0, size=(20, code_length)).astype(np.float32)

Ys = session.run([gen],
                 feed_dict={
                     input_z: Z,
                     is_training: False
                 })

Ys = np.squeeze((Ys[0] + 1.0) * 0.5 * 255.0).astype(np.uint8)
```

The result is shown in the following screenshot:

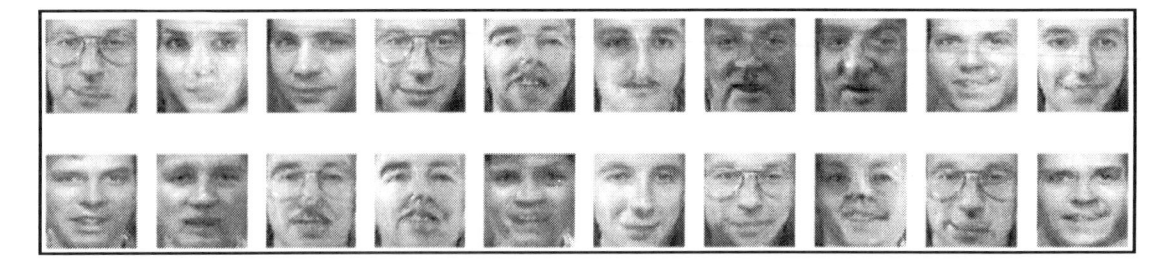

Sample faces generated by the DCGAN

As it's possible to see, the quality is extremely high, and a longer training phase would be helpful (along with a deeper hyperparameter search). However, the GAN has successfully learned how to generate new faces by using the same set of attributes. Both the expressions and the visual elements (for example, the eye shape, the presence of glasses, and so on) are reapplied to different models, in order to yield potential faces drawn from the same original data generating process. For example, the seventh and eighth are based on a single person, with modified attributes. The original pictures are as follows:

Original pictures corresponding to one of the Olivetti people

The structure of the mouth is common to both generated samples, but looking at the second one, we can confirm that many elements (the nose, eyes, forehead, and orientation) have been extracted from other samples, yielding a picture of a non-existing person. Even if the model works properly, a partial mode collapse is present, because some faces (with their relative attributes, such as the glasses) are more common than others. Conversely, a few female faces (a minority in the dataset) have been merged with male attributes, producing samples such as the second one of the first row or the eighth in the bottom row of the image containing the generated samples. As an exercise, I invite the reader to retrain the model with different parameters and other datasets (containing both grayscale and RGB images, such as Cifar-10 or STL-10).

> The screenshots that are shown in this and other examples in this chapter are often based on random generations; therefore, in order to increase the reproducibility, I suggest setting both the NumPy and TensorFlow random seed equal to 1000. The commands are: np.random.seed(1000) and tf.set_random_seed(1000).

Wasserstein GANs

Given a probability distribution $p(x)$, the set $D_p = \{x : p(x) > 0\}$ is called **support**. If two distributions, $p(x)$ and $q(x)$, have disjointed supports (that is, $D_p \cap D_q = \{\emptyset\}$), the Jensen-Shannon divergence becomes equal to $log(2)$. This means that the gradient is null, and no corrections can happen anymore. In a generic scenario where a GAN is involved, it's extremely unlikely that $p_g(x)$ and p_{data} are fully overlapped (however, you can expect a minimum overlap); therefore, the gradients are very small, and so are the updates to the weights. Such a problem could block the training process and trap the GAN in a suboptimal configuration that cannot be escaped. For this reason, Arjovsky, Chintala, and Bottou (in *Wasserstein GAN, Arjovsky M., Chintala S., and Bottou L., arXiv:1701.07875 [stat.ML]*) proposed a slightly different model, based on a more robust divergence measure called **Wasserstein distance** (or Earth Mover's Distance):

$$D_W(p_{data}\|p_g) = inf_{\mu \sim \prod(p_{data}, p_g)} E_{(x,y)\sim\mu}[\|x - y\|]$$

In order to understand the previous formula, it is necessary to say that $\Pi(p_{data}, p_g)$ is the set containing all possible joint distributions between the data generating process and the generator distribution. Therefore, the Wasserstein distance is equal to the infimum of the set of expected values of the norm $||x - y||$, assuming that the couple (x, y) is a sample from a distribution $\mu \sim \Pi(p_{data}, p_g)$. Such a definition is not extremely intuitive, even if the concept is straightforward, and can be summarized by thinking about two bidimensional blobs whose distance is the distance between the two closest points. It's evident that the problem of disjoint supports is completely overcome, and, moreover, the measure is also proportional to the actual distributional distance. Unfortunately, we are not working with finite sets; therefore, the computation of the Wasserstein distance could be very inefficient, and almost impossible to employ in real-life tasks. However, the **Kantorovich-Rubinstein theorem** (not fully analyzed because it's beyond the scope of this book) allows us to simplify the expression through the use of a special support function, $f(x)$:

$$D_W(p_{data}||p_g) = \frac{1}{2} sup_{||f|| \leq L} \, E_{\bar{x} \sim p_{data}}[f(\bar{x})] - E_{\bar{x} \sim p_g}[f(\bar{x})]$$

The main constraint imposed by the theorem is that $f(x)$ must be an L-Lipschitz function, which is to say that given a non-negative constant, L, the following applies:

$$|f(x_2) - f(x_1)| \leq L \, ||x_2 - x_1|| \quad \forall \, x_1, x_2 \in X$$

Considering a function $f(\cdot)$, parameterized using a neural network, the global objective becomes as follows:

$$D_W(p_{data}||p_g) = max_{\bar{\theta}_c \in \Theta_c} \, E_{\bar{x} \sim p_{data}}[f(\bar{x}; \bar{\theta}_c)] - E_{\bar{z} \sim p_{noise}}[f(g(\bar{z}; \bar{\theta}_g); \bar{\theta}_c)] = max_{\bar{\theta}_c \in \Theta_c}(W_{data} - W_{noise})$$

In this particular context, the discriminator is often called the critic, so $f(x; \theta_c)$ plays this role. As such a function must be L-Lipschitz, the authors suggested clipping all of the variables θ_c just after applying the corrections:

$$\bar{\theta}_c^{(t+1)} = clip(\bar{\theta}_c^{(t+1)} + \alpha \nabla_{\bar{\theta}_c} D_W, -c, c)$$

The method is not extremely efficient, because it slows down the learning procedure; however, as the function performs the manipulation of a finite set of variables, the output is assumed to always be bound by a constant, and the Kantorovich-Rubinstein theorem can be applied. Of course, as the parameterization often requires many variables (sometimes millions or more), the clipping constant should be kept very small (for example, 0.01). Moreover, as the training speed of the critic is compromised by the presence of the clipping, it's also necessary to increase the number of critic training steps during each iteration (for example, 5 times for the critic, 1 for the generator, and so on).

Transforming the DCGAN into a WGAN

In this example, we will implement a DCGAN based on the Wasserstein distance, using the Fashion MNIST dataset (as provided directly by Keras). This set is made up of 60,000 28 × 28 grayscale images of clothes, and it was introduced by Zalando as a replacement for the standard MNIST dataset, whose classes are too easy to separate with many classifiers. Considering the training time required by this kind of network, we have decided to limit the process to 5,000 samples, but a reader with enough resources can choose to increase or remove this constraint.

The first step consists of loading, slicing, and normalizing the dataset (in the range (-1, 1)), as follows:

```
import numpy as np

from keras.datasets import fashion_mnist

nb_samples = 5000

(X_train, _), (_, _) = fashion_mnist.load_data()
X_train = X_train.astype(np.float32)[0:nb_samples] / 255.0
X_train = (2.0 * X_train) - 1.0

width = X_train.shape[1]
height = X_train.shape[2]
```

A few samples are shown in the following screenshot:

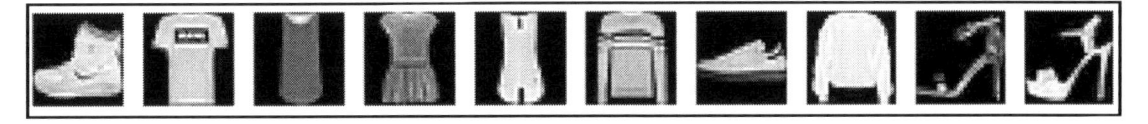

Samples extracted from the Fashion MNIST dataset

We can now define the generator DAG based on the same layer of the DCGAN, as follows:

- 2D convolution with 1,024 (4 × 4) filters with (1, 1) strides, valid padding, and linear output
- Batch normalization and leaky ReLU activation
- 2D convolution with 512 (4 × 4) filters with (2, 2) strides, the same padding, and linear output
- Batch normalization and leaky ReLU activation
- 2D convolution with 256 (4 × 4) filters with (2, 2) strides, the same padding, and linear output
- Batch normalization and leaky ReLU activation
- 2D convolution with 128 (4 × 4) filters with (2, 2) strides, the same padding, and linear output
- Batch normalization and leaky ReLU activation
- 2D convolution with 1 (4 × 4) filter with (2, 2) strides, the same padding, and hyperbolic tangent output

The code is shown in the following snippet:

```
import tensorflow as tf

def generator(z, is_training=True):
    with tf.variable_scope('generator'):
        conv_0 = tf.layers.conv2d_transpose(inputs=z,
                                            filters=1024,
                                            kernel_size=(4, 4),
                                            padding='valid')

        b_conv_0 = tf.layers.batch_normalization(inputs=conv_0,
training=is_training)

        conv_1 =
tf.layers.conv2d_transpose(inputs=tf.nn.leaky_relu(b_conv_0),
                                            filters=512,
                                            kernel_size=(4, 4),
                                            strides=(2, 2),
                                            padding='same')

        b_conv_1 = tf.layers.batch_normalization(inputs=conv_1,
training=is_training)

        conv_2 =
tf.layers.conv2d_transpose(inputs=tf.nn.leaky_relu(b_conv_1),
                                            filters=256,
```

```
                                    kernel_size=(4, 4),
                                    strides=(2, 2),
                                    padding='same')

      b_conv_2 = tf.layers.batch_normalization(inputs=conv_2,
training=is_training)

      conv_3 =
tf.layers.conv2d_transpose(inputs=tf.nn.leaky_relu(b_conv_2),
                                    filters=128,
                                    kernel_size=(4, 4),
                                    strides=(2, 2),
                                    padding='same')

      b_conv_3 = tf.layers.batch_normalization(inputs=conv_3,
training=is_training)

      conv_4 =
tf.layers.conv2d_transpose(inputs=tf.nn.leaky_relu(b_conv_3),
                                    filters=1,
                                    kernel_size=(4, 4),
                                    strides=(2, 2),
                                    padding='same')

      return tf.nn.tanh(conv_4)
```

The DAG for the critic is based on the following set of layers:

- 2D convolution with 128 (4 × 4) filters with (2, 2) strides, the same padding, and leaky ReLU output
- 2D convolution with 256 (4 × 4) filters with (2, 2) strides, the same padding, and linear output
- Batch normalization and leaky ReLU activation
- 2D convolution with 512 (4 × 4) filters with (2, 2) strides, the same padding, and linear output
- Batch normalization and leaky ReLU activation
- 2D convolution with 1,024 (4 × 4) filters with (2, 2) strides, the same padding, and linear output
- Batch normalization and leaky ReLU activation
- 2D convolution with 1 (4 × 4) filters with (2, 2) strides, valid padding, and linear output

The corresponding code block is as follows:

```
import tensorflow as tf

def critic(x, is_training=True, reuse_variables=True):
    with tf.variable_scope('critic', reuse=reuse_variables):
        conv_0 = tf.layers.conv2d(inputs=x,
                                  filters=128,
                                  kernel_size=(4, 4),
                                  strides=(2, 2),
                                  padding='same')

        conv_1 = tf.layers.conv2d(inputs=tf.nn.leaky_relu(conv_0),
                                  filters=256,
                                  kernel_size=(4, 4),
                                  strides=(2, 2),
                                  padding='same')

        b_conv_1 = tf.layers.batch_normalization(inputs=conv_1, training=is_training)

        conv_2 = tf.layers.conv2d(inputs=tf.nn.leaky_relu(b_conv_1),
                                  filters=512,
                                  kernel_size=(4, 4),
                                  strides=(2, 2),
                                  padding='same')

        b_conv_2 = tf.layers.batch_normalization(inputs=conv_2, training=is_training)

        conv_3 = tf.layers.conv2d(inputs=tf.nn.leaky_relu(b_conv_2),
                                  filters=1024,
                                  kernel_size=(4, 4),
                                  strides=(2, 2),
                                  padding='same')

        b_conv_3 = tf.layers.batch_normalization(inputs=conv_3, training=is_training)

        conv_4 = tf.layers.conv2d(inputs=tf.nn.leaky_relu(b_conv_3),
                                  filters=1,
                                  kernel_size=(4, 4),
                                  padding='valid')

        return conv_4
```

Chapter 9

As there are no particular differences with the DCGAN, there's no need to add further comments. Hence, we can move on to the definition of the graph and the overall DAG, as follows:

```
import tensorflow as tf

nb_epochs = 100
nb_critic = 5
batch_size = 64
nb_iterations = int(nb_samples / batch_size)
code_length = 100

graph = tf.Graph()

with graph.as_default():
    input_x = tf.placeholder(tf.float32, shape=(None, width, height, 1))
    input_z = tf.placeholder(tf.float32, shape=(None, code_length))
    is_training = tf.placeholder(tf.bool)

    gen = generator(z=tf.reshape(input_z, (-1, 1, 1, code_length)), is_training=is_training)

    r_input_x = tf.image.resize_images(images=input_x, size=(64,64), method=tf.image.ResizeMethod.BICUBIC)

    crit_1_l = critic(x=r_input_x, is_training=is_training, reuse_variables=False)
    crit_2_l = critic(x=gen, is_training=is_training, reuse_variables=True)

    loss_c = tf.reduce_mean(crit_2_l - crit_1_l)
    loss_g = tf.reduce_mean(-crit_2_l)

    variables_g = [variable for variable in tf.trainable_variables()
                   if variable.name.startswith('generator')]
    variables_c = [variable for variable in tf.trainable_variables()
                   if variable.name.startswith('critic')]

    with tf.control_dependencies(tf.get_collection(tf.GraphKeys.UPDATE_OPS)):
        optimizer_c = tf.train.AdamOptimizer(0.00005, beta1=0.5, beta2=0.9).\
                            minimize(loss=loss_c, var_list=variables_c)

        with tf.control_dependencies([optimizer_c]):
            training_step_c = tf.tuple(tensors=[
                                tf.assign(variable,
tf.clip_by_value(variable, -0.01, 0.01))
```

[343]

Generative Adversarial Networks and SOMs

```
                                             for variable
    in variables_c])

        training_step_g = tf.train.AdamOptimizer(0.00005, beta1=0.5,
beta2=0.9).\
                            minimize(loss=loss_g,
    var_list=variables_g)
```

As usual, the first step consists of declaring the placeholders, which are the same as the DCGAN. However, as the model (in particular, the sequence of convolutions or transpose convolutions) has been optimized for 64 × 64 images, we are going to resize the original samples by using the method tf.image.resize_images(). This operation will cause a limited quality loss; therefore, in production applications, I strongly suggest that you work with models optimized for the original input dimensions. After the declaration of both the generator and critics (as we discussed in the previous example, we need two instances sharing the same variables, as the loss functions are optimized separately), we can set the losses. In this case, they are extremely simple and fast to compute, but we pay the price for this simplification with the smaller corrections that this network will be able to apply. In fact, in this case, we are not minimizing the critic loss function directly; rather, we are first computing and applying the gradients with the operator optimizer_c, and then we are clipping all of the critic variables by using the operator training_step_c. As we only want to call this operator, we have declared it inside the context defined using the instruction tf.control_dependencies([optimizer_c]). In this way, when a session is requested to compute traning_step_c, TensorFlow will take care to first run optimizer_c, but only when the results are ready will execute the main command (which simply clips the variables). As we explained in the theory, this step is necessary to guarantee that the critic remains an L-Lipschitz function, and, consequently, to allow for the use of the simplified Wasserstein distance expression derived from the Kantorovich-Rubinstein theorem.

When the graph is completely defined, it's possible to create a session and initialize all of the variables, as follows:

```
import tensorflow as tf

session = tf.InteractiveSession(graph=graph)
tf.global_variables_initializer().run()
```

Now, all of the components have been set up, and we are ready to start the training procedure, which is split into `nb_critic` (five, in our case) iterations of the critic training step and one execution of the generator training step, as follows:

```
import numpy as np

samples_range = np.arange(X_train.shape[0])

for e in range(nb_epochs):
    c_losses = []
    g_losses = []

    for i in range(nb_iterations):
        for j in range(nb_critic):
            Xi = np.random.choice(samples_range, size=batch_size)
            X = np.expand_dims(X_train[Xi], axis=3)
            Z = np.random.uniform(-1.0, 1.0, size=(batch_size,
code_length)).astype(np.float32)

            _, c_loss = session.run([training_step_c, loss_c],
                                    feed_dict={
                                        input_x: X,
                                        input_z: Z,
                                        is_training: True
                                    })
            c_losses.append(c_loss)

        Z = np.random.uniform(-1.0, 1.0, size=(batch_size,
code_length)).astype(np.float32)

        _, g_loss = session.run([training_step_g, loss_g],
                                feed_dict={
                                    input_x:
np.zeros(shape=(batch_size, width, height, 1)),
                                    input_z: Z,
                                    is_training: True
                                })
        g_losses.append(g_loss)

    print('Epoch {}) Avg. critic loss: {} - Avg. generator loss:
{}'.format(e + 1,
np.mean(c_losses),
np.mean(g_losses)))
```

At the end of this process (which can be very long, especially without any GPU support), in order to get visual confirmation we can generate a few samples again, as follows:

```
import numpy as np

Z = np.random.uniform(-1.0, 1.0, size=(30, code_length)).astype(np.float32)

Ys = session.run([gen],
                 feed_dict={
                     input_z: Z,
                     is_training: False
                 })

Ys = np.squeeze((Ys[0] + 1.0) * 0.5 * 255.0).astype(np.uint8)
```

The results are shown in the following screenshot:

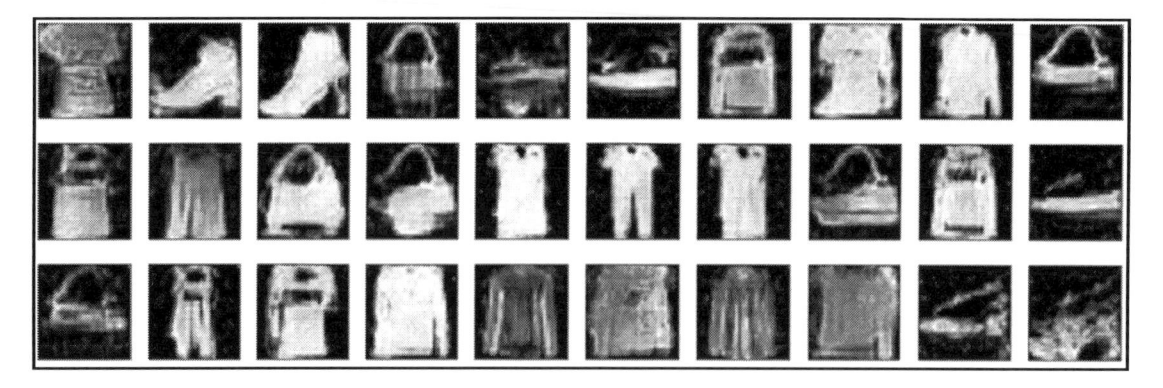

Samples generated by the WGAN

As it's possible to see, the WGAN has converged to a reasonably good final configuration. The quality of the images is strongly influenced by resize operation; however, it's interesting to observe that the generated samples are, on average, more complex than the original ones. The textures and the shapes of the clothes, for example, are influenced by the other factors (for example, bags and shoes), and the results are less regular models with an increased number of novel samples. Contrary to the Olivetti faces dataset, however, in this case it's more difficult to understand whether a sample is made up of a mixture of heterogeneous attributes, because the data generating process, such as the standard MNIST, has at least 10 dominant modes corresponding to the original classes.

The WGAN does not fall into a mode collapse, but the strong separation of the different regions prevents the model from easily merging elements, as we observed with the faces. As an exercise, I invite the reader to repeat this example with the Olivetti faces dataset, finding the optimal hyperparameter configuration and comparing the results with those achieved by the standard DCGAN.

Self-organizing maps

A self-organizing map is a model that was proposed for the first time by Willshaw and Von Der Malsburg (in *How Patterned Neural Connections Can Be Set Up by Self-Organization, Willshaw, D. J. and Von Der Malsburg, C., Proceedings of the Royal Society of London*, B/194, N. 1117, 1976), with the goal of finding a way to describe different phenomena that happen in the brains of many animals. In fact, they observed that some areas of the brain can develop internally organized structures whose subcomponents are selectively receptive, with respect to specific input patterns (for example, some visual cortex areas are very responsive to vertical or horizontal bands). The central idea of an SOM can be synthesized by thinking about a clustering procedure aimed at finding out the low-level properties of a sample, thanks to its assignment to a cluster. The main practical difference is that in an SOM, a single unit becomes representative of a part of the sample population (that is, a region of the data generating process) through a learning process called **winner-takes-all**. Such a training procedure starts by eliciting the responses of all units (which we are going to call neurons) and strengthening all of the weights and proceeds by reducing the area of influence around the most active units, until a single one becomes the only responsive neuron for a given input pattern.

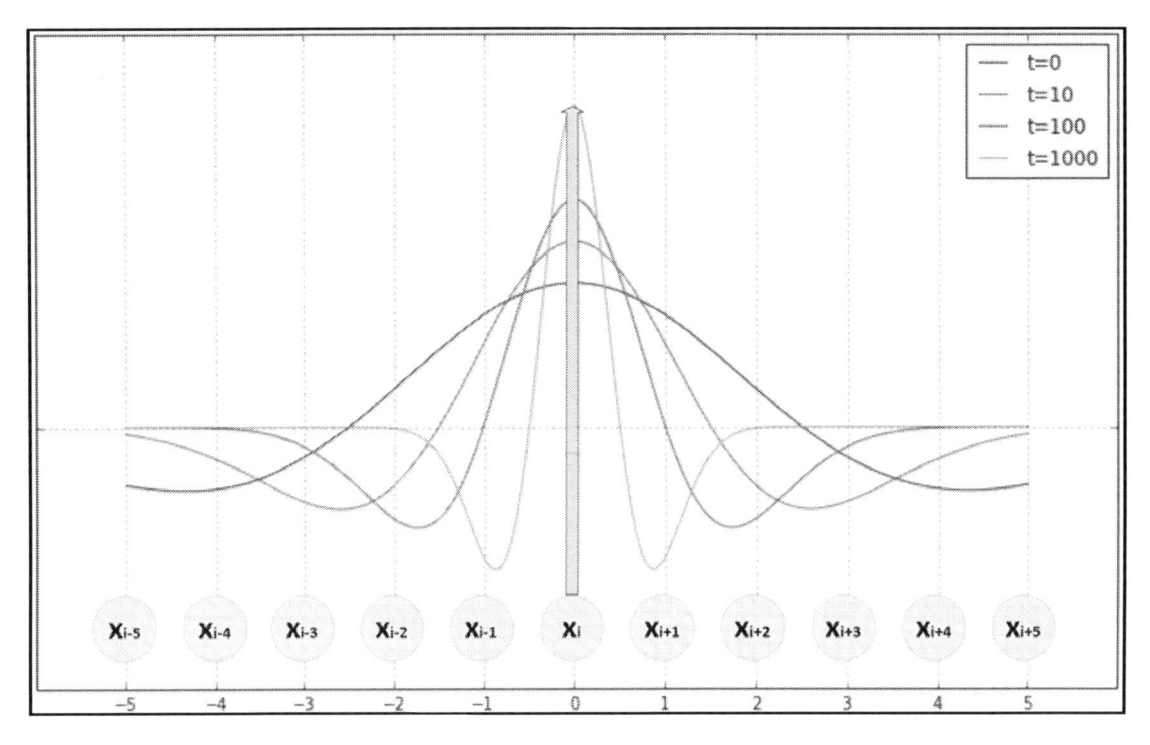

The process is synthesized in the following diagram:

Mexican hat selectivity developed by an SOM

During the initial steps, many units respond to the same input pattern, but we can already observe a dominance around x_i. Picking this unit immediately, however, could lead to a premature convergence with a consequent loss of accuracy. That's why the radius around the winning unit is progressively reduced (observing a phenomenon called **Mexican hat**, because of its characteristic shape). Of course, an initial winning unit could not remain stable during this process; that's why it's important to avoid a fast reduction of the radius that could prevent other potential units from being elicited. When a neuron keeps on being the most active when a specific pattern is presented, it will be slightly converted into an actual winner, and consequently, it takes all, because no other units will be strengthened anymore.

Some very famous and helpful SOMs are **Kohonen maps** (presented for the first time in *Self-Organized Formation of Topologically Correct Feature Maps, Kohonen T., Biological Cybernetics*, 43/1, 1982). They are structured like flat surfaces projected onto bidimensional manifolds (the most classical case is a flat bidimensional area) made up of N neurons. From now on, for simplicity, we are going to consider surfaces mapped onto matrices containing $k \times p$ units, each of them modeled using a synaptic weight, $w_{ij} \in \Re^n$ (the dimensionality is the same of the input patterns, $x_i \in \Re^n$). Hence, the weight matrix becomes $W(i, j) \in \Re^{k \times p \times n}$. From a practical viewpoint, in this model, a neuron is represented through the corresponding weight vector, because no internal transformations are performed. When a pattern, x_i, is presented, the winning neuron, n_w (as a tuple), is then determined by using the following rule:

$$n_w = argmin_{(k,p)} \|W(k,p) - \bar{x}_i\| \quad where \quad n_w \in \{(1,k),(1,p)\}$$

The training process is usually split into two distinct stages: **adjustment** and **convergence**. During the adjustment phase, the updates are extended to all of the neighbors of a winning unit, while, during the latter, only the weight, $W(n_w)$, will be strengthened. However, a smooth and progressive decrease is preferable to a rapid one; therefore, a common choice for the size of the neighborhood, $n_s(i,j)$, is based on a **radial basis function** (RBF) with an exponentially decaying variance:

$$\begin{cases} n_s(i,j) = e^{-\frac{\|n_w - (i,j)\|^2}{2\sigma(t)^2}} \\ \sigma(t) = \sigma_0 e^{-\frac{t}{\tau}} \end{cases}$$

The initial variance (which is proportional to the largest neighborhood) is σ_0, and it decays exponentially, according to the time constant, τ. As a rule of thumb, $\sigma(t) \approx 0$ when $t > 4\tau$, so τ should be set equal to $1/4^{th}$ of the number of training epochs of the adjustment phase: $\tau = 0.25 \cdot t_{adj}$. Once a neighborhood has been defined, it's possible to update the weights of all members according to their dissimilarity with each sample, x_i:

$$\Delta \bar{w}_{ij} = \eta(t) n(i,j)(\bar{x}_i - \bar{w}_{ij})$$

Generative Adversarial Networks and SOMs

In the previous formula, the learning rate, $\eta(t)$, is also a function of the training epoch, because it's preferable to impose a greater flexibility at the early stages (in particular, during the adjustment phase), while it's better to set a smaller η during the convergence phase, in order to allow for slighter modifications. A very common choice for a decaying learning rate is analogous to the neighborhood size:

$$\eta(t) = \begin{cases} \eta_0 e^{-\frac{t}{\tau}} & if\ t < t_{adj} \\ \eta_\infty & if\ t \geqslant t_{adj} \end{cases}$$

The effect of the learning rule is to force the weights of the winning units to get closer to a specific pattern, so that at the end of the training process, each pattern should elicit the response of a single unit representing a well-defined feature set. The adjective self-organizing derives from the ability that such models have to optimize units, in order to move similar patterns close to each other (for example, if a vertical bar elicits the response of units, a slightly rotated one should elicit the response of neighbors).

Example of a Kohonen map

In this example, we want to train a square 8 × 8 Kohonen map to become receptive to the Olivetti faces dataset. As each sample is a 64 × 64 grayscale image, we need to allocate a weight matrix with a shape equal to (8, 8, 4,096). The training process can be very long; therefore, we will limit the map to 100 random samples (of course, the reader is free to remove this limit and train the model with the whole dataset).

As usual, let's start by loading and normalizing the dataset, as follows:

```
import numpy as np

from sklearn.datasets import fetch_olivetti_faces

faces = fetch_olivetti_faces(shuffle=True)
Xcomplete = faces['data'].astype(np.float64) / np.max(faces['data'])
np.random.shuffle(Xcomplete)
X = Xcomplete[0:100]
```

Now, let's define the exponentially decaying functions for the variance of the distance function, $\sigma(t)$, and for the learning rate, $\eta(t)$, as follows:

```
import numpy as np

eta0 = 1.0
```

```
sigma0 = 3.0
tau = 100.0

def eta(t):
  return eta0 * np.exp(-float(t) / tau)

def sigma(t):
  return float(sigma0) * np.exp(-float(t) / tau)
```

In this example, we are employing the initial learning rate $\eta(0) = 1$ and the radius variance $\sigma(0) = 3$. The time constant has been chosen as equal to 100, because we are planning to perform 500 adjustment iterations and 500 convergence ones (1000 total iterations). The corresponding values are declared in the following snippet:

```
nb_iterations = 1000
nb_adj_iterations = 500
```

At this point, we can define the weight matrix (initialized so that $w_{ij} \sim N(0, 0.01)$) and the function responsible for computing the winning unit, based on the L_2 norm of the difference $w - x$, as follows:

```
import numpy as np

pattern_length = 64 * 64
pattern_width = pattern_height = 64
matrix_side = 8

W = np.random.normal(0, 0.1, size=(matrix_side, matrix_side, pattern_length))

def winning_unit(xt):
    distances = np.linalg.norm(W - xt, ord=2, axis=2)
    max_activation_unit = np.argmax(distances)
    return int(np.floor(max_activation_unit / matrix_side)), 
max_activation_unit % matrix_side
```

Before starting the training cycle, it's helpful to precompute the distance matrix, $dm(x_0, y_0, x_1, y_1)$, where each element represents the square Euclidean distance between (x_0, y_0) and (x_1, y_1). This step, as shown in the following snippet, avoids a computational overhead when the neighborhood of the winning unit must be determined:

```
import numpy as np

precomputed_distances = np.zeros((matrix_side, matrix_side, matrix_side, matrix_side))

for i in range(matrix_side):
```

```
        for j in range(matrix_side):
            for k in range(matrix_side):
                for t in range(matrix_side):
                    precomputed_distances[i, j, k, t] = \
                        np.power(float(i) - float(k), 2) + np.power(float(j) -
float(t), 2)

    def distance_matrix(xt, yt, sigmat):
        dm = precomputed_distances[xt, yt, :, :]
        de = 2.0 * np.power(sigmat, 2)
        return np.exp(-dm / de)
```

The function `distance_matrix()` computes a square matrix containing the exponentially decaying influence of all neurons whose center is (xt, yt). We now have all of the building blocks necessary to create the training procedure, which is based on the weight update rule that we previously described, and is shown as follows:

```
import numpy as np

sequence = np.arange(0, X.shape[0])
t = 0

for e in range(nb_iterations):
    np.random.shuffle(sequence)
    t += 1

    if e < nb_adj_iterations:
        etat = eta(t)
        sigmat = sigma(t)
    else:
        etat = 0.2
        sigmat = 1.0

    for n in sequence:
        x_sample = X[n]

        xw, yw = winning_unit(x_sample)
        dm = distance_matrix(xw, yw, sigmat)

        dW = etat * np.expand_dims(dm, axis=2) * (x_sample - W)
        W += dW

    W /= np.linalg.norm(W, axis=2).reshape((matrix_side, matrix_side, 1))

    if e > 0 and e % 100 == 0:
        print('Training step: {}'.format(t-1))
```

In each cycle, the following steps are performed:

1. The sequence of input samples is shuffled, in order to avoid intercorrelations.
2. The learning rate and the distance variance are computed (the convergence values are $\eta_\infty = 0.2$ and $\sigma_\infty = 1$).
3. For each sample, the following apply:
    1. The winning unit is computed.
    2. The distance matrix is computed.
    3. The weight updates are computed and applied.
4. The weights are renormalized, in order to avoid overflows.

We can now show the weight matrix at the end of the training process, as follows:

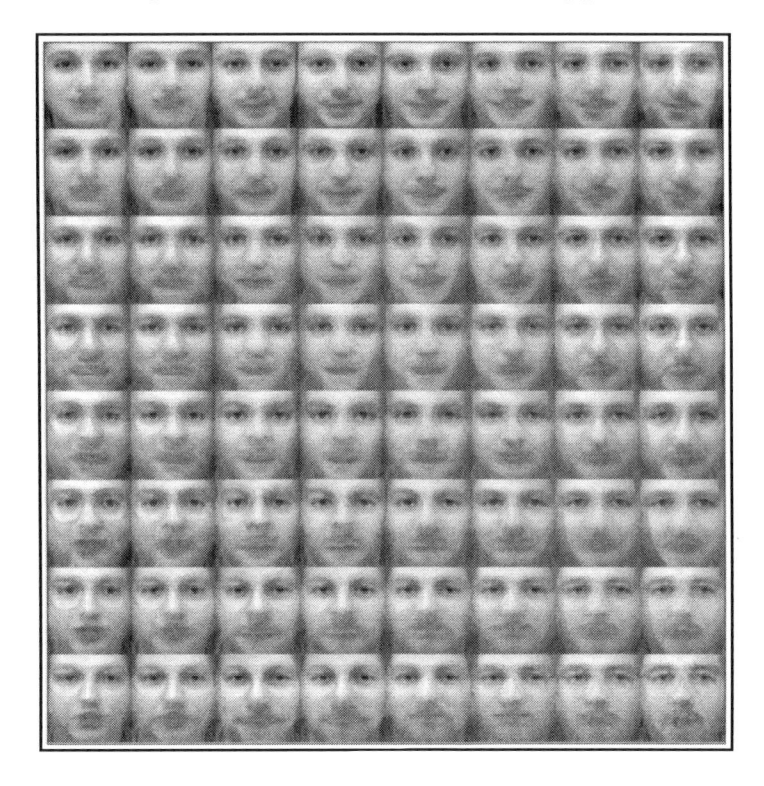

Kohonen map weight matrix at the end of the training process

As it's possible to see, every weight is centered on the generic structure of a face (as the dataset contains only this kind of pattern); however, different weights have become more responsive to specific input attributes. I suggest that you start looking at an element (for example, the eyes or the mouth) of the top-left face and rotating in a clockwise direction along a spiral that ends on the central weight. This way, it'll be easy to see the modifications in the receptive fields. As an exercise, I invite the reader to test the model with other datasets (for example, MNIST or Fashion MNIST) and to perform manual labeling of the final weight matrix (for example, considering this example, a specific weight can represent a smiling face with glasses and a big nose). After each element has been labeled, it will be possible to project the original samples and check which neurons are more receptive by directly providing the label as output.

Summary

In this chapter, we introduced the concept of GANs, discussing an example of a DCGAN. Such models have the ability to learn a data generating process through the use of two neural networks involved in a minimax game. The generator has to learn how to return samples that are indistinguishable from the others employed during the training process. The discriminator, or critic, has to become smarter and smarter in only assigning high probabilities to valid samples. The adversarial training approach is based on the idea of forcing the generator to win against the discriminator, by learning how to cheat it with synthetic samples with the same properties as the real ones. At the same time, the generator is forced to win against the discriminator by becoming more and more selective. In our examples, we also analyzed an important variant, called WGAN, which can be employed when a standard model fails to reproduce valid samples.

An SOM is a structure based on the functioning of specific areas of the brain that force their units to learn particular features of the input samples. Such models auto-organize themselves, so that units responding to similar patterns get closer. Once a new sample is presented, it's enough to compute the winning unit, which is the one whose weights have the shortest distance from the sample; and, after a labeling process, it's possible to immediately understand which features elicited the response (for example, vertical lines or high-level features, such as the presence of glasses or a mustache, or the shape of the face).

Questions

1. In a GAN, the generator and discriminator play the same roles as the encoder and decoder in an autoencoder. Is this correct?
2. Can a discriminator output values in the range *(-1, 1)*?
3. One of the problems with GANs is the premature convergence of the discriminator. It this correct?
4. In a Wasserstein GAN, is the critic (the discriminator) slower than the generator during the training phase?
5. Considering the previous question, what is the reason for the different speeds?
6. What is the value of the Jensen-Shannon divergence between *U(-1, 0)* and *U(1, 2)*?
7. What is the goal of the winner-takes-all strategy?
8. What's the purpose of the adjustment phase of the SOM training process?

Further reading

- *Generative Adversarial Networks, Goodfellow I. J., Pouget-Abadie J., Mirza M., Xu B., Warde-Farley D., Ozair S., Courville A., and Bengio Y., arXiv:1406.2661 [stat.ML]*
- *Unsupervised Representation Learning with Deep Convolutional Generative Adversarial Networks, Radford A., Metz L., and Chintala S., arXiv:1511.06434 [cs.LG]*
- *Wasserstein GAN, Arjovsky M., Chintala S., and Bottou L., arXiv:1701.07875 [stat.ML]*
- *How Patterned Neural Connections Can Be Set Up by Self-Organization, Willshaw, D. J. and Von Der Malsburg, C., Proceedings of the Royal Society of London, B/194, N. 1117, 1976*
- *Self-Organized Formation of Topologically Correct Feature Maps, Kohonen T., Biological Cybernetics, 43/1, 1982*
- *Mastering Machine Learning Algorithms, Bonaccorso G., Packt Publishing, 2018*

Assessments

Chapter 1

1. Unsupervised learning can be applied independently from supervised approaches, because its goal is different. If a problem requires a supervised approach, often unsupervised learning cannot be employed as an alternative solution. In general, unsupervised methods try to extract pieces of information from a dataset (for example, clustering) without any external hint (such as the prediction error). Conversely, supervised methods require hints in order to correct their parameters.
2. As the goal is finding the causes of the trend, it's necessary to perform a diagnostic analysis.
3. No; the likelihood of n independent samples being drawn from the same distribution is obtained as a product of the single probabilities (see question 4 for the main assumption).
4. The main hypothesis is that the samples are **independent and identically distributed (IID)**.
5. The gender can be encoded as a numerical feature (for example, one-hot encoding); hence, we need to consider two possibilities. If the gender is not present among the attributes and the other features have no correlations with it, the result of the clustering is perfectly justified. If the gender if present, as a general clustering approach is based on the similarities between samples, a 50/50 result means that the gender is not a discriminative feature. In other words, given two randomly selected samples, their similarity is not affected (or slightly affected) by the gender, because other features are dominant. In this particular case, for example, the average mark or the age have larger variances, so their influence is stronger.
6. We can expect more compact groups, where each dominant feature has a smaller range. For example, a group can contain students in the age range 13-15, with all possible marks, and so on. Alternatively, we can observe a segmentation based on single features (for example, the age, mark average, and so on). The final result depends on the numerical structure of the vectors, the distance function, and, of course, the algorithm.

7. If every customer is represented by a feature vector containing a summary of his/her interests (for example, based on the products that he/she has bought or seen), we can find the cluster assignment, check which elements characterize the cluster (for example, books, movies, clothes, specific brands, and so on), and use these pieces of information in order to recommend potential products (that is, products bought by similar users). This concept is based on the main idea of sharing the information among members of the same cluster, thanks to their similarities.

Chapter 2

1. The Manhattan distance is the same as the Minkowski distance with $p=1$; hence, we expect to observe a longer distance.
2. No; the convergence speed is primarily influenced by the initial position of the centroids.
3. Yes; k-means is designed to work with convex clusters, and its performances are poor with concave ones.
4. It means that all clusters (except for a negligible percentage of samples), respectively, only contain samples belonging to the same class (that is, with the same true labels).
5. It indicates a moderate/strong negative discrepancy between the true label distribution and the assignments. Such a value is a clear negative condition that cannot be accepted, because the vast majority of the samples have been assigned to the wrong clusters.
6. No, because the adjusted Rand score is based on the ground truth (that is, the expected number of clusters is fixed).
7. If all of the base queries require the same time, they are executed in $60 - (2 \times 4) - 2 = 50$ seconds. Hence, each of them requires $50 / 100 = 0.5$ seconds. With a *leaf size*=50, we can expect to halve the execution time of both *50-NN* queries, while there's no impact on the base queries. So, the total time available for the base queries becomes $60 - (2 \times 2) - 2 = 54$ seconds. Therefore, we can execute *108* base queries.
8. No; ball tree is a data structure that doesn't suffer the curse of dimensionality, and its computational complexity is always $O(N \log M)$.

9. The Gaussians $N([-1.0, 0.0], diag[0.1, 0.2])$ and $N([-0.8, 0.0], diag[0.3, 0.3])$ are overlapped (even if the resulting cluster is very stretched), while the third one is sufficiently far (considering the mean and variance) to be captured by a separate cluster. Hence, the optimal cluster size is 2, and it's extremely difficult for k-means to correctly separate the large blob into two cohesive components (in particular, for a large numbers of samples).
10. VQ is a lossy compression method. It can only be employed when the semantics are not altered by small or moderate transformations. In this case, it's impossible to swap a token with another one without modifying the underlying semantics.

Chapter 3

1. No; in a convex set, given two points, the segment connecting them always lies inside the set.
2. Considering the radial structure of the dataset, the RBF kernel can generally solve the problem.
3. With $\varepsilon=1.0$, many points are not density-reachable. When the radius of the balls is reduced, we should expect more noisy points.
4. No; k-medoids can employ any metric.
5. No; DBSCAN is not sensitive to the geometry, and can manage any kind of cluster structure.
6. We have shown that the performance of mini-batch K-means is slightly worse than k-means. Therefore, the answer is yes. It's possible to save memory by using a batch algorithm.
7. Considering that the variance of the noise is $\sigma^2=0.005 \rightarrow \sigma \approx 0.07$, which is about 14 times smaller than the cluster standard deviation, we cannot expect such a large number of new assignments (80%) in a stable clustering configuration.

Chapter 4

1. In the agglomerative approach, the algorithm starts from each sample, considered as a cluster, and proceeds to merge the sub-clusters until a single cluster has been defined. In the divisive approach, the algorithm starts from a single cluster containing all of the samples, and proceeds by splitting it until every sample makes up a cluster.

Assessments

2. The closest points are *(0, 0)* and *(0, 1)*, so the single linkage is $L_s(a, b) = 1$. The farthest points are *(-1, -1)* and *(1, 1)*, so the complete linkage is $L_c(a, b) = 2\sqrt{2}$.
3. No; a dendrogram is a tree representation of a hierarchical clustering procedure, given a metric and a linkage.
4. In an agglomerative clustering, the initial part of a dendrogram contains all of the samples as autonomous clusters.
5. The *y* axis reports the dissimilarity.
6. The dissimilarity increases when merging smaller clusters into larger ones.
7. Yes; that's the definition of the cophenetic matrix.
8. Connectivity constraints allow for imposing, so merging constraints to the aggregation process, so to force it to keep some elements in the same cluster.

Chapter 5

1. Hard clustering is based on fixed assignments; hence, a sample x_i will always belong to a single cluster. Conversely, soft clustering returns a degree vector whose elements represent the membership level, with respect to each cluster (for example, (0.1, 0.7, 0.05, 0.15)).
2. No; fuzzy c-means is an extension of k-means, and it's not particularly suitable for non-convex geometries. However, the soft assignments allow for evaluating the influence of neighboring clusters.
3. The main assumption is that the dataset has been drawn from a distribution that can be efficiently approximated with the weighted sum of a number of Gaussian distributions.
4. It means that the first model has a number of parameters that is the double of the second one.
5. The second one, because it can achieve the same result with fewer parameters.
6. Because we want to employ such a model for the auto-selection of the components. This means that we want to start with a larger number of weights, expecting that many of them will be forced to close to 0. As the Dirichlet distribution has the property of being very sparse and works on a simplex, it is the best choice for the prior.
7. If they have been collected from the same sources and the labeled ones are verified, we can employ a semi-supervised approach (for example, a generative Gaussian mixture), in order to find the most appropriate label for the remaining samples.

Chapter 6

1. As the random variables are clearly independent, *P(Tall, Rain) = P(Tall)P(Rain) =* $0.75 \cdot 0.2 = 0.15$.
2. One of the main drawbacks of histograms is that when the number of bins is too large, many of them start to be empty, because there are no samples in all of the value ranges. In this case, either the cardinality of X can be smaller than 1,000, or, even with more than 1,000 samples, the relative frequencies can be concentrated in a number of bins smaller than 1,000.
3. The total number of samples is 75, and the bins have equal lengths. Hence, $P(0 < x < 2) = 20/75 \approx 0.27$, $P(2 < x < 4) = 30/75 = 0.4$, and $P(4 < x < 6) = 25/75 \approx 0.33$. As we don't have any samples, we can assume that $P(x > 6) = 0$; therefore, $P(x > 2) = P(2 < x < 4) + P(4 < x < 6) \approx 0.73$. We have an immediate confirmation, considering that $0.73 \cdot 75 \approx 55$, which is the number of samples belonging to the bins with $x > 2$.
4. In a normal distribution, $N(0, 1)$, the maximum density is $p(0) \approx 0.4$. After about three standard deviations, $p(x) \approx 0$; therefore, a sample x with $p(x) = 0.35$ cannot generally be considered an anomaly.
5. As $min(std(X), IQR(X)/1.34) \approx 2.24$, the optimal bandwidth is $h = 0.9 \cdot 2.24 \cdot 500^{-0.2} = 0.58$.
6. Even if a Gaussian kernel could be employed, given the description of the distribution, we should initially opt for the exponential kernel, which allows for very rapid drops around the mean.
7. That would be the most logical conclusion. In fact, in the case of novelties, we should expect the new samples to alter the distribution, in order to model the novelties, too. If the probability density remains very low after retraining the model, the sample is very likely to be an anomaly.

Chapter 7

1. The covariance matrix is already diagonal; therefore, the eigenvectors are the standard x and y versors $(1,0)$ and $(0, 1)$, and the eigenvalues are 2 and 1. Hence, the x axis is the principal component, and the y axis is the second one.
2. As the ball $B_{0.5}(0, 0)$ is empty, there are no samples around the point $(0, 0)$. Considering the horizontal variance $\sigma_x^2 = 2$, we can imagine that X is broken into two blobs, so it's possible to imagine that the line $x = 0$ is a horizontal discriminator. However, this is only a hypothesis, and it needs to be verified with actual data.

3. No, they are not. The covariance matrix after PCA is uncorrelated, but the statistical independence is not guaranteed.
4. Yes; a distribution with Kurt(X) is super-Gaussian, so it's peaked and with heavy tails. This guarantees finding independent components.
5. As X contains a negative element, it's impossible to employ the NNMF algorithm.
6. No; as the dictionary has 10 elements, it means that the documents are made up of many recurring terms, so the dictionary is under-complete (10 < 30).
7. A sample, $(x, y) \in \Re^2$, is transformed by a quadratic polynomial into $(ax, by, cx^2, dy^2, exy, f) \in \Re^6$.

Chapter 8

1. No, they don't. Both the encoder and decoder must be functionally symmetric, but their internal structures can also be different.
2. No; a part of the input information is lost during the transformation, while the remaining one is split between the code output Y and the autoencoder variables, which, along with the underlying model, encode all of the transformations.
3. As $min(sum(z_i)) = 0$ and $min(sum(z_i)) = 128$, a sum equal to 36 can imply both sparseness (if the standard deviation is large) and a uniform distribution with small values (when the standard deviation is close to zero).
4. As $sum(z_i) = 36$, a $std(z_i) = 0.03$ implies that the majority of values are centered around 0.28 (0.25 ÷ 0.31), the code can be considered dense.
5. No; a Sanger network (as well as a Rubner-Tavan one) requires the input samples $x_i \in X$.
6. The components are extracted in descending order, from the largest to the smallest eigenvalue (that is, from the first to the last principal component); hence, there's no need for further analysis to determine the importance.
7. Yes; starting from the last layer, it's possible to sample the values of each internal layer until the first one. The most likely input value is obtained by selecting the $argmax(•)$ of every probability vector.

Chapter 9

1. No; the generator and discriminator are functionally different.
2. No, it can't, because the output of a discriminator must be a probability (that is, $p_i \in (0, 1)$).
3. Yes; it's correct. The discriminator can learn to output different probabilities very quickly, and the gradients of its loss function can become close to 0, reducing the magnitude of the correction feedback provided to the generator.
4. Yes; it's normally quite slower.
5. The critic is slower, because the variables are clipped after every update.
6. As the supports are disjointed, the Jensen-Shannon divergence is equal to $log(2)$.
7. The goal is to develop highly selective units whose responses are only elicited by a specific feature set.
8. It's impossible to know the final organization during the early stages of the training process; therefore, it's not a good practice to force the premature specialization of some units. The adjustment phase allows for many neurons to be candidates, and, at the same time, progressively increases the selectiveness of the most promising one (which will become the winner).

Other Books You May Enjoy

If you enjoyed this book, you may be interested in these other books by Packt:

Building Machine Learning Systems with Python - Third Edition
Luis Pedro Coelho, Wilhelm Richert

ISBN: 978-1-78862-322-3

- Build a classification system that can be applied to text, images, and sound
- Employ Amazon Web Services (AWS) to run analysis on the cloud
- Solve problems related to regression using scikit-learn and TensorFlow
- Recommend products to users based on their past purchases
- Understand different ways to apply deep neural networks on structured data

Machine Learning Algorithms - Second Edition
Giuseppe Bonaccorso

ISBN: 978-1-78934-799-9

- Study feature selection and the feature engineering process
- Assess performance and error trade-offs for linear regression
- Build a data model and understand how it works by using different types of algorithm
- Learn to tune the parameters of Support Vector Machines (SVM)
- Explore the concept of natural language processing (NLP) and recommendation systems

Leave a review - let other readers know what you think

Please share your thoughts on this book with others by leaving a review on the site that you bought it from. If you purchased the book from Amazon, please leave us an honest review on this book's Amazon page. This is vital so that other potential readers can see and use your unbiased opinion to make purchasing decisions, we can understand what our customers think about our products, and our authors can see your feedback on the title that they have worked with Packt to create. It will only take a few minutes of your time, but is valuable to other potential customers, our authors, and Packt. Thank you!

Index

A

adjusted mutual information (AMI) score 64
adjusted Rand score 66
adjustment 349
adversarial training 322
agglomerative clustering
  about 131
  average linkage 135
  complete linkages 133
  on water treatment plant dataset 145, 147, 151, 153
  single linkages 133
  Ward's linkage 135
Akaike Information Criterion (AIC) 181
anomalies
  about 200
  as novelties 200, 201
  as outliers 200, 201
anti-Hebbian rule 308
association rules 24
autoencoders
  about 280, 281, 282
  deep convolutional autoencoder, example 282, 286, 287
  denoising autoencoders 287, 288
  sparse autoencoders 290, 291
  variational autoencoders 292, 293, 294

B

Balanced Iterative Reducing and Clustering using Hierarchies (BIRCH)
  about 85, 119
  versus mini-batch k-means 122, 124
ball-tree 69
bandwidth 93, 206
Bayesian Information Criterion (BIC) 181
bias of an estimator 13
bias-variance trade-off 12
bimodal 326
branching factor 120
Breast Cancer Wisconsin dataset
  analysis 45, 48, 51
building atoms 259

C

Calinski-Harabasz score 100
centroids 42
Characteristic-Feature (CF) 120
city block distance 132
cluster analysis 22
clustering
  about 22, 36, 38, 119
    distance function 39
    distance functions 41
cocktail party 265
complete linkages 133
completeness score 60, 62
conjugate prior 185
connectivity constraints 154, 157, 159
connectivity matrix 154
contingency matrix 67
Contrastive Divergence 314
convergence 349
convexity 38
cophenetic correlation coefficient (CPC) 143
cophenetic correlation
  as performance metric 143
cophenetic matrix 143
core point 97
corpus 270
cosine distance 132
critic 322
Cumulative Distribution Function (CDF) 27

D

data science
  Python, used 31
dataset
  structure 202
deep belief networks (DBN)
  about 280, 312, 314, 315
  example 315, 316, 317, 318
  Restricted Boltzmann Machine (RBM) 312, 313, 314
deep convolutional autoencoder
  example 282, 286, 287
deep convolutional GAN
  example 328, 329, 331, 334, 337
deep convolutional variational autoencoder
  example 294, 296
dendrogram
  about 136
  analyzing 136, 139, 142
denoising autoencoders
  about 287, 288
  noise, adding to deep convolutional autoencoder 288, 289, 290
Density-based Spatial Clustering of Applications with Noise (DBSCAN)
  about 85, 97
  Calinski-Harabasz score 100
  cluster instability, as performance metric 109, 112
  used, for analysing absenteeism at work dataset 101, 103, 107
density-connected 98
descriptive models 9
diagnostic analysis 11
dictionary learning algorithms 259
directly density-reachable 98
distance function 39, 41
divisive approach 131
Dunn's Partitioning Coefficient 167

E

Epanechnikov kernel 208
estimator 13
Euclidean distance 39, 132

evaluation metrics
  about 51
  adjusted mutual information (AMI) score 64
  adjusted Rand score 66
  completeness score 60, 62
  contingency matrix 67
  homogeneity score 62
  inertia, minimizing 51, 54, 57
  silhouette score 58, 60
Evidence Lower Bound (ELBO) 293
Expectation Maximization (EM) 257
Expectation step (E-step) 175
Exponential kernel 209, 210

F

factor analysis 257
factors 11
fast Independent Component Analysis (FastICA) 266
Fuzzy c-means 166, 167, 168, 169, 170, 171
fuzzy clustering 37

G

Gaussian kernel 207
Gaussian mixture
  about 172, 173, 174
  component selecting, Bayesian Gaussian mixture used 184, 185, 186, 188, 190
  EM algorithm 174, 175, 176, 177, 178, 179, 180
  generative Gaussian mixture 190, 191, 192, 193, 195
  performance, assessing with AIC 181, 182, 183, 184
  performance, assessing with BIC 181, 182, 183, 184
Generalized Hebbian Learning (GHL) 300
generative adversarial network (GAN), components
  discriminator 322
  generator 322
generative adversarial network (GAN)
  about 23, 322, 323, 324, 337
  analyzing 324, 325, 326
  deep convolutional GAN, example 328, 329, 331, 334, 337

mode collapse 326, 327
Wasserstein GANs 337, 338, 339
generative models 23
Gram-Schmidt orthonormalization procedure 301

H

hard clustering 36
Harmonium 312
Hebb's rule 299
Hebbian learning 299
Hebbian-based principal component analysis
    about 299
    Rubner-Tavan's network 307, 308, 309
    sanger's network 300, 301, 302
heteroscedastic 256
hierarchical clustering 130
hierarchical lateral connection 307
histograms 203, 204, 205, 206
homogeneity score 62
homoscedastic 256

I

independent and identically distributed (IID) 17, 175, 198
Independent Component Analysis 264, 265, 266, 267, 268, 269, 270
indicator vector 90
inertia
    about 42
    minimizing 51, 54, 57
instance-based learning 68
interquartile range (IQR) 204

J

Jensen-Shannon divergence 325

K

K-means 42
k-means++ 43
k-medoids 112, 117
K-Nearest Neighbors 68, 70, 73
Kantorovich-Rubinstein theorem 338
kd-trees 68
kernel density estimation (KDE)
    about 197, 206, 210
    Epanechnikov kernel 208
    Exponential kernel 209, 210
    Gaussian kernel 207
kernel principal component analysis (kernel PCA) 280
kernel trick 255
Kohonen map
    about 349
    example 350, 353, 354
Kullback-Leibler divergence D_{KL} 19
kurtosis 265

L

Latent Dirichlet Allocation (LDA)
    about 271
    used, for topic modeling 270, 271, 272, 274, 275
leptokurtic 266
linkage 132
Lloyd's algorithm 43
logcosh 267

M

machine learning
    algorithms, types 17
    diagnostic analysis 11
    need for 8
    predictive analysis 12, 15
    prescriptive analysis 16
    Python, used 31
    reinforcement learning algorithms 30
    semi-supervised learning algorithms 29
    supervised learning algorithms 17
    unsupervised learning algorithms 21
Manhattan 132
Markov random field (MRF) 313
Maximization-step (M-step) 176
maximum cohesion 37
Maximum Likelihood Estimation (MLE) 25, 175
maximum separation 37
mean integrated square error (MISE) 209
mean shift 92, 94, 96
medoids 113
meta-face 269

Mexican hat 348
mini-batch k-means
    about 118
    versus Balanced Iterative Reducing and
        Clustering using Hierarchies (BIRCH) 124
    versus BIRCH 122
minimax game 323
Minkowski distance 132
mode 326
mode collapse 326, 327
multimodal 326
mutual information (MI) 64

N

Nash equilibrium point 324
Natural Language Processing (NLP) 132
negentropy 266
noise point 99
Non-Negative Matrix Factorization (NNMF) 262, 263
novelties 201
novelty detection 201

O

Oja's rule 300
online clustering
    about 117
    Balanced Iterative Reducing and Clustering using
        Hierarchies (BIRCH) 119
    mini-batch k-means 118
    mini-batch k-means, versus BIRCH 122
outlier detection 201
outliers 201
over-complete 259
overfitted 14

P

Parzen windows 93
platykurtic 266
predictive analysis 12, 15
predictive models 9
prescriptive analysis 16
Principal Component Analysis (PCA)
    about 242, 243, 244, 245, 299
    dictionary learning 259, 260, 261
    Independent Component Analysis 264
    kernel 253, 254, 255, 256
    Non-Negative Matrix Factorization (NNMF) 262, 263
    robustness, adding to heteroscedastic noise with
        factor analysis 256, 257, 258, 259
    Sparse PCA 259, 260, 261
    whitening 246, 247, 248
    with MNIST dataset 249, 250, 251, 252
    with Singular Value Decomposition 245, 246
principle components 244
probabilistic clustering 37
Probability density function 198, 199, 200
probability density function (PDF) 92
proximity matrix 132
Python
    used, for data science 31
    used, for machine learning 31

R

Radial Basis Function (RBF) 87, 349
reassignment ratio 118
regression problem 18
reinforcement learning algorithms 30
Restricted Boltzmann Machine (RBM) 312, 313, 314
Rubner-Tavan's network
    about 307, 309
    example 309

S

sanger's network
    about 300, 301, 302
    example 302, 303, 304, 305, 306
self-organizing maps
    about 347, 348, 349, 350
    Kohonen map, example 350, 353, 354
semi-supervised learning algorithms 29
silhouette score 58, 60
single linkage 133
Singular Value Decomposition (SVD) 245
soft clustering 37, 164
sparse autoencoders
    about 290, 291
    sparseness constraint, adding to deep

    convolutional autoencoder 291, 292
spectral clustering 86, 89, 91
Stochastic Gradient Descent (SGD) 18, 293
supervised 17
supervised learning algorithms
    about 17
    example 20
support 337
Support Vector Machine (SVM) 30
Survival Function (SF) 27

T

t-Distributed Stochastic Neighbor Embedding (t-SNE) 48
threshold 120
topic modeling
    Latent Dirichlet Allocation (LDA), used 270, 271, 272, 274, 275
trusted guides 195

U

unbiased estimators 13
under-complete 259
underfitted model 14
unimodal 326
unsupervised learning algorithms
    about 21
    association rules 24
    cluster analysis 22
    example 24, 28
    examples 27
    generative models 23
Unweighted Pair Group Method with Arithmetic Mean (UPGMA) 135

V

variational autoencoders
    about 292, 293, 294
    deep convolutional variational autoencoder, example 294, 296
Variational Bayesian Inference 185
variational posterior 184
Vector Quantization 77, 80

W

Ward's linkage 135
Wasserstein distance 337
Wasserstein GANs
    about 337, 338, 339
    DCGAN, transforming 339, 341, 342, 343, 345, 346, 347
weight concentration parameter 185
whitening 246
winner-takes-all 347
Within-Cluster Dispersion (WCD) 100

Printed in Poland
by Amazon Fulfillment
Poland Sp. z o.o., Wrocław